S0-FJH-732

Dictionary of

PERSONNEL and INDUSTRIAL RELATIONS

ESTHER R. BECKER

Dictionary
of
PERSONNEL
and
INDUSTRIAL
RELATIONS

HF
5549
B3418

79778

PHILOSOPHICAL LIBRARY   New York

Copyright ©, 1958,
by Philosophical Library, Inc.
15 East 40th Street, New York, N. Y.
All rights reserved.
Type set at The Polyglot Press, New York.
Printed in the United States of America.

GLENN L. GARDINER
who, in my opinion, has made the greatest contribution to industrial relations in the first half of the century. He was given the Award of Merit "for outstanding achievement in the field of Personnel Relations" by the New York Personnel Management Association.

Bus. (grad.) 2/63 McClurg 6.80

Dictionary of

PERSONNEL and INDUSTRIAL RELATIONS

A

Abilities, Inc. An organization started in September 1952 by four handicapped men in West Hempstead, N. Y., headed by Henry Viscardi, Jr. who became president. The first production of the new company was that of lacing cable assemblies. To do this work the four pooled their usable physical resources—one leg and five arms. The company has grown rapidly and received wide recognition. The plant operates as a job shop. The work is mostly of a subcontract nature. All work is obtained on competitive bidding. Employees include amputees, blind and deaf, and over age, arthritic, tubercular, cardiac, cerebral palsy, hemiplegic, paraplegic, triplegic, quadraparetic and orthopedic deformities.

ability. In personnel terminology, ability designates (1) physical ability, usually meaning strength, energy, power of endurance or dexterity. It is generally used in context with a specific job, as requirements for physical ability vary. (2) mental ability, loosely used to denote intelligence, experience, education, skill, imagination, resourcefulness or power. A person possessing administrative, executive, managerial and supervisory ability is assumed to be able to handle adequately the problems connected with these duties and responsibilities.

ability to pay. A wage determination concept based on the employer's being able to pay certain wage rates. A capacity to pay.

abnormal reading. See ABNORMAL TIME.

abnormal time. The elapsed time for any element recorded during a time study which, being excessively longer or shorter than the majority or median of the elapsed times, is judged at the time of the study to be not representative for the element, and which may be excluded in determining the most typical elapsed time (or the average time) for the element.

absence or absenteeism. The state of not being present on the job or of not being available for work when needed. Absence may be (1) excused, when it is arranged for ahead of time or when a worker has notified his supervisor in accordance with established procedures; (2) unexcused when (a) a worker does not telephone or otherwise notify his supervisor; (b) the absence has not previously been arranged for; (c) there is a wilful disregard of the company policy

(1)

in respect to excused absence; (3) chronic, when it occurs as a habit. Much activity in the personnel field centers around the problem of absenteeism. This includes the study of rates of absence, duration, types of disability, cost of medical care, employee benefit plans, and economic impact on production. Extensive studies have been made by the National Industrial Conference Board and the Research Council for Economic Security, 111 West Jackson Boulevard, Chicago, 4, Illinois, as well as by the large insurance companies.

absentee. The person who is absent. Usually applied to an employee absent for a particular day.

absenteeism rate. A ratio of absences to work days available. Calculated by taking the total number of man-days (or hours) missed and divided by the total number of man-days (or hours) which were available for any specified period.

absenteeism, statistics of. Absenteeism statistics are studied by the Department of Labor, numerous colleges and associations, and specifically by the Research Council for Economic Security, 111 W. Jackson Blvd., Chicago, Illinois. Current statistics show that the average number of prolonged absences per 1,000 employees per year among men is 19 for salaried employees and 33 for production workers; among women, 34 among salaried employees and 73 for production workers.

acceleration premium. A method of computing incentive wage payments which provides for the increase of percentage premiums in progressively higher levels of production. Wages are increased above the basic wage rate, not in proportion to the output above the production standard, but in proportion to the increase in output. Thus a worker exceeding the production standard by 10% may be given a 10% premium, while a worker exceeding the standard by 20% may receive a 30% premium.

"Acceptance." A term used by the United States Employment Service. See APPLICANT-HOLDING OFFICE ACCEPTANCE.

accession. The hiring of a new worker, or the rehiring of a former employee.

"Accession Notice." A term used by the United States Employment Service, to designate an employer's report of workers hired, showing for each worker such data as the name, social security number, and the date on which he began work.

accession rate. The total number of accessions, or newly hired workers, per hundred employees; usually computed on a monthly basis, but sometimes determined as a yearly rate.

"Accessions." A term used by the United States Employment Service to designate all permanent and temporary additions to the employment roll, whether of new or rehired employees. Accessions include all employees returning from layoffs, military leave, and other absences who have been counted as separations. Transfers from one plant or department, or shifts within the establishment or from regular activities to force-account construction activities or vice versa, or from one establishment to another operated by the same employer, are not to be considered as accessions.

accident analysis. A study of the causes of accidents. Distinction is made between human and mechanical causes. Other factors considered are the type of accident, as falls, burns, striking against object; the agency causing the accident, as drill press, conveyor; the type of operation and identifying the hazards (See ACCIDENT HAZARDS). Accident analysis may also take into consideration the states of mind or body which account for the fact that some persons are more safe than others in the same environment or that accidents may occur more frequently at certain times of the day. A formula for handling accidents is: (1) Analyze the Accident. Check the work area, material handled, machine or tools used, and clothing worn. Look for "unsafe acts" and "unsafe conditions." Review job instructions issued. Investigate immediately. Don't wait. Get all the facts. (2) Determine Its Cause. Spot the unsafe act, physical hazard, or both. Consider possible remedies. Think of the effect on the individual, group, production, and economy. "Careless" is not a "cause"—it is an alibi word. Consider all aspects. (3) Take Action. For each hazard found do one of three things: Remove the hazard. Protect the worker against the hazard. Set up a safe practice for the worker to avoid injury from the hazard. Accept your responsibility. "Don't pass the buck." (4) Follow Through. Check all other similar operations. Have more than one look at how things turned out. Watch attitudes and relationships of persons.

accident frequency rate. Number of lost-time accidents per million man-hours worked. Only disabling injuries, as arbitrarily defined in the American Standard Association Code, are counted. The Code provides that any injury involving death, permanent impairment, or loss of time

beyond the day or shift on which the injury occurred will be counted. Frequency rates for various industries, computed in accordance with the ASA Code, are available from the U. S. Bureau of Labor Statistics, the National Safety Council, certain local safety councils and state labor departments.

accident hazards. Hazards fall into well-defined categories: (1) handling objects accidents, as bruised toes, hands, backstrain, hernia; (2) falling objects, particularly from a higher level; (3) falls of persons, either from one level to another or on the same level; (4) machinery operation accidents, as members of the body caught between moving parts, between moving part and stationary part of object, in contact with part moving at high rate of speed, loss of control of material in process of being fed into or withdrawn from machine; (5) hand tools, either improperly used, or wrong tool used for the job; (6) contact with dangerous facilities, as electricity, acids, materials of high temperature; (7) exposure to extremes of heat, cold, or dangerous conditions; (8) foreign body in the eye. The National Safety Council, Chicago, Illinois publishes literature to help both employees and employers avoid accidents.

accident hazard spots. To insure safety, many companies check every step of every job against the hazard spots, which can be considered as: (1) Work Area: Housekeeping—tripping, slipping; Illumination; Storage—piling, floor loads; Cramped quarters—corners; Stairs—inclines; Blind exits; Aisles; Ventilation; Holes, excavations; Exposed surfaces (electric; sharp; hot; etc.) (2) Material Handling: Heavy; Rough; Sharp; Long;

Poisonous; Hot; Explosive; Slippery; Fragile; Acid; Alkali; (3) Machines: Point of operation—cutting, punching, forming, etc.; Power transmission—line shafts, other shafting, belts, gears; Pinch points; Projections—flying particles; (4) Tools: Proper tools; Proper use of tools; Proper condition of tools; Proper place for tools; (5) Improper Clothing: Loose, ragged; Oil-soaked, flammable; Neckties, jewelry; High heels, thin soles.

accident prevention. A term generally used to designate a planned program for job safety. Four recognized responsibilities in connection with accident prevention are: (1) instruct each employee thoroughly in the safety precautions of his job; (2) follow up safety training constantly; (3) keep all safety devices in proper use; (4) Set a good safety example. See also ACCIDENT HAZARDS.

accident proneness. The tendency of certain people habitually to have a higher rate of accidents than others; usually to an abnormally high degree. Also called accident recidivism. Sometimes accident proneness is caused by physical condition, poor eyesight, etc. But if that is not the case, the accident prone person can usually be identified by certain personality characteristics. He is believed to have an instinct of rebellion and resentment and to demonstrate a show-off, don't care type of psychology. He is usually impulsive, and likely to act on the spur of the moment, and concentrates on what he wants to do rather than considering others.

accident severity rate. Number of working days lost through accident per thousand man-hours worked. The American Standards Association sets down certain

definitions and rules which must be followed if the figures obtained are to be credible.

accidental death benefit. A feature added to some group life insurance policies providing for payment of an additional death benefit in case of death as a result of accidental means. It is often called "double indemnity."

accidents, cost of. The cost of accidents may be figured in terms of: (1) Human suffering; (2) Medical and surgical attention; (3) Hospital fees and expense; (4) Loss of wages; (5) Time lost from production; (6) Spoilage of materials and damage to machines.

"Account Number." A term used by the United States Employment Service. See SOCIAL SECURITY ACCOUNT NUMBER.

"Accounts." A term used by the United States Employment Services. Types of accounts are: *Benefit Payment Account:* An account maintained in a State unemployment fund in which are recorded (1) amounts transferred from the Unemployment Trust Fund in the United States Treasury, and receipts from any other source, and (2) amounts of benefits paid. *Clearing Account:* An account maintained in a State unemployment fund in which are recorded (1) amounts of all contributions or other items paid into the Unemployment Fund, and (2) amounts transferred to the Unemployment Trust Fund in the United States Treasury, refunds to employers, or other items of withdrawal. *Experience-Rating Account:* An account of an employer which is maintained by the State employment security agency for the purpose of determining the contribution rate of that employer. *Partially Pooled Ac-*

(4)

count: An account maintained within a State unemployment fund from which benefits are payable to a claimant whose employer's reserve account is exhausted or is otherwise unavailable. Such an account is maintained only in those States whose employment security law provides for separate employer reserve accounts. See also RESERVE ACCOUNT below. *Reserve Account*: An account maintained in a State unemployment fund with respect to a subject employer to which are credited contributions paid by such employer and from which, if solvent, are payable all and only those benefits which are based on services performed for such employer. See also POOLED FUND under FUNDS. *Unemployment Trust Fund Account*: An account maintained in a State unemployment fund in which are recorded amounts transferred to and from the Unemployment Trust Fund in the United States Treasury and the amount of interest earned on the account. See also UNEMPLOYMENT TRUST FUND under FUNDS.

accumulative timing. A time-study technique utilizing two stop watches connected so that when one is stopped the other is simultaneously started. Each watch is thus read alternatively while its hand is stationary.

accuracy. Degree of correctness, exactness or precision. Used in industrial engineering terminology to denote the relationship between the mean value of a large number of measurements and the objective true value of the quality measured.

acquire. A THERBLIG (which see) which is defined as: to obtain by search or endeavor; to search, find and select. This therblig covers the duty and activity of the three therbligs, *search, find,* and *select.* By the use of this term, a series of impulses may be defined under one heading.

across - the - board increase. A general wage increase affecting simultaneously all or most of the employees within a plant, company, or industry. Such an increase may be granted in uniform percentage or cents-per-hour terms. In the former case, the absolute amount of increase will differ among employees in accordance with their original rate levels.

"Active Application." A term used by the United States Employment Service. See APPLICATION CARD.

"Active File." A term used by the United States Employment Service to designate a file of active application cards.

"Active File Clearance." A term used by the United States Employment Service to designate the systematic removal from the active file of the cards of those applicants considered as unavailable for referral.

"Active Opening." A term used by the United States Employment Service. See OPENING.

activity. (Time-Study Usage) The number of times a given operation or occurrence is repeated during a given period, usually a year.

actual cost. An acceptable approximation of the true cost of producing a part, product, or group of parts or products including all labor and material costs and a reasonable allocation of overhead charges.

actual earnings. See AVERAGE EARNED RATE.

actual time. The time taken by a workman to complete a task or an element of a task.

actuarially sound pension plan. A plan under which the funds already deposited in the reserve and the current contributions are sufficient to meet the liabilities already accrued and those which are being accrued. The contributions required to fund the pensions are determined by an actuary on the basis of various assumptions such as interest rates, mortality experience, and composition of the working force.

actuary. A specialist, trained in the science of mathematics, statistics, and legal accounting methods, who applies the probabilities of longevity to financial operations, epecially insurance and pensions. Recognized professional standing through the Society of Actuaries.

actual hours. See HOURS, ACTUAL.

Adamson Act. A federal law passed in 1916. It stipulates the 8-hour day as the basis for computing railway employees' rates, and maintains that the wage shall not be cut because of the shorter eight-hour day. It does not, however, limit the working-day to eight hours.

"Additional Application." A term used by the United States Employment Service. See APPLICATION CARD.

"Additional Claim." A term used by the United States Employment Service. See CLAIM.

"Additional Credit Allowance." A term used by the United States Employment Service. See CREDIT ALLOWANCE.

"Additional Occupational Classification." A term used by the United States Employment Service. See OCCUPATIONAL CLASSIFICATION.

"Adjusted Contribution Rates." A term used by the United States Employment Service. See CONTRIBUTION RATES.

administration. The function of management which is concerned with the determination of the general objectives or goals; major policies; organizational structure of the enterprise. Administration effectively commands and coordinates human and physical resources, and provides for continuous unification of data, facts, and opinions collected from varied sources; and through which there must be channeled a free flow of information, suggestions and ideas and plans to and from all levels,—up and down, as well as across. Administration determines the pattern of relationships and causes it to be modified as required. Widely accepted text is, "The Elements of Administration," L. Urwick, (Harper & Bros., 1944).

"Administrative Fund, Employment Security." A term used by the United States Employment Service. See FUNDS.

"Administrative Funds." A term used by the United States Employment Service. See FUNDS.

"Administrative Office" (State). Same as CENTRAL OFFICE, a term used by the United States Employment Service.

adult vocational education. Instruction offered to adults or out-of-school youth over 16 years of age who are already engaged in or are preparing to enter an occupation. Vocational education for adults is chiefly of an up-grading nature, offered on a part-time basis.

advance on wages. In general, refers to any practice by which employees are entitled to draw wages or salaries in advance of actual work performance; e.g., wage advances during slack seasons to workers on commission basis of wage payment etc. Also applies to the payment of wages in advance of the regular pay day for services already rendered.

affiliation. The process whereby a union associates itself with, and becomes a constituent part of, a larger labor organization.

"Agent State." A term used by the United States Employment Service to designate the State in which a worker claims benefits against another (liable) State through the facilities of the State employment security agency. See also LIABLE STATE.

aggregate funding. Method of figuring cost of pension plan over period of years in the future. Current assets of pension fund taken into consideration, and then amount of payments that will be needed to meet future needs figured and cost distributed over regular intervals in the future.

agreement, collective. An agreement, signed by union representatives and an employer, group of employers or their representatives, stipulating terms and conditions of employment.

agreement, master. A substantially identical contract signed by a large number of employers in an industry.

agreement, sweetheart. Statement in a collective agreement expressing the desire and intention of both union and management to maintain harmonious relations.

agreement, trade. Same as AGREEMENT COLLECTIVE.

"Agricultural Placement." A term used by the United States Employment Service. See PLACEMENT.

"Agricultural Referral." A term used by the United States Employment Service. See REFERRAL.

alcoholism. Alcoholism is costing industry a billion dollars a year. There are about 4½ million alcoholics in the U. S.; about 2 million hold down jobs in industry. Alcoholics lose an average of 22 workdays a year from drinking and they are responsible for around 1,500 fatal on-the-job accidents. Other factors bring up the total loss. Drinking is said to be a factor in 10 per cent of discipline cases in many organizations. Alcoholics Anonymous are active in most cities. Their General Service Headquarters are located at Box 459, Grand Central Annex, New York 17, N. Y.; the National Council on Alcoholism is located at 2 East 103d Street, New York City. Studies are under way at the Yale University Center of Alcohol Studies, which has published *Profile of the Problem Drinker*, in 1957.

all-day trade classes. Courses conducted for persons regularly enrolled in a full-time school who have selected a trade or industrial pursuit and who wish to prepare for useful employment in that occupation. Training is comprehensive and includes instruction in manipulative processes and also in those technical and other related subjects which are needed by the skilled and competent worker.

"Allotment." A term used by the United States Employment Service to designate

(7)

the amount of funds made or to be made available to a State employment security agency for a specific period from funds appropriated by Congress for the administration of the employment security program.

allowance. A time increment included in the standard time for an operation to compensate the workman for production lost due to fatigue and normally expected interruptions such as for personal and unavoidable delays. It is usually applied as a percentage of the normal or leveled time.

allowed hours. See ALLOWED TIME.

allowed time. Under incentive wage systems, the total time allowed or set as standard to complete a task or element thereof. Also relates to the amount of time permitted a worker for the care of tools, for rest periods, or for other reasons. This time is added to operating time in computing the standard time allowed for a particular operation as the basis for establishing piece rates or production bonuses.

all-round mechanic. A trained person possessing the knowledge and skills necessary to do practically all of the jobs within a specified trade or occupation.

alternate time standard. A standard allowed time developed for use with a method of performing a task other than the established standard method.

American Accounting Association. The American Accounting Association is the successor to the American Association of University Instructors in Accounting. The latter organization was established in 1916 by a group of accounting teachers who saw in the Association an opportunity to promote acquaintanceship and to stimulate the exchange of ideas. In 1926 the *Accounting Review* was started as the official quarterly journal. In 1935 the name of the organization was changed to American Accounting Association; new by-laws were adapted; and the objectives of the organization were revised to a somewhat broader scope. Membership was opened to all persons interested in the advancement of the objectives of the Association. Members receive without additional charge, the following: the *Accounting Review*, the annual index to the *Review*, the membership directory, and research monographs.

American Arbitration Association. A private, non-partisan, non-profit membership corporation organized in 1926 for the purpose of carrying on research and education for the promotion of the knowledge and practice of arbitration as a method of adjudicating controversies and providing facilities therefore. It maintains panels of arbitrators composed of members chosen from all trades and professions and occupational groups from which parties may select arbitrators to hear and determine their controversies. Through cooperative arrangements with trade and commercial organizations throughout the world, it has available facilities and arbitrators for the determination of international trade disputes. It publishes *The Arbitration Journal* issued quarterly; a monthly Arbitration News bulletin; books and pamphlets regarding the arbitration process. Its headquarters are at 477 Madison Avenue, New York City, and it maintains 14 other offices located in Boston, Charlotte, Chicago, Cleveland, Dallas, Detroit,

Hartford, Los Angeles, Philadelphia, Atlanta, Buffalo, Indianapolis, San Francisco and Washington, D.C.

The American Bankers Association. A national trade organization of banking representing in its membership more than 98 per cent of the banks in the United States by number and over 99 per cent of the nation's banking resources. Its membership on September 1, 1955 totalled 17,140, including 14,020 banks, 2,939 branches, and 181 members in foreign countries. The Association was organized in 1875, and its aim "to promote the general welfare and usefulness of banks" remains unchanged. Members of the Association may belong to divisions, such as national bank, state bank, trust, or savings and mortgage divisions; or be active in working groups, including many commissions, departments, councils, sections, committees, and subcommittees, each of which covers its specialized field in detail as, for example, agriculture, bank management, economic policy, credit policy, or executive development. The governing body of the Association is its membership which meets annually in convention to choose officers and determine policy. Between conventions, the Association is governed by its Executive Council, the members of which are elected by member banks in the various states. Between meetings of the Council, Association affairs are in charge of an Administrative Committee, including officers of the Association, presidents of the four divisions and two sections, three immediate past presidents of the A.B.A., and four members of the Executive Council, representing four different Federal Reserve Districts. The American Institute of Banking

is the educational section of the Association and offers courses to bank people through chapters and study groups in 437 cities and towns throughout the country and through correspondent study. Membership of the Institute on January 1, 1956 was 114,209, with 47,-386 student enrollments. In addition to the American Institute of Banking, the A.B.A. also sponsors The Graduate School of Banking at Rutgers University, New Brunswick, New Jersey. The Graduate School, organized in 1935 as a school of advanced study for bankers on the officer level, is attended by more than 1,000 bank executives who attend three two-week resident sessions on Rutgers campus and complete two years of extension study. One of the qualifications for graduation is the writing of an acceptable thesis on a banking or economic subject. The educational activities of organized banking are also carried on in approximately 80 banking schools, clinics, and conferences, sponsored by regional and state bankers associations. The national headquarters of the American Bankers Association is located at 12 East 36 Street, New York 16, New York.

American Economic Foundation. Founded 1939 by Fred G. Clark. Located at 295 Madison Avenue, New York 17, N. Y. The work of the Foundation has four goals: (1) The discovery of the need for a new simplified economic vocabulary; (2) the development and testing of that vocabulary; (3) preparation of a basic body of literature employing that vocabulary; (4) application of that literature to editorial material, visual aids, and motion pictures for use in free discussion in factories, offices, schools and colleges.

(9)

AFL-CIO. (See entries under American Federation of Labor and Congress of Industrial Organizations.) These two powerful unions merged on November 30, 1955. Highlights of the merger, which brought together 15,000,000 members, are as follows: Each national or international union, organizing committee or directly chartered local union affiliated to CIO or AFL at the time of merger shall be an affiliate of the new federation. The integrity of each union is confirmed. Present union jurisdictions are preserved; unions with conflicting or duplicating jurisdictions will be helped and encouraged to work out their problems through voluntary merger or agreement. The principles of both industrial and craft unionism are recognized. The AFL-CIO No-Raiding Agreement will be preserved and extended with the consent of the signatories. The CIO Organizational Disputes Agreement and the AFL Internal Disputees Plan are continued for the signatories. The principle of non-discrimination because of race, creed, color or national origin is recognized in the constitution, as is the principle of opposition to corruption and communism in all forms. Officers will be a president, secretary-treasurer and 27 vice-presidents, initially 17 from the AFL and 10 from the CIO, who will constitute an Executive Council. There will be an Executive Committee, composed of the president, secretary-treasurer and six vice presidents, three from CIO unions, three from AFL; and a General Board consisting of the Executive Council and one principal officer from each union, which will meet once a year. The president will appoint a director of organization from a CIO union. State and local central bodies of both CIO and AFL are continued as affiliates of the new organization, and are directed to merge within two years of adoption of the draft constitution. Per capita taxes of 4c a month are authorized for each member of all national and international unions and organizing committees, and of 80c per month per members of directly affiliated unions. Appropriate departments, including an industrial union department, are established, and the president is directed to appoint members of 14 named standing committees and such others as necessary. Resolution on the Achievement of Labor Unity: *Whereas* the combination of the American Federation of Labor and the Congress of Industrial Organizations into a single labor federation is a long-cherished goal of the trade union movement of this country, and *whereas* on Feb. 9, 1955, the Joint AFL-CIO Unity Committee agreed upon and recommended to the two federations the adoption of the "Agreement for the Merger of the American Federation of Labor and the Congress of Industrial Organizations" attached hereto as Annex A, and *whereas* the Agreement of Feb. 9 was ratified by the Executive Council of the American Federation of Labor on Feb. 10, 1955, and by the Executive Board of the Congress of Industrial Organizations on Feb. 24, 1955, and *whereas*, pursuant to the provisions of the Agreement of Feb. 9, 1955, a proposed constitution for the combined federation was drafted by the Joint AFL-CIO Unity Committee for submission to the two federations, and *whereas* the Executive Council of the American Federation of Labor and the Executive Board of the Congress of Industrial Organizations reviewed this draft constitution on several occasions, and made various changes therein, and *whereas* the "Constitution of the American Federation of Labor and Congress of Industrial Organizations" attached hereto as Annex B was approved by the Executive Council of the American Federation of Labor on Nov. 30, 1955, and by the Executive Board of the Congress of Industrial Organizations on Nov. 30, 1955, and *whereas* the Agreement of Feb. 9 provides that upon approval by the Executive Council of the American Federation of Labor and the Executive Board of the Congress of Industrial Organizations of that Agreement and of a Constitution for the combined federation, that the Agreement and the Constitution, and any other agreements necessary to accomplish the combination of the two federations, shall be submitted to the separate conventions of the American Federation of Labor and of the Congress of Industrial Organizations; and that upon approval by the separate conventions of the Agreement and of the Constitution of the combined federation, a joint convention shall be held, and *whereas* the Implementation Agreement dated Nov. 30, 1955, attached hereto as Annex C, was approved by the Executive Council of the American Federation of Labor on Nov. 30, 1955, and by the Executive Board of the Congress of Industrial Organizations on Nov. 30, 1955, and is necessary and appropriate to dispose of various matters arising out of the combination of the two federations, and *whereas* the Constitution of the "American Federation of Labor and Congress of Industrial Organizations," attached hereto as Annex B, provides in Articles XIX and XX that it shall become effective upon approval by the separate conventions of the two federations and shall

govern the joint conventions of the combined federations, NOW THEREFORE BE IT RESOLVED: (1) The "Agreement for the Merger of the American Federation of Labor and the Congress of Industrial Organizations," attached hereto as Annex A, is ratified, approved and adopted. (2) The Constitution of the "American Federation of Labor and Congress of Industrial Organizations," attached hereto as Annex B, is ratified, approved and adopted as the Constitution of the "American Federation of Labor and Congress of Industrial Organizations," and as an amendment to and substitute for the Constitution of this federation heretofore in effect. (3) The Implementation Agreement dated Nov. 30, 1955, and attached hereto as Annex C, is ratified, approved and adopted. (4) The adoption of this Resolution by this convention is conditional upon the adoption of an identical Resolution by the present separate convention of the other federation; *provided, however,* that this Resolution, the Agreement for Merger, the Constitution of the "American Federation of Labor and Congress of Industrial Organizations" and the Implementation Agreement shall become effective upon the opening of the initial convention of the "American Federation of Labor and Congress of Industrial Organizations" on Dec. 5, 1955. *The following Implementation Agreement, a step toward effectuation of merger of AFL and CIO, was approved by the 17th CIO Constitutional Convention:* Implementation Agreement. Made this 30th day of November, 1955, by and between the American Federation of Labor, sometimes referred to hereinafter as the AFL, and the Congress of Industrial Organizations, sometimes referred to hereinafter as the CIO.

(11)

Whereas, the AFL and the CIO, by their duly constituted executive bodies, have concluded an agreement entitled "Agreement for the Merger of the American Federation of Labor and the Congress of Industrial Organizations" to combine and continue both organizations into a single organization, the "American Federation of Labor and Congress of Industrial Organizations" (sometimes referred to hereinafter as the AFL-CIO), and *whereas*, the executive bodies of the AFL and the CIO have approved a proposed constitution for such combined organization, and *whereas*, the agreement to combine and the proposed constitution will be submitted for approval to the forthcoming constitutional convention of the AFL and of the CIO, and *whereas*, the combination of the AFL and the CIO into the AFL-CIO will become effective, in accordance with the agreement to combine and the proposed constitution of the AFL-CIO, on the effective date of the approval of such agreement and such constitution by the separate conventions of the AFL and of the CIO, and *whereas*, the duly constituted executive bodies of the AFL and the CIO have authorized the undersigned Officers of the respective organizations to enter into this agreement to implement the combination of the AFL and the CIO. *Now, therefore, the American Federation of Labor and the Congress of Industrial Organizations do hereby agree as follows*: (1) The AFL-CIO shall be deemed, for all purposes, to be a combination and continuation of the American Federation of Labor and the Congress of Industrial Organizations. Neither of such organizations shall be deemed for any purpose, to be dissolved, terminated or discontinued, but upon the effective date of the combination they shall be combined and continued as a single organization, the AFL-CIO, to be governed by the constitution of the AFL-CIO, which shall be an amendment to and substitute for the present separate constitutions of the AFL and the CIO. (2) Immediately prior to the effective date of the combination of the American Federation of Labor and the Congress of Industrial Organizations, the CIO shall, in accordance with Paragraph 4(a) of the "Agreement for the Merger of the American Federation of Labor and the Congress of Industrial Organizations" transfer to an appropriate account or other depository, for the benefit of, and to be the sole property of, the Industrial Union Dept. of the AFL-CIO, a sum in cash or securities estimated to be equal to the difference between the value of the net assets of the CIO and $1,238,536.00. Any errors in this estimate of the amounts due to the AFL-CIO and to the Industrial Union Dept. under the said Paragraph 4(a) shall be corrected subsequently by an appropriate adjustment between the AFL-CIO and the Industrial Union Dept. (3) On the effective date of the combination, all the property, real and personal and mixed and all right, title and interest, either legal or equitable, in any monies, funds or property tangible and intangible, of the American Federation of Labor and the Congress of Industrial Organizations, and their respective separate names, trademarks, and emblems, and all debts due to each of them, and all the rights, privileges and powers and every other interest of each of them, of whatever nature, except for the sum transferred to the Industrial Union Dept. as provided in Paragraph 2 of this Agreement, shall by virtue of the combination of the AFL and the CIO, be transferred to and vested in the AFL-CIO and all such rights and properties shall thereafter be as effectually the property of the AFL-CIO as they were of the AFL and the CIO. Title to any property, real, personal or mixed, legally or beneficially vested by deed or otherwise in the AFL or the CIO, shall not be in any way impaired by reason of the combination but shall in all respects be vested in the combined organization by virtue of the combination. The AFL-CIO shall, on and after the effective date of the combination, be responsible, by virtue of the combination, for all the debts, liabilities and obligations of the AFL and the CIO, and all such debts, liabilities and obligations shall from that time forth attach to the combined organization and may be enforced against it to the same extent as if the said debts, liabilities, and obligations were incurred or otherwise contracted by it. (4) The present executive officers, the present members of the Executive Council of the AFL and any trustee holding property for the AFL, and the present executive officers, the present members of the Executive Board of the CIO and any trustee holding property for the CIO shall be empowered to and shall from time to time after the effective date of the combination, execute and deliver or cause to be executed and delivered, upon request of the combined organization, all such deeds, authorizations, or other instruments as the combined organization may deem necessary or desirable in order to confirm the right and title of the combined organization to the property, rights and privileges referred to in Paragraph 3 above, and shall take such further and

other action as may be requested by the combined organization for such purposes. (5) In accordance with the provisions of Article III of the proposed constitution of the AFL-CIO, each national and international union and each Federal Labor and Local Trade Union and each State and Territorial Federation of Labor and Local Central Body affiliated with the AFL, and each department of the AFL and each national and international union, organizing committee and Local Industrial Union, and each State and Local Industrial Union Council affiliated with the CIO, and the Industrial Union Dept. provided for in Article XII of the constitution of the AFL-CIO, shall on the effective date of the combination of the AFL and the CIO, and by virtue of such combination, be an affiliate of the AFL-CIO unless, in the case of a national or international union, it expressly disaffiliates therefrom. (6) The combination of the AFL and the CIO into the AFL-CIO shall not affect, interrupt or change in any way the continuing status or the rights or duties with respect to third persons, of any organization affiliated with the AFL or the CIO, or any of their subordinate or affiliated bodies, whether such organization be a national or international union, organizing committee, national council, federal labor or local trade union, local industrial union, state or territorial federation, city central labor union, state or local industrial union council, or trade and industrial department, and, further, shall not impair the status of such organizations, or any of their subordinate or affiliated bodies, in any pending action or proceeding or any right, title or interest in any property or arising from any deeds, bonds, mortgages, leases or contracts of any kind, or the continuity thereof; and, further, shall not impair any federal, state or territorial certification or any rights or obligations of such organizations, or any of their subordinate or affiliated bodies, under their existing collective bargaining agreements or checkoff authorizations. (7) The combination of the AFL and the CIO is not intended to affect any presently existing collective bargaining agreement or any federal, state or territorial certification of the AFL or the CIO, but all rights, privileges, duties and responsibilities vested in either the AFL or the CIO pursuant to such contracts or certifications are intended to be vested in the AFL-CIO by virtue of the combination. (8) The combination of the AFL and the CIO is not intended, nor shall it be deemed, in itself to terminate the employment of any employee of either the AFL or the CIO. All employees of the AFL and the CIO initially shall, upon the effective date of the combination, and by virtue thereof, be deemed to be employees of the AFL-CIO without interruption of their employment status. (9) The combination of the AFL and the CIO shall not terminate or affect in any way any existing pension or insurance plan which may be in effect with respect to the employees of the AFL or the CIO but such plans shall be maintained in force by the AFL-CIO with respect to the employees covered thereby on the effective date of the combination until such time as consolidated pension and insurance plans shall be substituted therefor. (10) This Agreement is subject to and shall not become effective unless the agreement to combine the AFL and the CIO and the proposed constitution of the

AFL-CIO are approved and made effective by the separate conventions of the AFL and the CIO.

American Federation of Labor. See AFL-CIO. The American Federation of Labor was founded in 1881 as the first federation of trade unions. Reorganized and organization strengthened in 1886. Samuel Gompers first President, 1866-1924. William Green, President, 1924-1952. George Meany, President, 1952-1955, when merger with CIO took place. Financed by worker membership. At time of merger had 110 affiliated national unions with 45,000 local unions, with total membership of more than 10 million. Has local and state bodies as well as national headquarters.

American Institute of Industrial Engineers. This organization was founded in Columbus, Ohio, by Dr. Wyllys G. Stanton, and was incorporated as a nonprofit institution on September 9, 1948. Headquarters are 145 North High Street, Columbus, 15, Ohio. Official publication is *Journal of Industrial Engineering.* Purposes of the American Institute of Industrial Engineers are: (1) To maintain the practice of Industrial Engineering on a professional status; (2) To foster a high degree of integrity among the members of the industrial engineering profession; (3) To encourage and assist education among members of the profession; (4) To promote the interchange of ideas and information among members of the profession; (5) To serve in the public interest by the identification of men qualified to practice as Industrial Engineers; (6) To promote professional registration of Industrial Engineers.

American Institute of Management. A non-profit foundation, incorporated in

1948, located at 125 East 38th Street, New York City. Its objectives include: (1) To use funds exclusively for charitable, scientific, literary or educational purposes, so that no part thereof shall inure to the benefit of any member or individual having a personal interest in the activities of the corporation. (2) To promote, carry on, conduct and foster scientific research, education, training and publication in the fields of finance, economics, government administration and the political and social facts and principles relating to questions of local, national or international significance. (3) To make studies of corporate management. Publications include: *Manual of Excellent Managements; AIM Management Audit; The Corporate Director; Industry Audit; National Biographic* plus periodical studies.

American Management Association. An association originally organized in 1922 as the National Personnel Association by the merging of the National Association of Corporation Schools and the Industrial Relations Association; its present title was adopted March 14, 1923. Its services are subdivided into the eight different areas of Finance, Insurance, General Management, Marketing, Manufacturing, Office Management, Personnel, and Packaging. Services include national conferences for each division in major cities across the nation; workshop seminars; orientation seminars; management courses; executive communication courses; marketing management courses. It also supplies library service and information to management; has a confidential executive compensation service and a supervisory development service. Services of the American Management Association: (1) National Conferences: AMA holds national conferences for each Division in major cities across the nation, so that top operating executives can answer the questions of its members and report experiences that bear directly on their problems. Headquarters of the American Management Association are at 1515 Broadway, New York City. It also has a resident training facility for business executives—the A.M.A. Academy for Advanced Management, at Saranac Lake, New York. (2) Orientation Seminars: to supply its members with rapid-fire job fundamentals, AMA conducts intensive three-day courses covering such subjects as Sales Forecasting, Supervisory Development, Quality Control, and many others. Ideal for the seasoned executive undertaking new areas of responsibility. Orientation Seminars accommodate up to 35 members. (3) Workshop Seminars: limited to 15 operating executives who discuss a specific problem for three days in a round-table atmosphere, comparing facts, poring over business data, and leaving with a collective knowledge that could be gained in no other way. More than 250 management topics are covered in one year of workshop seminar activity. (4) Management Course: A curriculum of advanced study of the principles, skills and tools of effective management. Instruction is given at a rapid pace by outstanding operating executives. Assists the experienced executive in employing his fullest abilities. The four weekly units may be taken over a year's time. (5) Marketing Course: Intensive instruction is given with a balance of lecture, presentations and group discussions supported by practical working materials. Prime emphasis is placed upon scientific and realistic situations. For the experienced marketing executive only. Course consists of three one-week units. (6) Executive Communication Course: A three-week program for operating executives whose position requires communication skills of a high order. Teaches the executive to identify and clarify ideas, secure participation of others, transmit ideas and decisions, motivate others to act on these decisions, and to measure the effect of communication on those concerned. (7) Publications Service: AMA publishes for its members *The Management Review, Supervisory Management, Management News, Personnel, Conference Proceedings, Research Reports,* and other special publications, which together are widely recognized as the best business editorial service of its kind anywhere. (8) Management Information Service: When management problems arise, many members use this service to find tested ideas and procedures. AMA's Management Information Service draws upon a vast amount of published material, private reports and original source materials from industrial firms. AMA's Library of 12,000 volumes on every business subject may be used by members doing their own research or studies. (9) Special Services: (a) Executive Compensation Service: A confidential research service that supplies specific data on executive compensation practices, providing a sound basis for evaluation and comparison with similar firms and positions. (b) Intra-Company Management Program: A service to plan and present your company's internal management meetings. Complete program includes arrangements for speakers, presentations, and all physical accommodations and facilities.

American Marketing Association. An association composed of teachers of marketing, marketing-research and distribution specialists, government officials and the like, interested in promoting the development and advancement of marketing and securing on the part of the public a broader recognition of marketing as a science.

American Medical Association. An association, organized in 1847 primarily for the purpose of promoting the science and art of medicine and the betterment of public health. It now maintains a section on preventive and industrial medicine and public health. Abbreviation A.M.A.

American Personnel and Guidance Association, Inc. (APGA). The APGA is a professional association of 7,500 persons engaged in the various phases of guidance and personnel work. Its main purpose is to bring together in one organization all qualified workers in the field, so that mutual acquaintance may be cultivated, and so that principles, practices, and professional standards may be advanced. The APGA is the result of the unification of several associations which formerly were allied in the Council of Guidance and Personnel Associations, of which the APGA is the legal and historical successor. To further the development of personnel and guidance work in educational institutions, community agencies, government organizations, and business and industry, the association holds an annual convention, assists regional groups in conducting regional conferences, provides field services, conducts a placement service for guidance and personnel workers, coordinates the work of a variety of committees concerned with training, ethical standards, placement, and related matters, and provides its membership with such publications as a journal, a directory of approved vocational counseling agencies and studies and reports of interest in their professional field. The official journal, sent to all members nine times a year, is *The Personnel and Guidance Journal.* The headquarters office, under the direction of an executive secretary, is located at 1534 O Street, N.W., Washington 5, D. C., and serves both the Association and its Divisions. All members of the Association hold membership in one or more of the following Divisions according to their special interest: American College Personnel Association (ACPA); American School Counselors Association (ASCA); National Association of Guidance Supervisors and Counselor Trainers (NAGSCT); National Vocational Guidance Association (NVGA); Student Personnel Association for Teacher Education (SPATE).

American Public Health Association. An association founded in 1872 to protect and promote personal and public health through the application of biology and the medical and sanitary sciences. With its 13,000 members, organized in 13 Sections representing the various health disciplines, it is today the largest professional public health organization in the world. Included in its membership are 34 state affiliates and two regional branches. It holds an annual scientific meeting. The American Journal of Public Health is its monthly scientific journal.

American Society of Training Directors. Headquarters at 2020 University Avenue, Madison, 5, Wisconsin. Founded in 1944. 3,100 members in 53 chapters.

The ASTD operates to discover, develop and expand the skills, standards and perspective of those engaged in training as a creative, practical and developmental service to business, industry and its related professions, through developing increased knowledge, more and better skill and helpful right attitudes of all employees, from porters to presidents. It attempts to effectively: (1) Promote and conduct worthwhile projects of interest to the profession. (2) Aid, promote and improve the stature of ASTD members. (3) Hold an annual international conference of ASTD and regional conferences to present and discuss topics pertinent to effective training in business and industry and report the newest developments in adult educational techniques. (4) Publish and distribute *The Journal of ASTD* which keeps the membership up-to-date on professional progress. *The Journal* is published bi-monthly and is the official publication of the Society. *The Journal* provides a medium whereby ideas are exchanged, and wide communication given to results of special studies, training programs and analyses of training and related activities. (5) Publish and distribute to all members the proceedings of the annual ASTD conference. (6) Furnish members with special reports and manuscripts covering committee findings, results of research in program development, new techniques, procedures, standards and related data. (7) Cooperate with other professional organizations. The Society is an active member of the Council of National Organizations and the Council of International Progress of Management. (8) Issue a Directory of Membership classifying the Society's members alphabetically, geographically and by employer. (9) Develop and conduct a high degree of communication between members, chapters and business and industrial world. (10) Develop and maintain the ASTD Library located at Purdue University, Lafayette, Indiana. The Library's free Program Information Exchange to members is promoting and disseminating training "know-how" by exchanging and borrowing works and publications dealing with training. (11) Provide a valuable placement service to members seeking training positions and to organizations interested in locating capable training personnel. (12) Develop training personnel, procedures, techniques and programs. (13) Disseminate information concerning the Society, its members, programs, and activities, to the press, radio, trade and professional publications. (14) Exchange training program information on an international scale. (15) Offer the benefits of 30 ASTD Committee Activities. (16) Offer the privilege and opportunity of attending, participating in, and directing the Society's Annual Conferences. (17) Conduct a two week Annual Institute to provide a curriculum of study for all Training Directors. *Personnel*, published by the American Management Association, annually publishes each fall a list of all local groups which occupy the status of affiliated chapters of the American Society of Training Directors.

American Vocational Association. The national, professional organization of teachers, administrators, supervisors, and teacher-educators engaged in the various phases of vocational and practical arts education. Its objectives are the promotion of sound vocational and practical

arts education programs and the professional advancement of its members.

"Annual Benefit Amount." A term used by the United States Employment Service. See MAXIMUM ANNUAL BENEFITS under BENEFITS.

annual earnings. The total amount of compensation received for services by a worker during the year, including wages, salaries, and bonuses. The total annual earnings of a worker may be the result of work performed for a single employer or a number of employers in a given year.

"Annual Pay Roll (Experience-Rating)." A term used by the United States Employment Service. See PAY ROLL, ANNUAL (EXPERIENCE-RATING).

annual reports. More and more companies are popularizing their annual reports for employee consumption. Some companies publish booklets on how to read annual reports. Various publicity "stunts," such as putting the reports on records, in fancy covers, illustrated with cartoons, are in fashion. See *How to Read A Financial Report* published by Merrill Lynch, Pierce, Fenner & Beane, 70 Pine Str., New York, N. Y.

annual wage or employment guarantee. An arrangement under which any employer guarantees his workers a minimum amount of wages or employment during the year. Under the Fair Labor Standards Act, as amended in October 1949, employers may enter agreements, with certified labor unions, which set a maximum of 2,240 hours of employment in a specified 52-week period and which guarantee not less than 1,840 hours (or not less than 46 weeks at the normal number of hours worked per week, but not less than 30 hours per week) and not more than 2,080 hours. Under such agreements, employers are relieved from the overtime pay requirement for the first 12 hours of work in a day, or 56 in a week, during the guarantee period. Thereafter they are liable for overtime pay at time and one-half for all hours after 40 in a week up to 2,080 hours, and for *all* hours or work after 2,080 hours in the 52-week period. If the 2,240-hour maximum limit is exceeded, the entire agreement is made retroactively ineffective. See also GUARANTEED WAGE PLAN and WAGE ADVANCE PLAN.

"Annual Wage Formula." A term used by the United States Employment Service. See BENEFIT FORMULA.

annuitant. One who receives annuity benefit payments.

annuity. Periodic payments made to the retired employee either for life or until the fund accumulated in his behalf is exhausted.

annuity, cash refund. Pension paid after retirement until death of annuitant. If, upon death, the total amount to his credit at retirement exceeds his pension payments, the balance is paid to his beneficiary.

annuity, certain. Fixed annuity, which is to run a specified number of years regardless of outside circumstances. It may be a terminable annuity, or it may be a perpetuity, which means that it is, barring unforeseen and extraordinary accidents, to last forever.

annuity, certain and continuous. An annuity which is regulated by two factors,

the refund provision and the deferred life annuity.

annuity, contingent. A contingent annuity depends upon some uncertain outside event, usually upon the death of one or more people. The event is, in a sense, both certain and uncertain, since it is certain that it will take place; the uncertain element is the time at which it shall take place. In other words, pension benefits may be paid to a worker and payments continue to his beneficiary after his death. Usually such benefits are smaller than normal benefits payable to the worker only. Also known as joint survivor annuity or last survivor annuity.

annuity, deferred life. See DEFERRED LIFE ANNUITY.

annuity, five or ten years certain. The guarantee of a specified number of pension payments. If the annuitant dies before he receives all of the payments, the balance is continued to his beneficiary.

annuity, immediate life. An annuity which immediately pays income for life, but with nothing payable in event of death.

annuity, joint and survivor. Annuity, payable during life of annuitant, is continued either in part or in its entirety to his named beneficiary until the death of the latter.

annuity, last survivor.
See ANNUITY, CONTINGENT.

annuity, life. Periodic payments made after retirement and ceasing with the death of the annuitant.

annuity, modified cash refund. Pension paid after retirement until death of an-

(19)

nuitant. If, upon death, the amount of his contributions and interest exceeds the pension payments, the balance is paid to his beneficiary.

annuity, temporary life. An annuity which pays immediate income for a specifically stipulated number of years. In case the employee dies prior to the expiration of the stipulated payment years, nothing more is payable.

Anti-Injunction Act. (Norris-LaGuardia Act) passed March, 1932 and subsequently modified. The Anti-Injunction Act declares it to be a public policy that the worker shall have full freedom of association, self-organization, and designation of representatives of his own choosing to negotiate the terms and conditions of his employment, free from employer interference in these or other concerted activities for mutual aid or protection. The act defines and limits the powers of the Federal courts to issue injunctions in labor disputes in conformity with this policy. When injunctions may not be issued: No Federal court may issue an injunction, temporary or permanent, in any case involving or growing out of a labor dispute, to prohibit any individual worker or group of workers acting in concert from doing any of the following acts, (except as modified by the Labor Management Relations Act, under which the General Counsel has the power to seek a Federal Court injunction to stop either an employer or a labor organization from committing any unfair labor practice): (1) Ceasing or refusing to work; (2) Joining or continuing membership in a union; (3) Aiding or refusing to aid financially or by other lawful means any person participating in or interested in

a labor dispute; (4) Giving publicity to the existence of or the facts involved in any labor dispute whether by advertising, speaking, patrolling, or by any other method not involving fraud or violence; (5) Assembling peaceably to act or to organize to act in promotion of their interests in a labor dispute; (6) Advising or notifying any person of intent to do any of the above, agreeing or refusing to do any of the above, or inducing others to do any of the above acts, without fraud or violence. Except as otherwise indicated below, a Federal court may issue a temporary or permanent injunction in cases involving or growing out of a labor dispute only after hearing the testimony of witnesses in open court with opportunity for cross-examination. Such hearings shall be held only after personal notice to all known persons involved including the public officers responsible for protecting the complainant's property. The court must also find that: (1) unlawful acts have been threatened and will be committed unless restrained or have been committed and will be continued unless restrained; (2) Substantial and irreparable property damage will follow; (3) Greater injury will result to the complainant from denying the injunction than to the defendant from granting it; (4) The complainant has no adequate remedy at law; (5) Public officers are unable or unwilling to furnish adequate protection; (6) The complainant has complied with every legal obligation involved in the dispute and has made very reasonable effort to settle the dispute by negotiation or with the aid of available Government machinery. The injunction or temporary restraining order may be issued only against the person or persons, association, or organization making the threat or committing the unlawful act or actually authorizing or ratifying the act. Under special circumstances a Federal court may issue a temporary restraining order for a maximum of 5 days without an open court hearing, on the basis of sworn testimony sufficient to sustain a temporary injunction issued on hearing after notice, and on condition that the complainant posts a bond. See INJUNCTIONS IN SPECIAL CASES.

anti-injunction law. A type of State or Federal legislation which restricts the issuance of injunctions in labor disputes. See ANTI-INJUNCTION ACT.

Anti-Kickback Law and Copeland Act. Act of June, 25, 1948. These laws cover not only direct Federal public building and public work but also all work financed in whole or in part with Federal funds, loans, or grants. The Government agencies that let the contracts are primarily responsible for obtaining compliance with these laws and the regulations of the Secretary of Labor. *Anti-Kickback Law.* This law makes it punishable by a fine up to $5,000 or by imprisonment up to 5 years, or both, for anyone, by force, intimidation, threat of procuring dismissal from employment or by any other manner whatsoever, to induce an employee on work covered by the law to give up any part of the compensation to which he has a right under his contract of employment. *Copeland Act.* This act authorizes the Secretary of Labor to make reasonable regulations for contractors and subcontractors engaged in construction covered by the act. These regulations (29 CFR 3, as amended 29 CFR [1955 Supp.] 3)

show under what conditions deductions from wages are and are not permitted, require the contractors to present evidence that proposed deductions are proper ones, and require approval of the Department of Labor for such deductions. The act and the regulations also require the contractors to file weekly affidavits showing wages paid and deductions made. The regulations also require payroll records showing the information needed to determine whether required wages are being paid. The requirements of these regulations are made a part of every contract for a Federal or Federal-aid job. For further information write the Office of the Solicitor, U.S. Department of Labor, Washington 25, D. C.

Anti-Racketeering Law. (Hobbs Act) passed June 18, 1934 and subsequently amended. The anti-racketeering law makes it a felony to obstruct, delay, or affect commerce, or the movement of any article or commodity in commerce, by robbery or extortion. The act also makes it a felony to act in concert with others to do anything in violation of the above, or to participate in any attempt at such violation, or to commit or threaten physical violence to any person or property in furtherance of any plan to commit such violation. The provisions of the Anti-Injunction Act, Railway Labor Act, and National Labor Relations Act are specifically preserved.

The U. S. Department of Justice is charged with prosecuting violators, who are subject to a maximum fine of $10,000, imprisonment for a maximum of 20 years, or both.

Anti-Strikebreaker Law. (Byrnes Act) passed June 24, 1936 and subsequently

79778

amended. The anti-strikebreaker law makes it a felony to transport in interstate commerce any person employed for the purpose of interfering by force or threats with: (a) Peaceful picketing during any labor dispute affecting wages, hours, or working conditions, or (b) exercise of employee rights of self-organization or collective bargaining. This act applies to persons who wilfully transport others or cause others to be transported, and to persons knowingly transported for these purposes. It does not apply to common carriers. The U. S. Department of Justice is charged with prosecuting violators, who are subject to a maximum fine of $5,000, imprisonment up to 2 years, or both.

"Appeal Administrative." A term used by the United States Employment Service to designate a request for a review by an appeals authority of a State employment security agency's determination on a claim for benefits, on a status report, or on an employer's contribution rate, or a request for a review by a higher appeals authority of a decision made by a lower appeals authority. *Appeal Board*: The title given in some States to the higher appeals authority. See also BOARD OF REVIEW. *Appeal Tribunal*: The title given in some States to the lower appeals authority. *Appeals Authority*: An administrative authority provided by the State employment security law to make decisions with respect to appeals. *Appeals Referee*: The title given in some States to the lower appeals authority.

"Applicant." As used by the United States Employment Service, designates a person who contacts a local office for the purpose of obtaining employment.

Clearance Applicant. An applicant (1) who desires employment in another State and for whom a search for a clearance job opening has been initiated; or (2) who cannot be placed locally and accepts referral to a clearance job opening. *Handicapped Applicant.* An applicant who has a physical, mental, or emotional impairment or condition included in the list of coded disabilities; or who has an impairment or condition not included in the list and is in need of one or more of the specialized services to obtain a suitable job; or who is a veteran currently rated 10 percent or more disabled by the Veterans Administration or retired for physical disability by a branch of the armed services.

"Applicant-Holding Office." A term used by the United States Employment Service to designate a local office which (1) attempts to locate and refer applicants from its local office administrative area to job openings located outside that area in response to a request by an order-holding office, or (2) initiates action to locate suitable job openings outside its local office area for its applicants who desire employment in another locality or who cannot be placed locally and will accept employment elsewhere.

"Applicant-Holding Office Acceptance." A term used by the United States Employment Service to show that an applicant-holding office acceptance has occurred when (1) as a result of an interview with an employer (or his representative, including the Employment Service when hiring authority has been delegated to the agency) an offer of employment has been made and the applicant agrees to accept the job; or (2) the order-holding office notifies the applicant-holding office that the employer, after reviewing the information regarding the applicant (mail referral), wishes the applicant to report at a specified place for an interview or to commence work, and the applicant agrees to report at the specified place for the purpose indicated; or (3) after direct referral or telephone referral when the applicant-holding office receives notification that the employer has offered employment and the applicant agrees to accept the job.

"Applicant Identification Card." A term used by the United States Employment Service. See IDENTIFICATION CARD, APPLICANT.

"Application." As used by the United States Employment Service designates the act by which a job seeker informs an employment service interviewer of his ability and qualifications for referral to job openings. *Clearance Application.* A form submitted by an applicant-holding office to an order-holding office which contains (1) a record of an applicant's qualifications for referral to a definite job opening, and (2) provision for reply by the order-holding office. *Self-Application.* The partial filling out of an application card by the applicant.

application blank. A form for recording data furnished by one who applies for employment. Some companies require the application blank to be filled out when an employee appears in the personnel office; others have the blank filled out after the applicant has passed a preliminary interview and is being considered for the job. Some concerns require only the factual details necessary for their records. Others explore an employee's interests and capabilities.

"Application Card," as used by the United States Employment Service, describes the basic local office record for an applicant. *Active Application Card:* The application card of a person who has indicated his availability for referral to job openings during the established validity period. See also VALIDITY PERIOD. *Additional Application Card:* A partial copy of the primary application card which is classified for an additional occupational classification assigned to an applicant. *Inactive Application Card:* The application card of a person who is currently not considered by a local office as available for referral to job openings. *New Application Card:* The application of a person for whom a local office has no previously prepared application card. *Primary Application Card:* The application card which is classified under the primary occupational classification assigned to an applicant.

application interview. A part of the application process, usually the more formal or complete interview in which the prospective employee's background is explored. Frequently employees are interviewed both by the personnel department staff and by the supervisor under whom they will work.

"Application Interview." A term used by the United States Employment Service. See INTERVIEW.

apprentice. A person who is learning a skilled trade by means of supervised work experience, supplemented in some cases by related classroom instruction. An apprentice is usually employed in accordance with the terms of an agreement defining his rights and obligations and those of his employer. Satisfactory completion of a formal apprenticeship is a requirement for membership in many craft unions. In view of the relative decline in the number of skilled artisans and in the level of skills required for modern industry, the importance of apprenticeship has been declining. Formal technical education, particularly in public and vocational schools, has also minimized the need for apprenticeships. A description of the apprenticeship system in the United States appears in *Educating for Industry Through Apprenticeship*, by William Patterson and Marion Hedges, 1946.

apprentice rate. The schedule of rates applicable to workers being given formal apprenticeship training for a skilled job, in accordance with set standards. The rate schedule is usually established in such a manner as to permit the gradual achievement of the minimum journeyman rate.

apprentice scale. See APPRENTICE RATE.

apprenticeship, indentured. Apprentice training under terms of a contractual agreement specifying types and length of training and graduated pay increases.

apprentice training. An organized system for providing young people with the manipulative skills and technical or theoretical knowledge needed for competent performance in skilled occupations. The program usually involves cooperation among school, labor and management, since apprentices learn the skills of the craftsman through on-the-job work experiences and the related information in the classroom. The minimum terms and conditions of apprenticeship are regulated by state and local statutes or agreements.

Apprentice Training Service. A bureau of the Department of Labor which develops and formulates standards of apprenticeship for the training of skilled workers by industry. It is assisted by the Federal Committee on Apprentice Training composed of representatives of labor, management and government.

"Approved Budget." A term used by the United States Employment Service. See BUDGET, APPROVED.

approved pension plan. Pension or profit-sharing plan which meets the provisions of the Internal Revenue Code and accompanying regulations. An approved plan is advantageous taxwise from the standpoint of the employer, employee and the trust.

aptitude. A term used in employment testing. The potentiality for acquiring, with appropriate training and experience, a recognized degree of skill.

"Aptitude." A term used by the United States Employment Service to designate the potentiality for acquiring vocational proficiency after appropriate training and experience.

aptitude test. A method of measuring present performance as a means of estimating future potentialities of the one tested for success in a contemplated course of training or study. Aptitude tests in business and industry are usually given for skilled trades, clerical occupations or executive positions.

aptitude test, offered by United States Employment Service. The U.S.E.S. offers employers a "General Aptitude Test Battery." The aptitudes measured by this Battery are: *Learning Aptitude*—The ability to "catch on" or understand instructions and underlying principles; the ability to reason and make judgments. Is closely related to doing well in school. *Verbal Aptitude*—The ability to understand meaning of words and ideas associated with them, and to use them effectively. The ability to comprehend language, to understand relationships between words and to understand meanings of whole sentences and paragraphs. The ability to present information or ideas clearly. *Numerical Aptitude*—Ability to perform arithmetic operations quickly and accurately. *Spatial Aptitude*—Ability to comprehend forms in space and understand relationships of plane and solid objects. May be used in such tasks as blueprint reading and in solving geometric problems. Frequently described as the ability to "visualize" objects of two or three dimensions, or to think visually of geometric forms. *Form Perception*—Ability to preceive pertinent detail in objects or in pictorial or graphic material. Ability to make visual comparisons and discriminations and see slight differences in shapes and shadings of figures. *Clerical Perception*—Ability to perceive pertinent detail in verbal and tabular material. Ability to observe differences in copy, to proofread words and numbers, and to avoid perceptual errors in arithmetic computation. *Finger Dexterity*—Ability to move the fingers and manipulate small objects with the fingers, rapidly and accurately. *Manual Dexterity*—Ability to move the hands easily and skillfully. Ability to work with the hands in placing and turning motions. *Motor Coordination*—Ability to coordinate eyes and hands or fingers rapidly and accurately in making precise movements with speed. Ability to make a movement response accurately and swiftly.

aptitude test battery. A term used in employment testing. A combination of aptitude tests used to measure the potentiality of an applicant for acquiring one or more occupational skills. Examples: (1) For specific occupations—TRANSMITTER TESTER B-75; (2) For groups of occupations—CLERICAL OCCUPATIONS B-3; (3) For fields of work —GENERAL APTITUDE TEST BATTERY B-1001.

arbiter. An individual who has the power to settle a dispute. (more commonly called arbitrator)

arbitration, labor. The American Arbitration Association (which see) describes the arbitration process as follows: Voluntary arbitration of disputes arising out of collective bargaining agreements is today accepted almost unanimously by both labor and management. There is also a growing tendency to submit to arbitration disputes regarding the terms of such agreements, including wage reopenings and other conditions upon which parties are unable to agree in their contract negotiations. But despite this widespread use of arbitration and possibly due to the rapidity of its growth, it is evident from reports in the daily press and in both management and labor papers that there is considerable misunderstanding regarding arbitration practice and procedure. It is essential that management and labor be familiar with the arbitration process, in order to utilize it most expeditiously, with the greatest saving of time, money and good will. Arbitration is frequently confused with conciliation and mediation and is sometimes referred

(25)

to as a step in the collective bargaining process. It is not conciliation, mediation, or compromise; nor is it an extension of collective bargaining. Parties providing for the settlement of a dispute by a third person should understand and be in agreement as to the process to be used or confusion and dissatisfaction will be the result. The term arbitration should be used only when arbitration in its accurate meaning is desired. For this reason, it is important that parties have a clear definition of arbitration and do not apply the term to processes such as mediation or fact finding, nor any other process that does not meet the essential requirements of arbitration. A definition follows: Arbitration is the reference of a dispute by voluntary agreement of the parties to an impartial person for determination on the basis of evidence and arguments presented by such parties, who agree in advance to accept the decision of the arbitrator as final and binding. Arbitration is a judicial process. The arbitrator is the judge. The parties present their evidence, witnesses or documents and each is permitted to cross examine the evidence of the other. Upon the evidence submitted by the parties and the arguments advanced by them, the arbitrator makes his decision. The parties having voluntarily agreed to arbitrate are bound to accept and carry out the decision. *Preparation for the Hearing*: Under a collective bargaining agreement, the facts regarding the grievance will be known by the parties through the course of the grievance procedure. The arbitrator, however, will know nothing whatever of what has previously transpired, and it is essential, therefore, that a case be prepared carefully and completely. The following is a suggested course of *preparation*: (1) Study of the grievance. (2) Review the contact thoroughly and note carefully all clauses that apply to the grievance. (3) Examine all records that have any bearing on the grievance. (4) Interview all witnesses. (5) Take down summaries, at least of their statements, in order that you may know what testimony you have to offer and how it will cover the essential facts. (6) Secure copies of any documents or papers (other contracts, etc.) that the arbitrator should receive. ("Photostats" are most convenient.) If these are in the possession of the other party, notify him that they will be required at the hearing. (7) The arbitrator is usually empowered to issue a subpoena for persons or documents at the request of a party. (8) When you have prepared an outline of your case, discuss it with other officials of your organization, in order that you may have other viewpoints on the matter. (9) Endeavor to prepare an outline of your opponent's case so that you may anticipate what proof he will offer and how you may examine it and answer it. In preparing the case for arbitration, it is frequently desirable to obtain information as to condition and practices in competitive plants or the industry generally, and to secure publications or other documents which may support any statement made in regard to such information. In planning to offer documents and data, parties should be prepared to have them substantiated and identified by witnesses, if required. If any attorney is to be present, the rules require that at least three days' notice thereof shall be given to the other party, in order that he may avail himself of a like privilege. *The Award*: The award is the decision of the arbitrator upon the matters submitted to him under the arbitration agreement. Its purpose is to dispose, finally and conclusively, of the controversy. The award must be within the limits of the arbitration agreement, must rule on each claim submitted, and be definite and final. It may be accompanied by an Opinion discussing the evidence and setting forth the reasoning of the arbitrator. An award may not be changed by the arbitrator, once it is made, *unless the parties mutually agree to reopen the proceeding and to restore the power of the arbitrator.* The power of the arbitrator ends with the making of the award. When the parties do agree to request the arbitrator to reopen a proceeding in order to obtain a clarification or interpretation of a disputed ruling, the agreement to reopen must be in writing and must set forth precisely the question submitted. Such agreement is filed with the Association which then proceeds to make the necessary arrangements with the arbitrator. Unless the parties have otherwise agreed, the award may be made by a majority of the arbitrators.

arbitration, compulsory. See ARBITRATION.

arbitration, voluntary. See ARBITRATION, LABOR.

arbitration, terminal. The use of arbitration specified in a contract as a final step in grievance procedure.

arbitrator. An individual to whom disputing parties submit their differences for decision.

"Area Actively Served," a term used by the United States Employment Service to designate the geographic portion of the local office total administrative area, (normally encompassing the city in which the office is located, plus its immediate environs) which can be effectively served for placement purposes on a continuing basis. See LABOR MARKET; LOCAL OFFICE ADMINISTRATIVE AREA.

area, industrial. A district, of a town, city, county, state or region devoted predominantly to manufacturing.

area vocational school. A school offering specialized training to prospective students in a large geographical territory, usually involving more than one school district, and often operated or sponsored by the state.

area-wide bargaining. The process of arriving at a collective bargaining agreement between a union and one or more employers whose establishments are within a specified geographical area.

artisan. One who is skilled in the industrial arts. An artisan is sometimes classified as a journeyman or a master in contradistinction to an apprentice.

assemble. The basic element employed when one or more objects are put on or into another object so that they fit or contact each other in a predetermined relation in order to form a unit.

assemble. A THERBLIG (which see) which is defined as: to collect; to fit or join together; to place in proper position relative to other parts; to secure in a desired relationship. *Assemble* may define an entire operation such as "assemble four screws," or "place two hundred screws in a carton." However, when used as a THERBLIG, it means the contacting of two or more parts.

(27)

assembly. A term used to denote the collection of parts or units which have been put together, or assembled, into a finished unit: sometimes applied to parts put together into a series of smaller units, or sub-assembly. The term may also apply to a meeting or forum, when groups of people are called together for training, lectures, or similar purposes.

assembly line. In personnel work, a term describing machine-paced and repetitive work. Morris S. Viteles ("Science of Work," W. W. Norton & Company, Inc.) describes the assembly line worker as follows: "As an attendant of the machine he must surrender himself to its time and rhythm. He supplements whatever human faculties the machine lacks . . . at a pace set by the machine and under its direction and command. Man not only works at the speed and rhythm imposed by the machine but he is forced by it into the repetition, hour after hour, day after day, of the same limited series of movements constituting his task." The assembly line of the automobile industry furnishes perhaps the most striking illustration of the high degree of specialization of work into repetitive tasks which the machine has brought into modern industry. See JOB SPECIALIZATION. One of the most thorough-going studies of assembly line and other repetitive work was made by Dr. Charles W. Walker and Robert H. Guest, of the Institute of Human Relations at Yale University. The characteristics of the assembly line work in an auto plant which a large majority of the workers interviewed said they found most frustrating are: mechanical pacing, repetition and monotony, too little demand for skill and judgment and social isolation.

assessment. A charge levied by a union on each member for a purpose not covered by the regular dues. Assessments may be either one-time or periodic charges.

"Assignment." A term used by the United States Employment Service to designate the placing by an employer of a worker in a specific position in his establishment.

assignment of wages. An action instigated by a worker which designates that his wages are to be turned over to a creditor, or which authorizes the employer to turn over specified amounts to charitable organizations, or to be applied to dues, etc.; the agreement is in writing and is duly signed by the employee.

association. An organized group formed in pursuit of some common interest with its own self-contained administrative structure and functionaries, as American Management Association.

association agreement. An agreement negotiated and signed by an employers' association on behalf of its members, usually with a union or a board representing several unions. An association agreement may cover all or most of the employers within an industry throughout the country or in a particular locality.

Association of Consulting Management Engineers. Organized informally in 1929, articles of incorporation were drawn up and temporary officers elected in 1932, and the first official meeting was held in early 1933. The purpose of the association is to raise the standards of management consulting, to give it the status of a recognized profession, and to make it worthy of the trust of the business managers it serves. Every member of the association is pledged to observe and maintain this code of ethics: (1) In presenting our qualifications for carrying out an engagement, we will make representations and employ means that conform to the highest professional standards. (2) We will accept engagements that we are qualified to undertake, and will assign to a client's work personnel fitted to give effective service in solving problems involved. (3) We will regard as confidential all information concerning the business and affairs of a client coming to us in the course of our professional engagement. (4) We will maintain an objective and unbiased attitude and will always be governed by the best interest of the client. (5) We will endeavor so to serve our clients that our work will bring about permanent benefits. In striving for these results we will supply the client's employees with information as to principles applied and techniques in such a manner that improvements suggested may be most effectively administered by them after completion of our assignment. (6) We will be guided in our work by the increasingly preponderant importance of human relations and accordingly so formulate our recommendations and pave the way for their introduction that the cooperation of all employees substantially affected may be reasonably expected. (7) We will maintain an impartial attitude toward the work of our professional colleagues and will refrain from making comments, either solicited or unsolicited, which will be detrimental to the standing of our profession. (8) We will charge reasonable fees or rates for services appropriate to

the character of the work and preferably agreed upon in advance of an engagement. (9) If we should at any time employ in our work methods devised by and generally credited to colleagues, we will do so only with their permission and giving due credit. (10) We will not accept fees, commissions, or any other valuable considerations from organizations the use of whose equipment, supplies or services we may recommend to our clients.

associations, personnel and management. See PERSONNEL ASSOCIATIONS.

attitude scale. A series of indices of attitudes, each of which has been given a quantitative value relative to that of each other. The usual indices are propositions which are ranked or rated in reference to the degree of antagonism or protagonism expressed toward some object of thought. The indices may be selected so that the interval between each two consecutive ones appears to equal that between each other two consecutive ones.

attributes, supervisory. See SUPERVISORY ATTRIBUTES.

attitude, measurement of employee. A technique for determining how employees feel about their job, their supervisor, company policies, working conditions, and so forth. Questionnaires or personal interviews, or both combined are used. Frequently attitude surveys are conducted by outside agencies, as colleges or opinion pollsters, so employees feel free to register their attitudes. See MORALE SURVEY.

audio-visual aids. Implements or devices which enable the learner to experience by seeing and hearing the best patterns after which to form his own performances in the skills he is learning. Such aids include motion pictures, slides, flannel board presentations, charts, and closed television, used for highly technical material.

"Augmented Weekly Benefit Amount." A term used by the United States Employment service. See BENEFIT AMOUNT.

authorization card. A statement signed by an employee authorizing a union to act as his collective bargaining agent.

automatic checkoff. An agreement between a union and a company for deducting union dues from employees' wages.

automatic progression. A policy by which rates of pay of workers in jobs with established rate ranges are increased automatically and at set time intervals. The width of the rate ranges and the number of steps within each range may vary among occupations, establishments, and industries, but under all fully automatic plans increments are received at specified time intervals until the maximum rate for the job is reached. Some plans combine automatic progression up to a specific point (for example, the midpoint) within the range, with discretionary increases, usually based on some type of merit review, up to the top of the range. Also refers to the automatic movement from a trainee rate to a job classification single rate or to the minimum of a job classification rate range.

automaticity. The ability to perform hand, arm, leg or body motions or mo-

tion patterns without apparent mental direction as a result of practice.

automation. The modern-day engineer's word for the state of being automatic. Formerly automation referred to machine tool applications. But it has come to mean the act or method of making a manufacturing—or processing—system fully or partially automatic. Automation has the following characteristics: (1) Linking together various conventionally separate operations –known as integrated data processing. (2) The use of "feed back" control devices or servo-mechanisms to allow operations to be performed without any necessity for human control. With feed back, there is always some built-in electrical, mechanical, or electronic automatic device for comparing the way in which the work is actually being done with the way it is supposed to be done and for making automatically any adjustments in the work process that may be necessary. In other words, feed back exists when information about the output at one stage of a process is returned, or fed back to an earlier stage so as to influence its action and hence to change the output itself. (3) Development of general and special purpose computing machines capable of recording and storing information (usually in the form of numbers) and of performing both simple and complex mathematical operations on such information. Automation is conceived as a philosophy of design of the product, a manufacturing method and a control within a machine. Although popularly referred to as a "push-button factory," its definition and application is much broader.

auxiliary department. A staff department in the line organization that provides services such as maintenance, material handling, warehousing, and the like to the production departments. It rarely performs manufacturing operation on the product to be marketed.

average earned rate. The total earnings of an individual or group of individuals for a period divided by the number of manhours worked during the period. Total earnings include all of the components which are a function of pay per hour such as base rate earnings, shift differentials, incentive earnings, overtime premiums and the like but not profit sharing bonuses, Christmas bonuses, or other bonuses that are not a function of pay per hour.

average earnings. The total earnings of an individual or group of individuals during a specified period divided by the number of man-hours, man-days, man-weeks, man-pay periods, or any similar measure of the time elapsed during the specified period.

average elemental time. (1) The sum of all the unleveled, individual actual times recorded for an element (which see) divided by the number of unleveled, individual actual times. (2) The sum of all the consistent unleveled actual times recorded for an element divided by the number of consistent unleveled individual actual times.

average hourly earnings exclusive of overtime payments. In general, average hourly earnings from which the effect of premium payments for overtime work has been eliminated. Also, a measure of average hourly earnings published by the Bureau of Labor Statistics in which gross average hourly earnings in manu-

facturing are adjusted statistically to eliminate the influence of premium overtime payments at time and one-half the regular rate of pay after 40 hours of work a week. The adjustment does not compensate for other forms of overtime payment nor for other types of premium pay. See also AVERAGE STRAIGHT TIME. HOURLY EARNINGS and GROSS AVERAGE HOURLY EARNINGS.

average pay plan. Pension based upon the individual's pay averaged over his years of participation in the plan.

average selected time. See AVERAGE ELEMENTAL TIME and AVERAGE TIME.

average straight-time hourly earnings. Average wages earned per hour excluding premium overtime payments and shift differentials. Commissions, production bonuses, and cost-of-living bonuses are included, but nonproduction bonuses (such as Christmas, profit-sharing, attendance, and service), tips, and allowances for room or board or other payments in kind are excluded. This concept is used by the Bureau of Labor Statistics in virtually all of its occupational wage rate studies and by numerous private organizations engaged in wage survey work. This definition, however, is not universally accepted. There appears to be general agreement on the elimination of overtime premium payments; but differences are found as to the treatment of shift differentials and the monetary value of some other wage and related practices. See also AVERAGE HOURLY EARNINGS EXCLUSIVE OF OVERTIME PAYMENTS and GROSS AVERAGE HOURLY EARNINGS.

average time. The arithmetical average of all the actual times, or of all except the abnormal times, taken by a workman to complete a task or an element of a task.

"Average Weekly Wages." A term used by the United States Employment Service. See WAGES.

average working force. An average (monthly or annual) number of employees, sometimes obtained by adding the number on the payroll at the beginning of the period to the number at the end of the period and dividing by two.

avocational interests. Pursuits or hobbies distinct from the regular work or occupation of the individual and which are followed for recreational purposes.

avoidable delay. Any time during an assigned work period which is within the control of the workman and which he uses for idling or for doing things unnecessary to the performance of the operation. Such time does not include allowance for personal requirements, fatigue, and unavoidable delays.

avoidable delay. A THERBLIG (which see) which is defined as: a temporary stoppage which can be avoided; an unnecessary movement or sense organ service. These pauses are a direct choice of the operator. They may be the result of unnecessary care, being too fussy, refusal to learn an improved method, or produced by poor mental processes of mental discipline. AVOIDABLE DELAY may occur as a delay within a rhythmic motion or a body member movement. It may be caused by insufficient tools or supplies, or tools or supplies not the best for the purpose. It may be fostered by the attitudes of executives and may be a result of favoring or protecting certain individuals. It may also be a means of using up accumulated time where the operator must fulfill a rigid policy of keeping busy.

award. Written decision of an arbitrator or arbitration board on questions submitted for their consideration.

award, arbitration. A decision of an arbitration board concerning questions or points of dispute which have been submitted for consideration. It usually is in formal, written form.

award, to employees. A form of employee recognition for suggestions, service, long employment or unusual performance. May be a certificate, citation, pin, watch, money or attendance at some special function or dinner.

(32)

B

B. A unit of time, used in measurement of productive activity, designating one minute of work at normal skill and with normal expenditure of effort. In computing a B time for required rest and relaxation is included.

Back pay. Delayed payment of part of the wages for a particular period of time, arising from arbitration awards, grievance procedure regarding particular rates, errors in computation of pay, or current legal interpretation of wage legislation. See also RETROACTIVE PAY.

back-to-work movement. Demand among workers for terminating a strike and returning to work, sometimes instituted by an employer.

Bacon-Davis Act. See PREVAILING WAGE LAW.

balance. That quality of a motion sequence in an operation which promotes the development of rhythm and automaticity. As applied to progressive related operations, it is the condition in which the standard times required for each successive operation are approximately equal and the work flows steadily or at a desired rate from one operation to the next.

balanced line. A series of progressive related operations with approximately equal standard times for each arranged so that work flows at a desired steady rate from one operation to the next.

balanced motion pattern. A motion sequence that promotes the development of rhythm and automaticity.

balance sheet reserve. A reserve set up by the employer for the payment of future pensions. These funds may be recaptured by the employer. Usually these reserves are not actuarily determined.

balancing delay. The delay which occurs when one body member performs its work faster than another body member because of different motions, due to the requirements of the layout or the required sequence of motions, and therefore must wait for the slower member or must work more slowly so as to finish its work simultaneously with the slower body member.

bank. In industrial engineering terminology, a planned accumulation of work-in-process to permit reasonable fluctuations in performance times of coordinated or associated operations.

bargaining agent (or agency) for members only. A union which acts and bargains only for its own members in a plant where non-union members are also employed.

bargaining, area-wide. Collective bargaining between union and employer representatives to establish the terms and conditions of employment through negotiation by an employer or employers and an employee organization, union or unions.

bargaining, collective. See COLLECTIVE BARGAINING.

bargaining, industry-wide. Collective bargaining between management and union representatives for an entire industry. See "PATTERN-FOLLOWING BARGAINING."

bargaining representatives, rights of, National Labor Relations Act (which see). The labor organization or individual winning a majority among the employees casting valid ballots in a representation election shall have the exclusive right to bargain for the employees in the unit covered. In regard to the exclusive right of the bargaining agent, section 9 (a) of the statute reads: Representatives designated or selected for the purposes of collective bargaining by the majority of the employees in a unit appropriate for such purposes, shall be the exclusive representatives of all the employees in such unit for the purposes of collective bargaining in respect to rates of pay, wages, hours of employment, or other conditions of employment : Provided, That any individual employee or a group of employees shall have the right at any time to present grievances to their employer and to have such grievances adjusted, without the intervention of the

bargaining representative, as long as the adjustment is not inconsistent with the terms of a collective-bargaining contract or agreement then in effect: Provided further, that the bargaining representative has been given opportunity to be present at such adjustment.

bargaining steps to change or terminate a contract, under National Labor Relations Act (which see). In the negotiation of new contracts to replace existing ones, the law provides four specific steps which must be observed. The section states that where there is in effect a collective-bargaining contract covering employees in an industry affecting commerce, the duty to bargain collectively shall mean that no party to such contract shall terminate or modify such contract, unless the party desiring such termination or modification—(1) serves a written notice upon the other party to the contract of the proposed termination or modification sixty days prior to the expiration date thereof, or in the event such contract contains no expiration date, sixty days prior to the time it is proposed to make such termination or modification; (2) offers to meet and confer with the other party for the purpose of negotiating a new contract or a contract containing the proposed modifications; (3) notifies the Federal Mediation and Conciliation Service within thirty days after such notice of the existence of a dispute, and simultaneously therewith notifies any State or Territorial agency established to mediate and conciliate disputes within the State or Territory where the dispute occurred, provided no agreement has been reached by that time; and (4) continues in full force and effect, without resorting to strike or lock-out, all the terms and conditions of the existing contract for a period of sixty days after such notice is given or until the expiration date of such contract, whichever occurs later. It further provides that: Any employee who engages in a strike within the sixty-day period specified in this subsection shall lose his status as an employee of the employer engaged in the particular labor dispute, for the purposes of sections 8, 9, and 10 of this Act, as amended, but such loss of status for such employee shall terminate if and when he is reemployed by such employer.

bargaining theory of wages. An obsolete theory which held that labor is a commodity the price of which is determined by bargaining between the employer and the employee. The theory was advocated by John Davidson in *"The Bargaining Theory of Wages,"* 1898.

bargaining unit. A group of employees accepted or designated by an authorized agency or an employer as appropriate for representation by one union.

Barth Variable Sharing Plan. An incentive wage plan based on standard time but which does not establish any wage guarantee. Pay is figured by multiplying the standard number of hours by the number of hours really taken for the job, extracting the square root of the product, and multiplying it by the hourly rate of pay. The plan provides for shares of varying nature at various levels of production or standard. A formula for figuring a worker's earnings under the Barth Plan is:

$$E = \sqrt{(H_s \times H_a)} \times R_h$$

where: E = earnings

H_s = hours standard

H_a = hours actual

R_h = rate per hour

or dividing by $H_a R_h$;

$$E = E/H_a R_h = \sqrt{H_s/H_a} \text{ or}$$

$y = \sqrt{x}$ and $y^2 = ax$ where a = unity.

When $H_a = H_s$, the formula can become either $H_a R_h$ time wages, or $H_s R_h$ piece wages.

base pay. See BASE RATE. Also used to denote the product of a workman's base rate and the time he worked during a pay period when expressed in the proper measurement units.

"Base Period." A term used by the United States Employment Service to designate a period of time prior to the benefit year (or a period similar to the benefit year) in which the claimant must have had a specified minimum amount of insured work in order to qualify for benefits. Wages earned during this period are used in determining a claimant's weekly benefit amount and his maximum annual benefits. *Individual Base Period*: A base period which varies as to starting date for individual claimants. *Uniform Base Period*: A base period which starts on the same calendar date for all claimants.

base points. (1) The minimum point values assigned to the factors of a job evaluation system. (2) The minimum points assigned to any job by an evaluation system.

base rate. The amount of pay for a unit of time; e.g., hour, day, week, month, or year, exclusive of premium pay for overtime or other premium payments. Under incentive wage systems, other than piece-rate systems, the term may refer to the rate to be paid for production at "standard," before the addition of extra earnings for production above standard; more generally, under piece rate or other incentive systems, the term may refer to the amount guaranteed per hour or other time period. See also GUARANTEED RATE.

base time. (1) See STANDARD TIME. (2) In the piece work system of wage payment, that time value which, when multiplied by the applicable base wage rate, gives the piece rate.

base wage rate. See BASE RATE.

"Base Year." A term used by the United States Employment Service. Same as BASE PERIOD.

basic division of accomplishment. The smallest elements of human activity or inactivity used in any particular system of motion analysis. See THERBLIG.

basic element. See BASIC DIVISION OF AC- COMPLISHMENT.

basic motion. See BASIC DIVISION OF AC- COMPLISHMENT.

basic motion timestudy. A system of predetermined motion time standards. The essence of the system lies in the arbitrary definition of a basic motion as one that commences from rest and ends at rest. The system's purpose is to establish time standards for procedures that are composed of human motions controlled only by the individual perform-

ing them, and to do so without resorting to time study. An allied purpose is to facilitate the analysis of methods. Abbreviated as BMT.

"Basic weekly Benefit Amount." A term used by the United States Employment Service. See BENEFIT AMOUNT.

Baum System. A wage incentive plan which provides for a by-step type of bonus in a multiple piece-rate system. It has low piece-rates for high production, or standard; similar to bonus steps of the MERRICK DIFFERENTIAL BONUS PLAN.

Bayle System. A wage incentive plan, resembling the Rowan plan, which see. It is computed in the same way as the Rowan plan, after percentage of earnings has in addition been squared and multiplied by two.

Bedaux Plan Formula. The formula for computing a worker's earnings under the Bedaux Plan, usually calculated as follows: Extra pay at the rate of one minute basic pay for each Bedeaux unit over standard.

Bedaux Point System. An incentive wage system, introduced by Charles E. Bedaux, for determining earnings in terms of the number of "man minutes" required to perform each operation or job. Output is measured in time units instead of in pieces completed. The amount of work per minute, together with allowance for fatigue, etc. is called a "B," or a point. Operations are rated in accordance with the amount of work that the average man is able to perform. The worker is guaranteed a basic rate for each job and a bonus is paid for anything that he does over and above the established standard.

Bedaux Point System Formula. A prescribed formula for computing an employee's earnings under the Bedaux Point System is: Earnings up to high task$=H_a \times R_h$, or $E = H_a R_h$. Earnings up to and above task$=H_a R_h + \frac{3}{4}$ earning saved, or $E = H_a R_h + \frac{3}{4}(H_s - H_a)R_h$
$E = R_h/4(H_a + 3H_s)$
where: $E =$ earning in dollars
(vertical variable)
where: $H_s =$ hours standard
(horizontal variable)
where: $H_a =$ hours actual
(a constant)
where: $R_h =$ rate per hour in dollars
(a constant)
where: $H_a R_h =$ time wages

Bedaux unit. A work unit, under the Bedaux Point System, used as a measure of human productivity which represents the standard amount of work that can be done in one man-minute or one man-hour, depending on which is simpler to use in the given case. This conception is such that the average group of men in temperate zones, properly trained and supervised and with reasonable incentive, whether money or other kind, will eventually develop under normal working conditions a productivity averaging 33 percent above the standard, unless productivity is impaired by process or machine limitations. (Standard performance always represents 100 per cent.) Each work unit is made up of two components: (1) the element of work itself; (2) a rest allowance. The proportion of one to the other varies considerably in different cases, but the total of both components always forms one work unit which is equal to any other work unit whatever type of work or the circumstances.

beneficiary. The person named in a policy, to whom the insurance money is to be paid at the death of the insured.

"Beneficiary." A term used by the United States Employment Service. Designates a claimant who has received unemployment benefits.

"Benefit Amount," a term used by the United States Employment Service. *Augmented Weekly Benefit Amount*: The weekly benefit amount of a claimant with dependents, including the allowance for dependents. *Basic Weekly Benefit Amount*: The weekly benefit amount of a claimant excluding any allowance for dependents. *Maximum Weekly Benefit Amount*: The highest weekly benefit amount provided in a State employment security law. *Minimum Weekly Benefit Amount*: The lowest weekly benefit amount for a week of total unemployment provided in a State employment security law. *Weekly Benefit Amount*: The full amount of benefits a claimant is entitled to receive for a week of total unemployment.

"Benefit Balance." A term used by the United States Employment Service, to designate the unpaid portion of the total benefits payable with respect to a claimant's unemployment during a given benefit year.

benefit, death. See DEATH BENEFIT.

"Benefit Decision." A term used by the United States Employment Service to designate the decision reached by a lower or higher appeals authority with respect to an appealed claim. See also BENEFIT DETERMINATION, under DETERMINATION.

"Benefit Determination." A term used by the United States Employment Service. See DETERMINATION.

"Benefit Eligibility Conditions." A term used by the United States Employment Service to designate statutory requirements which must be satisfied by an individual with respect to each week of unemployment for which he claims benefits before he may receive benefits. See also DETERMINATION; DISQUALIFICATION PROVISIONS; QUALIFYING EMPLOYMENT; WAGES, QUALIFYING.

"Benefit Formula." A term used by the United States Employment Service to designate the combination of mathematical factors specified in the State employment security law as the basis for computing an individual's weekly benefit amount and maximum annual benefits. *Annual-Wage Formula.* A benefit formula which uses the claimant's total wages in insured work for a one-year period for computing his weekly benefit amount. *High-Quarter Formula.* A benefit formula which uses, for determining a claimant's weekly benefit amount, the quarter of the base period in which his wages in insured work were highest.

"Benefit Ledger." A term used by the United States Employment Service to designate a record maintained by a State employment security agency, showing for a claimant the weekly benefit amount, maximum annual benefits, benefits paid, and the benefit balance.

"Benefit Payment Account." A term used by the United States Employment Service. See ACCOUNTS.

benefit plan, definite. A pension plan that sets a percentage of an employee's salary or earnings he will receive as a pension at retirement age. Benefits may be determined: (1) by a fixed percentage of the employee's highest (or last) annual salary or earnings; (2) by a fixed percentage of the employee's average salary or earnings over a definite period of years; (3) by a fixed percentage of each year's salary or earnings during the period during which the employee is a member of the plan. In other words, the pension is equivalent to a definite percentage of pay multiplied by years of service or by years of participation in the plan.

"Benefit Rate." A term used by the United States Employment Service. Same as WEEKLY BENEFIT AMOUNT—See BENEFIT AMOUNT.

"Benefit Wages." A term used by the United States Employment Service. See WAGES.

"Benefit Year." A term used by the United States Employment Service to designate that period to which the limitation of maximum duration of benefits is applicable, a year or approximately a year. *Individual Benefit Year.* A benefit year for which individual claimants varie as to starting date. The starting date is usually the day as of which the claimant first files a valid claim or request for determination of insured status. *Uniform Benefit Year.* A benefit year which starts on the same date for all claimants.

"Benefits." A term used by the United States Employment Service to designate money payments to an individual with

(38)

respect to his unemployment. *Maximum Annual Benefits.* For an individual claimant, the largest amount of benefits he may receive in a benefit year under a State employment security law. *Maximum Potential Benefits.* The largest amount of benefits any claimant may receive in a benefit year under a State employment security law. *Minimum Potential Benefits.* The maximum annual benefits for a claimant who has only minimum qualifying employment, and is entitled to the minimum weekly benefit amount under a State employment security law. *Partial Benefits.* Benefits for partial unemployment. See WEEK OF PARTIAL UNEMPLOYMENT under WEEK OF UNEMPLOYMENT. *Part-Total Benefits.* Benefits for part-total unemployment. See WEEK OF PART-TOTAL UNEMPLOYMENT under WEEK OF UNEMPLOYMENT.

benefits, Social Security, Table of. The following examples show the benefits payable to retired or disabled workers with different wage earnings, and also to their wives, children, or survivors. In each of these examples it is assumed that the wage earner earned $240 or more each year in covered occupations.

Retirement and Disability Insurance Payments

Retirement benefit starting at age 65 or later, or disability benefit starting at age 50—man or woman:

Average monthly earnings after 1950*	
$50	$30.00
100	55.00
150	68.50
200	78.50
250	88.50
300	98.50
350	108.50

Retirement benefit for woman worker, starting at age—

Average monthly earnings after 1950*	62	63	64
$50	$24.00	$26.00	$28.00
100	44.00	47.70	51.40
150	54.80	59.40	64.00
200	62.80	68.10	73.30
250	70.80	76.70	82.60
300	78.80	85.40	92.00
350	86.80	94.10	101.30

Retirement benefit for couple—man 65 or over, wife's benefit starting at age—

Average monthly earnings after 1950*	62	63	64	65
$50	$41.30	$42.50	$43.80	$45.00
100	75.70	78.00	80.30	82.50
150	94.30	97.10	100.00	102.80
200	108.80	111.30	114.60	117.80
250	121.80	125.50	129.20	132.80
300	135.50	139.60	143.70	147.80
350	149.30	153.80	158.30	162.80

Survivors Insurance Payments

Average monthly earnings after 1950*	Widow, widower, child, or parent	Widow and one child
$50	30.00	45.00
100	41.30	82.60
150	51.40	102.80
200	58.90	117.80
250	66.40	132.80
300	73.90	147.80
350	81.40	162.80

---

*After dropping out as many as 5 years of lowest earnings or of no earnings.

Average monthly earnings after 1950*	Widow and two children	Lump-sum death payment
$50	$50.20	$90.00
100	82.60	165.00
150	120.00	205.50
200	157.10	235.50
250	177.20	255.00
300	197.10	255.00
350	200.00	255.00

*After dropping out as many as 5 years of lowest earnings or of no earnings.

A worker may continue to build up insurance credits regardless of his age as long as he remains in employment covered by the program. However, wages received from 1937 to 1939 count toward old-age benefits only if they were earned before a worker's 65th birthday in the case of a man, and 62nd birthday in the case of a woman.

Benefits, types of, and insured status, under Social Security Act. The following table shows, for each type of old-age and survivors insurance benefit, whether the worker must be fully insured, currently insured, or both:

Types of Old Age and Survivors Insurance Benefits and who is entitled to them

	Payable to—	At age—	If retired worker is—
MONTHLY RETIREMENT BENEFITS	retired worker	65 or over / 62-64, reduced benefit	woman or man, fully insured / woman, fully insured
	dependent husband	65 or over	woman, BOTH currently and fully insured
	wife	65 or over / 62-64, reduced benefit	man, fully insured
	wife, caring for child entitled to benefits	any age	man, fully insured
	dependent child, unmarried	under 18	woman or man fully insured
	dependent child, unmarried, disabled before reaching 18	any age	

	Payable to—	At age—	If disabled worker is—
MONTHLY DISABILITY BENEFITS	disabled worker	50 or over	woman or man, both currently and fully insured, who has 20 quarters of coverage out of the 40 before becoming disabled, and who meets other disability conditions

	Payable to—	At age—	If deceased worker was—
MONTHLY SURVIVOR BENEFITS	dependent widower	65 or over	woman, BOTH currently and fully insured
	widow	62 or over	man, fully insured
	widow, caring for child entitled to benefits	any age	man, fully OR currently insured
	dependent child, unmarried	under 18	woman or man, currently or fully insured
	dependent child, unmarried, disabled bfore reaching 18	any age	
	dependent parent: mother	62 or over	woman or man, fully insured and leaving neither spouse nor child entitled to monthly benefits
	father	65 or over	
LUMP-SUM DEATH BENEFITS	spouse living with insured worker or, in absence of such spouse, person paying burial expenses	any age	woman or man, currently OR fully insured

(40)

benefits, under Social Security Act.
Monthly benefits are figured according to a formula that takes into account the worker's average monthly wage on covered jobs. His average wage cannot be calculated exactly until he retires or dies; but on the basis of his usual pay in covered jobs, he can figure out roughly what his benefits may be. Workers who retire will have their benefits computed by the following formula: 55 percent of the first $110 of average monthly wages, plus 20 percent of the next $240. This formula is applicable to monthly earnings up to a maximum of $350. For example, a certain worker averages $240 a month steadily. The calculation of his benefit would be:

55 percent of the first $110............60.50
20 percent of the remaining $130.26.00
                                    ——————
                                     86.50

This is called the primary insurance benefit. It is the benefit to which the worker himself is entitled when he reaches 65, on the basis of the wages or self-employment income he has earned in covered employment. All other benefits under the old-age and survivors insurance program are figured on the basis of the primary benefit. No primary benefit will ever be less than $30. In other words, if the benefit calculation should come to less, the amount will be raised to $30.

bibliographies, personnel and industrial relations. These include: Personnel Management and the Professional Employee, Industrial Relations Section, Princeton University, Princeton, N. J. Bibliography of Outstanding Books in Industrial Relations, Industrial Relations Section, Princeton University. Industrial Training, A Guide to Selected Readings, New York State School of Industrial and Labor Relations, Cornell University, Ithaca, N. Y. Industrial Relations Bookshelf, Industrial Relations News, 230 West 41st St., New York, N. Y. (periodically) Film Guide for Industrial Training, National Metal Trades Association, 337 West Madison Street, Chicago, 6, Illinois. Library Accessions Bulletins, Industrial Relations Library, Massachusetts Institute of Technology, Cambridge, Mass. Business Literature (Monthly Note) The Business Library, Newark, N. J. The Executive—guide to reading for top management. Baker Library, Harvard University, Graduate School of Business Administration.

Bidding. Application of present employees for vacant jobs on the basis of seniority.

Bigelow-Knoeppel Efficiency Bonus Plan. This plan begins with a "hiring" or learner's rate 40% below the usual day wages. As they increase production, new employees are advanced on a straight line scale from the hiring rate to day rate. This line is the average of a reverse curve called the effort line. An employee below 70% task "should be considered as an apprentice and rewarded in terms of his attainment of skill." When he reaches 70% of the high task, he is given a 5% bonus. From 70% to 100% of high task, employees are paid according to an empiric bonus—efficiency scale—which is terminated at task with a small step bonus amounting to 5% of day wages, or about 4% of wages at 99% of task. Above the point (100, 130) the earning is a straight line falling away from the piece rate of (100, 130) but parallel to basic piece rate as in the case of the original Emerson earning curve. By virtue of the two small steps and the empiric bonuses, the location of this earning curve for above task productions is high. If the plan can hold the average response just above task, it will succeed in combining high wages and reasonably low unit total costs.

Bigelow Plan. A wage incentive system which provides for a step bonus between the minimum, or base, wage and standard wage, along with more than one percent added pay for one percent added production at exceptionally high levels. Somewhat like the Emerson Efficiency Wage Plan.

blackleg. A British labor term applied to a person who works for a plant after a strike has been called. The American equivalent is "scab."

black list. A compilation of the names of workers considered undesirable by employers. Use of a black list to facilitate discrimination in employment has been viewed as an unfair labor practice under the National Labor Relations Act.

Blue Cross and Blue Shield plans. Nonprofit plans for individual or group prepayment of hospital service. These plans are recognized by local hospitals. The Blue Cross plans make group hospitalization insurance available to workers. The Blue Shield plans provide surgical operations insurance.

blue-sky bargaining. A term sometimes used in labor relations to characterize excessive and unreasonable demands made by union representatives.

"Board of Appeals." A term used by the United States Employment Service to designate the title given in some States to the higher appeals authority.

"Board of Review." A term used by the United States Employment Service to designate the title given in some States to the higher appeals authority.

bogey. A term sometimes applied to limits on output informally maintained by employees.

bonus. A broad term which refers to any payment above regular or base rates. It includes extra payments for night work, hazardous work, regular attendance, and overtime, as well as any annual or regular allotment such as a Christmas bonus. It also refers to extra earnings of incentive workers above the base or guaranteed rate. Specific forms of bonuses are usually preceded by descriptive terms such as "Christmas bonus," "attendance bonus." In sales compensation, bonus is generally paid when a definite point of sales is reached; that is, when a certain quota is sold.

bookkeeper. (1) general. Keeps a complete and systematic set of records of all business transactions of an establishment, examining and recording the transactions in proper record books and on special forms; balances books and compiles reports at regular intervals to show the receipts, expenditures, accounts payable, accounts receivable, profit or loss, and many other items pertinent to the operation of a business; calculates wages of employees from plant records or time cards, and makes up checks or draws cash from bank for payment of wages. May prepare, type, and mail monthly statements to customers. May perform other duties, such as taking telephone orders and making bank deposits. May operate an adding machine. (2) Keeps a record of and works with only one phase or section of a complete set of records pertaining to business transactions, such as accounts receivable or the accounts payable section.

bootleg wages. The wages above those at the prevailing rate or the union scale which an employer may pay in a tight labor market to hold or attract employees. May also refer to wages at rates below the prevailing or union rate which an employee may accept in order to obtain employment. See also KICK-BACK.

boycott. Concerted effort by a union to prevent the sale or use of products or services of an employer with whom the union is in dispute. "Boycott" is derived from the name of a Captain Boycott, a British merchant in Ireland to whom no one would sell and from whom no one would buy.

boycott, primary. Involves only a refusal to trade with an employer with whom a labor dispute is current, and then only on the part of his own workers. It is a permissible form of collective pressure. Should the workers of this employer with whom they have a dispute go beyond merely refusing to deal themselves; should they attempt to secure sympathetic refusal by labor generally, the public or customers of the employer, the primary boycott becomes a secondary boycott, which see.

boycott, secondary. The act, on the part of a union involved in a labor dispute, of causing, or attempting to cause, by inducement, persuasion, or coercion, third persons not directly involved in the dispute, to refrain from business dealings with the adversary employer. Such acts may try to keep suppliers and customers to refrain from business dealings; may seek sympathetic pressure by other labor organizations, as where they are induced to refuse to cross a picket line or refuse to work with nonunion men or materials. Under the provisions of the Taft-Hartley Labor Act of 1947, secondary boycotts have been made illegal.

boycott, tertiary. Involves the coercion of suppliers or customers of a supplier or customer of an employer with whom a labor difficulty exists. This form of boycott is uniformly held to be an illegal weapon and is rarely resorted to by labor organizations.

"braceros." A Mexican laborer who legally enters the United States to do work in the fields, under the provisions of Public Law 78, enacted in 1941. This law specifies that braceros must be pulled off jobs if domestic labor is available. Bracero labor is used primarily with fruits, nuts, vegetables, sugar beets and cotton, rather than with ordinary field crops, which are usually mechanized.

"brainstorming." A term used to designate a problem-solving process. "Brainstorming" is based on the principle that, faced with a given need, several people voicing any ideas that enter their heads can produce an amazing number of solutions. One suggestion triggers another until the group is so stimulated, suggestions simply pour forth. No criticisms are allowed and no evaluations. "Brainstorming" was initiated by Alex F. Osborn, co-founder of Batten, Barton, Durstine and Osborn, advertising agency. It has been used regularly by his company and many other business organizations. Brainstorming has three distinguishing characteristics: (1) It depends upon free association to produce ideas. One idea suggests a variation which in turn suggests a different idea, and so on. (2) It concentrates on quantity rather than quality of answers. (3) Evaluation of ideas is postponed until later, because pausing to evaluate sidetracks the session from its objective of piling up alternatives. When a group member introduces criticism, the leader rings a desk bell, shutting him off. Criticisms of brainstorming are: (1) It may tend to produce superficial ideas. (2) The job of sorting useless from useful suggestions becomes tedious and evaluations may be put off indefinitely. Participants feel the sessions are not taken seriously. (3) Brainstorming may tend to be haphazard and disorderly.

break-even chart. A graphic representation of the relation between total income and total costs for various levels of production and sales indicating areas of profit and loss. See BREAK-EVEN POINT.

break-even point. That point at which the level of balance is equal, as the level of production at which there will be no profit or loss, or the volume of sales required to balance all expenses so that there will be neither profit nor loss on the portion of operation being measured, and so forth.

The Brookings Institution, Washington, D.C. The Institution is named in honor of Robert Somers Brookings, a St. Louis businessman who retired in middle life to devote himself and his fortune to education and the public service. From 1896 to 1928, he was President of the

Board of Directors of Washington University in St. Louis. During the First World War, he served as a member of the War Industries Board as Chairman of the Price Fixing Committee. Mr. Brookings' experience in government intensified his interest in public affairs. He was one of the original trustees of the Institute for Government Research in 1916, and after the First World War, he worked energetically to promote the work of the Institute and to finance its activities. He was largely responsible for founding the Institute of Economics in 1922, for which he obtained financial support from the Carnegie Corporation. He established the Robert Brookings Graduate School of Economics and Government in 1924 and contributed to its capital resources. Upon the amalgamation of these organizations in 1927, the trustees named the resulting Institution in his honor. Brookings Institution was founded to fulfill three related purposes: (1) To study with scientific objectivity the expanding structure of government—federal, state, and local—and to promote efficiency and economy in public administrations. A group of educators and business leaders joined in 1916 with this end in view—in the establishment of an institute for government research in the nation's capital. This agency was financed for a number of years by contributions from interested individuals and business enterprises. (2) To make available to the public a wider knowledge of the working of economic forces. In response to an appeal to the Carnegie Corporation of New York, a sustaining grant was made to make this possible. (3) To provide a more realistic and practical type of research training than that provided by existing institutions, more closely related to the requirements of the public service. To meet this need a research training program for advanced graduate students of economics and government was begun in 1924.

brotherhood. A term sometimes used as a synonym for "union." It was originally used by railroad labor organizations established for fraternal and benefit purposes.

budget. An organized statement of expected or estimated income and expenditures for a definite future period, usually a month or a year, made in order to assist in controlling expenditures and to provide a criterion for judging performance during that period.

"Budget, Approved." A term used by the United States Employment Service to designate a statement showing the amount approved by the Bureau of Employment Security for the administrative expenditures of a State employment security agency during a given period of operation, and setting forth the general and special limitations governing the expenditure of such amount.

budget, cash. A statement designating the systematic organization of anticipated receipts and disbursements for a stipulated forecasted period of time.

budget, control. Same as budget, flexible.

budget, fixed. A systematic organization of anticipated results, usually established on the basis of past experiences, and weighted to allow for the future. It usually makes no provision for variation in levels of activity, as in the flexible budget. The fixed budget is based upon the

concept that sales can be anticipated within close limits of approximation. Inventory, production, and expenses can, as a result, be budgeted within comparable limits.

budget, flexible. Same as budget, variable.

budget, forecast. Same as budget, fixed.

"Budget Request." A term used by the United States Employment Service to designate a request from a State employment security agency for funds in an amount estimated as necessary to cover administrative costs for a given period of operation, supported by a detailed statement of such costs.

budget, variable. A systematic measurement of actual results based on provision for varying levels of activity. In the variable budget concept, future expenses are budgeted in relation to anticipated levels of production, two or three levels or more, or even a probable range of variation between a probable maximum and a probable minimum. In this concept of budgeting, the emphasis is on the need for accurate prediction of the relationship of expense to production, rather than on the need for accurate prediction of the expense itself.

budgets. As used in labor negotiations, or for personnel purposes, the amount of income required to maintain certain standards of living. Most generally used are "Thirteen State Minimum Cost-of-Living Budgets for Single Working Women," (See SINGLE WORKING WOMAN BUDGET); "Heller Committee Budgets for Three Income Levels" (See HELLER COMMITTEE BUDGETS); and "City Worker's Family Budget for Four Persons," (See

CITY WORKER'S FAMILY BUDGET.) Current budget data is available through The *Economic Almanac*, published by the National Industrial Conference Board.

bug. See UNION LABEL.

bulletin boards. A board on which notices are posted whereby management communicates with its employees. Rules and regulations, announcements, accident prevention and health posters, are most frequently found on bulletin boards.

bumping. Replacement of a worker by and on the demand of an employee with greater seniority whose job is no longer available to him. Thus, the employee with greater seniority takes the job of one with less seniority.

burden. See OVERHEAD.

burden center. See COST CENTER.

Bureau of Apprenticeship and Training. The purpose of the Bureau of Apprenticeship and Training is to improve the working conditions of wage earners of the United States and to advance their opportunity for profitable employment through a program of promoting training for workers in industry. The apprenticeship service of the Bureau of Apprenticeship and Training is concerned with the promotion of the National Apprenticeship Program (Act of August 11, 1937). The objectives of this program are determined with the assistance of the Federal Committee on Apprenticeship which is representative of employers, labor, and government. An effective apprenticeship program, as recommended by the Federal Committee on Apprenticeship, should contain provisions for the following: (1) The starting age of an apprentice to be not less than 16. (2) A schedule of work processes in which an apprentice is to be given training and experience on the job. (3) Organized instruction designed to provide the apprentice with knowledge in technical subjects related to his trade. (A minimum of 144 hours per year of such instruction is normally considered necessary.) (4) A progressively increasing schedule of wages. (5) Proper supervision of on-the-job training with adequate facilities to train apprentices. (6) Periodic evaluation of the apprentice's progress, both in job performance and related instruction, and the maintenance of appropriate records. (7) Employee-employer cooperation. (8) Recognition for successful completions. Program recogniton by those States having apprenticeship agencies, or in other States by the Bureau of Apprenticeship and Training, is available to those who wish it. Certificates of Completion of Apprenticeship, attesting to the all-round training received by the individual apprentice, are likewise available through State apprenticeship agencies or the Bureau of Apprenticeship and Training. For Further Information: Write to Bureau of Apprenticeship and Training, U. S. Department of Labor, Washington 25, D. C., or its representative in the major cities.

Bureau of Employment Security. The Bureau of Employment Security of the United States Department of Labor carries out the Federal Government's responsibilities in connection with the administration of two coordinated programs —the public employment service program and the unemployment insurance program. Through the United States Employment Service established in 1933 under the Wagner-Peyser Act (see below), the Bureau promotes and develops a nationwide system of public employment offices to bring workers and employers together. In its performance of the unemployment insurance functions authorized by the Social Security Act of 1935, the Bureau assists the States in carrying out their unemployment insurance programs by which qualified workers are paid insurance benefits during limited periods of unemployment. The Bureau issues two monthly publications, the *Employment Security Review*, which furthers the exchange of operating experiences among State employment security agencies, and *Labor Market and Employment Security*, which provides economic and labor market information. It also issues "A Bimonthly Summary of Labor Market Developments in Major Areas." The Railroad Retirement Board administers another program providing both unemployment and sickness benefits for qualified railroad workers under the Railroad Unemployment Insurance Act. See also: UNITED STATES EMPLOYMENT SERVICE; UNEMPLOYMENT INSURANCE and RAILROAD UNEMPLOYMENT INSURANCE ACT.

Bureau of Labor Standards. The Bureau of Labor Standards is a service agency promoting sound labor standards as a means for improving working conditions and increasing the well being, efficiency, and productivity of wage earners. It does this mainly through bringing about better understanding of labor laws by giving technical assistance to the States in improving labor laws and their administration, conducting research on employment conditions affecting minors, and helping develop and strengthen State occupational safety programs and providing training courses for safety personnel. The Bureau serves as a center of information on State labor standards and administrative practices. It prepares and publishes reports on various aspects of State labor legislation. It also issues technical and popular safety bulletins and training materials, and publishes the bimonthly periodical, *Safety Standards*. In cooperation with administrators of State labor laws, the Bureau works out suggested principles or standards for labor law and administrative practices. Upon request it gives technical assistance to State labor officials on specific labor law problems and assists such officials, labor organizations, and other interested groups and individuals in their efforts to improve labor standards. The Bureau also seeks to improve working and living conditions for migratory agricultural workers through encouragement and stimulation of State and local action. It cooperates with the President's Committee on Migratory Labor, an interagency committee which mobilizes the resources of the Federal government and assists the States in improving migrant labor conditions. The Bureau conducts research and advises on employment conditions and problems affecting working minors. It works with national organizations concerned with youth employment programs and through them with State and local affiliates. Under the Fair Labor Standards Act, it develops standards and proposes regulation for issuance by the Secretary under which employment of children 14 and 15 years of age is permitted under certain conditions. The Bureau also develops standards for proposed hazardous occupations orders issued by the Secretary. It carries on cooperative programs with the States for use of State employment and age certificates as proof of age under the Fair Labor Standards Act. In the field of occupational health and safety, the Bureau aids the State labor departments in the development and promotion of statewide and industrywide safety programs. It conducts safety training courses for the benefit of union, management, and Federal safety personnel. It serves as headquarters and secretariat for the Federal Safety Council. It provides direct consultative safety service to employers and workers subject to the Federal Longshoremen's and Harbor Workers' Compensation Act. The Bureau services the President's Conference on Occupational Safety and other national and regional conferences on various aspects of labor law and administration. The Bureau administers the provisions of the Labor Management Relations Act of 1947 relating to the filing of organization and financial data by labor organizations. In cooperation with the Office of International Labor Affairs, the Bureau participates in the Department's international activities particularly in connection with the International Labor Organizations. It gives technical information and consultant services to the States regarding State action on international labor standards. It carries on training programs for foreign trainees and gives technical assistance in the field of labor law and occupational safety to other countries. The President's Committee on Employment of the Physically Handicapped (in the Bureau for budget purposes only) enlists public support for equal job opportunities for the physically impaired. The services of field consultants in the various areas of the Bureau's program

are available and publications are sent on request. Inquiries should be addressed to the Bureau of Labor Standards, U. S. Department of Labor, Washington 25, D. C.

Bureau of Labor Statistics. The Bureau of Labor Statistics is a fact-finding and research agency covering all fields of labor economics and statistics. The Bureau regularly publishes information in the following major fields: Monthly data on industrial employment. Information on changes in labor productivity, technological development, labor turnover, unemployment, size and composition of the labor force, and the employment outlook for specific occupations and industries. Labor requirements and volume of activity in construction. Monthly data on hourly and weekly earnings, by industries. Information on wage rates nationally and for local areas by occupation and industry, and wage rates in union agreements in selected industries and areas. Studies of union status, paid vacations, sick leave, seniority, pensions and other customary provisions of union agreements. Studies of collective bargaining in specific industries. Monthly statistics on work stoppages. Quarterly reports on accident frequency, and studies of the causes of industrial injuries. Monthly data on hours of work. Monthly Consumer Price Index (cost-of-living) for moderate-income city families for the United States as a whole, and for selected cities. Data on wholesale and retail prices. Information on labor developments in other countries. The Bureau's three monthly periodicals, the *Monthly Labor Review, Employment and Earnings,* and the *Construction Review,* (the last published jointly with the Department of Commerce), and bulletins are on sale by the Superintendent of Documents, Washington 25, D. C., or from the Bureau's regional offices. Free publications are available on request to the Bureau of Labor Statistics, U. S. Department of Labor, Washington 25, D. C., or to its regional offices in Boston, New York, Atlanta, Chicago, and San Francisco.

Bureau of Labor Statistics index. See COST-OF-LIVING INDEX.

business. Business is often differentiated from the professions on the one hand and from finance on the other. It involves the assumption of ownership and/or management, and is therefore sharply contrasted to the contribution made by labor, or the passive participation of the landlord or simple capitalist. More specifically, a business is a productive unit, organized according to whatever pattern is characteristic of any particular culture, or permitted by its mores.

business agent, union. Usually a worker from the factory or trade who has been active in union affairs and is elected (or appointed) by the workers of his plant or local union to a full-time job. He represents the union's interest in relations with employers and is generally responsible for adjusting grievances, bargaining with employers, enforcement of agreements, organization of membership drives and the union's financial affairs.

business education. A program of education which equips a person with marketable skills, knowledges and attitudes needed for initial employment and advancement in business occupations. The business curriculum includes such subjects as stenography, typing, bookkeeping, office machine operation, clerical practice.

Byrnes Act. See ANTI-STRIKEBREAKER LAW.

C

"Calendar Week." A term used by the United States Employment Service. See WEEK.

call pay. Same as call-in pay.

call-back pay. The pay (usually at premium rates) received by a worker called back to duty after completing his regular assignment. Union agreements frequently provide for pay for a minimum number of hours for workers called back to duty, usually at premium rates.

"Call-Backs." A term used by the United States Employment Service to designate workers rehired during the calendar month as a result of recall by the employer after previous separation.

call-in pay. The amount of pay guaranteed to a worker who is called to work on a day on which he otherwise would not have reported, and finds no work available or is not given a full or half shift's employment. Call-pay may be higher than the amount of reporting pay, and may be provided for at premium rates on specified premium days, such as Saturdays, Sundays, and holidays. See also REPORTING PAY.

camera study. See MICROMOTION STUDY, DEFINITION 2.

"Canceled Opening." A term used by the United States Employment Service. See OPENING.

"Canceled Order." A term used by the United States Employment Service. See ORDER.

"Cancellation of Application." A term used by the United States Employment Service to designate the removal from the active file, for any reason other than placement, of the application for a person no longer considered available for referral to job openings.

captive shop. An establishment or production unit whose output is used chiefly by the company which owns it.

Careers Unlimited. An organization founded in 1956 by San Francisco businessmen to help women over 40 find jobs. See FORTY-PLUS CLUBS.

case studies. A method of training which seeks to develop increased skills for diagnosing and solving concrete problems in human relations. The use of case studies for training has been perfected at the Harvard School of Business Administration, and has found wide appli-

(50)

cation in business and industry. Advantages of case studies are: (1) Case studies are no substitute for actual experience, which is still "the best teacher." But they are the next best thing, and permit learning more quickly and more painlessly than through experience itself. (2) The employee is constantly and repeatedly presented with realistic situations. He has opportunity to think for himself, projecting himself into the problems of others. In handling case studies: (1) The leader should know exactly what he wants to bring out, and the case should be so worded as to highlight this point. (2) The leader should refrain from forcing his own diagnosis or solution upon the group. (3) He should not state a problem in such a way that the solution is suggested. For example, if the leader says, "The company feels that the quality of the work turned out is poor," the obvious solution which someone in the group will suggest is better quality. No real participation will result. (4) Cases should not be too extreme. Care should be taken that they are practical and reasonable. (5) Cases involving people and events in the company should be disguised. Otherwise the group devotes more attention trying to guess the personalities involved than to the problems. The leader can avoid this by saying, "This did not actually happen in our company . . . but it's the type of situation that might arise." (6) The leader should be willing to learn from the group in order to strengthen his future presentations. Some people will give a new interpretation to a case or will ask questions that give a new slant to a problem. See, for example, "The Case Method: A Technique of Management Development." Society for Personnel Administration, 5506 Connecticut Avenue, N. W., Washington, D. C.

Cash Sickness Benefit plans. Some states protect employees against loss of time for non-occupational disability through compulsory insurance plans. Generally, the employer may meet the requirements of the law by taking out a group policy with a privately operated insurance company or through self-insurance, or he may accept protection through a government-operated fund. The Railroad Unemployment Act also provides for compulsory sickness insurance.

casual labor. (1) Labor which has no special trade, skill, or qualification. Casual laborers drift from one industry to another, as farm workers, dock employees, or fruit pickers. Although casual laborers are unskilled, not all unskilled labor is casual. Maintenance men may be unskilled, but do not necessarily drift from job to job, but may be on the payroll of the same employer for years; (2) labor which is employed for only a few days at a time; (3) labor which is needed only at certain seasons.

"Catalog of Tests and Test Materials." A term used by the United States Employment Service to designate a reference work which lists and describes the various aptitude and proficiency tests and related materials developed by the Bureau of Employment Security in cooperation with the State employment security agencies.

"Catalog of Expenditures." A term used by the United States Employment Service to designate the classification of expenditures of State employment security agencies by defined groups, such as personal services, equipment, etc.

cease and desist order. An order issued by a court or a government agency instructing an employer or union to cease an unfair labor practice. See UNFAIR LABOR PRACTICE.

Central Labor Union. An association of local unions of the American Federation of Labor in a city, county or metropolitan area.

"Central Office." A term used by the United States Employment Service to designate the State administrative office of an employment security agency.

centralization. Concentrating activities of the same type, or which have a similar function in one department, or under the direction of one executive. Purchasing, stenographic pools, and data processing centers are well known examples. See also DECENTRALIZATION.

centralization and decentralization. As a rule an industrial organization is neither completely centralized nor completely decentralized, but it may, depending upon the spirit which guides its management, have more of a centralized or decentralized character. Raymond Villers, in his "The Dynamics of Industrial Management," (Funk & Wagnalls Company) says, "There has been a growing recognition, especially since the end of World War II, of the need for giving more independence to the members of the industrial organization. Their increased and unavoidable specialization tends to prevent them from gaining a sense of accomplishment. The interaction of relationships is so complex, the need for coordination so pressing, that

the temptation is great to play safe by centralizing management. It is true that a centralized management involves less immediate risk than a decentralized one. If members of the industrial organization, and more specifically the junior executives and supervisors, are not permitted to exercise their own judgment, but are told by their superiors *what* to do, *when* to do it, and *how* to do it, and if in addition they are continuously asked to report upon their performance, 'Did you write this letter? Did you check if the shipment has been made?' etc., the coordination of efforts can be effected in a shorter time than in a decentrailzed organization. In the long run, such methods break down for the essential reason that they put too much reliance upon one man or a small group of men on the one hand, and on the other they slowly but surely destroy the vitality of the organization. When men have spent five, ten, or fifteen years of their lives at various levels of industrial management receiving, obeying, or transmitting orders, they have lost their dynamism; if they ever had pride in taking responsibility, they have forgotten it; they have learned how to ask the insidious question that will clearly place the problem in the lap of their superior; they have also learned how to pass to another, in an inconspicuous way, the burden of a decision; their deal is not so much to be useful but rather to be promoted; their actions are not guided by the consideration of the general interests of the organization but rather by their desire to satisfy the requirements of the often mechanistic rules that govern their selection and advancement. This does not make them happy; their attitude represents submission to their environment, rather than deliberate choice. There is a growing recognition that it is a challenge to maintain the necessary coordination between the specialized activities of the members of the industrial organization and to give them at the same time a chance to show their sense of responsibility and develop their initiative. The increasing trend toward decentralization, which is recognizable throughout industry, is based upon the recognition of the fact that to give more independence to every member of the organization stimulates their desire for responsibility, their pride and their sense of accomplishment and thus, in the long run, benefits the organization itself. The difficulty, however, is to organize this decentralization without endangering the necessary unity of action. The big problem of our time is that of building large organizations and of retaining, at the same time, the quality and strength of small, well integrated work groups."

certificate of completion. Written recognition granted to members of vocational classes upon satisfactorily completing the requirements of a course of instruction. Such certificates are presented when courses are not taken for credit towards graduation.

certificate of training. See CERTIFICATE OF COMPLETION.

certification. Designation by an appropriate federal or state agency of a union which is to act as the collective bargaining agent for the employees in a bargaining unit. See also BARGAINING AGENT; BARGAINING UNIT.

"Certification for Additional Credit Allowance." A term used by the United States Employment Service. *To the Secretary of the Treasury*: The certification by the Secretary of Labor to the Secre-

tary of the Treasury at the end of each taxable year listing those States under whose laws reduced rates were allowable with respect to such year only in accordance with the conditions for additional tax credit established by the Federal Unemployment Tax Act. *To a State*: The certification by the Secretary of Labor to a State that the provisions of its employment security law for reduced employer contributions rates are in accordance with the conditions for additional credit allowance established by the Federal Unemployment Tax Act.

"Certification for Payment." A term used by the United States Employment Service to designate the certification from the Director, Bureau of Employment Security, (pursuant to a delegation by the Secretary of Labor) to the Secretary of the Treasury that the amount specified for grant to a State has been determined in accordance with the provisions of the Wagner-Peyser Act and of title III of the Social Security Act, that the law of the State meets the conditions for grants set forth in those acts, and that such amount is payable to the State.

"Certification for Waiting Period." A term used by the United States Employment Service. Same as *Waiting-Period Claim*. See CLAIM.

"Certification of Approval." A term used by the United States Employment Service. *To the Secretary of the Treasury*: The certification by the Secretary of Labor at the end of each taxable year listing those States whose employment security laws and administration have, during the year, met the conditions for tax credit to employers established by the Federal Unemployment Tax Act.

certified union. A union designated by appropriate federal or state authorities as the bargaining agent for a group of employees.

Chamber of Commerce of the U.S. Founded in 1912. Located at 1615 H St., N.W., Washington 6, D.C. A federation of business organizations composed of 3,200 chambers of commerce, trade and professional associations, with an underlying membership of 2 1/3 million business and professional men and women. The Washington office prepares extensive material of general business and economic nature. Included are *The Nation's Business*, a monthly publication, and *Economic Intelligence*.

changes, in business and industry. Changes are always taking place in an expanding economy, and some of them have a direct influence on personnel. Chief among the changes are: (1) changes in the duties and responsibilities of personnel; (2) the introduction of new personnel embracing new functions; (3) changes in building, layout, etc.; (4) introduction of new designs; (5) changes in method throughout the whole business (6) introduction of new machinery and plant; (7) changes in marketing policy.

change direction. An industrial term meaning the basic element employed to change the line or plane along which a Reach or Move (or a Transport Empty or Transport Loaded) is made. See THERBLIG; TRANSPORT EMPTY; TRANSPORT LOADED.

check-off. The practice whereby the employer, by agreement with the union, regularly withholds from the wages of his union workers assessments and dues, and transmits these funds to the union. Under the Labor Management Relations Act of 1947, the employer must receive from each employee a written assignment which shall not be irrevocable for a period of more than 1 year, or beyond the termination date of the agreement, whichever occurs sooner.

checkoff, automatic. See AUTOMATIC CHECKOFF.

checkoff, compulsory. See AUTOMATIC CHECKOFF.

checkoff, voluntary. See VOLUNTARY CHECKOFF.

check study. Any study of the performance time for an operation that is made to verify or disprove a previous study. The technique used may be the same or different from that used in the previous study.

child labor. "Child labor" means different things at different times in different places. In our country child labor has long meant the employment of boys and girls too young to work for hire, or at jobs unsuitable or unsafe for children of their ages, or under conditions injurious to their health and welfare. It is any employment that robs them of their rightful heritage of a chance for healthful development and full educational opportunity. It does not mean the school activities of boys and girls. Nor does it include home chores and those tasks which boys and girls can and should be called upon to do as their contribution to their family, school, and community. Child labor legislation in the United States is rooted in the American principle that a free people need education. In the early part of the nineteenth century, with the beginnings of the textile

(54)

industry in New England, manpower was scarce and child labor was cheap. Children of 8 or 9 years, or even younger, were employed in the mills. They worked 12 or 13 hours a day from dawn to dark. For these children there was much work and little education. Such schooling as these working children received was usually obtained in Sunday School or at night after the long workday. It was this lack of education that brought the first effort to control child labor by law. In 1813, Connecticut passed a law requiring mill owners to have the children in their factories taught reading, writing, and arithmetic. In 1836, Massachusetts required that children under 14 working in factories attend school for 3 months of the year. Similar laws were passed in other States. These were followed by laws regulating the hours of work of very young children. Massachusetts, in 1842, limited children under 12 years of age to 10 hours of work a day. In the same year, Connecticut passed a 10-hour-day law for children under 14. The next development was to set a minimum age for employment. Pennsylvania adopted the first such law in 1848, with a 12-year minimum age for work in cotton, woolen, and silk factories. By 1860, a number of States prohibited employment in factories of children under a certain age, usually 10 or 12 years. Following the Civil War, the number of employed children increased as business grew and new machines were developed. But this country was becoming increasingly aware of the results and causes of child labor. In 1881, the American Federation of Labor, at its first convention, urged complete abolition by the States of the employment of children under 14 in

any capacity. The National Consumers League, organized in 1899, and the National Child Labor Committee, in 1904, aroused public interest in safeguarding working children. Improvements in child labor laws were made gradually, as the public became more aware of the evils of child labor. From the first early requirements that a child have schooling for a certain number of months, and that the hours he might work be limited, our present State and Federal child labor laws have developed. Many groups, including labor unions, women's organizations, civic and church groups, through the years have actively supported child labor legislation and worked for better enforcement of child labor laws. Much progress has been made in controlling the undesirable employment of children. Many of the early evils of child labor are a thing of the past. But some child labor—some undesirable employment— still exists. Some children still work at too young an age. Some boys and girls work for overlong hours; others work at late night hours that interfere with their schooling the next day. Many still work at dangerous jobs, or under other unsuitable conditions. Many work at a sacrifice of their education. Child labor is most likely to be found in employments not covered by the child labor laws or not adequately regulated by them. Work in industrialized agriculture is the most significant of these. Thousands of boys and girls still work at early ages harvesting fruits and vegetables. Children working in agriculture have the protection of the child labor provisions of the Fair Labor Standards Act only during school hours. After school hours and during summer months when school is not in session, they are not protected by the Federal act. And children can work under the child labor laws of most States at any age and for long hours at back-breaking and monotonous farm jobs. Work in agriculture either during or after school hours is usually exempted under State child labor laws. This exemption in State laws of agricultural work stems from the time when the work of children on the farm was generally limited to their home farms. The pattern and pace of industrialized agriculture is different. Many of the children engaged in harvesting crops are migrants. The employment and living conditions for these children today are often deplorable. The schooling which these migrant children receive is often negligible. They travel with their families, usually by truck or car, from State to State. They neither claim, nor are claimed by, any community. Child labor also still crops up in other occupations where standards set by child labor laws are still too low. Sometimes it results from violations of existing laws. Each year enforcement of State and Federal child labor laws brings to light thousands of violations.

child labor provisions, under Fair Labor Standards Act. The act's child-labor provisions directly prohibit the employment of "oppressive child labor" in commerce or in production of goods for commerce —including any closely related occupation or process directly essential to such production. Also prohibited is the shipment or delivery for shipment in interstate commerce by any producer, manufacturer, or dealer of any goods produced in establishments, in or about which minors have been employed contrary to the minimum-age standards set by the act within 30 days prior to removal of the goods. An exception to the prohibition of such shipments is provided under specified conditions for certain purchasers acting in good faith, in reliance on written statements of compliance. Agricultural employment is subject to the child-labor provisions of the act during school hours. "Oppressive child labor" is defined as: (1) Employment of a child under 16, except employment of children between 14 and 16 years of age in such nonmining and nonmanufacturing occupations and under such conditions as the Secretary of Labor determines not to interfere with their schooling, health, or well-being. (2) Employment of minors between 16 and 18 years of age, in occupations found and by order declared by the Secretary of Labor, to be partially hazardous or detrimental to their health or well-being. The employment of a child under 14 in any occupation is "oppressive child labor," unless specifically exempt. The following hazardous occupations orders, each establishing a minimum age of 18, have been issued to deal with: (1) Occupations in or about plants manufacturing or storing explosives or articles containing explosive components. (2) Occupations of motor-vehicle driver and helper. (3) Coal-mine occupations. (4) Logging occupations and occupations in the operation of any sawmill, lath mill, shingle mill, or cooperage-stock mill. (5) Occupations involved in the operation of power-driven woodworking machines. (6) Occupations involving exposure to radioactive substances. (7) Occupations involved in the operation of elevators and other power-driven hoisting apparatus. (8) Occupations involved in the operation of power-driven metal forming, punching, and shearing machines. (9) Occupations in connection with mining, other than coal. (10) Occupations in slaughtering and meatpacking establishments and rendering plants. (11) Occupations involved in the operation of bakery machines. (12) Occupations involved in the operation of paper products machines. (13) Occuations involved in the manufacture of brick, tile, and kindred products. The following are exempt from the child-labor provisions of the act: (a) Children employed in agriculture outside of school hours for the school district where such child is living while so employed. (b) Children employed as actors or performers in motion-picture or theatrical productions or in radio or television productions. (c) Children under 16 years of age employed by their parents, or persons standing in place of parents, in an occupation other than manufacturing or mining or an occupation found by the Secretary of Labor to be particularly hazardous. (d) Children delivering newspapers to the consumer. Employers can protect themselves from unintentionally employing a minor under the legal age by having on file a certificate of age issued in accordance with regulations of the Secretary of Labor showing that the minor is above the legal age for employment in the occupation in which he is engaged. Age or employment certificates issued under State child-labor laws are accepted as proof of age in 44 States, the District of Columbia, Puerto Rico, and Hawaii. Federal certificates of age are issued in Idaho, Mississippi, South Carolina, and Texas.

child labor provisions, under Walsh-Healey Public Contracts Act. The law

prohibits employment of boys under 16 and girls under 18.

Certified Professional Secretaries program. A certifying examination developed by the Institute for Certifying Secretaries, sponsored by The National Secretaries Association, which see.

chronograph technique. A special type of cyclograph technique in which an interrupter is placed in the electric circuit with a light bulb, and the light is flashed on and off. The slow cooling of the filament causes the path of the bulb to be photographed to appear to be pear-shaped dots which indicate the direction and the path of the motion. Since the spots of light are spaced according to the speed of the movement, being widely separated when the worker moves fast and close together when the worker's movement is slow, it is possible, from the photograph, to obtain an approximation of time, speed, acceleration, and retardation and to show direction and the path of motion.

City Worker's Family Budget for Four Persons. Designed for an employed father, a housewife not gainfully employed and two children under 15, to represent the estimated dollar cost required to maintain this family at a level of adequate living in respect to health, efficiency, the nurture of children and for participation in community activities. The budget makes provision for housing, clothes, food, including 189 meals away from home and modest amount for alcoholic beverages, life insurance, taxes. Detailed data are available from the Bureau of Labor Statistics.

civil service. A system providing for and regulating the impartial selection by examination or with regard to fitness, ability and experience, the tenure, advancement, compensation and conditions of employment of governmental employees.

Civil Service Commission. An agency of the government to administer civil services, usually presided over by commissioners. In the United States, the Civil Service systems were established during the latter part of the nineteenth century in order to overcome the evil effects of the spoils system, to give government employees the security of a career and to supply the government with properly trained and experienced workers and to meet the growing need for technically trained personnel.

"Claim." A term used by the United States Employment Service to designate a request for a benefit payment; also used to mean any notice filed by an individual to establish his insured status or to obtain credit for a waiting week, or a notice filed by an individual to inform the administrative agency of his unemployment. A claim may be filed under any one or more of the following programs: (1) The State program of unemployment insurance (UI), (2) The Federal program of unemployment compensation for Federal employees (UCFE) established by title XV of the Social Security Act, and (3) The Federal program of unemployment compensation for veterans (UCV) established by title IV of the Veterans' Readjustment Assistance Act of 1952. Unless otherwise specified, the term "claim" as used in the following definitions is applicable equally to each of the three programs. *Additional UCV Claim*: A notice filed at the beginning of a new spell of unem-

ployment, second or subsequent to the one for which the claimant's new UCV claim was filed, when a break in job attachment has occurred since the last claim was filed, concerning which State procedures require that separation information be secured. *Additional UI or UCFE Claim*: A notice filed at the beginning of a second or subsequent series of claims within a benefit year, when a break in job attachment has occurred since the last claim was filed, concerning which State procedures require that separation information be obtained. *Appealed Claim*: See APPEAL, ADMINISTRATIVE. *Combined-Wage Claim*: A claim filed under the basic or the extended interstate wage-combining plans. See INTERSTATE ARRANGEMENTS. *Compensable Claim*: A request for benefit payment. *Contested Claim*: A claim which has not yet reached an appeal stage but regarding which the claimant's right to benefits is questioned by the agency or by an interested party. *Continued Claim*: A request for waiting-period credit or benefit payment. Continued claims are either (1) waiting-period claims or (2) compensable claims. *Initial Claim*: Either a new or an additional claim. *Interstate Claim*: A claim filed in one State (agent State) against another State (liable State). *Mail Claim*: A claim filed by mail instead of being filed by a claimant in person at an employment office. *New UCV Claim*: A request for determination of title IV veteran status, normally filed only once by any veteran. *New UI or UCFE Claim*: A request for determination of insured status for purposes of establishing a new benefit year. *Reopened Claim*: The first continued claim in a second or subsequent series of claims in a benefit year when no additional claim is reportable. *Transitional Claim*:

A new claim dated as of any day in the 7-day period immediately following a week for which waiting-period credit or benefits were claimed. *Valid UI or UCFE Claim*: A new claim on which a determination has been made that the claimant has met the wage or employment requirements (and, under some laws, other eligibility conditions) to establish a benefit year. *Waiting-Period Claim*: A request for waiting-period credit.

claim, appealing of, under Social Security law. If a claimant thinks that the decision in his case is incorrect, he can appeal as follows: Either ask for a reconsideration by the Bureau of Old-Age and Survivors Insurance, or ask for a hearing before a referee of the Appeals Council of the Social Security Administration, who is independent of the Bureau of Old-Age and Survivors Insurance. A request in writing for a reconsideration or hearing must reach the nearest Social Security Administration office within 6 months from the date the Bureau's decision was mailed to the claimant. If the claimant chooses to ask for a reconsideration by the Bureau first and then is not satisfied, he can still obtain a hearing before a referee. If he thinks the referee's decision is wrong, he may ask to have it reviewed by the Appeals Council in Washington. If he still is not satisfied, he may file a civil service suit in a United States District Court.

claim, filing of, under Social Security law. When a worker is ready to file a claim, he should either go or write to the nearest Social Security office saying that he wishes to file a claim for benefits. A member of his family who may have a claim should, of course, do the same

thing. Any Social Security office will help the claimant file the necessary papers. It is not necessary to pay for an attorney's services in connection with a claim. If the claim is a proper one under the law, it will be approved and certified to the United States Treasury by the Social Security Administration. The United States Treasury sends out the benefit checks.

"claimant." A term used by the United States Employment Service to designate an individual who has filed a request for determination of insured status or a new claim.

"Claim Record Card." A term used by the United States Employment Service to designate the record of a claimant's claim history maintained in the local office.

"Claim Series." A term used by the United States Employment Service to designate a series of claims filed for continuous weeks of unemployment or for a period of unemployment during which the lapse in compensability or in reporting is deemed by the State to be insufficient to interrupt the series.

clean hands. A principle held by some union members restricting them from handling work not union-made.

"Clearance." A term used by the United States Employment Service to designate activities of the regular placement process involving joint action of an order-holding office and an applicant-holding office in (1) the location and selection of an applicant and the referral of the applicant to a job opening, or (2) the location of a suitable job opening for an applicant and the referral of the applicant.

(59)

"**Clearance Applicant.**" A term used by the United States Employment Service. See APPLICANT.

"**Clearance Application.**" A term used by the United States Employment Service. See APPLICATION.

"**Clearance Job Opening.**" A term used by the United States Employment Service. See OPENING.

"**Clearance Order.**" A term used by the United States Employment Service. See ORDER.

"**Clearance Placement.**" A term used by the United States Employment Service. See PLACEMENT.

"**Clearance Referral.**" A term used by the United States Employment Service. See REFERRAL.

"**Clearing Account.**" A term used by the United States Employment Service. See ACCOUNTS.

clerical practice. A business subject dealing with the various duties of office workers other than stenographic, e.g., typing, filing, keeping records, handling office forms, and using duplicating, computing and other office machines.

clerical tests. Clerical tests vary from the measurement of a single function, such as comparison of numbers or comparison of names, to test instruments which sample other aspects of clerical work, such as arithmetic reasoning, filing, grammar, substitution, spelling, vocabulary, business information, classification, and other requirements of clerical occupations. Clerical tests include: *Division of Applied Psychology, Purdue University, Lafayette, Indiana*: Purdue Clerical Adaptability Test—Moore, Lawshe

and Tiffin; *Psychological Corporation*: Blackstone Stenographic Proficiency Test; The Short Employment Tests; Bennett & Gelink, Wide Range Vocabulary Test, Atwell and Wells; D.A.T. Clerical Speed and Accuracy Test; General Clerical Test; Thurstone Examination in Clerical Work; D.A.T. Language Usage Test, Bennett, Seashore and Wesman; Seashore-Bennett Stenographic Proficiency Tests; *Science Research Associates*: Kimberly-Clark Typing Ability Analysis, Jurgensen; SRA Test of Dictation Skill, Richardson and Pedersen; SRA Test of Typing Skill, Richardson and Pedersen; SRA Clerical Aptitudes Test, Richardson, Bellows Henry & Co.; *World Book Company*: Elwell-Fowlkes Bookkeeping Test; Otis Employment Tests; Otis General Intelligence Examination; Thompson Business Practice Test; Thurstone Employment Tests; Turse-Durost Shorthand Achievement Test; Turse Shorthand Aptitude Test; *Acorn Publishing Company, Inc.*: Clerical Aptitude Test; *Martin Publishing Company*: Aptitude Tests for Office Clerks; *Education Test Bureau*: Clerical Perception Tests; *Remington Rand, Inc.*: Typewriting Employment Tests; *Western Psychological Services*: Clerical Aptitude Tests; *Joint Committee on Tests, National Office Management Association*: National Business Education Tests; *California Test Bureau*: Ruch Survey of Working Speed and Accuracy. See PUBLISHERS, PERSONNEL TESTS.

clerk, general. According to the Dictionary of Occupational Titles, (which see) a classification title for the clerical jobs, which require little or no previous training, which involve the performance of routing clerical duties, such as addressing envelopes, keeping simple records, and gathering and delivering messages and assisting in operating office machines, and which may require the ability to do simple typing.

clock card. (1) Any form designed for use with a time clock. (2) Any form used by a workman to record by means of a time clock the date and times of day when he starts or stops a job assignment or just the times of day that mark the beginning and end of his period of attendance at his place of employment.

"Closed Order." A term used by the United States Employment Service. See ORDER.

closed shop. An agreement whereby employees in the bargaining unit must be members of the union in good standing and new employees must be hired through the union. If the union cannot supply new employees, management may hire from the open market, but such new employees must become union members.

closed union. A union, which is a party to a closed shop contract, and which "closes its book," refusing to admit additional members. This limitation of membership may be achieved by the use of high initiation fees or other restrictive rules in order to reduce competition for jobs.

closed union shop. See CLOSED SHOP.

clothing allowance. An allowance granted by an employer to those of his employees who are required to buy special clothing, such as uniforms and safety garments, in connection with the performance of their work.

coaching. See JOB INSTRUCTION.

"coffee break." A word which has become part of the language to signify an established custom in business and in-

dustry. According to surveys made by the Pan-American Coffee Bureau, 75% of all workers in this country and Canada have opportunities for coffee breaks.

cold-storage training. Training of employees for higher level jobs in advance of the need for them in such positions.

Cole, George Douglas Howard (1889–) is a British academician. Cole's views of the proper function of organized labor and its role in the world of the future were most fully stated in his book, *The World Of Labour*, published in 1913. He sees the responsibility of the trade unions as the "control of industry" by the true producers, the workers, in partnership with the state. The principal union development necessary to this end is industrial unionism, with "all workers working together under a single employer or group of employers . . . organized in a single Union." This is arguable only upon the assumption that trade unionism is regarded as a class movement based upon the class struggle. If that is not the meaning of the labor movement, then there is good reason for the skilled worker to hold aloof from those less advantageously situated than himself and so maintain his monopoly of jobs and pay. On the other hand, if the labor movement is a part of the class struggle, then mass formations of labor are needed to combat the mass formations of capital, and the requirements of unity deny sectional groupings based on class or craft. Cole himself apparently believed that trade unionism exists today to carry on the class strruggle.

collective agreement. See AGREEMENT, COLLECTIVE.

collective bargaining. The right and process of negotiation between an employer, or a group of or association of employers, and representatives of workers organized in a union. The National Industrial Recovery Act established this right in the United States by providing that "employees shall have the right to organize and bargain collectively through representatives of their own choosing." (73rd Congress, Public No. 67, H.R. 5755, approved June 16, 1933, Section 7 (a).) The right was further defined as follows in the act creating the National Labor Relations Board: "Employees shall have the right to self-organization, to form, join, or assist labor organizations, to bargain collectively through representatives of their own choosing, and to engage in concerted activities, for the purpose of collective bargaining or other mutual aid protection." (74th Congress, Public No. 198, S. 1958, approved July 5, 1935, Section 7). The National Labor Relations Board was established by the National Labor Relations Act (which see). "Collective bargaining" differs from employees' representation, or "company unions" in that it is self-organized by workers in more than one establishment, while employees' representation is limited to one company. The phrase, "collective bargaining" was first used by Beatrice Webb in her writings on trade unions in England. In collective bargaining, there is both a political settlement between the union and management over the division of authority and an economic settlement between the workers and management over the share which the workers receive from the proceeds of the business. The combined settlement is formalized in a collective bargaining contract. Collective bargaining implies that both sides are free to organize and choose representatives without interference from the other and that they deal in good faith with each others' representatives. See "SINGLE FIRM," "PATTERN-FOLLOWING" and "MULTI-EMPLOYER" BARGAINING. The process of collective bargaining has a number of distinctly separate phases which may be described as: (1) spirit in which negotiations are carried on; (2) preparations preliminary to negotiations; (3) method of procedure during negotiations; (4) negotiation techniques.

collective bargaining, as defined under the National Labor Management Relations Act (which see). Section 8 (d) of the Act defines collective bargaining for the purpose of section 8 as the performance of the mutual obligation of the employer and the representative of the employees to meet at reasonable times and confer in good faith with respect to wages, hours, and other terms and conditions of employment, or the negotiation of an agreement, or any question arising thereunder, and the execution of a written contract incorporating any agreement reached if requested by either party, but such obligation does not compel either party to agree to a proposal or require the making of a concession. The Board has held that pensions and group insurance plans come within the scope of subjects on which the law requires an employer to bargain with the representative of his employees.

collective bargaining representative, determination of, under National Labor Management Relations Act follows the principle of majority rule in determining the representation of employees bargaining with their employer as a group. The representative may be an individual or a labor organization, but not a supervisor or other representative of an employer. The act requires that an employer bargain with the representative selected by a majority of his employees in a unit appropriate for collective bargaining. The act does not require that the representative be selected by any particular procedure, as long as the representative is clearly the choice of a majority of the employees. As one method for employees to select a majority representative, the act authorizes the Board to conduct representation elections. However, the Board may conduct such an election only when a petition has been filed by the employees or any individual or labor organization acting in their behalf, or by an employer who has been confronted with a claim of representation from an individual or labor organization. Under the law, the Board may certify the choice of the majority of employees for a bargaining representative only after a secret-ballot election. In a representation election, the employees are given a choice of one or more bargaining representatives or no representative at all. To be chosen as bargaining representative, a labor organization or an individual must receive a majority of the valid votes cast.

commercial education. See BUSINESS EDUCATION.

commission earnings. Compensation to sales personnel based on a percentage of value of sales. Commission earnings may be in addition to a guaranteed salary or may constitute total pay. Sales personnel on straight commission usually have a fixed drawing account which is balanced against actually realized commission earnings at specified periods. See also DRAWING ACCOUNT.

Committee for Industrial Organization. A union body organized in 1935 by the officers of seven national unions of the AFL, who favored industrial unionization of mass-production industries, as opposed to the craft union approach of the AFL. The Committee for Industrial Organization became the Congress of Industrial Organizations in 1938. (which see)

common labor rate. In general, the hourly rate paid to adult males for physical or manual labor of a general character and simple nature, requiring no special training or skill and requiring little or no previous experience. In some establishments, this rate may apply to a common labor crew or pool who are assigned to specific tasks as required, while in other establishments it may refer to the rate paid for specific unskilled tasks, such as sweeping, hand trucking, loading and unloading.

Commons, John Rogers. (1862-1944) Professor of political economy at the University of Wisconsin, dean of American labor scholars, and founder of the "Wisconsin school" of institutional economists. His most influential books were *Trade Unionism and Labor Problems,* (1905); *History of Labour in the United States* (4 vols., 1918-1932); *Institutional Economics* (1934); and with John B. Andrews, *Principles of Labor Legislation* (several editions, 1916 to 1936). His greatest contribution to the study of the American labor movement was to arouse the enthusiasm of gifted graduate students and set them to work, individually and in platoons, producing masterpieces of research. Commons himself regarded the labor movement as an aspect of the class struggle and his method of investigation indicated a firm belief in the influence of political and economic institutions upon the thoughts and actions of

(63)

men. He regarded the labor movement in America as delayed and thwarted by a number of factors, the first of which was *free land*. Free land, he felt, was influential in producing a labor movement based on the ideas of a "middle class" or the "producing classes," rather than the "wage class," which held trade unionism back for half a century. Ranking next as a major influence upon the labor movement of the nineteenth century was the tremendous *expansion of markets* which changed the character of competition, intensified its pressure, separated manufactures from agriculture, introduced the middleman, produced new alignments of social classes, and obliterated the futile lines that distinguish the jurisdiction of the States. The chief products of this competitive melee were two: the *merchant-capitalist*, who acted as middleman between the manufacturer and the retailer and drove a hard bargain with each, and the *financier*, who aided the merchant in his extension of credits. This produced a series of "sweated" trades and drove employees to their first conscious combination with others of their class in "trade" unions, and away from the guildlike associations of earlier days, which included masters as well as journeymen. A fourth important influence was found in the *organs of government*. The confused pattern of state and Federal law made extensive legislative reforms impracticable. The main effect of these obstacles was to turn labor away from political action to reliance upon organization and economic power. Additional influences of great importance have been *immigration*, with its influx of races, nationalities and languages, thrown together in a single competitive area, and *cycles of prosperity and depression*, which Commons found

to have a positive correlation with the rise and fall of union activity.

communication, in business and industry. There has been a definite trend in training and utilization of communications skills. The current concept of face-to-face communication may said to have originated from Paul Pigor's study "Effective Communication in Industry," launched by the National Association of Manufacturers, in 1949, The Public Opinion Index for Industry on "How to Make the Communication Dollar Work," and the American Management Association's "Effective Communication on the Job."

communism. Labor organizations (or employers) found to be "Communist-infiltrated" will have no legal rights and privileges before the National Labor Relations Board (Public Law 637—[83rd Cong., 2d sess.]: Communist Control Act of 1954, approved August 24, 1954.) Upon petition by not less than 20 percent of the employees in such a bargaining unit, the NLRB must direct an election for determining whether the unit desires to rescind any representation authority previously granted and to select any representative the unit desires for collective bargaining purposes. The Communist Control Act was designed in part to assist labor organizations in resisting and expelling Communist influences. Any labor organization which is an affiliate in good standing of a national federation or other labor organization whose policies and activities have been directed against Communism will be presumed prima facie not to be "Communist-infiltrated." Adoption of this provision gave emphatic recognition to the unswerving loyalty to the United States of the many bona fide labor organizations—AFL, CIO, UMW, the railroad brotherhoods, and similar national labor federations. Both the effectiveness and the possibility of early enforcement of the Communist Control Act were uncertain. Determination of whether an organization is "Communist-infiltrated" as well as the due course of judicial review proceedings would, obviously, take considerable time.

community college. A composite of all educational opportunities extended by the local public school system free to all persons who, having passed the normal age for completing the twelfth grade, need or want to continue their education. Vocational courses are emphasized in these community colleges.

"Community Employment Program." A term used by the United States Employment Service to designate a program of concerted action undertaken by community groups and organizations and concerned with employment problems to achieve (1) maximum utilization of the community's labor force in regular employment, and (2) full development of the community's industrial resources.

community relations. In more than half of companies in the U. S., according to surveys, community relations are handled by the personnel department. These range from "open house" events, work with schools on vocational opportunities, cooperation with local charities, sponsoring sports events, welcoming newcomers to the organization.

community wage survey. A general term used to describe a survey to reveal the structure and level of wages within a particular geographical area for a given industry or, more typically, for broad categories of industry.

"Commuter." A term used by the United States Employment Service to designate a worker who travels regularly across a State line from home to work and comes under the Interstate Benefit Payment Plan.

company-financed pension plan. See NON-CONTRIBUTORY PENSION PLAN.

company stores. Stores maintained by a company for the use of its employees. Such stores have in the past been common in industries removed from cities, as mining towns.

company town. A community usually created by a company because its plant is isolated. The company usually controls the town's housing facilities, stores, etc. Company towns range from "boxcar" villages in Southern timber tracts, rows of "tenements" in New England textile towns to planned communities with parks and recreation facilities as at Hershey, Pennsylvania.

company union. A labor union whose membership is confined to the employees of one company and which is sometimes organized by and always dominated by management. Company unions are generally considered unfair labor practice, and hence illegal.

comparable rate. A rate paid for work agreed or determined to be comparable within a plant or within an area. Comparisons of this type may be limited to virtually identical occupations within a specific industry or be broadened to include occupations with similar characteristics in various industries. Such comparisons are used in wage negotiations and wage determinations.

"Compensable Claim." A term used by

the United States Employment Service. See CLAIM.

"Compensable Week." A term used by the United States Employment Service. See WEEK.

"Compensating Bank Balances." A term used by the United States Employment Service to designate Treasury funds deposited by the United States Treasury in banks, the interest on which compensates the banks for the cost of handling State employment security funds. Such interest is in lieu of the payment-of-service charges which are ordinarily levied by banks against depositors.

compensation. Payments for goods, services, sacrifice or loss.

"Compensation." A term used by the United States Employment Service. See BENEFITS.

compensation, methods of, under job evaluation systems. The relative worth of jobs to be evaluated is determined by assigning to each a number of points (arithmetic units). The procedures for the design of a point plan are as follows: (1) Determine the types of job to be evaluated. (2) Determine the factors to be used in the plan and prepare a suitable definition for each. (3) Determine the number of degrees to be allocated to each factor and prepare a suitable definition for each. (4) Determine the weightings of the factors and assign points to each degree of each factor. (5) Select between 15 and 25 key jobs and evaluate each, using the plan developed. (6) Establish: (a) a single rate for each individual job; (b) a rate range for each individual job; (c) a single rate for groups of jobs (labor grades); (d) a rate range for groups of jobs (labor grades).

competitive wage. In economic theory, the wage within a given labor market required to balance the demand for and supply of labor of a particular type. More popularly, the wage level a company must maintain to compete with other firms in the same labor market for particular types of labor. Also used in the sense of the wage level that is required by a company to maintain a competitive price position with other firms in the same industry.

comprehensive (composite) general shop. A school shop designed and equipped to offer two or more areas of instruction in industrial arts. Such a shop may contain facilities for teaching drawing, woodworking, metalworking, graphic arts, and electricity, or a similar combination of teaching areas. It is sometimes called general shop, multiple-activity shop, or laboratory of industries.

comprehensive high school. A secondary school that offers both general education courses and vocational education courses in its program.

compulsory arbitration. See ARBITRATION, LABOR.

compulsory checkoff. See AUTOMATIC CHECKOFF.

compulsory membership. Eligible employees are required, as a condition of employment, to join a contributory plan. Compulsory membership usually is required only of workers who are employed after the effective date of the plan.

"Computation Date, Experience-Rating." A term used by the United States Employment Service. Under a pooled fund law, the date as of which employers' experience with respect to unemployment or unemployment risk is measured for the purpose of determining contribution rates; or, under a reserve account law, the date as of which the balances in employers' reserve accounts are determined for the purpose of rate computation.

conciliation. A method of restoring peaceful relations between employers and employees. It is an attempt to bring together two or more parties that are involved in a dispute or have differences of opinion through prevailing upon them to compromise on their original demands so that a settlement can be reached. See ARBITRATION.

conciliator. An individual who undertakes conciliation of a labor dispute.

conference method. A training technique extensively used for supervisory and management training. Basically the conference method is a procedure in which several persons meet to contribute their experiences and opinions, focusing on a situation or problem. The nature of any such conference depends upon its objectives. Perhaps the conferees want to: (1) pool their experiences; (2) establish a standard procedure or policy; (3) agree upon a course of action; (4) correct some unsatisfactory practice or attitude; or (5) report, recapitulate, and evaluate some activity. In the conference method, groups of usually not over 20 people are brought together under conditions which permit them to be comfortable and at ease. The relationship of teacher and learner is carefully avoided. The conference program is not presented to conferees in such a way that they feel that they are not making good on their jobs and that the job of the conference leader is to teach them how to do better.

On the other hand, the conference program is presented to them as an opportunity to pool their experiences, and through discussion of them, to develop better methods of dealing with their problems. The function of the conference leader under this method is not directly to instruct but to guide discussion and see that it leads into constructive ideas which will, for example, result in improved supervision in the plant.

Congress of Industrial Organizations. See AFL-CIO. An outgrowth of the Committee for Industrial Organization, formed in 1935, which see. John L. Lewis was its first President, 1935-1940. He was succeeded by Philip Murray, 1940 till his death in 1952. Third President was Walter Reuther, 1952 till 1955 when the CIO merged with the AFL. At the time of their merger the CIO had 32 affiliated unions, and some 5,000,000 members.

consent election. An election for the determination of a bargaining agent, held at the joint request of an employer and union. See also BARGAINING AGENT.

consistency. A time-study term which indicates the degree of uniformity or agreement which exists among the actual times recorded for two or more repetitions of the same element.

constant element. An industrial engineering term: (1) An element for which the leveled or normal time is always the same regardless of the characteristics of the parts being worked upon, as long as the method and the working conditions are unchanged. (2) An element for which, under a specified set of conditions, the standard time allowance should always be the same. Example: Raise spindle a definite distance on a drill press of a certain size and make.

(67)

constant time element. See CONSTANT ELEMENT.

consultant. A recognized expert, or group of experts, in a specialized field. Consultants are not vested with authority, but give advice and suggestions. In personnel work, most frequently encountered are management consultants (which see); personnel consultants, industrial psychologists, labor relations counselors; management engineers. A "Code of Professional Ethics" has been adopted by the Association of Consulting Management Engineers, Inc. 347 Madison Avenue, New York, 17, N. Y. (which see)

consumer education. Understandings concerning the financial problems of the buying public, e.g. credit, insurance, budgeting, buying procedures, specifications and standards for products, determination of prices, etc. aimed at helping the public to make choices, to buy more wisely, and to make intelligent use of purchases.

consumers' price index. See COST-OF-LIVING INDEX.

"Contested Claim." A term used by the United States Employment Service. See CLAIM.

"Contingency Fund." A term used by the United States Employment Service. See FUNDS.

continuation school or class. See PART-TIME PROGRAMS.

"Continued Claim." A term used by the United States Employment Service. See CLAIM.

continuous method. The procedure of timing, used in making time studies, whereby the watch is permitted to run continuously throughout the period of study while the observer notes and records the reading of the watch at the end of each element, delay or any other occurrence happening in the study regardless of whether or not it has a direct bearing on the job. The elapsed times are secured by subtracting the successive readings after the timing has been completed.

continuous method timing. See CONTINUOUS METHOD.

continuous reading. See CONTINUOUS METHOD.

continuous timing. See CONTINUOUS METHOD.

contract. Same as agreement, collective.

contract, master. Same as agreement, master.

contract wage payment. An arrangement whereby the worker contracts to perform a specific job for a predetermined amount of compensation.

"Contribution Rates." A term used by the United States Employment Service. *Adjusted Contribution Rates*: Rates of contribution that differ from the standard contribution rate, computed for individual employers under the experience-rating provisions of a State employment security law. *Reduced Contribution Rates*: Rates of contribution less than the standard contribution rate, computed for individual employers under the experience-rating provisions of a State employment security law. *Standard Contribution Rate*: The basic rate of contributions from which variations are computed under the experience-rating provisions of a State employment security law.

"Contribution Report." A term used by the United States Employment Service to designate an employer's report of the amount of contributions due to a State pay roll.

"Contributions." A term used by the United States Employment Service to designate payments required by a State employment security law to be made to the State unemployment fund by reason of insured work.

contributory pension plan. A pension plan for the benefit of the employee under which the cost is shared by both the employer and the employee. Employee contributions are almost always made through periodic pay-roll deductions.

control, supervisory. See SUPERVISORY CONTROL.

convict labor provisions, under Walsh-Healey Public Contracts Act. The law prohibits the employment of convict labor.

cooling-off period. A required period of delay after legal notice of an intended strike or lockout, during which no strike or lockout can legally be called.

cooperative education (cooperative part-time instruction). A training program that provides for alternation of study in school with a job in industry or business, the two experiences being so planned and supervised by school and employer that each contributes definitely to the student's development in his chosen occupation. Work periods and school attendance may be on alternate days, weeks, or other periods of time, but the hours at work equal or exceed the hours spent in school during the regular school year. This plan of training is used extensively in business, distributive, and trade and industrial courses. See also WORK EXPERIENCE EDUCATION.

coordinator. A member of the school staff responsible for integrating the classroom instruction and the on-the-job activities of the employed student in a vocational training program. The coordinator acts as liaison between the school and employers in programs of cooperative education or other part-time job training.

coordinator-teacher (or teacher-coordinator). A member of the school staff who teaches the related and technical subject matter involved in work experience programs and coordinates classroom instruction with on-the-job training.

Copeland Act. See ANTI-KICKBACK LAW.

correspondence schools, offering courses in supervision. Approved correspondence schools have been listed by the National Home Study Council, Washington, D. C. Information is also available from the National University Extension Association, 152 Nicholson Hall, University of Minnesota, Minneapolis, Minn. Approved schools include: American School, Drexel Avenue at 5th St., Chicago, 37, Illinois Commercial Trades Institute, 1400 W. Greenleaf Avenue, Chicago 26, Illinois; International Correspondence Schools, Scranton 9, Pennsylvania; Lasalle Extension University, 417 S. Dearborn St., Chicago 5, Illinois; Lincoln Extension Institute, 1401 West 75th St., Cleveland 2, Ohio.

cost center. Any subdivision of an organization comprised of workmen, equipment, areas, activities, or combination of these that is established for the purpose of assigning or allocating costs.

(69)

cost and savings form. See COST REDUC-
TION REPORT.

cost-of-living adjustment. An adjustment
of wages or salaries in accordance with
changes in the cost of living as measured
by an appropriate index of the retail
prices of goods and services that enter
into the consumption of low- or moderate-income families. Limitations as to the
extent of wage adjustment are sometimes
provided for. See also ESCALATOR CLAUSE.

cost-of-living index. This term generally
refers to an index prepared by the Bureau of Labor Statistics of the U. S. Department of Labor, which indicates price
changes of a selected list of commodities
and services used by families of wage
earners and lower-salaried workers in representative cities and in the country as
a whole. The purpose is to measure periodically the cost of maintaining a fixed
scale of living.

cost reduction report. A form designed
to allow easy comparison of two or more
methods, plans, designs, and the like on
the basis of known and/or anticipated
costs and savings, usually used in connection with industrial engineering studies.

costs, turnover. See TURNOVER COSTS.

Council of Economic Advisers. A body
created by the federal Employment Act
of 1946 for purposes of maintaining and
continuing appraisal and forecast of economic conditions. It prepares and submits a report to the President of the
United States each December. The President, in turn, presents an Economic
Report to Congress in the early part of
each year. The Council was reorganized
in 1953 and an Advisory Board on Economic Growth and Stability was established under it. Ten divisions of the

government have Cabinet or other high-
level officials on this Board, including
the Council; Agriculture; Commerce;
Health, Education and Welfare; Labor;
State; Treasury; Federal Reserve System;
Bureau of the Budget and the White
House. The Board meets every Thursday
at 11:00 A.M. It publishes no minutes
and issues no releases. The following
day, the Chairman of the Council of
Economic Advisors meets with the Cabinet. He sees the President on the following Monday morning.

"Counseling." A term used by the United
States Employment Service. See EMPLOY-
MENT COUNSELING.

counselor, guidance. An experienced and
trained person, frequently a psychologist,
who assists an individual to understand
himself and his opportunities, to make
appropriate adjustments to the job, and
choices and decisions in the light of his
own unique characteristics. Where training programs or educational facilities are
available, the guidance counselor may
work out a suitable training program or
help in its selection.

"Counseling Interview." A term used by
the United States Employment Service.
See INTERVIEW.

"Coverage Determination." A term used
by the United States Employment Service. See DETERMINATION.

Coverage, under Social Security Act. The
original social security law, which went
into effect January 1, 1937, covered people who were employed in business and
industry. In 1950 about 10 million more
people were brought under the law, including people who were self-employed
in a trade or business, or regularly employed farm and household workers, and
some employees of nonprofit organiza-

tions and of State and local governments. In 1946, 1947, and 1951, amendments to the Railroad Retirement Act providing for combining, under certain conditions, the wage credits earned in the railroad industry with social security wage credits. In 1954 the social security law was extended so that beginning January 1, 1955, more than 90 percent of those who were gainfully employed were covered. The largest groups brought under the law by the 1954 amendments and the principal changes in the coverage provisions of the law were: Most people self-employed in a trade or business, brought under the law beginning in 1951. Net earnings from self-employment as an architect, professional engineer, accountant, or funeral director, for taxable years ending after December 31, 1954, were covered by the law, provided the annual net earnings were $400 or more. In 1956 the social security law was further extended so that in the case of a self-employed lawyer, dentist, osteopath, veterinarian, chiropractor, naturopath, or optometrist, earnings for taxable years ending after 1955 count toward old-age, survivors, and disability insurance benefits. Like other self-employed people, it is necessary to report earnings and pay the social security self-employment tax if net earnings amount to $400 in a year. The 1950 law provided for covering State and local government employees under voluntary agreements between the individual State and the Federal Government. It excluded from coverage under such an agreement, however, employees in positions covered by a State or local retirement system. Under the 1954 revisions, a State can bring members of a State or local retirement system (except policemen and firemen who are under a State or local retirement system) under

its old-age and survivors insurance agreement, if a referendum is held among the members of the system and a majority of the members eligible to vote in the referendum vote in favor of old-age and survivors insurance coverage. The law states it is the policy of the Congress, in making coverage available to retirement system members, that the protection of members and beneficiaries of the retirement system not be impaired by reason of coverage of the members under old-age and survivors insurance. The 1954 law permits ministers, Christian Science practitioners, and members of religious orders who have not taken a vow of poverty to secure coverage by filing with the Internal Revenue Service a certificate indicating their desire to be covered on the same terms as self-employed persons. In general, such a person had two years after 1954, or after he became a minister, Christian Science practitioner, or a member of the religious order, in which to take advantage of this provision. The 1954 law provided that a domestic worker's wages from any employer for work in a private household is covered if they amount to $50 or more in cash in a calendar quarter. People who do industrial work at home—piecework, quilting, needlework products, etc. —are also covered regardless of whether or not their work is subject to licensing under State law. Beginning with 1955 certain employees of the Federal Government not covered by another retirement system were covered by the 1954 amendments to the Social Security Act. United States citizens employed by United States employers aboard vessels and aircraft of foreign registry were brought under the law by the 1954 amendments. United States citizens working abroad for a foreign subsidiary of a

(71)

United States corporation may be covered by the law if the parent corporation makes an agreement with the Secretary of the Treasury to pay the social security taxes for all United States citizens employed abroad by the foreign subsidiary. The 1954 amendments covered fishermen and some other employees in the fishing industry. Farmers, farm operators were brought under the law by the 1954 amendments; farm workers received extended coverage under this law. The 1956 amendments were even more extensive. (1) A self-employed farmer has optional methods of figuring his earnings for social security purposes. This method can be used both by individual farmers and by members of partnerships and can be used with records kept on the cash or accrual basis. Under the optional method, for taxable years ending on or after December 1956: If the gross income from agricultural self-employment is not more than $1800, he may count as his net earnings from farm self-employment either his actual net earnings or two-thirds of their gross farm income. If the gross farm income is more than $1,800 and the net farm earnings are less than $1,200, the farmer may use either his actual net earnings from farming or $1,200. If the gross farm income is more than $1,800 and his net farm earnings are $1,200 or more, he must use the actual amount of his net farm earnings. (2) If a person farms land owned by someone else on a share basis, and the crops or livestock he produces are divided between him and the landlord with the share he receives depending on the total amount produced, then such a person is considered a self-employed farmer for social security purposes. This rule is effective for all taxable years ending after 1954. (3) If a person has land which is farmed by someone else, and he takes part in the management or production of the crop, his income from that land for taxable years ending after 1955 may count toward social security benefits for him and his family. Under the 1956 amendments, the cash or crop shares he receives from a tenant or share-farmer will count for social security purposes if under his arrangement with the tenant or share-farmer he "participates materially" in the production of the crops or livestock or in the management of the production. In order to "participate materially" a person must take an important part in the management decisions or in the actual production. (4) If a person works for a farmer, beginning with 1957, his earnings from farmwork will count toward social security benefits under either of these conditions: If a farm employer pays him $150 or more in cash during the year, his cash pay from that employer is covered by the law. If he does farmwork for an employer on 20 or more days during a year for cash pay figured on a time basis (rather than on a piece-rate basis), his cash pay from that employer is covered by the law. (5) If a person is a leader of a farm labor crew, the crew members he furnishes and pays are his employees, unless he and the farmer for whom he does the work have entered into a written agreement which shows that the crew leader is the farmer's employee. (6) If a farm operator uses crew workers, and has entered into a written agreement with the crew leader which shows that he is the farm operator's employee, then the crew members are also the farm operator's employees. These provisions are effective for work performed after December 31, 1956. (7) Workers temporarily admitted to the

United States from any foreign country to do agricultural labor will not be covered by the social security law after 1956. Members of the uniformed services are covered by the social security law beginning with 1957. Their basic pay will count toward old-age, survivors, and disability insurance benefits, and the social security tax will be deducted from their pay just as if they were civilians. Service between September 15, 1940, and January 1, 1957, can generally count toward benefits if it is not counted toward certain other Federal benefits.

"Covered Employment." A term used by the United States Employment Service. Same as INSURED WORK.

"Covered Worker." A term used by the United States Employment Service to designate an individual who has earned wages in insured work.

craft. Employment requiring skilled mechanical or manual workmanship, independent judgment, thorough knowledge of processes, and often responsibility for expensive equipment and material.

craft advisory committee. A group of local craftsmen selected from a specific trade or occupation appointed to advise the school on matters pertaining to teaching the particular occupation. When appropriate, the committee should include an equal number of representatives of labor and management.

craft union. A trade union which limits membership to persons following the same specific craft or skill in related trades, regardless of the industry or business in which they may be working. The object of such a union is to bargain collectively with the employer for favorable conditions of employment for members of the craft. The power of the craft union comes from its monopoly of a particular skill which is made possible by control over apprenticeship and licensing. In opposition to the craft principle of trade union organization is the idea of the industrial union which aims to incorporate into one union all workers in a given industry regardless of skill or craft differences. Generally speaking, craft unions characterize the former A.F. of L. unions (now A.F. of L.-C.I.O.) and are considered "horizontal" bargaining.

creative engineering. A method of conducting creative thinking sessions (which see) by the orderly or step-by-step approach. A four-step procedure consists of (1) Definition: amassing all of the possible ways of stating the problem; (2) Search: amassing of possible solutions; (3) Evaluation: choosing the best approach; (4) Solution: engineering the plan down to a practical stage. Engineers particularly favor this method of solving problems because: (1) By stressing specialized knowledge, the approach leads to a more thorough understanding of technical principles. (2) Solutions tend to be highly practical. (3) By carrying solutions to a completed stage, participants learn how to impart their ideas effectively. (4) By thoroughly examining the definitions of problems, the participants are able to avoid superficial answers. Criticisms are: (1) It is a long and costly process; (2) Time is also required outside of the sessions; (3) Some critics feel that an orderly approach may hinder the formation of "inspired" or highly original thinking.

creative thinking. Creative thinking is a term used to describe a method of encouraging groups of people to develop imaginative solutions to problems, unhampered by the barriers of convention, stereotype and precedent. To achieve this objective, creative thinking sessions establish three ground rules: (1) Instead of looking for one "right" answer, participants try to amass a multitude of possible answers; (2) Ideas are not required to be logical; (3) Problems are tackled en masse, that is, by groups of people rather than by one individual. The idea behind these rules is that creativity cannot be fully realized if it depends entirely upon the logical, analytical process normally associated with thinking, because: (1) Logical thinking often leads to single-answer "deadlock." By assuming that all problems have one right answer, standard methods of thinking tend to focus attention on only one of many possible solutions. As a result, conferees spend time debating whether the answer at hand is the right one instead of searching for other solutions. (2) Standard methods of thinking fail to harness the creative faculty of intuition; (3) The "lone-wolf" method of attacking problems is too restricted. By working together people can complement one another's creative powers. There are three types of creative thinking sessions: (1) The free association process (See BRAINSTORMING); (2) The orderly step-by-step approach (See CREATIVE ENGINEERING); (3) The broad field approach (See CREATIVE THINKING-BROAD FIELD APPROACH). In creative thinking sessions, group leaders try to help the session along by following ten fundamental rules: (1) Take time to define the problem. (2) Avoid single-answer deadlock. (3) Phrase questions in terms of "how many." (4) Use significant problems. (5) Avoid technical terms. (6) Form a pattern. (7) Encourage adaptation and borrowing. (8) Do not promise to put any ideas into effect. (9) Keep the number of participants down to fifteen. (10) Fit the method to the objective of the session.

creative thinking, broad field approach. A method of conducting creative thinking sessions which has two distinguishing characteristics: (1) The group attacks the underlying concept of the problem rather than the problem itself. For example, if a new principle for a can opener is wanted, the group leader introduces the general subject of *opening*. When a cutting device is wanted, the subject *severing* is introduced. (2) Underlying concepts are explored at length, and subjects are examined from many angles —social and economic as well as mechanical. The broad field approach is said to have two advantages: (1) It prevents early closure of the problem. It keeps participants from thinking they have already seen the obvious answer. (2) It encourages radical applications of old techniques. Limitations are: (1) It is an extremely roundabout way of reaching solutions. (2) Since subjects are explored at great length, it becomes time consuming. (3) Because concepts are explored broadly and abstractly, the sessions require participants to have broad knowledge and highly conceptual aptitudes.

"Credit Allowance." A term used by the United States Employment Service to designate credit allowed an employer against the Federal Unemployment Tax. *Additional Credit Allowance*: Credit for the difference between the employer's liability at the standard rate in the State and the contributions required of him by the State law, where the State permits reduced rates only in accordance

with the conditions of the Federal Unemployment Tax Act. *Normal Credit Allowance*: Credit for payments into a
State unemployment fund.

"Credit Offset." A term used by the
United States Employment Service. Same
as CREDIT ALLOWANCE.

**credits, building up, for Social Security
benefits.** To qualify for monthly benefits
(become fully insured) at retirements, to
make payments possible for survivors in
case of death, or to receive disability
insurance, a worker must have been in
work covered by the social security law
for a certain length of time. The amount
of work required is measured in "quarters of coverage." A quarter of coverage,
in a general way, corresponds with a
calendar quarter of work. A calendar
quarter is a three-month period beginning January 1, April 1, July 1, or October 1. The exact meaning of a quarter
of coverage is different, however, for
certain different kinds of work. A worker
gets 4 quarters of coverage for a year in
which he has $400 or more in net earn-
ings from self-employment. He gets 1
quarter of coverage for each $100 of
wages paid him in a year as a farm employee (but no more than 4 in a year).
For all other kinds of employment, he
gets one quarter of coverage for each
calendar quarter in which he is paid
$50 or more in wages. He can also earn
quarters of coverage through railroad
employment and active military service.
He may have earned quarters of coverage by working as an employee at any
time after 1936 and by self-employment
after 1950. The number of quarters of
coverage a worker has, is used only in
figuring whether or not a payment can
be made. The amount of the payment
is figured from the average monthly

earnings. If at the time of "retirement
age" (65 for a man or 62 for a woman)
a person has enough quarters of coverage to be "fully insured," he is eligible
for retirement payments. A person also
may earn needed quarters of coverage
after they reach retirement age. "Fully
insured" means only that some benefits
may be paid, not necessarily that the
maximum will be paid. Additional needed
quarters of coverage after retirement age
may be earned in covered employment
or self-employment. If at the time of
death a person is "fully insured" or "currently insured," his survivors may be
eligible for benefit payments. For certain
kinds of benefits to be paid the worker
must be both fully and currently insured. If a person becomes totally disabled, he may ask to have the period of
disability left out in figuring the amount
of work he needs and the amount of
his payments. See FULLY INSURED, CUR-
RENTLY INSURED. *Two special provisions*:
A person who reaches 65 before October
1, 1958, or a person who dies after
March 31, 1956, and before October 1,
1958 will be "fully insured" even if he
does not meet the "fully insured" requirements if: (1) he has a quarter of
coverage for every calendar quarter after
1954 and until he reaches 65 or dies, and
(2) at least 6 of his quarters of coverage were earned after 1954. Workers
who died after June 30, 1940, and before
September 1, 1950, are fully insured if
they had 6 quarters of coverage (1½
years of work) or more.

credit union. A cooperative savings and
loan association, incorporated under federal or state law, composed of employees
in the same firm, trade, industry, or
other groups with common interests. The
operation of credit unions is regulated

by state legislation. In 1934 a federal law was passed providing for the incorporation of credit unions. In an industrial credit union, the operation usually is set up so that members are required to buy at least one share of stock in the authorized corporation. The management of the credit union and its funds is generally in the hands of a board of directors, composed of five or more members elected by the membership. There may also be a credit committee and other supervisory officers elected by the credit union members. The treasurer in most credit unions is a member of the board of directors and is bonded. He collects and dispenses the funds, which in most states must be deposited in a state or national bank. Members can borrow from these funds, but approval from the credit committee or a committee made up of directors is usually required. Companies frequently provide office space, legal advice and assistance by making payroll deductions, but prefer to place responsibility for membership savings and other funds on the board of directors of the credit union. See PERSONNEL HANDBOOK (Ronald Press) for details.

"Critical Score." A score on a test or a battery of tests which distinguishes between those applicants who are apt to be satisfactory in an occupation and those who would be less likely to be satisfactory. Also called the "minimum," "cutting," or "passing" score.

"Current Intake." A term used by the United States Employment Service to designate those applicants present in a local office at a given time, except those who have been called in.

"currently insured." A term used in the Social Security Act. See CREDITS, BUILD-ING UP, FOR SOCIAL SECURITY BENEFITS. A person is currently insured when he has become entitled to retirement payments or at death if he has at least 6 quarters of coverage within the preceding three years. See FULLY INSURED.

cutback. A sudden reduction of work, resulting in a decrease in the work force through layoffs.

cutting rate. See CUTTING SPEED.

cutting speed. The relative velocity, usually expressed in feet per minute, between a cutting tool and the surface of the material from which it is removing stock.

cybernetics. A new field of science which attempts to relate the operation of automatic functioning of the human body's nervous system. Once accomplished, it hopes to evolve a theory blanketing the field of control and communication—both in machines and men. The word "cybernetics" has a definite origin. Dr. Norbert Wiener, professor of mathematics at MIT, and Arturo Rosenblueth, of Harvard University, coined it in the summer of 1947. Said Dr. Wiener at the time, "We have decided to call the entire field of control and communication theory, whether in the machine or in the animal, by the name of Cybernetics, which we form from the Greek word, steersman." See Cybernetics (New York: John Wiley and Sons, Inc., 1948).

cyclograph technique. The method devised by the Gilbreths and used in motion study by which a three-dimensional pattern of a motion path may be recorded by attaching a small electric light bulb to the finger, hand, or other part of a worker's body and photographing, with a stereoscopic camera, the path of the light as it moves through space.

cycle timing. (1) Observance of the total time required to complete a cycle. (2) A time-study technique used to time work elements that are too short to time in the usual manner. It consists of timing a cycle or periodically recurring series of elements, first including and then excluding the element for which the time is needed. The needed time for this element is then obtained by subtraction.

cyclic timing. See CYCLE TIMING.

D

daily rate. For a worker hired on a daily rate basis, the rate of pay is normally expressed as a rate for a standard number of work hours per day. Like the hourly rate, the quotation of a daily rate normally excludes premiums that may be paid for late-shift work or overtime hours, as well as bonuses for special conditions of work or of other reasons unrelated directly to production.

damage, equipment and machine. Monetary loss incurred through carelessness, error or other fault of an employee. Damage is reflected in costs for repair, replacement, down time, etc.

danger zone bonus. A bonus paid to employees who are required to work in an area where either the material or machinery is particularly hazardous. Such bonuses are common in the explosives manufacturing industry and in the work of longshoremen. During the war, special payments were made to members of the merchant marine as war-risk bonuses.

"Day-Haul Operation." A term used by the United States Employment Service to designate the daily transporting of workers, assembled at a pick-up point, to farm employment and return.

day-rate. See DAILY RATE.

day work. Work compensated for at a specified rate per hour or per day, for which the compensation is not directly dependent upon the quantity of production as is the case in piece work or incentive work. (2) a shift that falls during the daylight hours; casual labor hired a day at a time when needed.

deadheading pay. A special payment to a transportation worker who is required to report for work at a point far removed from his home terminal. "Deadheading" refers to the extra time consumed in traveling to and from the place of work, as transporting railroad crewmen from one terminal to another, with or without pay.

dead time. Time lost by a worker because of lack of materials, a break-down of machinery, or from causes beyond his control. An incentive worker usually receives his guaranteed or base rate during this period. See also DOWN TIME.

dead work. A term used in mining, referring to nonproductive work, including the removal of rock, debris, and other waste matter from the product mined.

death benefit. The benefits provided under a pension plan for the beneficiary or estate of a participant upon the death of the latter. Frequently these benefits are paid both prior to or after retirement.

death, discounts for. The anticipated cost of providing pensions may be reduced by assuming that a certain number of employees will die before retirement. A recognized mortality table is used as the basis for these assumptions.

decasualization. Removing the casual element from certain types of labor, in order to reduce or eliminate unemployment or loss in irregular or unstable jobs. See CASUAL LABOR. Methods of decasualization include shifting of workers in groups from areas of unemployment to areas of higher employment; expansion of employment exchanges for registering employees seeking work, such as the use of a centralized hiring hall for the hiring of longshoremen or dock workers; and the guaranteed annual wage.

deceased. A person who has died. The term is used to denote that employment service has been severed by the death of the employee.

decentralization. The distribution of similar types of work, activities or functions to various offices or departments. Thus, work is thereby located close to the course initiating the activity. Decentralization of filing would mean that each executive has his own files, rather than all files being consolidated in a centralized office. See also CENTRALIZATION.

decimal-hour stop watch. A two-handed timing device whose movement may be started or stopped manually and whose large outer dial is divided into 100 spaces each of which represents 0.0001 hour. The position of the large hand on the large dial indicates time in hours to four decimal places and the position of the small hand on a smaller, inner dial indicates time in hours to two decimal places.

decimal-minute stop watch. A two-handed timing device whose movement may be started or stopped manually and whose large outer dial is divided into 100 spaces each of which represents 0.01 minute. The position of the large hand on the large dial indicates time in minutes to two decimal places and the position of the small hand on a smaller, inner dial indicates time in whole minutes.

decision-making. A term that usually refers to a management function, involving recognition of the problem to be faced, accumulation of facts or data, arranging or classifying evidence so as to throw some light on a tentative answer, weighing evidence or data, picturing alternative eventualities, formulating a trial solution, testing the solution to see if it is practicable or effective, and adopting or accepting the trial solution as valid and useful as long as the fundamental facts of the situation remain substantially unchanged. Also implied is the willingness of the person who makes the choice to stand by his decision. A scientific approach to decision-making is known as OPERATIONS RESEARCH, which see. Says Dr. Arthur Lesser, Jr., Prof. of Industrial Engineering, Stevens Institute of Technology, "A study of the steps gone through in making any real decision about the most trivial matters, shows that a final decision is preceded by a myriad of minor decisions, one related to the other, and each one of these minor decisions calls for a valuing procedure."

deductions. Amounts withheld from the pay check. They may be fixed, or non-fluctuating, which means they are taken out with scheduled regularity, as union dues; or variable, which means they fluctuate with the amount of the gross pay, as withholding taxes. Insurance deductions may be either fixed or variable, depending on the individual situation.

defense base act. Act of August 16, 1941, as amended. Extends the Longshoremen's and Harbor Works' Compensation Act to employees of private employers on defense bases or employees engaged in public works outside the continental United States under contract with the Federal Government.

Defense Housing and Community Facilities and Services Act of 1951. The prevailing wage provisions of this law cover housing for defense workers or for military personnel, and also cover community facilities such as sewers, waterlines, streets, and other facilities in defense areas, outside military installations.

deferred life annuity. An annuity which becomes effective at a future date. If death occurs before the beginning of income from annuity, nothing is paid; after income from the annuity has started, it continues for the balance of the life of the insured, but nothing is payable upon death.

definite benefit plan. See BENEFIT PLAN, DEFINITE.

delay. A period during which conditions (except those which intentionally change the physical or chemical characteristics of an object) do not permit or require immediate performance of the next planned action.

delay allowance. (1) A time increment included in a time standard to allow for contingencies and minor delays beyond the control of the worker. (2) A separate credit (in time or money) to compensate the worker on incentive for a specific instance of delay not covered by the piece rate or standard.

"Delegated Hiring Authority." A term used by the United States Employment Service. See REFERRAL.

"Demand List." A term used by the United States Employment Service. See SHORTAGE LIST.

department. An organizational unit established to operate in and be responsible for a specified activity or physical or functional area.

department or plant incentive systems. Such systems differ from group systems in that the requirement of interdependence of operations does not necessarily apply, and in that whereas under group systems the amount of production is measured and the earnings of the group are calculated at short intervals, under department or plant systems the measurement of production and the calculation of bonuses may be carried out at relatively lengthy intervals, generally once a month. The bonuses are frequently paid to the individual workers in proportion to their time rates. Thus, provision can be made for not only direct but also indirect workers to participate.

"Dependents ' Allowances." A term used by the United States Employment Service to designate special allowances provided in a State employment security law to beneficiaries by reason of their family responsibilities.

depletion. A lessening of the value of an asset due to a decrease in the quantity available. It is similar to depreciation except that it refers to such natural resources as coal, oil, and timber in forests.

Deposit Administration Plan. A type of pension plan, usually under a master group annuity contract, providing for the accumulation of contributions in an undivided fund out of which annuities are purchased as the individual members of the group retire. The contributions needed to fund the benefits are determined either by the insurance company's actuary or an independent actuary. The sums so deposited are not allocated to the account of any individual, but are accumulated to purchase an annuity when the employee retires.

depreciable unit. An asset or group of assets which is recorded and depreciated separately from the other units.

depreciable value. (1) The difference between the first cost of an asset to the current owner and the net recoverable value at the time of its disposal. (2) The recorded or book value of an asset at any time.

depreciation. The actual decline in the value of an asset due to exhaustion, wear and tear, and obsolescence.

depreciation base. The actual or adjusted initial cost of an asset to which a depreciation rate is applied in computing depreciation cost or expense.

depreciation expense. A periodic accounting charge or operating cost arising from the systematic writing off of assets in the accounting records.

"Designation of Hiring Agent." A term used by the United States Employment

Service to designate a contractual form executed by the employer delegating hiring authority to the United States Employment Service and its affiliated State Employment Services.

"Determination." A term used by the United States Employment Service. *Benefit Determination*: A decision with respect to a request for determination of insured status, a notice of unemployment, of insured status, a notice of unemployment, a certification for waiting-period credit, or a claim for benefits. *Coverage Determination*: A determination as to whether an employing unit is a subject employer and whether service performed for it constitutes employment as defined under a State employment security law. See STATUS DETERMINATION, below. *Determination of Insured Status*: A determination as to whether an individual meets the employment requirements necessary for the receipt of benefits; and, if so, his weekly benefit amount and maximum annual benefits. *Initial Determination*: The first determination with respect to a claim or a request for determination of insured status. *Monetary Determination*: Same as DETERMINATION OF INSURED STATUS. *Nonmonetary Determination*: A determination as to whether a claimant is barred from receiving benefits or waiting-period credits for reasons other than those affecting his insured status. *Predetermination*: A determination of insured status made prior to the filing of a new claim. *Reconsidered Determination*: Same as REDETERMINATION. *Redetermination.* A determination made with respect to a claimant after reconsideration by the initial determining authority. *Seasonal Determination*: The determination made by a State employment security agency as

(81)

to the seasonal nature and the period of seasonal operations of an industry, occupation, establishment, or employer for the purposes of determining whether the seasonal provision of the State law shall be applied to the benefit rights of workers employed in such industry, occupation, or establishment, or by such employer. *Status Determination*: A determination as to whether an employing unit whose status is not known is a subject employer. See COVERAGE DETERMINATION, above.

determination of collective bargaining representatives, under Railway Labor Act (which see). Section 2 (3) of the act states that collective bargaining representatives *shall be designated by the respective parties without interference, influence, or coercion by either party over the designation of representatives by the other; and neither party shall in any way interfere with, influence, or coerce the other in its choice of representatives.* It is specifically provided that employee representatives for collective bargaining shall not be required to be employees of the employer. The act states that *the majority of any craft or class of employees shall have the right to determine who shall be the representative of the class or craft* [sec. 2(4)]. While the Board has no power to establish crafts or classes or employees, it may designate who may participate in representation elections. Such determinations are usually made in the light of accepted practice in employee self-organization over a period of years. Where any labor organization, committee, or employee representative asserts that a dispute exists concerning representation of employees for the purposes of the act, it is the duty of the National Mediation Board to investigate

such a dispute and conduct an election by secret ballot or any other suitable method to determine who is the collective bargaining representative of the employees [sec. 2 (9)]. If a majority of the employees in a craft or class chooses an individual or a labor organization, the Board then issues a certification of that fact to the parties and the carrier. Interference by carriers in the designation of employee representatives is a misdemeanor. Employees may also appeal to the Federal courts for an injunction to restrain the carrier from violating the act.

deviate. A THERBLIG (which see) which is defined as: to turn aside as from a straight path; to bring out of or aside from a straight line; to use a curved irregular, or abrupt turn. The *deviate* therblig applies in turning through motion paths of the arm, forearm, hand, finger, foreleg, or foot movements. The path of turning may occur as an arc, as an angular movement, or as a reversal of the movement.

Dictionary of Occupational Titles. An inclusive source of occupational information and techniques, usually in Volumes I and II, with supplements added periodically, published by the United States Employment Service, Division of Occupational Analysis. It includes descriptions and definitions of over 20,000 jobs listed alphabetically.

Diemer Plan. A wage incentive plan which provides for the payment of regular day rates up to task and then of an increase of one half percent added wage for each one percent production above task along with a 10% bonus.

differential piece work. A wage incentive plan that employs two or more piece rates. One piece rate is paid if the expected output is not attained. A higher rate is paid if the expected output is attained or exceeded. While originally devised by F. W. Taylor to provide only two piece rates, modifications of the plan provide for more than two. Synonym: MULTIPLE PIECE RATE PLAN.

differential time plan. See MULTIPLE TIME PLAN.

differentials. Differences in wage rates because of hours of work, certain undesirable days, or other working conditions. Differentials may include evening and night differentials, Christmas Eve and New Year's differentials, time differential tricks or shifts, and in-charge differentials.

differential timing. See CYCLE TIMING.

direct labor. (1) Work which alters the composition, condition, conformation, or construction of the product; the cost of which can be identified with and assessed against a particular part, product, or group of parts or products accurately and without undue effort and expense. (2) Workers directly engaged in or identified with some process or work of converting direct materials into finished products.

direct labor standard. A specific output or a time allowance established for a direct labor operation.

direct material. All material that enters into and becomes part of the finished product (including waste); the cost of which can be identified with and assessed against a particular part, product, or group of parts or products accurately and without undue effort or expense.

"Direct Referral." A term used by the United States Employment Service. See REFERRAL.

disability benefit. A feature added to some group life insurance policies providing for payment of monthly or weekly income upon the furnishing of proof that the insured has become totally and permanently disabled.

disability "freeze," under Social Security Law. The social security law protects the old-age and survivors insurance rights of people who have had a certain amount of work covered by social security but have since become totally disabled for work. If a person has been totally disabled for six months or longer, and the disability is expected to be of a long-continued and indefinite duration, he can apply to have his earnings "frozen." When earnings are frozen, the period in which the worker is totally disabled or has low earnings or no earnings need not be counted at all in figuring his average earnings or in figuring the amount of work he needs to be eligible for payment. To qualify for the disability freeze, a person must have been working regularly in a job covered by the social security law before he was disabled and he must have become totally disabled for work before reaching 65. (1) He must have been working regularly. In order to have earnings "frozen," he must have social security credit for both: Five years of work out the ten years before he was disabled, and one-and-one half years of work out of the three years immediately before he was disabled. (2) He must be totally disabled. Only a disability severe enough to keep him from doing any substantial gain for work can be considered. The disability may have been caused by injury, bodily sickness, mental sickness, or blindness—anything that can be medically determined. After he has been disabled for six months, if it appears that he will be disabled for an indefinite period, then he may be considered disabled for purposes of the "freeze." Application to have the record frozen, if it is made by June 30, 1957, can fully cover the period of a person's total disability back to the time it started. If application is made after June 30, 1957, the freeze can go back no more than one year. Persons who are unable to visit the social security office, may telephone or write, or someone else may take the call for them. The extent of disability will ordinarily be determined by an agency of the State. The social security office will refer the worker to the proper State agency for medical determination of the extent of his disability. The State vocational rehabilitation agency may be able to help a person in restoring or replacing lost skills and hastening his return to productive work. See also DISABILITY INSURANCE BENEFITS, UNDER SOCIAL SECURITY ACT.

"Disability Insurance." A term used by the United States Employment Service. See TEMPORARY DISABILITY INSURANCE.

disability insurance payments, under Social Security Act. If a person is disabled, he may have rights under one or more of three different parts of the social security law: (1) He may be eligible for disability insurance payments after 1957, if he is: 50 years of age or older, has had enough work under social security law, is so severely disabled that he is unable to do any substantial work, has been disabled for at least 6 months, and the disability is expected to continue indefinitely. At least 5 years of work under the law in the 10 years before the be-

ginning date of disability are required. At least 1½ years of this work must have been in the 3 years before the beginning date of disability. Persons temporarily disabled, or only partly disabled, are not eligible. If a person believes he may be eligible for disability insurance but has not previously applied for a disability freeze (as explained below) he should get in touch with his social security office immediately. (2) If a person is disabled and disability began before 18 years of age, he may be eligible (after 1956) to receive child's insurance benefits even after reaching age 18 if either father or mother is receiving old-age insurance benefits or if he has lost the support of a parent through death. To get social security benefits as a disabled child over 18 years of age, a person must (a) be unable to do any substantial work because of a disability that began before he reached 18 and has continued, (b) be dependent on a parent, stepparent, or adopting parent who is entitled to old-age insurance benefits under the social security law, or have been dependent on a parent who died after 1939 and was insured for survivors insurance benefits at the time of his or her death. (c) Be unmarried. (3) If a person is disabled and has not yet reached 50 years of age, he may be eligible to have his social security earnings "frozen" to protect his own and his family's right to future benefit payments because of old-age, disability, or death. To be eligible for a disability freeze, a person must (a) have at least 5 years of work covered by the social security law in the 10 years before the beginning date of disability. At least 1½ years of this work must have been in the 3 years before the beginning date of disability.

(b) Be so severely disabled that he is unable to do any substantial work. If a person believes he is eligible for a disability freeze he should get in touch with his social security office immediately unless he has already done so. See also: BENEFITS, SOCIAL SECURITY, TABLE OF; DISABILITY "FREEZE," under SOCIAL SECURITY LAW.

disability pension. Pension payable in the event that the employee becomes totally and permanently disabled before age of normal retirement.

disability retirement. Retirement necessitated before the normal retirement age because of a disability. Under many plans, an employee must have a minimum number of years of service and must have reached the minimum age required under the plan. Benefit payments are usually somewhat lower than at normal retirement.

"Disabled Veterans." A term used by the United States Employment Service to designate a veteran who (a) has a service-connected disability (see definition) and is currently rated 10% or more disabled by the Veterans Administration; or (b) has been retired for physical disability by a branch of the Armed Forces; or (c) meets the United States Employment Service definition of a "handicapped applicant" regardless of how or when the disability was incurred. (See APPLICANT).

disassemble. The basic element denoting the removal of a part or a unit or assembly.

disassemble. A THERBLIG (which see) which is defined as: to take apart, demount, as part of a machine. Disassemble may be considered as a reversed assemble.

discharge. Termination of employment initiated by the employer with prejudice to the employee. See LAYOFF, QUIT, SEPARATION.

"Discharges." A term used by the United States Employment Service. See SEPARATIONS.

discipline clause. A provision written into a union contract established through collective bargaining, stipulating the means of disciplining workers for violation of management or union rules and regulations.

discipline, foundations of good. Company policy should include, in order to achieve good discipline: (1) A clear and reasonable list of plant rules, with uniform penalties for their violation. (2) Instruction of all employees in what is expected of them, in terms of both observance of plant rules and established standards of job performance. (3) A procedure for telling employees how well they are meeting job standards and rules of conduct. (4) Investigation of the background and circumstances of each case before taking disciplinary action, when apparent breaches of conduct or expected performance do occur. (5) Prompt, consistent application of disciplinary measures by the employee's immediate superior, when guilt has clearly been established. (See particularly, *Personnel Administration*, by Paul Pigors and Charles A. Myers, Massachusetts Institute of Technology, McGraw-Hill Book Company, 1956.)

discipline. The ideal type of industrial discipline is "self-discipline," where employees by their own free will follow the rules. Such discipline is the result of constructive, positive leadership, exercised within the framework of a · clear, consistent disciplinary policy. An appeal to reason is much superior to an appeal to fear. Authority should not be used as a whip. The supervisor who has authority but who depends, rather, upon his leadership to control his subordinates will find his authority is more highly regarded than if he made use of it at every opportunity. Authority should be thought of as reserve power to be used only after all else fails. There are, of course, occasions and situations which justify the use of full authority. It requires fine judgment to know where to draw the line—to know when an appeal to reason has failed and rigid authority must be asserted.

discipline, ten practical points for maintaining. Following suggestions from "When Foreman and Steward Bargain," Glenn Gardiner, McGraw-Hill. (1) Be factual. Don't act or make decisions until you have all the facts. (2) Be friendly. Make people feel you are interested in them and their interests. (3) Be firm. With your friendliness, be sure you are firm—not "soft." Having gotten all the facts, be firm in carrying out decisions. (4) Be fearless. If you know you are right, do not be afraid of the results. Just be careful to take action in the most diplomatic way. (5) Act promptly. Having once made the decision as to what you're going to do, carry out your decision with promptness. (6) Be fair. Make certain that all your actions are based on fairness. Be sure that you are absolutely impartial in enforcement of rules and regulations. (7) Do not be finicking and fussy. In administering discipline, do not be small and petty. Do not fuss about unimportant details. Have as few rules and regulations as possible, but enforce them. (8) Do not be fault-

finding. Avoid nagging and finding fault about unimportant details. (9) Do not favor friends. Be sure that you treat all employees alike. Never let it appear that you are doing things for certain people who are thought to be special friends of yours. Be consistent. (10) Discharge only as last resort. Do not carry your authority like a club. Do not resort to discharge until every reasonable means has been used to correct a man. It takes no ability to fire a man but it takes a good supervisor to correct one who needs discipline.

discontinuous timing.   See SNAPBACK METHOD.

discrimination. Distinctions in hiring, promotion, layoff, discharge, or other employment practices based upon differences in race, religion, or national origin, or upon other reasons not related to job performance.

"Discriminatory Order." A term used by the United States Employment Service. See ORDER.

disengage. An industrial engineering term meaning the basic element employed to break the contact between one object and another. It is characterized by an involuntary recoil caused by the sudden ending of resistance.

dismissal compensation. A specific payment, in addition to regular wages, which is given an employee upon permanent termination of employment through no fault of his own. This dismissal compensation, or wage, may be paid in one sum at the time employment is terminated, or it may be spread over a period of time. The amount of the payment to any one employee is usually related to the amount of his regular wages and his length of service.

dismissal pay. See DISMISSAL COMPENSATION.

disposable income. See SPENDABLE EARNINGS and TAKEHOME PAY.

dispose. An industrial engineering term meaning an element of a total operation that involves the laying aside and releasing or otherwise getting rid of a part, assembly, tool or other object during or at the end of the operation.

"Disqualification Provisions." A term used by the United States Employment Service. Those provisions of a State employment security law that set forth the conditions that bar an individual from receiving benefits or waiting-period credit for a specified period and/or cancel or reduce the individual's benefits or credits. See also BENEFIT ELIGIBILITY CONDITIONS.

distributive education. A program of education offering training in the selling, marketing, and merchandising of goods and services, for the purpose of improving distribution and upgrading distributive workers, including employees, managers and owners engaged in distributive occupations.

distributive occupations program (diversified, cooperative, training). A high school course in which students are given supervised work experience in any of a variety of occupations combined with related classroom instruction. This type of program is especially suited to communities where the need for workers in any occupation is too limited to justify separate courses for each trade. The diversified occupations program is usually under the direction of the trade and industrial education division.

distributive occupations. Occupations followed by workers directly engaged in merchandising activities or in contact with buyers and sellers when (1) distributing to consumers, retailers, jobbers, wholesalers, and others the production of industry or the products of farms, or selling services, or (2) managing, operating or conducting a retail, wholesale or service business.

do. An industrial engineering term meaning the basic element accomplished in full or in part the purpose of the operation. It includes the basic elements Use and Assemble and may sometimes be expressed in terms of other basic elements. See THERBLIG; USE; ASSEMBLE.

docking of pay. A deduction from wages as a penalty for tardiness, spoilage of work through carelessness, or similar causes.

dole. A donation given by a private or public relief agency to supplement the income of an individual or family, generally at regular intervals and in standardized amounts determined by some established law or policy. The term applies specifically to the British system of unemployment relief, but is loosely used to cover any systematic allotment made without corresponding return in labor or otherwise.

doubleheading pay. Refers to the extra compensation given the railroad engineer where very steep grades require the use of more than one engine for some distance. The specific rules regulating payment under these conditions are found in the various union agreements.

double indemnity. An accidental death benefit providing for payment of double the face amount of the policy in case of death as a result of accidental means.

downgrading. The reassignment of workers to tasks with lower skill requirements and lower rates of pay. Usually resorted to when a marked change in products or in the methods of production occurs and a lesser degree of skill in work performance is required; also applied in reductions of force which require reassignments of workers to jobs of lower skills. Downgrading was used by some establishments after World War II when conversion from war work to the manufacture of civilian goods required less skilled operations. (See also UPGRADING.)

down time. Brief periods of idleness while waiting for repair, set-up, or adjustment of machinery. (See also DEAD TIME.)

drawing account. A weekly allowance usually the determining factor in establishing the amount of the drawing account. (See also COMMISSION EARNINGS.)

"Draft Bill." Suggested language published by the Bureau of Employment Security to assist States in drafting State employment legislation.

draftsman. According to the "Dictionary of Occupational Titles," prepares clear, complete, and accurate working plans and detail drawing, from rough or detailed sketches or notes for engineering or manufacturing purposes according to the specified dimensions: makes final sketch of the proposed drawing, checking dimensions of parts, materials to be used, the relation of one part to another, and the relation of the various parts to the whole structure. Makes any adjustments or changes necessary or desired; inks in all lines and letters on pencil drawings; exercises manual skill in the manipulations of triangle, T-square, and other drafting tools; lays tissue sheet on drawing and traces drawing on tissue paper; makes charts for representation of statistical data; makes finished designs from sketches; utilizes knowledge of various machines, engineering practices, mathematics, building materials, and other physical sciences to complete the drawings.

drawing account. An allowance, generally of a specified amount, to be paid weekly or at some other stated period, for people who work on straight commission basis. The account is balanced against the earnings of total commissions at designated periods of time and the size of the drawing account is generally determined on the basis of anticipated earning power.

drop delivery. (1) The method of introducing an object to the work place by gravity. (2) A method whereby a chute or container is so placed that, when work on a part in question is finished it will fall or drop into a chute or container or onto a conveyor with little or no "transport" by the workman. (3) The laying aside of a part by releasing it so that it falls or moves away from the work area either through the force of gravity or by mechanical or other means.

dual pay. A system of wage payment used by railroads under which employees are paid on a mileage or hours basis. A standard mileage is defined as a basic day, usually 8 hours, for the purpose of determining the daily rate. Wages are computed on the number of hours or miles, whichever yields the greater compensation to the employee.

dual union. See UNION, DUAL.

"Duration of Benefits." A term used by the United States Employment Service to designate the number of weeks for which benefits are paid or payable for total unemployment in a benefit year. Because there may be partial and part-time employment, duration is often described in terms of the total amount of benefits arrived at by multiplying the weekly benefit amount by the number of weeks of total employment. *Actual Duration*: The number of full weeks of benefits received by a claimant, or the equivalent thereof expressed in terms of dollars. *Individual Duration*: Same Variable Duration below. *Maximum Duration*: The highest number of weeks of total unemployment for which benefits are payable to any claimant in a benefit year under a State employment security law. See also MAXIMUM ANNUAL BENEFITS under BENEFITS. *Potential Duration*: The total number of weeks of total unemployment for which an individual claimant is qualified to receive benefits on the basis of his base-period insured work. *Uniform Duration*: A formula which provides varying numbers of weeks of potential duration, based on an individual's base-period insured work.

duties of carriers and employees to bargain collectively under Railway Labor Act (which see). Section 2 (1) states that it shall be the duty of all carriers, their officers, agents, and employees to exert every reasonable effort to make and maintain agreements concerning rates of pay, rules and working conditions, and to settle all disputes, whether arising out of the application of such agreements or otherwise, in order to avoid any interruption to commerce or to the operation of any carrier growing out of any dispute between the carrier and the employees thereof. Every carrier is required to file with the National Mediation Board a copy of every contract with its employees, as well as all changes when made.

Dyer System. A wage incentive plan which is an offshoot of the Haynes or Bedaux principle. The Dyer plan includes a machine rate in the computation for earning of machine operators. The machine rate is expressed as a fraction such as 65/60ths for a drill press. The formula for earning becomes:

$$E = H_a R_h + \tfrac{4}{5}(H_s - H_a) R_h R_m$$

or in terms of minutes instead of hours,

$$E = M_a R_h / 60 + \tfrac{4}{5}(M_s - M_a) R_h R_m / 60$$

this may be reduced to,

$$E = R_h / 60 [M_a + \tfrac{4}{5}(M_s - M_a) R_m]$$

which means that minutes actual are added to four-fifths of the minutes saved times the machine rate and all multiplied by the man rate per minute.

See: SYMBOLS, WAGE FORMULA.

Key to additional symbols:

M_a = Minutes actual = $60 H_a$

M_s = Minutes standard = $60 H_s$

R_m = Machine rate in per cent

E

early retirement. See RETIREMENT EARLY.

earned hours. An industrial engineering term meaning the time in standard hours credited to a worker or group of workers as a result of their completion of a given task or group of tasks.

earned period rate. See AVERAGE EARNED RATE.

earned rate. See AVERAGE EARNED RATE.

earnings. The total remuneration of a worker or group of workers for services rendered, including wages, overtime pay, bonuses, commissions, etc.

economic education, for supervisors. Increasing attention is given to economic education for supervisors, both so that supervisors themselves may understand our American economy system, and to help them pass along proper information to employees. Included are "packages" or commercially available programs, programs developed by companies, which may or may not be commercially available, and community programs. Organizations dealing specifically with economic education include: American Economic Association, American Economic Foundation, American Institute for Economic Research, National Bureau of Economic Research, Committee for Eco-

nomic Development. The Foremanship Foundation, of Dayton, Ohio, has published two all-inclusive booklets on the subjects: Survey of Economic Education and Economic Education—A Bibliography.

economic lot size. That number of units of material or a manufactured item that can be purchased or produced within the lowest unit cost range. Its determination involves reconciling the decreasing trend in preparation unit costs and the increasing trend in unit costs of storage, interest, insurance, depreciation and other costs incident to ownership as the size of the lot is increased.

economics. Economics has been defined (in "Dictionary of Modern Economics," Public Affairs Press) as "a systematic study of man's attempt to obtain the material means to satisfy his wants. Currently, economics is chiefly used in the applied sense, i.e., the application of the principles of economics to public policy or to particular problems of industry. It implies utilization of the best available data on wants, productive techniques and economic institutions for the purpose of achieving maximum effectiveness from material and human resources. See, for example, *Sources of Economic In-*

(90)

formation for Collective Bargaining, by Ernest Dale, American Management Association, Research Report Number 17.

efficiency. (1) The ratio of standard performance time to actual performance time usually expressed as a percentage. (2) The ratio of actual performance numbers (e.g. number of pieces) to standard performance numbers usually expressed as a percentage.

efficiency expert. A person, frequently from an outside consulting firm, who is to improve methods and procedures. He analyzes the situation or field where improvement is desired, to determine the performance of the right operation, at the right place, at the right time, by the right person.

efficiency rating. See RATING, EXPERIENCE MERIT.

effort. (1) The evidence of the will to work as manifested by a worker performing an operation. (2) The sum total of the mental absorption and physical participation which may be required by a worker on a given operation.

effort rating. (1) That part of any performance rating technique concerned with evaluating the extent or degree to which the will to work is exhibited by a worker. (2) See SPEED RATING.

Eight-hour day. This term may have three distinct meanings: (1) A straight eight-hour day with overtime eliminated or prohibited. (2) A shift of eight hours with three work periods of eight hours each for three or more different sets of workers. This arrangement may extend over six or seven days of the week. (3) A basic eight-hour day in which eight hours is made the measure for service

or payment, but under which overtime is permitted.

Eight-Hour Laws. Act of August 1, 1892, as amended, and Act of June 19, 1912, as amended. These laws apply generally to contracts, including contracts for services, made by agencies of the Federal Government, the District of Columbia, and the Territories which may require or involve the employment of laborers or mechanics. Some exceptions are made in the laws, such as contracts for transportation, for communications, for supplies or such other materials or for articles as may be bought in the open market, or the construction or repair of levees or revetments necessary for flood protection. Construction, alteration, and repair including painting and decorating of the kind covered by the Davis-Bacon Act are generally covered by these laws, regardless of the amount of the contract. These laws also cover laborers and mechanics employed by the Federal Government itself. Except for work under the Defense Housing and Community Facilities and Services Act of 1951, which has its own 8-hour law provision, work under federally assisted construction programs of non-Federal agencies or persons is not covered by the Eight-Hour Laws. These laws do not apply, for instance, to construction work under Federal-aid programs on projects for hospitals, schools, FHA-insured multi-family apartments, slum clearance, low-rent public housing, and airports. However, in the case of low-rent public housing, the contract in general use furnished by the Public Housing Administration which administers the program provides that time and one-half be paid for hours worked over 8 a day or 40 a week. The Eight-Hour Laws permit overtime work in excess of 8 hours in any calendar day by a covered laborer or mechanic employed on a covered contract if not less than time and one-half his basic rate of pay is paid him for the period of overtime work. Wages must be computed on a basic day rate of 8 hours a day and the basic rate can never be less than the wage rate predetermined for the classification of work by the Secretary of Labor, although it may be higher if the worker is actually paid at a higher rate. The Eight-Hour Laws provide for overtime pay only when a worker works more than 8 hours a calendar day. There is no provision for extra pay when he works more than 40 hours in the week, as there is in the Fair Labor Standard Act and in the Public Housing Administration contract mentioned above. Enforcement of these laws is the responsibility of the Government agency for which the work is performed, subject to standards, regulations, and procedures prescribed by the Secretary of Labor under Reorganization Plan No. 14 of 1950. The Eight-Hour Laws provide for the withholding from the contractor of a penalty of $5 per day for each violation and each employee involved. Intentional violation by an officer or agent of the Government or by a contractor or subcontractor of that part of the law which limits the hours of employment of laborers and mechanics employed on public works of the United States or the District of Columbia constitutes a misdemeanor, punishable by a fine or imprisonment. For further information write to the Office of the Solicitor, U.S. Department of Labor, Washington 25, D.C.

elapsed time. (1) The actual time taken by a worker to complete a task, an operation, or an element of an operation. (2) The total time interval from the beginning to the end of a time study.

"Election, Voluntary." A term used by the United States Employment Service.

element. A subdivision of the work cycle composed of a sequence of one or several fundamental motions, and/or machine or process activities, which is distinct, describable, and measurable. Two classes of elements are: (1) constant, for which the standard time allowance should always be the same for a specified set of conditions. On a drill press of a certain size and make, Raise Spindle, and Lock Speed are examples. (2) variable, for which the standard time allowance should change to compensate for variations in effort required according to a range in the dimensions of the product or equipment. Drill-press variables might be, Pick Up Piece, Hole to Hole, Turn Jig Over, and all machining time.

elemental motion. See BASIC DIVISION OF ACCOMPLISHMENT.

elemental time value. See ELEMENT TIME.

element breakdown. The subdivisions of an operation each of which is composed of a distinct, describable and measurable sequence of one or several fundamental motions and/or machine or process activities.

element time. The term used to indicate either the actual, observed, selected, normal, or standard time to perform an element of an operation.

"Eligibility Requirements." A term used by the United States Employment Service. Same as BENEFIT ELIGIBILITY CONDITIONS.

(92)

Emerson Efficiency Bonus Plan. See
EMERSON GRADUATED BONUS PLAN.

Emerson Efficiency Plan. A wage incentive plan providing a guaranteed base wage rate and an increasing rate of incentive payment beginning when performance reaches 67% of standard. Under the original plan, incentive payment became constant at 120% of the base wage rate when standard performance was reached. Modifications of this plan provide increasing incentive payment for performance above standard.

Emerson Efficiency System. See EMERSON GRADUATED BONUS PLAN.

Emerson Efficiency Wage Plan formulas. The formulas for figuring a worker's earnings in the Emerson plan: (1) From 66⅔% of task up to task: $E = RT + p(RT)$ A.T. (above task) $E = RS + 0.20(RT)$ Value of p is taken from an empirical table. See SYMBOLS, WAGE FORMULA. (2) a) Earnings up to 66% of high task: $E = H_aR_h$ or Hours actual $\times$ Rate per hour (b) Earnings between 66⅔% and 100% of high task:
$E = H_aR_h + B_o \times R_h$ or $(1 + B_o)H_aR_h$
(c) Earnings at and above high task:
$E = H_sR_h + .20\ H_aR_h$ or $\dfrac{(H_s + H_a)R_h}{5}$

where: E = earnings
RT, or H_aR_h = time wages
H_a = hours actual
R_h = rate per hour
H_s = hours standard
B_o, or P = certain bonus %
$(H_s - H_a)R_h$ = savings from basic piece rate
$.20$ = 20% time wages

Emerson Graduated Bonus Plan. An incentive plan developed by Harrington

Emerson, a contemporary of F. W. Taylor. Under the plan the worker's pay is based on a standard time rate, with a bonus for work performed above a point of efficiency equal to 66⅔% of standard. The standard is based on the experienced performance of other workers and not on time and motion study. A sliding scale of bonuses is used and operates as follows: when a worker reaches 66⅔% of his standard task, a very small bonus is paid for additional work. The bonus is gradually increased to 10% by the time 90% of the standard is attained. At 100% of efficiency, the bonus reaches 20%. Often called the Emerson Empiric Plan.

Emerson Graduated Bonus Plan empiric formula. A formula for figuring the empiric or bonus earnings for workers under the Emerson Graduated, or Empiric Bonus Plan is: (Computed to start at 67% of the high task efficiency.) E = time wages $\times$ the binomial $(1 + B_o)$, in which B_o is the empiric bonus as per the Emerson Efficiency-Bonus Scale, or Earning between 67% and high task:
$E = H_aR_h + B_o \times H_aR_h$
Reducing $E - H_aR_h(1 + B_o)$

employee appraisal. See MERIT RATING.

Employee Benefit Society. See MUTUAL BENEFIT ASSOCIATION.

employee class. See JOB CLASS.

employee communications. Of outstanding interest in current personnel activities is the subject of communicating with employees. Communication may be designated variously as two-way communication; line-and-staff communication; oral communication; written communication; formal communication; informal communication; face-to-face communication. Among the communication media are: annual reports, attitude surveys, bulletin boards, posters; reading racks; house organs; contests; letters, handbooks; interviews; group meetings; films; inter-communication systems. See SECTION 15, "EMPLOYEE COMMUNICATIONS," in *Personnel Handbook*, Ronald Press. *Sharing Information with Employees*, by Alexander Heron, Stanford University Press; *Making the Communications Dollar Work, Public Opinion Index for Industry*, Opinion Research Corporation; *Effective Communication in Industry*, National Association of Manufacturers; *Effective Communication On The Job*, American Management Association.

Employee elections, under National Labor Relations Act (which see). The act provides for three general types of elections among employees. These are: (1) Representation elections to determine the employees choice of a collective bargaining agent. These are held upon petition of an employer, employees, or a labor organization. (2) Decertification elections to determine whether or not the employees wish to withdraw the bargaining authority of a labor organization which they previously had designated as their representative. These are held upon petition of employees or labor organizations. (3) Deauthorization polls to determine whether or not the employees wish to revoke the authority of their bargaining representative to make a union-shop contract. These elections are held on petition of employees. Elections may be held by agreement between the employer and the labor organization or individual claiming to represent the employees. Under such an agreement, the election is authorized and conducted by the NLRB

Regional Director. If the parties are unable to reach an agreement, the Board has authority to order an election after a hearing. In petitioning for an election, a labor organization or individual seeking representation rights must show that at least 30 percent of the employees involved have indicated their support of such representation. This may be shown by authorization cards, petitions, or other means. An individual or group of employees petitioning to decertify an incumbent bargaining agent or deauthorize a union shop must also make a showing that 30 percent or more appear to favor decertification or deauthorization. An employer, however, has only to show that some labor organization has made a claim to represent his employees in order to obtain a representation election. In contested election cases, the evidence and arguments of the parties are recorded at a public hearing conducted by an agent of the Board. The Board then makes its decision upon the basis of this record. Only one valid representation election, whether for certification or decertification, may be held in a bargaining unit within any 12-month period. Employees on an economic strike (as distinguished from one caused by unfair labor practices) are not entitled to vote if they have been replaced by bona fide permanent employees or they are otherwise *not* entitled to reinstatement.

employee morale. An attitude combining interest, energy and initiative. Morale may apply to an individual employee's personal adjustment and job satisfaction; to his relationship and integration with the work group and to his acceptance of the company and identification with company goals. Among many attributes of morale covered by personnel writers are a positive goal, a feeling of "together-ness," an awareness of danger to a group, a conviction that conditions can be im-proved, a sense of advance toward group goals, enthusiastic and effective pursuit of group purposes, self-sustained, and in a measure self-directed performance. Morale is influenced by the employee's total experiences inside and outside the plant. In a sense, the state of the em-ployee's morale may be dependent upon the degree to which the employee's deep-rooted wants are affected by his work situation. By far the most important fac-tor, selected by 30 percent of employees in a survey ("Factors Affecting Employee Morale," National Industrial Conference Board) is job security. Compensation ranked next in importance, with 8.7% of the employees. Altogether 71 factors were listed by employees in responding to the Conference Board's questionnaire.

employee publication. See HOUSE ORGANS.

employee rating. See MERIT RATING.

Employees Annual Report. A report of company activities for a given year, chiefly an explanation and interpretation of the company's financial statement, prepared particularly for employees.

employee, superannuated. (1) An em-ployee who is to be retired because of old age or infirmities. (2) An employee who exceeds a certain retirement age limit, but is kept on for various reasons, such as the company needing his specific services, his economic need to earn money, or his long service record; (3) an employee over the normal age limit but who is retained at employee's status to comply with a collective bargaining agreement wherein the union may have

requested a provision that there be a specific ratio of older workers employed.

employer-employee relations. A term used to denote a democratic relationship between labor and capital. Former rela-tionships include slave-owner phase of relationship, then the lord-serf, followed by the master-man or mistress-maid re-lation.

"Employer Field Audit." A term used by the United States Employment Service. An examination of the books and records of an employing unit to determine the correct financial liability, if any, and the proper amount of contributions, interest, and penalty paid or payable.

employer liabilities, under Walsh-Healey Public Contracts Act. Possible damages to which a contractor is liable for violat-ing this law are: —A sum equal to the amount due employee under the law on account of underpayment of wages. (De-termination of the amount due is made by the Secretary of Labor. Sums recov-ered are held in a special deposit ac-count of the Government and are paid upon order of the Secretary of Labor directly to the employee concerned upon application of the employee within the statutory period of one year.)—Damages to the United States of $10 per day for each boy under 16, girl under 18, or convict laborer knowingly employed on the contract.

"Employer Order." A term used by the United States Employment Service. Same as ORDER.

"Employer-Prepared Job Specification." A term used by the United States Em-ployment Service. See JOB SPECIFICATION, EMPLOYER PREPARED.

(95)

"Employer Relations Record." A term used by the United States Employment Service. A record containing pertinent employment services operating information about an employer's establishment and about the local office working relationships and activities with that employer.

employers' association. A group of employers formed primarily for the purpose of presenting a united front in dealing with labor organizations.

"Employer, Subject." A term used by the United States Employment Service. See SUBJECT EMPLOYER.

"Employer Visit." A term used by the United States Employment Service. A visit made by a local office staff member to an employer's establishment (including union and employer organizations which are either employers or serve as hiring agents for employers) for one or more of the following purposes: to explain or emphasize the services available to the employer through the Employment Service, to discuss existing orders, to verify referrals, or to provide non-technical assistance in the solution of employment problems.

"Employing Unit." A term used by the United States Employment Service. An individual or organization which employs one or more workers.

Employment Act of 1946. The purpose of this Act, passed in 1946, was to provide study, research and advice to the federal government, to promote conditions which would result in the maximum of employment, production, and purchasing power. The Act created the Council of Economic Advisers and it authorized the Joint Congressional Committee on the Economic Report (which *see*.)

employment certificates. Necessary in connection with enforcement of child labor laws. These certificates show that the boys or girls for whom they are issued have met all the requirements of the child labor law for going to work. The certificate or permit also gives the employer permission to hire under legal conditions the young worker named in the certificate. See also FAIR LABOR STANDARDS ACT, WALSH HEALEY PUBLIC CONTRACTS ACT, CHILD LABOR. Also Bulletin No. 185, *Why—Child Labor Laws*, United States Department of Labor, Bureau of Labor Standards. The child must go in person to the office where certificates are issued and apply for a certificate or permit. His parents must consent to his employment. In order to be certain that the employment will be in accordance with the child labor law, the child must bring a statement from his prospective employer showing the type of work the employer expects him to do, and the hours that he will work. He must submit proof that he is of legal age for the job. To prove his age, he must present his birth certificate, or if this is not available, other reliable evidence. Many laws set up other conditions for issuing a certificate. For instance, some require that the child must pass a physical examination showing that he is fit for the intended work. Some laws also require the child to present a school record to prove he has completed a certain grade. Under the best laws the certificate or permit is issued to the employer, not to the young worker. These working papers are issued usually by the superintendent of schools. Issuance by school officials provides an opportunity for the school to discuss with the child the reason for cutting short his education, and to offer him guidance.

"Employment Counseling." A term used by the United States Employment Service. The process whereby (a) the present and potential qualifications of an applicant who has not made a satisfactory vocational choice are reviewed, evaluated, and related to the current and prospective occupational requirements and conditions so that the applicant may make an appropriate vocational choice and plan, and so that the Employment Service is provided with a realistic basis of referral, or (b) special assistance is given to an applicant who has made a vocational choice, in solving problems relating to obtaining or holding a job.

"Employment Counseling Interview." A term used by the United States Employment Service. See INTERVIEW.

"Employment Office." A term used by the United States Employment Service. See LOCAL OFFICE.

employment security. See BUREAU OF EMPLOYMENT SECURITY.

"Employment Security Administration Fund." A term used by the United States Employment Service. See FUNDS.

"Employment Security Law." A term used by the United States Employment Service to designate a body of law which established a free public employment service, or a system of unemployment insurance, or both, and which may also establish other systems compensating for wage loss, such as temporary disability insurance.

"Employment Security Program." A term used by the United States Employment

Service to designate the Federal-State program comprising public employment services and unemployment insurance.

employment selection forms. Used in connection with employment tests. Among these are: Application for Employment, Men; Application for Employment, Women; Application for Sales Position; Telephone Check with Previous Employers; Standard Selection Interview, Short Form. (Made by Robert N. McMurry and Company.) Specimen Packet: Application Interview Series—Industrial Psychology, Inc. See PUBLISHERS, PERSONNEL TESTS.

"Employment Service Job Specification." A term used by the United States Employment Service. See JOB SPECIFICATION, EMPLOYMENT SERVICE.

employer's liability. A legal term denoting responsibility of an employer for an accident to an employee. This responsibility would become the subject of court action in which the burden of proof was upon the employee to give evidence in justifying claim for damages from the employer. The term became obsolescent when workmen's compensation abolished the necessity for demonstration of negligence and established the injured employee's claim to damages as a right in accordance with the legally established system of insurance. Cf. WORKMEN'S COMPENSATION.

employment stabilization. Maintenance of employment for approximately the same work force throughout a year or a longer period.

"Encumbrances" (against administrative funds). A term used by the United States Employment Service. Obligations which have been incurred by a State employment security agency against the available administrative funds and for which there is documentary or other acceptable evidence of commitment, whether or not actual payment has been made thereon.

Engels, Friedrich. (1820-1895), social theorist and revolutionist, co-founder with Marx of scientific socialism. Engels was born in Barmen, Germany, of a prosperous commercial family with strong Protestant convictions. While at school, he broke with his family on religious grounds and began consorting with radical student groups. In 1842 he was sent to work in a factory of his father's in Manchester, England, where he became interested in economics. In 1844, visited Marx in Paris from which contact developed a long friendship and close collaboration. He took part in the Baden revolutionary outbreak in 1848 and after its suppression fled to England. From 1850 to 1869 he returned to work in his father's business in Manchester but in 1870 he devoted himself to a literary career. He wrote *The Conditions of the Working Classes;* collaborated with Marx on the *Communist Manifesto* and edited a major portion of Marx's *Das Kapital*. Much of Engels' work was published under Marx's name.

engineer. A general term used to designate one who pursues a branch of professional engineering. Specifically designated according to branch of engineering in which he specializes, such as Chemical Engineer, Civil Engineer, Electrical Engineer, Industrial Engineer, Mechanical Engineer.

engineers, unionization of. Groups such as the Engineers Joint Council, Engineers Council for Professional Development, National Society of Professional Engineers, are sources of information on the unionization of engineers. Reasons why engineers may consider unionization include: (1) Spread between engineers and wage earners in pay rates and fringes has narrowed. (2) Salaries for experienced engineers haven't kept pace with hiring rates for newly-graduated engineers. (3) Merit is sometimes subordinated to seniority in determining salary increases. (4) Some companies do not fulfill engineer's desire to be classified as part of management team. (5) The personal relationship that formerly existed between engineer and employer is disappearing. Basically, engineers seem to be against joining unions, and for the following reasons: (1) They feel their individual economic interests are best served through individual initiative. (2) They feel their professional status is better advanced by non-unionization. (3) They feel union membership has an adverse effect upon the creativity of the individual engineer. (4) They are conscious of the management status which engineering positions carry with them.

entrance rate. The hourly rate which a worker receives upon being hired into an establishment. In the case of a skilled worker, this may be slightly less than or equivalent to the minimum job rate; it may also be identical with the probationary rate. The entrance rate for unskilled workers may be synonymous with the minimum plant rate, and may be increased after designated time intervals. See also MINIMUM PLANT RATE and PROBATIONARY RATE.

"Entry Occupational Classification." A term used by the United States Employment Service. See OCCUPATIONAL CLASSIFICATION.

equalization pay. Same as COST-OF-LIV-ING ADJUSTMENT.

equal job opportunity. Executive Order 10479 (1953 Supp.); and Executive Order 10557 (1954 Supp.) Executive Order 10479, which created the President's Committee on Government Contracts, requires each contracting agency of the Federal Government to obtain compliance with the nondiscrimination clause included in Federal contracts. Executive Order 10557 strengthened the nondiscrimination clause by requiring, among other things, the posting of a notice by the contractor acknowledging his agreement to provide employment without discrimination because of race, religion, color or national origin. The particular contracting agency investigates complaints of alleged violations of the nondiscrimination provision and then submits a report of their findings to the Committee for review. For further information write to the President's Committee on Government Contracts, Washington 25, D.C.

equal pay for equal work. The payment of equal compensation to all employees within an establishment or other unit performing the same kind and amount of work, regardless of race, sex, or other characteristics of the individual workers.

equivalent annual rate. A measure used in making a monthly rate, such as that of labor turnover, comparable for each month, or comparable with an annual rate, regardless of variations in the number of working days.

Ernst and Ernst Wage Incentive Plan. This plan provides differential bonus changes for three production zones.

escape clause. A provision in a maintenance of membership agreement for an interval, usually of ten days or two weeks, during which an employee may withdraw from the union without loss of employment.

escalator clause. A provision in a union agreement allowing for the adjustment of wages in accordance with specified changes in the cost of living as measured by an appropriate index, or in the price of materials used in production, or in accordance with some other agreed-upon criterion, such as production index or price of product. See also COST-OF-LIVING ADJUSTMENT.

evaluated wage rate. A wage rate for a job or position determined through a job evaluation plan.

examine. In industrial engineering terminology, the basic element employed when comparing the quality of an object with a definite standard by means of any of the sense organs. (Examine was formerly called Inspect, but the name has been changed in order to avoid confusion with factory inspection operations.)

exceptions, under Walsh-Healey Public Contracts Act. Upon a written finding of the head of the contracting agency that operations of the Act will seriously impair the conduct of Government business the Secretary of Labor is authorized to make exceptions in certain cases *when justice or public interest will be served thereby.*

"Excluded Employment." A term used by the United States Employment Service. Service of the types which are excluded from employment as defined in a State employment security law.

exemptions, under Walsh-Healey Public Contract Act. The Act specifically exempts certain types of contracts, including contracts for transportation by common carriers under published tariffs; utility services; perishable agricultural products; rentals; and seasonal services.

executive. A person possessing the ability of executing, administering, governing and carrying out ideas, rules, laws and orders. An executive is anyone who is responsible for the direction and control of others and for the work performed by them. Certain traits and manners of conduct are essential to executive success. A few fundamental characteristics must be inborn, but others may be developed. See EXECUTIVE ABILITY, DEVELOPMENT OF; EXECUTIVE DEVELOPMENT.

executive ability, development of. Because of the need of managers in modern industry, the development of executive ability is both a personal problem to those who want to become executives and those who want to become better executives, and to companies, many of which have extensive programs. *How to Develop Your Executive Ability* by Daniel Starch, (Harper and Brothers) outline the following techniques: (I) Organizing the Ability to Think. (a) Five Basic Techniques in Thinking. 1) Ask questions: What, When, Where, Why, How and Who. 2) Define your problem precisely. 3) Get the necessary tools for thinking. 4) Keep your mind open and weigh calmly all factors in your problem. 5) Turn thought into action. (b) What You Must Think and Learn More About. 1) Your job and how to do it better. 2) The job ahead and how to get it. (c) The Most Valuable Thinking Business Men Do. 1) Start at your goal and work backward. 2) Nourish your creative

thinking. 3) Create new ideas. 4) Put new ideas to work. (II) Tackling the Work. (a) Stirring up the Inner Drive and Keeping it Going. 1) Two forces behind the inner drive of great men: i) all-consuming purpose, ii) anticipated satisfaction of achievement. 2) Concentrate on your goal. 3) Turn bad breaks into opportunities. 4) Make the first step to action easy. (III) Assuming Responsibility. (a) Two Ways of Acquiring Responsibility. 1) Get others to place more responsibility on your shoulders. 2) Assume leadership. (b) Testing Capacity to Shoulder Responsibility. 1) Seven tests to determine whether you would succeed in a business of your own. (IV) Handling People. (a) The First and Deepest Principle of Human Nature: each person is the center of his world of experience and action. (b) Six Techniques for Using the Law of Ego-Centrism in Dealing with People: 1) Respect and deal with each person as a person. 2) Show confidence and expect much. 3) The one way to get a man to do what you want: cause the man to want to do it. 4) Express what everyone deeply desires. 5) Save a man's face if he has made a mistake. 6) Avoid the commonest fault in dealing with others: failure to see the other person's point of view. (c) The Second Fundamental Principle of Human Nature in Dealing with People: Be and Do What You Want Others to Be and Do. (d) Techniques in Using the Law of Induction. 1) What you yourself must be and do to influence others. 2) The only way you can get another person to guide his own action: guiding his thinking.

executive development. The need for executive development programs to supplement the job experience of young men who are moving up in their companies has been widely accepted. Many companies have come to feel that it is more important to develop their young executives not only through experience on the job and company activities beyond these specific jobs, but also through experience outside of the environment of the company itself. It is felt that acquaintance with the basic policies and ways of thinking in other phases of the economy gives a broad perspective and lays a foundation for continuing personal growth and constructive action. To this end, a number of colleges, universities, and management associations, offer programs or seminars in executive development or management training. These programs are generally from several weeks to a year's duration. Frequently they require residence away from home. Participants are usually men who have been in charge of complex operations in some special phase of their companies' efforts and have proved their ability to make decisions requiring maturity and experience. Such men have become aware of business problems through their own jobs and have an intense desire to see the total picture. They have already required perspective so that they can weigh varying concepts judiciously; they welcome the opportunity to evaluate new opinions and approaches to problems. When they return to their companies they know more thoroughly the demands of production, personnel, marketing, financial control, all fit into a total operation. They should be able to make decisions that affect seemingly unrelated aspects of the organization, and they will understand the point of view of the men in other industries and in government with whom they must deal. See *Executive Development*, published by Industrial Relations Center, University of Chicago; *The Development of Executive Talent*, edited by M. Joseph Dooher and Vivienne Marquis, American Management Association. The American Management Association publishes an annual *Guide to Intensive Courses and Seminars for Executives*; the Industrial Relations News publishes a semi-annual *Conference Calendar for Industrial and Labor Relations Personnel and Related Fields;* the National Industrial Conference Board periodically publishes a Personnel Policy Report on *Executive Development Courses in Universities*, from which the following are taken:

Facility	Duration	Starting Dates	Estab.	Fee	Size of Group
BUFFALO...............	3 weeks	August	'53	$600	30
CARNEGIE TECH.......	9 weeks	March	'54	$950 and living	30
CASE TECH.............	8 weeks covering 23 week period	Three Sessions—Jan. March and Sept.	'56	$2,000	40
COLUMBIA.............	6 weeks	Two Sessions— June and Aug.	'52	$1,750	56
CORNELL —Executive Development.	6 weeks	June	'53	$1,200	42
CORNELL —Human Relations......	4 weeks	Two Sessions— Feb. and April	'53	$750 and living	20
GEORGIA...............	4 weeks	August	'53	$900	30

"Executive Development Courses in Universities" (*continued*)

Facility	Duration	Starting Dates	Estab.	Fee	Size of Group
HARVARD —Advanced Management.	3 months	Two Sessions— Spring and Fall	'43	$2,400 (approx.)	160
HARVARD —Middle Management...	7½ months	Jan. to Aug.	'54	$1,500 and living	60-70
HOUSTON...............	6 weeks	Three Sessions—Feb., June and Oct.	'53	$1,000	24
INDIANA................	3 weeks each 2 summers	June	'52	$600 per year	40
KANSAS.................	5 weeks	June	'55	$1,000	22
McGILL.................	4 weeks	May	'56	$560	30
M. I. T..................	10 weeks	Two Sessions— March and Oct.	'56	$2,500	16-20
MICHIGAN STATE......	4 weeks	February	'54	$500 and living	20-25
MICHIGAN —Executive Development.	4 weeks	June	'54	$750	50
MICHIGAN —Public Utility.........	4 weeks	Two Sessions— June and Aug.	'51	$750	60
NORTHWESTERN.......	4 weeks	Three Sessions— June, July and Aug.	'51	$1,000 and meals	37
OHIO STATE............	2 weeks each 2 summers	September	'55	$1,000	40
OHIO....................	4 weeks	July	'55	$700	30
OKLAHOMA.............	5 weeks	June	'57	$600 and living	35
PENNSYLVANIA STATE.	4 weeks	Two Sessions— June and Aug.	'56	$900	40
PENNSYLVANIA.........	2 weeks	June	'50	$600	35
PITTSBURGH............	8 weeks	Two Sessions— Fall and Spring	'49	$1,400 and meals	72
RICHMOND.............	3 weeks	June	'55	$600	35
STANFORD..............	8 weeks	July	'52	$1,600	50
SYRACUSE..............	4 weeks	July or Aug.	'54	$1,000	25
TEXAS A. & M...........	3 weeks	February	'53	$350 and living	35
TEXAS..................	5 weeks	February	'55	$975	24
WABASH................	10 weeks over 5 summers	July	'55	$3000	40
WASHINGTON..........	6 weeks	June	'52	$1200	30
WESTERN ONTARIO....	5 weeks	August	'48	$900	95

executive officer of the state board for vocational education. The legally designated state official directly responsible to a state board for vocational education for the administration of the policies of vocational education determined by the board.

"Exhaustion Ratio." A term used by the United States Employment Service. The proportion of beneficiaries who use up their maximum annual benefits in a benefit year.

exit interview. The type of interview which takes place when an employee's association terminates or separation from the company occurs. The purpose of the exit interview may be: (1) to learn pertinent facts regarding the attitude of the employee and determine exact reasons for leaving, (2) to arrange an adjustment, when desirable, in a similar position or by transfer, (3) to discover conditions which might affect other employees and which should be remedied, (4) to arrange for discussions between supervisors and employees who are leaving, (5) to provide an opportunity to explain personnel policies and practices which may have been misunderstood. Advantages of the exit interview are: (1) pinpoints faulty administration, poor personnel policies and practices, and unsatisfactory supervisors. (2) Prevents good employees from resigning. (3) Makes for better public relations with those who leave.

expected earning level. See TARGET.

expediting. See TROUBLE SHOOTING.

expense account. An account of expenses paid or incurred by an employee in connection with the performance of his services, usually covering such items as transportation, meals, and lodging while in a travel status and away from home. These expenses are reimbursable to the employee; payment is usually made after the expense account has been audited.

expense accounts, executive. Many companies reimburse their executives for travel, club and entertainment expenses, provided they are reasonable. To keep within the letter of the tax laws, executives are required to report expense re-

imbursements first as income and then as deductions when filing their personal income tax returns. In some situations companies can pay the bills directly. See STUDIES IN BUSINESS POLICY NO. 67, *Executive Expense Accounts*, NICB.

experience merit rating. See RATING, EXPERIENCE MERIT.

"Experience-Rating." A term used by the United States Employment Service. A method for determining the contribution rates of individual employers on the basis of the factors specified in the State employment security law for measuring employers' experience with respect to unemployment or unemployment risk.

"Experience-Rating Account." A term used by the United States Employment Service. See ACCOUNTS.

"Experience-Rating Computation Date." A term used by the United States Employment Service. See COMPUTATION DATE, EXPERIENCE-RATING.

exploratory courses. School subjects designed to provide the student with a broad, general overview of the knowledges and skills involved in a field of learning or an occupation. Courses which provide students with exploratory and introductory experiences in a wide range of occupations serve as an aid in choosing a vocation.

"Extending a Clearance Job Opening." A term used by the United States Employment Service. The submittal of a clearance job opening to other local offices in order to locate and utilize the labor supply of such other local offices.

explosive trucking bonus. A bonus paid to workers in the explosives manufacturing industry who are engaged in moving highly dangerous explosives by means of hand trucks.

"Extension of Application." A term used by the United States Employment Service. The posting of a date on an active application card to indicate continued availability of the applicant for referral.

extension training for employed personnel. Training programs which have as their general objective the extension of the knowledge and skill of employees in an organization are made necessary by such conditions as: (1) Changes in procedure which call for the use of new techniques, new types of equipment, or new or different materials. (2) Changes in the product, as in new designs or new models; or changes in the services rendered. (3) Recognition of a general need for upgrading in an organization because of the tendency of obsolete practices to persist. (4) No outside agency to give the special training needed. (5) Employees coming into the organization competent to perform the simpler classes of work, but inadequately equipped to handle more difficult jobs. (6) The existence in the organization of specific situations which are more or less unsatisfactory. Frank Cushman, in "Training Procedure," (John Wiley & Sons, Inc.) lists as situations which indicate the need for such training: Accidents to employees, excessive number of; Ambition, apparently lacking among employees; Authority of supervisors not commensurate with their responsibilities; Backed up, supervisors not adequately; Buck passing, excessive; Carelessness, too much; Complaints of employees, not satisfactorily handled; Cooperation, poor between individuals and departments; Data, business, supervisors or foremen unable to interpret; Duties, workers not adequately instructed on; Foreigners, working group includes many; Friction and misunderstanding in working group; Gossip, excessive plant or organization; Interest, too many examples of lack of; Job pride, absence of; Maintenance, cost of too high; Material, excessive spoilage of; Pep, organization lacks; Policies (of organization), too many employees ignorant of; Policies, uncertainty as to; Procedure, frequent changes in; Product, too large a percentage fails to meet standards; Production, cost of too high; Promotion, too few in organization qualified for; Promotions, made without sufficient preparation; Reports, importance of not recognized by those who make them; Responsibilities, of departmental supervisors very large; Responsibilities, joint, not well discharged; Responsibilities, lack of understanding of; Responsibilities, overlapping; Routine, new employees not adequately informed as to; Safe working practices, not sufficiently stressed; Seasonal work, skeleton organization for; Short-circuiting of minor executives; Staff members, hampered by lack of knowledge of how work is done; Star performers, too many of them in the organization; Supplies, wastage in use of; Team work, lack of effective; Technical knowledge, employees lack needed; Tools and equipment, loss and abuse of; Training, costs of too high; Transfers, excessive number of requests for; Turnover, high; Work, defective—goes out unchecked; Work, flow of—unsatisfactory between departments; Work, highly specialized; Work experience, supervisors lack adequate; Work force, anticipated expansion of; Work force, anticipated reduction of; Workers, competent ones hard to get; Workers, need to be brought up-to-date; Working relationships, not sufficiently close between executive and his staff.

external element. An element of a processing operation performed by a workman outside of the machine cycle. It usually begins with "stop machine" and ends with "start machine."

external time. See EXTERNAL ELEMENT.

F

Fabianism. The forms of socialism advocated by the Fabian Society which was founded by a small group in London, England, in 1884. The Fabians rejected Marxian socialism both in economics and in politics. Fabianism believes in the democratic way of life and uses education and conviction to attain its ends. George Bernard Shaw, Sidney and Beatrice Webb, G. D. H. Cole are among the notable names attached to the Fabian movement. Nearly all the leading Socialists and many of the foremost trade unionists of Britain have at one time or another become adherents. The policies of the British Labor Party have been based on Fabian principles.

fact-finding. The systematic and accurate assembling of data with reference to certain problems, policies. The Taft-Hartley law authorizes the President to request an injunction to restrain strike action for a maximum of eighty days pending impartial fact-finding and further negotiations.

fact-finding board. A group of individuals appointed, usually by a government agency or executive, to investigate, assemble, and make public the facts in a labor dispute.

factor comparison. A type of job evaluation plan in which relative values for each of a specified number of factors of a job are established by direct comparison with the values established for these same factors on selected key jobs.

factory. A building or group of buildings, with the facilities, mechanical equipment, tools, by which employees can produce goods. Also, implied is adequate facilities for the well-being of people employed.

factory system. The system of manufacturing characterized by the use of power driven machinery, housed under one roof and owned by the entrepreneur, or other owner, who hires men for wages to operate the machines. This system was the outgrowth of the discovery of new sources of power on the one hand and the invention of new types of machinery on the other. The origin of the factory system in England may be roughly placed at about 1750.

fair day's work. The amount of work that can be produced during a working day by a qualified individual with average skill who follows a prescribed method, works under specified conditions, and exerts average effort.

(106)

Fair Employment Practices Committee (FEPC). An independent federal agency established on June 25, 1941, by executive order to eliminate racial discrimination in employment by federal agencies and war industries. It was officially terminated in June 1946. See "EQUAL JOB OPPORTUNITY."

Fair Labor Standards Act of 1938 (Wage and Hour Law). The Federal Wage-Hour Law is administered by the Secretary of Labor through the Administrator of the Wage and Hour and Public Contracts Divisions. This law has been in effect since 1938 and sets minimum wage, overtime, and child-labor standards which apply to employees engaged in interstate commerce or in the production of goods for interstate commerce. Application does not deal in a blanket way with industries as a whole, but is determined on the basis of an employee's activities. The basic standards set by this act are: A minimum wage of one dollar an hour, except for industries in Puerto Rico and the Virgin Islands, where lower rates may be set by industry committees equally representing labor, management, and the general public; after July 1, 1956, the Amendments of 1955 require annual review of all wage orders for these islands; since August 8, 1956, when the American Samoan Labor Standards Amendments of 1956 were adopted, these provisions apply also in American Samoa; Time and one-half pay for overtime in excess of 40 hours worked in a workweek (except as otherwise specifically provided); A minimum age of 16 for general employment (except for occupations declared hazardous by the Secretary of Labor, where a minimum age of 18 applies; for certain occupations outside of school hours, where the minimum age is 14; and in agriculture outside of school hours). The act applies to all covered workers (unless specifically exempt) . . . male and female, whether employed in a factory, office, or at home. . . . It applies without regard to the number of employees. . . . It does not limit the number of hours of work in a day or in a week. . . . It does not require payment for days or hours not worked, such as holidays, vacations, or sick leave. . . . It does not provide for different rates of pay for work on Saturdays, Sundays, or holidays, as such. The minimum wage of one dollar an hour applies to all covered workers, irrespective of age or sex. Under certificates issued by the Wage-Hour Administrator, rates below the statutory minimum may be paid to certain learners, messengers, apprentices, and handicapped workers, subject to regulations issued under section 14 of the act, which provides for such rates in these instances, "to the extent necessary in order to prevent curtailment of opportunities for employment." Department of Labor; or from the Wage and Hour and Public Contracts Division, U. S. Department of Labor, Washington, 25, D. C. See also: under FAIR LABOR STANDARDS ACT for: rates, subminimum; workers, covered; workers, exempt; overtime, calculations of; child labor provisions; home work, regulated; records, required by; back wages, recovery of; penalties; "Hot Goods."

fall-down. An industrial engineering term. When used as a verb, it means to fail to meet the standard or expected performance level. As a noun, it describes a performance that is less than standard.

"Farm Clinic." A term used by the United States Employment Service. A meeting organized by the local office and scheduled in advance for employers and workers for on-the-spot referrals and placements; in some localities, farm clinics are referred to as "farm employment days" or "farm labor market days."

fatigue. Fatigue has been defined as the overuse of the mind or muscles, resulting in a lack of energy and an inability to continue a set pace or speed. It results from continual application or activity of either the nerves or body members. When more energy is delivered by a body member than can be replenished by the blood system, there is a resulting breakdown which is fatigue. The operator registers the effects of fatigue as a feeling of tiredness, or a realization of the exhaustion of strength. The voluntary muscular contraction is the effect of the stimulus sent out by the central nervous system to the various nerves; thus the fatigue culminates in the central nervous system. Carried to an extreme there may be serious damage to health. See FATIGUE ALLOWANCE, DETERMINATION OF; FATIGUE ALLOWANCE, PURPOSE OF.

fatigue allowance. Time included in the production standard to allow for decreases or losses in production which might be attributed to fatigue. (Usually applied as a percentage of the leveled, normal, or adjusted time.)

fatigue allowance, data based on judgment, arbitrary or comparative information. A method of determining fatigue allowances by systematic or unsystematic estimation, judgment, guess, trial and error, experience, tradition, trade practice, policy, arbitration, negotiation, or any combination thereof. Shumard* describes such a system. He suggests drawing up a list of work elements commonly

experienced in the plant. Where necessary, these may be sub-divided into degrees. For instance, the element of pushing a truck might be broken down to cover trucks of different weights. When this is done, fatigue values are assigned to the elements or element divisions. Values assigned are determined on the basis of judgment and experience with due care given to secure a logical relation between the amounts assigned and the fatiguing factor of the element. The assigned values presume normal working conditions in regard to dust, temperature, noise, etc. When a job is performed under conditions other than these, additions or subtractions are made to the allowance as necessary. The success of such a method as this depends entirely upon the skill, judgment and experience of the person assigning the values.

fatigue allowance, data taken from laboratory tests. This method of determining fatigue allowance consists of securing information from laboratory research tests. This information must then be translated to industrial conditions. It is possible in a laboratory test to obtain a degree of isolation of a factor of fatigue to be measured that would be impractical or impossible under other circumstances. This same isolation process, however, makes it difficult at times to apply the results directly to a practical industrial problem with any degree of accuracy. The adaptation process may require assumptions and estimates that destroy the original accuracy of the data. An example of a method of determination of fatigue allowance by the labora-

------
*Shumard, F. W. A *Primer of Time Study*, (New York and London, McGraw-Hill Book Company, Inc., 1940).

tory method is given by Holmes* who uses data on the efficiency and caloric consumption of the human body taken from the U.S. Department of Agriculture tests and other sources. This information is organized with the aid of several assumptions into a table listing fatigue allowance values for different conditions of caloric consumption. Vertical columns of the table are headed: Fatigue Allowance in Per Cent; Calories Consumed per Hour; Carry, Support, Push or Pull Factors; and Foot-Pounds of Work by Lifting. Fatigue allowances are determined from the table by individual elements of work corresponding to the proper headings. The calculations in each instance are relatively simple once the job is properly broken into its elements. This particular system of determining fatigue allowances accounts for only the energy-expended element of fatigue and not for the many other factors recognized as contributory. The chief value of these tests is not in their general application but in their specific application. Many industries with special problems, such as heat, pressure, fumes or dampness may find laboratory tests helpful in determining equitable allowances for such conditions.

fatigue allowance, data taken from production tests. This method of determining fatigue allowance consists of securing the information from special tests conducted on production jobs. The general advantage of this type of procedure is that the source and use of the information is the same—production work. A degree of practicality of results is thus possible that would be difficult to

obtain in the laboratory. At the same time, because the determination is a *test*, it is possible to control certain difficult and variable job elements that could not be controlled in a straight production study. Mundel* lists a number of job conditions known to affect the worker's fatigue, such as the amount of body used, foot pedals, room conditions, etc. These are subdivided into degrees, such as the different amounts of the body used; the number of pedals; the different working conditions in the room. Jobs are then selected, alike in every respect except for one condition. The one condition would be one of those listed known to affect fatigue. The two jobs are extensively studied. Differences in the results of the test are attributed to the fatiguing element. The tests are repeated on other jobs until the data obtained can be relied upon to predict results with reasonable accuracy. Other tests are then conducted until sufficient data is obtained to determine allowances for all conditions listed.

fatigue allowance, data taken from time studies. A method of determining fatigue allowances by comparing the actual production time of the time study with the total time. One procedure of this type is through the use of the Interruption Study as described by Morrow. The purpose of the interruption study is to obtain information on the productive time of the operator and the production delays and interruptions. From this study an average cycle time is determined from the production time and the number of cycles completed. This time is then compared with the average

* Holmes, Walter G., *Applied Time and Motion Study*, (New York, Ronald Press, 1945).

* Mundel, Marvin E., *Systematic Motion and Time Study*, (New York, Prentice-Hall, Inc., 1947).

cycle time from the regular time study of operation. The difference in the two is attributed to fatigue and an appropriate percentage is calculated. The regular time study under these conditions is a short study conducted at a time when the worker is rested and is producing at his best. The interruption study, being an all-day study, catches the full fatigue effect. Morrow, Robert Lee, *Time Study and Motion Economy* (New York, The Ronald Press Company, 1957).

fatigue allowance, determination of. Determination of a fatigue allowance requires that the subject of fatigue must be tied down, be measured and expressed as a number, be made a part of a given job, much as the materials and machines are a part of that job. In every work arrangement, there exists an implied fatigue allowance, due to the inseparability of the natures of work and fatigue. In many instances there is complete agreement between management and the worker on the workload of the job. This implies that there is agreement on the fatigue allowance. Whether workers accept the fatigue allowance as is, or whether they want to make some changes, some scientific method of setting the allowance is necessary. This requires separating the work and other elements of the job from the rest elements. This is usually quite possible within reasonable limits. Among the provisions that help in setting fatigue allowances are: (1) modern job study methods are employed by a skilled industrial engineer. (2) keen judgment is exercised by a qualified person with an adequate background and knowledge of the nature of fatigue. (3) a comparison is made of the results of the study in question and similar studies for the purpose of obtaining a logical and proper relationship of the results between jobs. (4) full consideration is given to the working conditions of the job that are known to affect fatigue. (5) attention is given to the sequence of the job elements to detect possible combinations of elements that serve to provide natural rest or that unduly affect fatigue. The methods of determining fatigue allowances break down into four groupings. These depend upon where the information for determining the fatigue allowance is secured. (1) The first group includes all the methods wherein the information for determining the allowance is taken from time studies of the job. See FATIGUE ALLOWANCE, DATA TAKEN FROM TIME STUDIES. (2) The second group includes the methods where the information is taken from simulated, controlled production studies. See FATIGUE ALLOWANCE, DATA TAKEN FROM SPECIAL PRODUCTION TESTS. (3) The third group includes all methods where the information is secured from laboratory research tests and which is then applied to production conditions. See FATIGUE ALLOWANCE, DATA TAKEN FROM LABORATORY TESTS. (4) The fourth group includes all methods based on judgment, arbitrary or comparative information. See FATIGUE ALLOWANCE, DATA BASED ON JUDGMENT, ARBITRARY OR COMPARATIVE INFORMATION.

fatigue allowance, purpose of. Fatigue allowance is a variable applied to variables. Fatigue allowance is an amount added to the basic time necessary for a qualified operator working at a normal gait to perform a given job, calculated to: (1) provide the worker with time necessary for rest to prevent undue fatigue. (2) provide the worker with the time necessary for rest enabling him to accomplish his task with equal facility compared to all other jobs in the plant. (3) provide the worker with the time necessary for rest enabling him to maintain the optimum productivity rate. (4) provide the worker with time necessary to enable him to work at a self-governed pace sympathetic to his natural working rhythm. (5) provide him with time necessary to compensate for his reduced efficiency as the time at the job continues. (6) provide the worker with time to enable him to maintain his productive effort. (7) to provide the worker with time to enable him to maintain the time specified for the element. (8) to increase the basic time to that which is considered to be a fair standard. . . . to provide the worker with proper reward for an hour of effort. (9) to provide the worker with the necessary recuperation to offset fatigue. Fatigue allowances vary with the methods, practices, and differences of various time study men or company policies. Some of the variables which must be considered are: Just what is meant by "rest to prevent undue fatigue?" How effective are present-day methods in selecting and placing workers in accordance with their physical, mental and temperamental make-up? How much energy does a worker contract to expend in the performance of a day's work? How much energy does a worker reserve for his own recreation and for other purposes after working hours? Is the amount of fatigue allowance that permits the worker to maintain the optimum productivity rate sufficient to prevent undue fatigue? To what extent would a fatigue allowance based on a maximum productivity concept permit the worker to govern his pace, according to his "natural working rhythm?" When incentive rates are used should the fatigue allowance be based on the normal pace of production or on the incentive pace? These—and other questions—must be answered before it is possible to determine fatigue allowances. See FATIGUE ALLOWANCE, DETERMINATION OF. Many authorities feel that allowances should be only for time for personal needs and that any adjustment for fatigue should be compensated for in the process of rating the operator's performance.

featherbedding. A term applied in connection with certain working rules which tend to pyramid pay even though all work is performed within the regular tour of duty, or rules by which an employee receives remuneration for work which he has not performed. According to legend, the term started early in the century when a local representative of the trainmen on a certain railroad brought in a grievance about the mattresses put in the road's cabooses for freight crews to sleep on when trains were at terminals away from home. When the union agent complained that the mattresses were filled with corn cobs, shucks and cottonseed hulls, the trainmaster retorted: "What do you brakemen want—feather beds?"
See table on p. 112.

Federal aid. See GRANT-IN-AID.

Federal Airport Act. Act of May 13, 1946. This law requires minimum wages as determined by the Secretary of Labor to be paid to skilled and unskilled labor employed on contracts of over $2,000 awarded by the State or local authorities for construction and repair of their airports with financial assistance from the Federal Government under a grant-in-aid program. For further information on

continued on p. 113

FEDERAL AGENCIES RESPONSIBLE FOR ADMINISTERING MAJOR LABOR LAWS

This chart shows the Federal agencies which administer major Federal labor laws or portions of such laws. For a few of the acts listed there is no specified administrative agency; these acts provide penalties, provide for injunctions, or give rights which may be enforced in a civil action.

Laws (column headings):

- Anti-Injunction Act (Norris-LaGuardia)
- Anti-kickback Law and Copeland Act [1]
- Anti-Racketeering Act (Hobbs)
- Anti-Strikebreaker Act (Byrnes)
- Apprenticeship Act
- Coal Mine Safety Act of 1952
- Davis-Bacon Act and Provisions in Other Acts Authorizing Wage Rates for Construction Work
- Defense Base Act
- Eight-Hour Laws [1]
- Fair Labor Standards Act
- G. I. Bill of Rights (Servicemen's Readjustment Act of 1944)
- Korean G. I. Bill of Rights (Veterans Readjustment Assistance Act of 1952)
- Labor Management Relations Act (Taft-Hartley)
- Longshoremen's and Harbor Workers' Compensation Act
- Miller Act
- Railroad Retirement Act
- Railroad Unemployment Insurance Act
- Railway Labor Act
- Smith-Hughes and George-Barden Acts
- Social Security Act
- Transportation of Migrant Workers
- Unlawful Practices in Radio Broadcasting (Lea Act)
- Veterans Reemployment Rights
- Vocational Rehabilitation Act
- Vocational Rehabilitation Act for Disabled Korean Veterans
- Vocational Rehabilitation Training Act for World War II Veterans
- Wagner-Peyser Act
- Walsh-Healey Public Contracts Act

Agencies (row headings):

DEPARTMENT OF LABOR
- The Solicitor of Labor
- Bureau of Apprenticeship and Training
- Bureau of Employees Compensation
- Bureau of Employment Security
- Bureau of Labor Standards
- Bureau of Veterans Reemployment Rights
- Wage and Hour and Public Contracts Divisions

DEPT. OF HEALTH, EDUCATION, AND WELFARE
- Bureau of Old Age and Survivors Insurance
- Bureau of Public Assistance
- Children's Bureau
- Social Security Admin.
- Office of Education (Vocational Division)
- Office of Vocational Rehabilitation

- Bureau of Mines, Department of Interior
- Federal Mediation and Conciliation Service
- Interstate Commerce Commission
- National Labor Relations Board
- National Mediation Board
- National Railroad Adjustment Board
- Railroad Retirement Board
- Veterans Administration

[1] Enforcement of these laws is the primary responsibility of contracting or financing agency in accordance with regulations prescribed by Secretary of Labor.

[2] The Bureau of Labor Standards administers only provisions relating to filing of organization and financial data by labor organizations.

wage standards for construction write to the Office of the Solicitor, U.S. Department of Labor, Washington 25, D. C.

Federal Coal Mine Safety Act. Act of July 16, 1952. The main objectives of the Division of Coal Mine Inspection, operating organizationally as part of the health and safety activities under the Bureau of Mines, whose province and duty, in turn, are subject to the approval of the Secretary of the Interior, are: (1) inspecting coal mines to determine the causes of accidents and occupational diseases therein; (2) reviewing reports and evaluating operations based on such inspections; (3) revealing, through personnel conferences with interested agencies, correspondence, and published reports, the unhealthful and unsafe conditions and practices in coal mines; (4) recommending practical means for correcting the conditions observed; (5) enforcing the mandatory provisions of Title II of the Federal Coal Mine Safety Act in order to forestall the occurrence of major disasters in coal mines in which 15 or more individuals are employed underground; and (6) promoting and sponsoring safety education programs in the industry. About 250 coal mine inspectors operate from geographically distributed district and subdistrict offices that are located near their actual field operations. Fourteen fully equipped rescue trucks and one fully equipped railroad rescue car are maintained by the Bureau of Mines' Division of Safety in the various mineral regions of the United States and Alaska and this equipment is available to the coal mine inspectors for giving aid in mine disasters. *For Further Information*: Write Bureau of Mines, U. S. Department of the Interior, Washington 25, D. C.

Federal Mediation and Conciliation Service, established under Labor Management Relations Act (which see). The Federal Mediation and Conciliation Service is an independent agency of the Federal Government. The policies of the Service are specified in Title II of the Labor Management Relations Act, 1947, as amended. Parties to labor disputes affecting commerce among or between the several States and within the District of Columbia and the Territories are encouraged to settle these disputes through their own processes of conference and collective bargaining. Should a dispute threaten to cause a substantial interruption of commerce, the Service may assist the parties in settling the dispute by making available its facilities of conciliation, mediation, and voluntary arbitration. It has no power or desire to compel settlement. The parties have a statutory obligation, however, to "participate fully and promptly in such meetings as may be undertaken by the Service under this Act for the purpose of aiding in a settlement of the dispute." There is also a statutory requirement that no party to a collective bargaining contract shall terminate or modify such contracts unless the party desiring such termination or modification serves a written notice upon the other party. The written notice must be served 60 days prior to the expiration date, or, if none, to the time of such termination or modification. The party desiring such changes must also offer to bargain collectively, and must notify the Federal Service as well as appropriate State or Territorial mediation agencies within 30 days after such notice to the other party that an unsettled dispute exists. A suggested form of notice to mediation agencies is available at the regional offices of the Federal Service.

Disputes having only a minor effect on interstate commerce are not mediated by the Federal Services if State or other conciliation services are available to the parties. Grievance disputes arising over the application or interpretation of an existing collective bargaining agreement are not mediated unless a work stoppage is imminent in an essential industry. A final adjustment by a method agreed upon between the parties is encouraged. The Service will supply a panel of qualified arbitrators, upon request, from which the parties may select the arbitrator whose decision will finally adjust the grievance. The arbitrator is paid by the parties. He is expected to conform with the procedures and policies of the Service as outlined in a pamphlet which is available in the regional offices of the Service. The functions and duties of the Federal Mediation and Conciliation Service are administered by a staff of commissioners working under the supervision of eight regional directors. Each regional director is responsible in his geographical area for the execution of the functions and policies of the Service, under the direction of the director of the Service. The director is appointed by the President, with the advice and consent of the Senate, and is assisted by a small staff in Washington, D. C. For further information, write or contact the Federal Mediation and Conciliation Service, Washington 25, D. C.

"Federal Unemployment Tax." A term used by the United States Employment Service. The excise tax of 3 percent imposed on employers by the Federal Unemployment Tax Act with respect to having individuals in their employ.

"Federal Unemployment Tax Act." A term used by the United States Employment Service. Subchapter C of chapter 9 of the Internal Revenue Code which relates to the Federal Unemployment Tax.

"Federal Unemployment Tax Return." A term used by the United States Employment Service. A report by an employer to the Bureau of Internal Revenue of the amount of Federal unemployment tax due and payable with respect to his wage payments to his workers during the calendar year.

Federal Highway Act of 1956. This act covers the construction of Federal-Aid highway systems including the Interstate System. Section 115 of the act provides for the application of the Davis-Bacon Act to all laborers and mechanics employed by contractors and subcontractors on the initial construction of highways on the Interstate System. Rates of wages paid to such laborers and mechanics may not be less than those which the Secretary of Labor, in accordance with the Davis-Bacon Act, determines to be prevailing on the same type of work on similar construction in the immediate locality. Such prevailing rates are required to be predetermined by the Secretary after consultation with the highway department of the State in which a project is to be performed and after giving due regard to the information so obtained. The Highway Act provides that the predetermined wage rates shall be set out in each project advertisement for bids and in each bid proposal form, and shall be made a part of the contract covering the project.

Federal Wage-Hour Act. Same as FAIR LABOR STANDARDS ACT.

FEPC. See FAIR EMPLOYMENT PRACTICES COMMITTEE.

Ficker Piece Rate Basis. A constant sharing wage incentive plan, where the earning will always be higher than the basic piece rate, but will vary depending upon the value of the machine rate.

Ficker Time Constant Sharing Plan. A plan like the high task Halsey plan (which see) but with an additional factor based on machine rate and figured similarly to the time rate in the Halsey plan. The machine rate is multiplied by time saved, and half of it is given to the employee.

"Field Audit, Employer." A term used by the United States Employment Service. See EMPLOYER FIELD AUDIT.

"Fields-of-Work Grouping." A term used by the United States Employment Service. A rearrangement of the fields of work presented in part IV of the Dictionary of Occupational Titles for use in analyzing the occupational composition of an industry or a community.

field trip. A planned visitation by a group of students to a plant or establishment for the purpose of observing and seeking firsthand information about its operation or of acquiring skills and experiences not possible in the classroom.

"Filled Opening." A term used by the United States Employment Service. See OPENING.

film analysis. A frame-by-frame study of a motion picture of an operation to determine the motions used, their sequence, and the time taken for each. See MICROMOTION STUDY, DEFINITION 2.

film analysis chart. A graphical representation of the activities of the various body members as determined by film analysis. Often referred to as right-and-left-hand chart or simo chart.

film analysis record. A tabular record of the data obtained from a film analysis.

financial incentive. A monetary inducement other than base or overtime wages, bearing some predetermined relationship to performance, such as quantity of work, reduction of spoilage, or some other desired result, paid to the worker as a reward for meeting or exceeding an established standard of performance.

final pay plan. A plan under which the pension is based upon the participant's pay immediately preceding retirement, or averaged over the last five or ten years preceding retirement.

financial incentive plan. A method of systematic financial remuneration in relation to specified standards of performance. Performance may relate to quantity, quality, control of waste, costs or other factors. Commonly, the systems provide extra remuneration for achievement in excess of a predescribed base. C. W. Lytle, in *Wage Incentive Methods,* (Ronald Press) has grouped wage incentive methods into four major groups: *Class I. Employer Takes All Gain or Loss:* (1) Time: hour, week, or any straight salary rate. Not an extra-financial incentive. (2) Standard time using two rates, on either side of task. A two-zone multiple time plan. (3) Multiple time: arithmetic steps in rate between production zones. (4) Multiple time: geometric steps in rate between production zones. *Class II. Employee Takes All Gain or Loss:* (5) Piece or straight commission rate. This subdivides into: punitive, basic and high. (6) Taylor (Multiple piece rate or multiple commission). (7) Merrick (Multiple piece rate or multiple commission). (8) Gantt (Combination of No. 1 and No. 5 with step between). Without step would be called piece rate with guarantee, Manchester, Standard Hour, 100% Premium or Haynes Manit. All five had identical earning curves. *Class III. Gain shared Between Employer and Employee but Day Wage Guaranteed, Excepting in Barth and "One-third Premium" Form of Halsey*: (9) Halsey. (10) Diemer. (11) Baum. (12) Bedaux, Dyer, Keays-Weaver, K.I.M., Shanley, and Stevens. (13) Ficker Time. (14) Ficker Piece. (15) Sherman Individual-Group. (16) Rowan, Mansfield, and Bayle. (17) Barth. *Class IV. Empiric Location of Points Between The Two Variables*: (18) Emerson. (19) Wennerlund (Piece work or commission above 100% production). (20) Knoeppel. (21) Bigelow. (22) Bigelow-Knoeppel. (23) Parkhurst. (24) Ernst and Ernst. (25) Sylvester (See SEPARATE ENTRIES)

find. A *therblig* (which see) which is defined as: to reach or arrive at; meet with accidentally, chance upon, fall in with. *Find* may be distinguished from *select* in that only one object is under consideration. The mental decision to accept the realized object is the true action of *find. Find* is the singular or unencumbered condition of *Select*; where only one object, part, or tool can be obtained at a time, there will be no *Find* in the sense of choice, but rather as an acceptance.

finish-go-home basis of pay. A practice under which employees are permitted to go home after completing a specific work assignment generally considered a standard day's work. An example of the "finish-go-home" basis of pay may be found in nonferrous smelters. Charging

the furnace in less than 8 hours permits more time for the actual smelting process and workers are encouraged to complete charging in less than 8 hours but are paid for a full shift. Similar standards for a day's work are set up in unloading of railroad cars or other shipping facilities, in shake-out work in foundries, and in other industries. Essentially, this may be considered an incentive method of pay; it generally involves making costly facilities available for use as quickly as possible.

fink. A person who makes a career of working in plants where workers are on strike.

first piece time. The time required to produce the first of a number of identical units including all necessary setup and make-ready time.

"First UI or UCFE Payment." A term used by the United States Employment Service. A payment issued to a claimant for his first compensable week of unemployment in a benefit year.

"First UCV Payment." A term used by the United States Employment Service to designate the first payment issued to a veteran from title IV funds.

"Fiscal Standards." A term used by the United States Employment Service to designate the basic principles adopted by the Bureau of Employment Security to govern the expenditure of administrative funds made available to a State employment security agency.

Fitzgerald Act. The National Apprenticeship Law, enacted in 1937, "to promote the furtherance of labor standards of apprenticeship, bring together employers and labor for the development of programs of apprenticeship and to cooperate with state agencies in the formulation of standards of apprenticeship." The act is administered by the Bureau of Apprenticeship, U.S. Department of Labor.

fixed benefit plan. See BENEFIT PLAN, DEFINITE.

fixed expense. Expenditures that remain constant with respect to time regardless of the volume of production such as taxes (on land and buildings), insurance, certain administrative salaries, and the like.

fixed shift. The term applied to the type of shift on which a group of workers maintains the same schedule of hours week after week rather than rotating time-of-day assignments periodically with other groups. See also ROTATING SHIFT, SHIFT, SPLIT SHIFT, and SWING SHIFT.

fixture. A device which: (1) holds material in a desired position but does not guide the machine or tools performing the necessary operations; or, (2) holds two or more parts in prescribed positions relative to each other while the parts are being assembled and/or joined together.

flannel board. A large, usually black, board covered with flannel to which cards or other items, specially treated, will adhere upon contact. Each step, or unit, of a talk or lecture is put in place at the exact moment when mentioned by the speaker. The board always shows the relationship between the steps in clear, graphic terms. When a talk is completed, the flannel board provides an immediate summary or review or may serve as a guide to returning to previous points for more discussion. If desired, the cards may be taken from the board singly or in groups, or may be moved to another part of the board, where they adhere on contact.

flat-percentage pension. A pension equivalent to a uniform percentage of compensation for all participants in the plan upon retirement.

flat rate (Auto Repair). A system of remuneration used in auto repair shops. The flat rate refers to the labor charge made for a repair job and is usually based on the standard time specified in an official automobile repair manual. The auto mechanic receives a percentage of the total labor cost, which is computed at a rate which allows a margin of profit for the employer. If the actual time spent on a job is greater than the standard allowance, the actual time is the determining factor in computing the labor cost.

flat-sum benefit. A benefit, or pension, of a specified uniform amount for all participants in the pension plan, regardless of the individual's earnings. Such plans ordinarily require a long service record before an employee is eligible.

flexible schedule. An arrangement of work periods whereby the number of hours worked for the over-all period do not exceed the amount of time for which straight-time wages are paid.

"Flexible Week." A term used by the United States Employment Service. See WEEK.

floor under wages. See MINIMUM WAGE.

flow diagram. A graphical representation on a floor plan of the work area involved of the locations of work stations and the paths of movement of men and/or materials.

(117)

flow process chart. A graphic representation of the sequences of all operations, transportations, inspections, delays, and storages occurring during a process of procedure. It includes information considered desirable for analysis such as time required and distance moved. (1) The material type presents the process in terms of the events which occur to the material. (2) The man type presents the process in terms of the activities of the man.

follow-up study, vocational. A survey to determine what occupations the students and graduates of vocational education courses enter and how effective their training was in relationship to actual needs of the job.

foreign element. An interruption which is not a regular occurrence in the work cycle or operation, and one for which no provision was made in the normal sequence of elements of a time study.

forelady. Performs the usual duties of a foreman (which see).

foreman. According to the DICTIONARY OF OCCUPATIONAL TITLES, (which see) a foreman is a boss; chief; head; leader; overlooker; overseer; principal; senior; supervisor. Supervises a group of workmen engaged chiefly in one craft, as Carpenters, or Electricians. Interprets blueprints, sketches, written or verbal orders; determines procedure of work; assigns duties to craftsmen and inspects their work for quality and quantity; maintains harmony among workers. May keep time, production, and other clerical records, employ, train, and discharge workers, assist subordinates during emergencies or as a regular assigned duty, ref. Working Foreman, set-up or inspect equipment preparatory to regular operations, per-form related duties of supervisory or minor administrative nature. Must be skilled in the particular craft in which he functions.

foremanship training. Foremanship or supervisory training has been in effect in American industry since Dr. Charles R. Allen, (See JOB INSTRUCTION) in 1914 was forced to develop a new approach in training factory foremen, simply because these men did not take kindly to listening to lectures on methods of improving their supervision. In method, training techniques have included lectures, case studies, conferences, "Training-Within Industry," role-playing, and combinations of these. Subject matter covered in foremanship training programs has been equally diversified. Charles Reitell, in "Training Workers and Supervisors," (The Ronald Press) suggests that Foremanship Training Courses include: (1) Those concerned with technical skills required for the job, such as Budget Control, Standards and Planning. (2) Those concerned with the general aspects of the job requirements—plant policies and organization, the plant product, labor legislation, and labor relations. (3) Those concerned with the requirements for good teaching and good leadership—human relations, teaching methods, group talking (public speaking).

forms. Business forms are instruments or tools of management by means of which something is performed or effected. Business forms show people what to do, when to do it, where to do it, how to do it, how much to do, and who is to do it. They provide a detailed record of transactions, events, and of people. See PERSONNEL RECORDS. The physical designing of forms is a job for the office systems expert. Some of the underlying principles of forms design are described in: *Design and Control of Business Forms*: President, Frank M Knox Co., Cleveland, Ohio National Office Management Association, 1952; *Manual of Business Forms*: Walace B. Sadauskas, The Office, 1955; Formcraft Library, Standard Register Co., Dayton, Ohio.

Forty-Plus Club. An organization formed in 1938 in Boston, Mass. Now there are Forty-Plus Clubs in 8 major cities, loosely held together through a liaison organization in Washington, D. C. The Forty-Plus clubs are composed of older unemployed executives who have banded together to help each other find jobs.

frame. In motion study work, the time which elapses between two successive exposures of a motion picture film, so called because a frame is the term used for an individual picture or space for a single picture on a motion picture film.

frame counter. A mechanical counter which can be used to determine the number of frames that have passed a predetermined point in a motion picture.

"Free Speech." A provision in the National Labor Management Relations Act (which see). Section 8 (c) of the Act states: The expressing of any views, argument, or opinion, or the dissemination thereof, whether in written, printed, graphic or visual form, shall not constitute or be evidence of an unfair labor practice under any of the provisions of this act, if such expression contains no threat of reprisal or force or promise of benefit. The Board has held that this section applies only to unfair labor practice cases and does not apply to conduct effecting elections. Examples of statements which this provision does not pro-

tect: (1) Implied threats by an employer that the organization of a union would result in the loss of benefits for employees. (2) Picket signs announcing to employees of one employer that another employer is "unfair" where an object is to induce the employees to engage in a secondary boycott. (3) A statement by a union official to an employee that the employee will lose his job if the union wins a majority in the plant.

frequency. In industrial engineering (1) the number of times an element occurs during an operation cycle. (2) The number of times a specific value occurs within a sample of several measurements of the same dimension or characteristic on several similar items.

frequency study. An industrial engineering term to describe a study made to determine the number of occurrences of elements during a given period.

frictional unemployment. Short term, or temporary unemployment of workers arising from delays involved in changing jobs, in the shifting of job seekers to occupations, industries and areas where there are employment opportunities or from personal, legal institutional and social barriers to mobility in the labor market, as employer age restrictions, union jurisdictional limitations, lack of personal qualities desired by employers at a particular time, etc.

fringe benefit. A benefit supplemental to wages received by workers, at a cost to employers. Among these benefits, commonly designated as "fringe," are paid holidays, paid vacations, pensions, and insurance benefits (life, accident, health, hospitalization, and medical). There is some disagreement as to whether a number of other payments to employees are "fringes." Some authorities consider as fringes everything that is over and above straight-time pay. Thus, within this framework, fringes would include overtime, travel time, wash-up time, shift premiums, bonuses, extra pay or hazardous work; in other words, any other conditions of employment for which employees receive compensation other than hourly or incentive pay.

fringe items. See FRINGE BENEFITS. Compensations, other than basic wages, for such things as holidays, vacations, benefits.

full crew rule. Government regulations requiring the presence of a certain number of crewmen on trains.

full employment. The availability of employment opportunities for all persons who are able and willing to work. Actually, this ideal state is never achieved because there are always some employees in transition between jobs.

Full Employment Bill. See EMPLOYMENT ACT OF 1946.

full-time earnings. Earnings received for working a regular schedule of hours over a stated period of time. Full-time earnings may be defined in terms of a day, week, month, or other period.

"Full-Time Wages." A term used by the United States Employment Service. See WAGES.

"Full-Time Week." A term used by the United States Employment Service. See WEEK.

full-time worker rate. A rate paid to a full-time or regular worker, as distinguished from that paid to a part-time or temporary worker.

"fully insured." A term used in the Social Security Act. See CREDITS, BUILDING UP, FOR SOCIAL SECURITY BENEFITS. A person is fully insured when he has reached 65 if a man, or 62 if a woman, or when he dies if he has at least one quarter of coverage for each 2 calendar quarters that have passed since December 31, 1950, or since he reached age 21, whichever is later. At least 6 quarters of coverage are necessary in each case. When a person has 40 quarters of coverage he is fully insured for life. See CURRENTLY INSURED.

functional layout. See PROCESS LAYOUT.

fundamental motion. See BASIC DIVISION OF ACCOMPLISHMENT.

funded fully. The cost of providing the ultimate benefits under a pension plan is determined actuarially. The funds necessary to meet the financial obligations under the plan are accumulated in a reserve during the individual's participation under the plan.

funded pension plan. A plan providing for accumulation of money over a period of years to meet pension obligations.

funding method. The procedure followed in accumulating money to pay for pensions under a pension plan. Used extensively are: (1) purchase of annuities from an insurance company; (2) payment of specified amounts to a pension trust fund for investment in securities or other property; (3) a combination of both.

"Funds." A term used by the United States Employment Service. *Administrative Funds.* Funds made available from Federal, State, local, and other sources

(120)

to meet the cost of State employment security administration. *Contingency Fund.* An amount of money appropriated by Congress to meet certain unpredictable increases in costs of administration by the State employment security agencies arising from increases in workload or other specified causes. *Employment Security Administration Fund.* A special fund in the State treasury, established by State law, in which are deposited moneys granted by the Bureau of Employment Security and moneys from other sources, for the purpose of paying the cost of administering the State employment security program. *Pooled Fund.* A State unemployment fund in which all contributions are mingled and undivided and from which benefits are payable to all eligible claimants. See also RESERVE ACCOUNTS under ACCOUNTS. *Reallotted Administrative Fund.* The amount of funds previously made available to State employment security agencies which remains unencumbered on the books of the agencies at the close of a budgetary period and which is reallotted by the Director, Bureau of Employment Security, for use in a subsequent budgetary period. *Title IV Funds.* Funds appropriated by Congress to pay unemployment benefits to veterans under title IV of the Veterans' Readjustment Assistance Act of 1952. *Title XV Funds.* Funds appropriated by Congress to pay unemployment benefits under title XV of the Social Security Act to Federal workers. *Unemployment Fund.* A special fund established under a State employment security law for the receipt and management of contributions and the payment of unemployment insurance benefits. Included in this fund are moneys in the benefit payment account, clearing account, and unemployment trust fund account. See ACCOUNTS. *Unemployment Trust Fund.* A fund established in the Treasury of the United States which contains all moneys deposited with the Treasury by State employment security agencies to the credit of their unemployment fund accounts and by the Railroad Retirement Board to the credit of the Railroad Unemployment Insurance Account.

furlough. A term which means the same as LAID OFF, FIRED or DISCHARGED. For all practical purposes, an employee who is furloughed, joins the ranks of the unemployed.

Future Business Leaders of America. A national organization of high school and college students of business education, which has for its purpose the promotion of better leadership opportunities for young people employed in the field of business.

future (current) service benefits. Pension credits provided for years of participation subsequent to the plan's adoption and prior to retirement, i.e. credits given to an employee for each year of service: (1) between the time the pension plan is set up and the time he retires; or (2) between the date he begins to participate in the plan and the day he retires.

future (current) service cost. Amount, determined actuarially, needed to fund pensions for present and future years of participation under the pension plan in effect.

(121)

G

gainful occupation. Any occupation for which a person receives compensation in money or in kind, or in which he assists in the production of marketable goods.

gainful worker. One who ordinarily follows a gainful occupation, regardless of whether or not the person is employed or seeking work.

gain sharing. A feature of some wage incentive plans which divides the bonus as computed by the wage incentive plan formula in some predetermined proportion between management and the workman.

Gantt Chart. A graphic representation on a time scale of the current relationship between actual and planned performance.

Gantt Task and Bonus Plan. Henry L. Gantt was the originator of a type of incentive plan which uses a step bonus for those attaining the standards. This plan was designed to use a low base rate. This was to be increased substantially, in cases 30 to 50 per cent, for the attainment of the time standards. All production above 100 per cent of efficiency was paid for at the increased base rate. The plan combines timestudy basis, standard times, individual payment and extra incentive. Today, a number of plants use a modified Gantt Plan with a 10 to 12 per cent jump in base rate at 100 per cent efficiency. The substantial increase is an added inducement to attain high performance. Everything over standard is paid for at the increased rate.

garnishment of wages. The practice of legally attaching the wages of a debtor and collecting the debt directly from his employer.

"General Aptitude Battery Tests." A term used by the United States Employment Service. See TESTS.

general aptitude tests. Aptitude has been defined (in Encyclopedia of Vocational Guidance) as ". . . a condition or set of characteristics regarded as symptomatic of an individual's ability to acquire with training (usually specified) knowledge, skill, or a set of responses such as ability to speak a language, etc." Aptitude tests include: General Aptitude Test Battery—Bureau of Employment Security, U. S. Dept. of Labor; Flanagan Aptitude Classification Tests—Science Research Associates; Purdue Industrial Training Classification Test—Science Research Associates; Aptitude Job Tests Program—Industrial Psychology, Inc.; Differential Aptitude

Tests—Bennett, Seashore and Wesman —Psychological Corporation. See PUBLISHERS, PERSONNEL TESTS.

general industrial course. A class organized to give specific preparation in a group where shop instruction in several closely allied trades is conducted simultaneously. Courses may be organized to give preparation for one or more production jobs that do not fall into the trade classification.

general shop course. A multi-activity program in industrial arts. See COMPREHENSIVE (COMPOSITE) GENERAL SHOP.

general strike. See STRIKE, GENERAL.

general unit shop. A school shop confined to industrial arts education within a family of occupations such as metalworking, woodworking or electricity. For example, a general metalworking shop would contain facilities related to the specific occupations of machine shop, foundry work, sheet metal, and the like.

geographical differential. The differences in wage rates for the same types of work between territorial divisions of the country—for example, between the Midwest and the East, between North and South.

George-Barden Act. The federal law enacted in 1946, which provides for "the further development and promotion of vocational education in the several states and territories." It authorizes a federal appropriation for grants-in-aid to states for use in vocational programs which meet certain minimum standards in agriculture, home economics, distributive education, trade and industrial education, and vocational guidance. The Act is administered by the U. S. Office of Education, Department of Health, Education and Welfare.

G. I. Bill of Rights for World War II Veterans. (Servicemen's Readjustment Act of 1944) Act of June 22, 1944, as amended. The Servicemen's Readjustment Act, commonly known as the "GI Bill of Rights," provides education and training benefits for those who pursue school, institutional on-farm, apprentice or other training on-the-job courses offered by approved educational institutions or business establishments. Included in the education and training benefits are subsistence allowances, tuition payments and necessary training supplies. Title III provides loan credit assistance to veterans for the purchase, construction, or improvement of homes, or farms and business property. In general, loan entitlement based on World War II service will not be available for use after July 25, 1958, although certain enlistees, or reenlistees, under Public Law 190, 79th Congress, October 6, 1945, have the benefit of a later deadline. Title V of that act established readjustment allowances. That program has, in the main, been executed. However, as in the case of Title III loan benefits, Public Law 190 extended the time limitations for certain persons. Education and training under Title II of the Servicemen's Readjustment Act came to an end on July 25, 1956, for all but a small handful of World War II veterans who enlisted or re-enlisted in the Armed Forces under Public Law 190, 79th Congress. During the 12 years that the Servicemen's Readjustment Act has been in effect, more than 7.8 million World War II veterans entered training. Of this number approximately 1.4 million veterans pursued programs of on-the-job training. On July 31, 1956, only 114 veterans who had enlisted or reenlisted under Public Law 190 were still pursuing programs of on-the-job training under the Servicemen's Readjustment Act.

Gilbreth Basic Element. A name given to each of the basic divisions of accomplishment defined and used by Frank B. and Lillian M. Gilbreth, by the American Society of Mechanical Engineers, to classify physical motions and associated mental processes. See also THERBLIG.

going wage. The wage commonly paid in a locality, community, area or industry for a specific type of work. See also PREVAILING WAGE.

goldbricking. A colloquial term, meaning to loaf on the job, usually for the purpose of reducing output.

"Good Housekeeping." In personnel work, a term used to describe the appearance of the shop, work-place or department. Disorderly, disarranged conditions affect work habits on the part of employees. Good housekeeping affects both safety and costs. A suggested check list for good housekeeping (Kress, Foremanship, Fundamentals) includes: (1) Have a good old-fashioned spring house cleaning. Start in and clean up the whole department. Get any necessary approval to junk some of the accumulation. (2) Mark off all aisles and passageways with paint. See that they are kept open. (3) Collect all mislaid tools. Get owners to identify them or send them to the tool crib. (4) Paint corners white to discourage spitting; furnish cuspidors. (5) Provide refuse containers. (6) Inspect lockers regularly. (7) Be on the alert for material not properly piled which may fall over. (8) See that trucks are kept out of aisles when not in use. (9) See that machines

are kept clean. Have a regular time for men to clean them. (10) Arrange to have your windows washed regularly. (11) Set a good example by keeping your own office or desk neat and clean. (12) See that your departmental washroom is kept clean. (13) Finally, sell your employees and keep them sold on the idea that good housekeeping means good workmanship. "The Value of Order," by Dr. Harry Myers, of Dayton, Ohio has for many years been a widely circulated pamphlet on "good housekeeping."

goon. A person hired by a union or employer to incite violence during a strike.

government regulation of industry. The control or supervision exercised by the government over business and industrial organizations and their methods of operation in order to protect the general public from improper economic exploitation. Characteristic regulatory measures are SHERMAN ANTI-TRUST ACT, the CLAYTON ACT, FEDERAL TRADE COMMISSION, and the INTERSTATE COMMERCE COMMISSION.

"Grant." A term used by the United States Employment Service. Moneys from Federal appropriations made available to States by the Bureau of Employment Security under the provisions of the Wagner-Peyser and Social Security Acts for the purpose of financing the State employment security administration.

Grant-in-aid. A financial grant, frequently in the form of periodic payments, made by a government or agency to another government or agency, by way of assistance for a special purpose. For example, funds are granted by the federal government to the states for the promotion of vocational education, under the terms of the SMITH-HUGHES and GEORGE-BARDEN ACTS.

grapevine. Generally associated with rumor. Word-to-mouth communication, usually among employees. It is differentiated from formal, or official communication, which is authentic.

graphic rating scale. A method of rating or appraising characteristics of individuals, jobs, organizations and the like. For each characteristic to be rated, several descriptive statements are arranged in either ascending or descending order of quality. A check mark placed opposite the statement best indicating the degree to which each characteristic is possessed permits a visual comparison with the extremes to which the characteristic could be possessed.

grasp. A THERBLIG (which see) which is defined as: to seize with the hand, hence, to embrace firmly; to take and hold in possession. Prepositioning reduces the *grasp* time. This may be accomplished by the previous operator placing the parts in a definite position as he disposes of them. It may be effected by the use of containers or trays. Mechanical means may be devised to place the part in the convenient position for the operator to grasp. A chute at the opening of a hopper, or from the previous operation, may deliver the part in a convenient position for *grasping* it. A power hopper may be designed to pick out the parts and deliver them to the operator in definite position which will facilitate *grasp*. A conveyor may deliver the part in a definite position, height, and location, and thus reduce the *grasp* movements. Holding devices for tools and appliances reduce *grasp* action. Tongs may be used to *grasp*

sharp, hot, acid-covered, very cold, dangerously positioned, or odd and peculiar-shaped parts. Tweezers may be used to hold small and delicate parts. Pliers may be used for a firm and small area grip.

grasp. In industrial engineering terminology, the basic element employed when the predominant purpose is to secure sufficient control of one or more objects with the fingers or the hand to permit the performance of the next required basic element.

graveyard shift. In multiple-shift operations, that shift of workers which is ployed from 11 p.m. or midnight until early morning. The graveyard shift is usually in effect in industries requiring around-the-clock operation.

gravity feed. A method of supplying materials into a machine or to a work station by the force of gravity. Generally, a hopper or chute is used to store and to guide the materials to the point of use.

"green." Used in connection with inexperienced workers, such as "green hands." Usually a newcomer, although an older employee may be "green" in connection with a new job.

grievance. Dissatisfaction, irritation, complaints or misunderstandings of an employee or the employer with respect to their relationship in the employment situation. Where a collective agreement exists, grievances frequently stem out of the interpretation and application of its provisions. In *How to Handle Grievances,* Glenn Gardiner defines what constitutes a grievance as follows: (1) Anything about a man's job which irritates him or tends to make his working con-

ditions unsatisfactory may be a grievance. (2) A grievance may exist even
though no verbal or written complaint is
presented. Such silent or unuttered
grievances may be as destructive of good
will as the grievance which is aired. (3)
Even though the grievance may be
imaginary, or based on lack of knowledge of facts, it is a grievance, none the
less, until properly cleared up. (4) If
a worker thinks he has a grievance, he
may be as discontented as though he had
a just grievance and the same careful
handling is necessary. (5) A grievance
may be trivial or important, affecting
an individual or a group, caused by
fellow-workers or management, financial
or non-financial, imaginary or real—but
is a grievance in any case, and requires
fair, open-minded, patient, considerate
treatment.

grievance committee. Grievance committees or shop, plant or labor relations
committees may be elected directly by
all the employees, indirectly through a
stewards' council, or may be composed
of a number of officials designated by
the union. The number of persons serving on the committee—usually three to
seven—is often stipulated in the agreement. The grievance committee comes
into action when more difficult grievances—those involving the interpretation
of the contract or determination of a new
policy—which cannot be settled either by
the steward or the business representative, arise. This committee usually has
authority to make decisions of policy on
behalf of the workers. Before an appeal
is taken up by the grievance committee,
authorization of the membership, either
through the stewards' council or the local
office, may be required. Grievance committees usually hold regular meetings

with management. They may meet with
a management committee of equal size
or with the industrial relations director
or other designated company officials.
How often the meetings are held usually
depends on the stage at which grievance
appeals are submitted to the committee.

grievance machinery. The grievance machinery provides an effective communications system for bringing an employee's complaints to management's attention or for management to register
its complaints against the union or
against individual employees. Most frequently it is considered a means of giving an employee, either directly or
through his union representative, the
opportunity to present orally or in writing his particular complaint. It enables
management with the help of the union
to discover and correct the sore spots
in working conditions and plant industrial relations before they are permitted
to spread and cause real trouble. (Machinery for handling grievances may also
exist where there is no union, although
usually in that case it is on a less formal
basis.) Union grievances fall into the
following broad categories: (1) wages,
demands for individual adjustment, complaints about job classifications or incentive systems; (2) supervision, discipline,
objection to a particular foreman, or to
general method of supervision; (3) seniority, discharge, loss, miscalculation or
misinterpretation of seniority, disciplinary discharge of lay-off, promotions,
transfer to other departments or shifts;
(4) general working conditions, safety
and health, inadequate eating facilities,
too much time lost waiting for materials;
(5) collective bargaining, violations of
contract, interpretations of contract,
settlement of grievances, disregard of

precedents, failure on part of company to take action in respect to supervisors. Management grievances include: (1) dissatisfaction with individual worker, discipline, poor work; (2) collective bargaining, violations of contract, disputes over interpretation of contract, complaints about grievance settlements and alleged lack of good faith on part of union; (3) union conduct, questionable methods of soliciting union members, union rules conflicting with terms of agreement; irresponsible charges against management by union leaders in press, leaflets, or public speeches.

grievance procedure. As established by union contract, grievance procedure usually includes the following essential provisions: (1) union management negotiations, starting with the aggrieved employee, his steward, (or other terminology as "chairman," "committeeman,") and his foreman or supervisor, and rising through successive stages, spelled out in the agreement, to the officers of the company and the union who are empowered to make final decisions. (2) Arbitration by an impartial agency or individual, if the above negotiations fail to secure a settlement. (3) A limitation on strikes and lock-outs until the above procedures have been exhausted. The first part of grievance adjustment—the union-management negotiations—has developed into a fairly standardized and formal type of procedure. This is true in two respects: (1) the orderly method of appeal through successive stages from foreman to top management, and (2) the practice of writing out grievances on special forms which are signed by each person who handles the case and used as the basis of appeal at each successive stage.

gross average weekly earnings. A measure of weekly wages typically obtained by dividing total compensation prior to pay-roll deductions for taxes, social security payments, or other purposes for a given weekly pay-roll period (or, by the use of a conversion factor for a period of longer duration) by total employment or, alternatively, by multiplying average hourly earnings by average weekly hours. Computed monthly on an industry basis for comprehensive groups of manufacturing and nonmanufacturing industries by the Bureau of Labor Statistics in its employment and pay-roll reporting program.

gross average hourly earnings. As used by the Bureau of Labor Statistics, a measure of hourly wages obtained by dividing total compensation prior to pay-roll deduction for social security, or other purposes for a given pay-roll period by man-hours worked plus hours paid for sick leave, holidays, and vacations. Total compensation includes premium payments for overtime and late shift work, as well as recurrent production and non-production bonuses. Computed monthly on an industry basis for comprehensive groups of manufacturing and non-manufacturing industries by the Bureau of Labor Statistics in its employment and pay-roll reporting program. See also AVERAGE STRAIGHT-TIME HOURLY EARNINGS and AVERAGE HOURLY EARNINGS EXCLUSIVE OF OVERTIME PAYMENTS.

group annuity insurance. See INSURANCE, GROUP ANNUITY.

group annuity pension plan. Provides annuities at retirement to a group of persons under a master contract. It is usually issued to an employer for the benefit of employees. The individual members of the group hold certificates as evidence of their coverage. The most common type of group annuity provides for the purchase each year of a paid-up deferred annuity for each member, the total amount received by the member at retirement being the sum of these deferred annuities. Another type is the DEPOSIT ADMINISTRATION PLAN, which see.

group annuity plan. A pension plan underwritten and administered by an insurance company under a master contract. The retirement benefit consists of a series of units of paid-up deferred annuities, one unit to be purchased each year for each eligible employee.

group dynamics. Group dynamics is the process by which people interact face-to-face in small groups. Several factors have contributed to the growth of group dynamics. In 1927 the Mayo group of researchers studied human relations at the Hawthorne plant of the Western Electric Company in Chicago and came to some conclusions which showed significant group inter-relationships. See HAWTHORNE EXPERIMENTS. Kurt Lewin, psychologist and philosopher, in 1944 became Director of the Research Center for Group Dynamics at the Massachusetts Institute of Technology. (The Center later moved to the University of Michigan.) One of the first instances of putting group dynamics into practice occurred at the First National Training Laboratory in Group Development held at Bethel, Maine, in the summer of 1947. Annual sessions have been held since. Group dynamics has brought to light the various roles played by people in an interacting group. These include starter, information giver, information seeker, opinion seeker, opinion giver, elabora-

tor, coordinator, tester, summarizer, encourager, the voice, census taker, nose counter, standard setter, follower, evaluator, diagnostician, mediator, reliever of tensions. The very same people may, however, slip Hyde-like into an entirely different set of roles which are non-functional. These include blocker, destroyer, self-confessor, competer, sympathy seeker, special pleader, clown, recognition seeker, nonparticipator. To Lewin the crucial determinant of group atmosphere lies in leadership. A successful resolution of social conflicts or creative accomplishments require in almost all instances the activity of trained democratic leaders. Such a leader plays a dominant part in getting ideas accepted. His job is to integrate ideas, bring out facts, and balance conflicts until agreement is reached. See "Applied Group Dynamics," publication of National Training Laboratories, 1201 Sixteenth St., N.W., Washington, D.C.

group incentive. Any financial incentive plan under which the output of workmen performing the same, related or interdependent operations is pooled and their earnings resulting from production above the established standard are distributed to the members of the group according to some predetermined plan.

group incentive systems. Systems where the earnings of each member of the group are determined first of all by measuring the amount of production which passes inspection as it leaves the group. The total earnings for the group are then determined and if all the members are of equal skill these earnings are usually divided among them equally. Frequently, however, the members of the group are not of equal skill. In these cases the total earnings of the group may be divided among the members in proportion to their individual time rates, or according to specified percentages, or in some cases among only a certain number of the group. Where, for example, the group consists of some highly skilled workers and some quite unskilled workers, or "helpers," the unskilled workers may receive their time rates and the skilled workers share the remainder of the total earnings.

group insurance. A master contract negotiated with an insurance company covering employees of a company. It may provide life insurance, accidental death and dismemberment benefits, annuities, nonoccupational accident and sickness benefits, hospitalization, medical and surgical benefits. The cost may be borne entirely by the employer or may be shared by employer and employees on some predetermined basis. Group insurance may be granted unilaterally by the employer or it may result from collective bargaining.

group leader. A member of a production unit or crew who is responsible for the coordination of the unit's efforts and who may assist other members in the performance of their assigned tasks.

group life insurance. Life insurance issued, usually without medical examination, on a group of persons under a master policy. It is usually issued to an employer for the benefit of employees. The individual members of the group hold certificates as evidence of their insurance.

group payment. See GROUP INCENTIVE.

group payment plan. A pension plan which includes both life insurance and annuity payments. The premiums are paid to the insurance company under the group plan, and the benefits are paid to eligible employees or beneficiaries by the insurance company. This plan is extensively used in larger industries. A policy is purchased for each participant under a group contract negotiated between the company and the employer. Life insurance protection equivalent to $1,000 for each $10 monthly annuity is usually provided. No physical examination is required unless the insurance underwritten for an individual exceeds a specified maximum.

guaranteed rate. The rate of pay guaranteed to an incentive worker. In the case of a production bonus worker, this rate may be equivalent to or higher than the base rate. When earnings at incentive are lower than the guaranteed rates, allowances are made to bring earnings up to the guaranteed levels. See also BASE RATE.

guaranteed time standard. An established expected performance level which management assures will not be changed regardless of workmen's earnings unless there is a significant change in quality requirements, method, materials, tools, layout, equipment, feeds, speeds, design, or working conditions.

guaranteed wage plan. An arrangement, written or unwritten, by which an employer guarantees or assures to some or all of his employees, in advance, a definite period of employment or a specific amount of wages. In a study conducted by the Bureau of Labor Statistics in 1945 and 1946, this term was defined to include guarantees of employment for at least 3 months a year or an equivalent amount of wages. In the ensuing years, a number of guaranteed wage plans with varying provisions, went into effect. What was termed a "historical" contract was signed June 1955 between the United Auto Workers and the Ford Motor Company. By this agreement the company will set up a trust fund to reach $55 million in three years. The fund is to be used to supplement unemployment insurance of laid-off workers in such a way that each worker, after his first week of unemployment, will get 65 percent of his take-home (after taxes) pay for the first 4 weeks, and 60 percent of take-home pay for another 22 weeks. First payments were to begin June 1, 1956. Workers with 90 days' service were eligible. Minimum benefit is $2 a week; maximum $25. This type of "guaranteed wage" plan is entirely different from the so-called guaranteed wage plans which have been adopted by a few companies in the past. Under the latter, guarantees were limited in a number of ways, among them: the amount of pay, the period for which benefits were to be paid, and the number of workers. In addition, many of these traditional plans were established and administered solely by management. See *Questions and Answers about the Guaranteed Annual Wage*, Employee Relations Dept., National Association of Manufacturers. Also, *Bibliography on Guaranteed Annual Wage and Employment Stabilization*, Research Division, California Management Association.

guarantee on trial rate. A minimum guaranteed rate that remains in effect during the time that trial or temporary piece rate is in effect. The level of these guaranteed rates is usually higher than plant minimum job or base rates and is related to past earnings of the individual or the group of workers affected. In order to provide an inducement to the worker to return on an incentive basis as soon as possible, the trial rate is frequently set at 95 or 98 percent of the average earnings of the worker for a given number of weeks prior to the trial run. See also TEMPORARY RATE.

guidance, vocational. The process of assisting individuals to understand their capabilities and interests, to choose a suitable vocation, and to prepare for, enter, and make successful progress in it.

H

halo effect. That tendency on the part of a rater to rate an individual the same on all traits because of the general impression he has, or forms immediately, or because of the effect of one particularly dominating characteristic of the person being rated. It is present in all ratings to a greater or lesser degree and is caused by the rater's inability to isolate and independently evaluate all of the various traits or characteristics which an individual may possess.

Halsey "50-50" plan. Also known as Halsey premium wage system. A method of paying wages by which employees are rewarded for time saved on the job. It represents a compromise between time work and piece work remuneration. Employees are paid a straight hourly wage plus a bonus for work completed in less than an agreed-upon standard time. The bonus usually presents some fraction of the straight-time wages for the time saved instead of the full wages. The plan was originated by F. A. Halsey of the Rand Quill Company of Quebec, Canada. The formula for figuring an employee's earnings under the Halsey plan is:

Up to 62½% of high task (low task):
$$E = H_a R_h \text{ or } E = RT$$

From 62½% of high task on:
$$E = H_a R_h + \text{fraction} \times \text{saving}$$
as $\quad E = H_a R_h + .50 \ (H_s - H_a) \ R_h$
or $\quad E = RT + p (s - t) \ R$
where: E = earnings
$H_a R_h$ or RT = time wages
p = fraction of
$s - t$, or $H_s - H_a$ = savings

"Handicapped Applicant." A term used by the United States Employment Service. See APPLICANT.

"Handicapped Veteran." A term used by the United States Employment Service. See DISABLED VETERAN.

handicapped worker rate. A lower rate of pay for a worker whose efficiency is impaired because of physical or mental handicaps. Under the Federal Fair Labor Standards Act, rates below the legal minimum wage may be established for handicapped workers in accordance with regulations issued pursuant to section 14 of the Act. See also SUBSTANDARD RATE.

handicapped workers. Much interest centers in helping the handicapped. The U. S. Department of Labor issues extensive literature, as do the state departments of labor. "Just One Break, Inc." care of Bellevue Hospital, N. Y. and Abilities, Inc. of West Hempstead, L. I.,

N. Y. are two among many organizations that have done outstanding jobs in hiring handicapped people and helping them to perform useful work. (which see) Information can also be obtained from the Office of Vocational Rehabilitation, Department of Health, Education and Welfare, Washington, D. C.

handling time. (1) The time required to perform the manual portion of an operation. (2) The time required to move materials, or parts, to and/or from a work station.

Hawthorne Experiments. A study made by the Harvard Business School of incentives at the Hawthorne, Illinois plant of the Western Electric Company. During the five-year study, researchers tried out all the known incentives—hours, rest pauses, wage rates, piecework, hot lunches, better lighting, heating, etc. Some of these increased productivity slightly and some did not. But productivity invariably shot up after interviews in which employees were encouraged to air freely their views and feelings about their work and about life in general. To double-check, researchers systematically took away all the other incentives, dimmed the lights or shone them in workers' eyes, made the work area too hot or too cold, increased noise to exasperating levels, and otherwise made working conditions hard. To everyone's astonishment productivity reached an all time high. The conclusion was inescapable: the test employees produced more because they felt they were being recognized and appreciated as individuals and that they were making an important contribution through their work. The studies proved that employees are social beings. Working groups established their own standards of output which were sometimes contrary to those set by management. These social standards were rigidly enforced by the group. The Hawthorne experiments are most extensively reported in "Management and the Worker: Technical vs. Social Organization in an Industrial Plant," by F. J. Roethlisberger and W. J. Dickson, Harvard University Graduate School of Business Administration.

Haynes incentive plan. A wage incentive plan providing premium pay for extra production, and utilizing the manit as in the Bedaux System. The original system provided 50% gain sharing but some adjustments provide up to 100%.

hazards. Exposure or conditions where a chance of loss or injury exists. See ACCIDENT HAZARDS.

Health, Education and Welfare, U. S. Department of. Set up in April, 1953, to replace the old Federal Security Agency. Like its predecessor, the Department of Health, Education and Welfare comprises the Social Security Administration, the Public Health Service, the Office of Education, the Food and Drug Administration and the Office of Vocational Rehabilitation. It has full Cabinet status.

Heller Committee budget. An attempt to measure the cost of maintaining the commonly accepted standard of living of three different occupational groups, designated as "Executive," "White-collar worker," and "Wage earner." The hypothetical budget families are composed of four persons—a man, wife, boy of 13 and girl of 8. The pilot study was made in San Francisco, but can easily be adjusted to the average community. Current data may be obtained from "The Heller Committee for Research in Social Economics," University of California at Berkeley, Cal.

helper. A person who is an assistant, or aide. Usually, by serving as a helper, the person learns the job through work performance and experience, although he may also just do some routine aspects of the job and never master the job itself. A trainee, student, or apprentice differs from a helper, in that they usually also receive formal instruction, and have a definite program of progression laid out for them.

"High-Quarter Formula." A term used by the United States Employment Service. See BENEFIT FORMULA.

hiring. The employment of a new worker. When hiring for the whole organization, or major parts thereof, is done in one office, such as an employment or personnel office, it is known as "centralized hiring"; when the various departments, divisions, or other individual units do their own hiring, "decentralized hiring" is said to be in effect. In many large companies with various branches, hiring may be centralized as far as executives and higher-level jobs are concerned; decentralized for local labor.

"Hiring Authority." A term used by the United States Employment Service. See DELEGATED HIRING AUTHORITY under REFERRAL.

hiring hall. An office used for referring union workers to employers.

Hiring Specifications. An employer's designation as to the characteristics of workers he will hire.

historical wage differential. See WAGE DIFFERENTIAL.

Hobbs Act. See ANTI-RACKETEERING LAW.

hold. An industrial engineering term describing the basic element employed when the hand maintains static control of an object while work is being performed on it.

hold. A THERBLIG (which see) which is defined as: to retain in any way as to prevent movement or escape; to keep in, bear up, restrict, confine, restrain, retain; to sustain or keep in position by means of a support; to maintain in a certain position, to endure, sustain; to remain or continue unchanged in regard to position, state, or condition. The length of time for holding the parts or tool, and the necessity of holding the part or tool for this length of time, must be carefully considered. The part must be held by one hand until it is grasped by the other hand or the part will fall from the hand which held the part.

holiday pay. Pay to workers, typically at regular rates, for holidays not worked. For work on such days payments are often provided at premium rates.

home work. Production carried on in the home of the worker or in a place outside the premises of the employer. The employer supplies the raw materials and usually pays the worker on a piece-time basis. Formerly, "home work" was particularly prevalent in the needle trades, making artificial flowers, working on feathers, cutting scallops on embroidery and similar jobs that could easily be carried from the factory to the home for processing. Home work is now restricted by law in many areas as being socially undesirable both from a labor and health standpoint.

home work defined, under Walsh-Healey Public Contracts Act. Industrial home work is prohibited under the definition of *manufacturer,* which provides that a manufacturer is a person *who owns, operates, or maintains a factory or estab-*

lishment that produces on the premises *the supplies required under the contract.*

home work, regulated, under Fair Labor Standards Act. The Act authorizes the issuance of regulations and orders, regulating, restricting, or prohibiting industrial home work. As of January 1950, the Wage-Hour Administrator had issued regulations restricting home work in the following industries: Jewelry manufacturing industry; Knitted outer-wear industry; Embroideries industry; Handkerchief manufacturing industry; Button and buckle manufacturing industry; Women's apparel industry; Gloves and mittens industry.

horizontal union. A workers' organization in which all the members are employed in the same or related craft. The carpenters' unions are typical of this type of union, in that most of the members are skilled workers. See CRAFT UNION.

"Hospital Dischargee." A term used by the United States Employment Service to designate a person discharged (or scheduled for discharge in the near future) from the armed services through a service hospital.

Hospital Survey and Construction Act. (Act of August 13, 1946) The prevailing wage provisions of this law cover construction contracts made by State or local authorities or private institutions under Federal grant-in-aid programs for the construction of hospitals and other medical facilities such as clinics and nurses' homes.

"Hot Goods." A term used in the Fair Labor Standards Act, which states that it is unlawful "to transport, offer for transportation, ship, deliver, or sell with knowledge that shipment or delivery or sale thereof in commerce is intended" any goods produced in violation of the Act's minimum-wage or overtime provisions. Exemptions are provided under specified conditions for common carriers, and for certain purchasers acting in good faith reliance on written statements of compliance.

hourly rate. Typically, the rate of pay expressed in terms of cents-per-hour, usually thought of as applying to manual and other workers remunerated on a time basis. Hourly rates are normally basic rates; i.e., exclusive of extra payments for shift work and overtime, and exclusive of production or nonproduction bonus payments. However, the term "hourly rate" is sometimes interpreted to mean "earned rate per hour" under incentive methods of wage payment.

hours, actual. Average number of hours worked by all employees per week or per month.

hours, nominal. Scheduled hours, i.e., the planned work day or work week.

hours of work, under Walsh-Healey Public Contracts Act. The basic hours of work are 8 in any one day, or 40 in any one week. Overtime is permitted provided that time and one-half the worker's basic hourly rate is paid for daily or weekly overtime, whichever results in the greater compensation.

hours, standard. Length of the work day or work week as specified in a collective bargaining agreement.

house organ. A company periodical containing articles and pictures about employees, recreation activities, news about new products and information of general interest about the organization. The "International Council of Industrial Editors," is a professional group whose headquarters moves with the current incumbent. Sources of information about house organs include "Employee Publications," Studies in Personnel Policy, No. 31, National Industrial Conference Board; New York, N. Y.; and Printers' Ink Monthly, New York, New York, which periodically issues "A Survey of House Magazines."

"How Supervise?" A personnel test (Quentin W. File and H. H. Remmers, Psychological Corporation. See PUBLISHERS, PERSONNEL TESTS.) Designed for use in selecting candidates for supervisory training or upgrading, in evaluating the results of supervisory training programs, and in counseling of supervisors. The test has three sections: Supervisory Practices, Company Policies, and Supervisor Opinions.

Hoxie, Robert Franklin. (1868-1916) A professor of economics at the University of Chicago. His principal published works were *Scientific Management and Labor* (1915) and *Trade Unionism in the United States* (1917) published after his death from notes. Hoxie's greatest contribution to the theory of unionism was to establish the idea of functional types of labor organization and to identify the principal ones to be found in this country. By "functional" he means a "common interpretation of the social situation," which produces agreement among the group as to the problem facing its members and the kind of remedial program which will solve it. The main types of unionism, according to Hoxie, were five: business, uplift, revolutionary, predatory, and dependent.

hundred per cent incentive. A feature of some wage incentive plans which gives the workman the entire monetary value of the time which he saves by exceeding a specified level of performance.

hundred per cent premium. See HUNDRED PER CENT INCENTIVE.

I

ideation. See "BRAINSTORMING."

"Identification Card, Applicant." A term used by the United States Employment Service. A card given to the applicant on which are recorded identifying information and dates of his visits to the local employment office for placements or benefits.

idle time. (1) A time interval during which either the workman, the equipment, or both do not perform useful work. (2) In motion study, the interval during which a body member does not perform useful work.

illness frequency rate. The number of cases of illness per one thousand employees which result in absences of more than one work day or shift; generally calculated on a monthly basis.

imagineering. See CREATIVE THINKING.

impartial chairman. An individual whose office is maintained jointly by a union and an employer in an industry to aid in the maintenance and interpretation of a labor agreement.

improvement factor. A term used in an agreement negotiated by the United Automobile Workers (CIO) with the General Motors Corporation in May 1948, describing an annual increase in wages of a stipulated amount during the life of an agreement. The improvement factor is designed to enable the wage earner to share in the benefits resulting from increased productivity in the economy. Cost-of-living adjustments were also provided for in this contract.

"Inactive Application Card." A term used by the United States Employment Service. See APPLICATION CARD.

"Inactive File." A term used by the United States Employment Service. A file of inactive application cards.

incentive. Any factor which motivates an employee to maintain or exceed an established standard of performance. An incentive may be financial or non-financial in nature. (which see)

incentive earnings. The amount of money paid to an employee in excess of the guaranteed hourly rate for performance at or above the established standard.

incentive, financial. A particular reward for a particular performance. Financial incentives may be based on direct production, as piecework, task or production bonus; or indirectly may be paid

(136)

for services other than those directly involved in the performance of the job, as bonus for attendance and promptness, length of service or for bringing other persons into the company's employment.

incentive operation. Work compensated for in a manner that motivates those executing it to maintain or exceed an established standard performance level.

incentive opportunity. The possibility for an individual to earn more than his guaranteed base wage rate by maintaining or exceeding the established standard performance level.

incentive pace. The performance level at which a qualified employee works when earning incentive pay.

incentive performance. The execution of work by a qualified individual following a specified method in such a way that his average output during a specified period of time equals or exceeds the established standard level of output.

incentive rate. The term "incentive rate" may apply to a piece rate, a rate of pay per unit for production above a predetermined minimum standard of output, a ratio of management-labor sharing of labor cost savings resulting from the operation of an incentive system, etc. The incentive plan may contain as an integral part of its operation one or more kinds of special rates which also influence the worker's pay: a guaranteed rate, a base rate, a down time rate, special rates for try-out on experimental work, etc.

incentive wage plan. A system providing compensation based on output for employees whose production is in excess of predetermined levels or standards.

Incentives, effect of. The effect of incentives on employees was researched and stated in a summary of a survey of 659 plants conducted by the Bureau of Labor Statistics of the United States Department of Labor, printed in the May, 1943 issue of *Monthly Labor Review*: "An analysis of statistics on hourly earnings of time and incentive workers in identical occupations in three important industries—machinery manufacture, cotton-textile manufacture, and primary fabrication of non-ferrous metals—reveals a definite and substantial margin in favor of workers paid under incentive plans. The data on median earnings show that this advantage ranged from 12.1 percent in the primary fabrication of non-ferrous metals to 18.2 percent in the manufacture of machinery. These findings are of significance for wage negotiations and in the stabilization of wages. They imply the maintenance of substantially higher levels of production under incentive systems of time payment. The higher earnings of incentive workers may result from more intensive effort by the workers themselves, or from greater efficiency on the part of management, or from both of these influences. Fragmentary evidence available for individual industries suggests that the incentive-wage advantage is to be found in both union and non-union establishments, in both the North and the South, and among women workers as well as men."

"Incident Process." A training term representing a technique for developing executive skills. It describes the work of Prof. Paul Pigors and his wife, Faith Pigors, introduced at Massachusetts Institute of Technology where he is associate professor of industrial engineering. Based on the do-it-yourself principle, incident process is designed to sharpen management ability in getting results with people, in organizational problems, in labor relations, and in other phases of leadership. Incident process presents only a bare incident. From this, those taking the course must make their own decisions, after digging for the facts on which the decision is to be based.

income level. The plane of living which any individual or family is able to enjoy, based on their earrnings or other sources of income. The term includes the following: (a) the subsistence level (the emergency or relief standard); (b) the minimum standard of health and decency; (c) the comfort standard; (d) the luxury standard.

income statement. A report of the revenue and expenses of an accounting entity for a specified period of time.

indentured apprenticeship. See APPRENTICESHIP, INDENTURED.

independent union. A labor union organized in a craft or industry which is not affiliated with a national or international union. The term should not be confused with "company unions."

index number wages. Wages which are raised or lowered in some fixed proportion to increases or decreases in the cost of living. See ESCALATOR CLAUSE.

indirect expense. Costs necessary in manufacturing which cannot readily be identified with or charged to a particular product, part, or groups of parts or products.

indirect labor. (1) Work which is performed rendering services necessary to production, the cost of which cannot be assessed against any product, part, or group of parts or products with any degree of accuracy unless undue effort or expense are involved. (2) Necessary work which does not alter the condition, conformation, or construction of the product.

indirect manufacturing expense. See OVERHEAD.

indirect material. Material consumed in the process of production or manufacture that does not become a part of the finished product and/or cannot be readily identified with or charged to a particular part, product, or group of parts or products.

"Individual Aptitude Profile." A term used by the United States Employment Service. The aptitude scores obtained by an applicant for the ten aptitudes measured by the General Aptitude Test Battery.

"Individual Base Period." A term used by the United States Employment Service. See BASE PERIOD.

"Individual Benefit Year." A term used by the United States Employment Service. See BENEFIT YEAR.

individual differences. Characteristics distinctive of one person which are not shared by others. Yet, in industry or business, such wholly dissimilar people are often treated as if they were identical. Management sometimes expresses surprises at the differences in their performance. Individuals, first of all have differences in their *drives*, or instinctive urges, as dominance, submission, creativeness, possessiveness, gregariousness, the homing instinct and the food instinct. Individuals cope with the problems in their everyday life in industry or business in various ways. They may ATTACK a problem, RUN AWAY from it, EVADE it, or SUBSTITUTE an alternate course of action. In substituting, particularly, they may rationalize, redirect activities, identify with others, project or blame someone else, regress to an infantile role, daydream or fantasize, over-compensate, sublimate, develop prejudices, become egocentric, seek sympathy, repress emotions, or become negativistic by refusing to act at all. Personnel executives and industrial psychologists are becoming increasingly aware of the importance of individual differences.

"Individual Duration." A term used by the United States Employment Service. See DURATION OF BENEFITS.

individual policy pension plan. Plan under which company buys an annuity policy for each employee. Usually requires the use of a trust. The plan is more popular in smaller organizations.

individual rate. In many establishments, there is no formal wage structure (either job or rate ranges), and the rates paid are known as individual rates. These rates may be based in a loose way upon the job being done, or may be related to the training, ability, skill, and bargaining power of the individual worker. The term "individual rate" is also used to indicate the rate actually received by the individual worker, as distinguished from the job rate shown in the rate structure maintained by an employer.

induction, of employees. See ORIENTATION.

industrial art. Application of principles of design and aesthetics to the planning and production of manufactured products.

industrial arts education. Instructional shopwork of a non-vocational type which provides general educational experiences centered around the industrial and technical aspects of life today and offers orientation in the areas of appreciation, production, consumption, and recreation through actual experiences with materials and goods. It also serves as exploratory experiences which are helpful in the choice of a vocation.

"Industrial Classification." A term used by the United States Employment Service. A system used in assigning code numbers to employers and/or establishments, based on the nature of their activities, in order that data reported by them may be grouped into industries and combinations of industries for purposes of analysis and publication. The system used by the State employment security agencies in the 1942 edition of the Social Security Board Industrial Classification Code for the nonmanufacturing industries, and the 1945 edition of the Standard Industrial Classification Manual, for the manufacturing industries.

industrial education. A generic term applying to all types of education related to industry, including general industrial education (industrial arts education), vocational industrial education (trade and industrial education), and technical education.

industrial engineer. A person with the necessary qualifications, through education, training, experience and personal characteristics, to perform the work included in the field of industrial engineering.

industrial engineering. The art and science of utilizing and coordinating men, equipment and materials to attain a desired quantity and quality of output at a specified time and at an optimum cost. This may include gathering, analyzing, and acting upon facts pertaining to building and facilities layouts, personnel organization, operating procedures, methods, processes, schedules, time standards, wage rates, wage payment plans, costs, and systems for controlling the quality and quantity of goods and services.

"Industrial Job Family." A term used by the United States Employment Service. See JOB FAMILY.

Industrial Management Clubs, National Council of. A project of the Industrial Committee of the National Young Men's Christian Associations; headquarters at 291 Broadway, New York, 7, N. Y. The 175 existing Industrial Management Clubs represent 4,500 companies in 30 states and Hawaii. The "Y" started industrial recreation in 1869; opened the first night schools and trade schools in 1900; organized the first Foremen's Club in 1903; sponsored the first conference on "Human Relations in Industry" at Silver Bay, N. Y. in 1919. These conferences are currently continuing on an annual basis. The objectives of an Industrial Management Club are: (1) To keep its members in touch with the best thought on industrial management and allied subjects. (2) To provide opportunity for the exchange of ideas and discussion of industrial problems. (3) To build character and good will in industry by recognition of the human element and by promoting a program of mutual service.

industrial relations. See INDUSTRIAL RELATIONS MANAGEMENT. To keep abreast of current studies in industrial relations and personnel administration, the American Management Association publishes an annual, two-part "Progress Report," on "Industrial Relations Research at Universities," in its publication, "Personnel."

industrial relations fraternity. See Iota Rho Chi.

industrial relations management. The planning, supervision, coordination, analysis, and appraisal of industrial relations for the purpose of securing the most efficient cooperation of all groups and persons engaged in the production and distribution of goods and the provision of services.

Industrial Relations Research Association. An organization formed in 1947, with the following purposes: (1) the encouragement of research in all aspects of the field of labor—social, political, economic, legal, and psychological—including employer and employee organization, labor relations, personnel administration, social security, and labor legislation; (2) the promotion of full discussion and exchange of ideas regarding the planning and conduct of research in this field; (3) the dissemination of the significant results of such research; and (4) the improvement of the materials and methods of instruction in the field of labor. The organization takes no partisan attitude on questions of policy in the field of labor, nor will it commit its members to any position on such questions. It holds annual meetings and publishes the proceedings of these meetings. The Board of Directors is drawn from industry, labor, the government and educational institutions.

industrial relations research at universities. Some highly significant findings of practical interest to personnel and industrial relations executives are emerging from the research work being done at a number of our universities. The American Management Association publishes an annual report, as a result of a survey, in an issue of *Personnel*. Many of the research centers publish booklets describing their activities. Almost all publish monographs, bulletins, proceedings; some hold meetings and conferences. Following are well known industrial relations research centers: A. and M. College of Texas, College Station, Texas—Department of industrial Engineering; University of Alabama, University, Alabama —School of Business Administration; University of Arkansas, Fayetteville, Arkansas—College of Business Administration; University of Arizona, Tucson, Arizona —College of Business Administration; University of Baltimore, Baltimore, Maryland—School of Business, Industry and Management; Baylor University, Waco, Texas—School of Business; Boston University, Boston, 15, Mass.—College of Business Administration; University of Bridgeport, Bridgeport, Conn.—Industrial Relations Section; Brown University, Providence, R. I.—Department of Economics; University of Buffalo, Buffalo, N. Y.—School of Business Administration: Department of Industrial Relations; University of California at Los Angeles— Institute of Industrial Relations—College of Engineering: Engineering and Management Course—College of Commerce— Organization Research Project; University of California at Berkeley, Cal.—Institute of Industrial Engineering, Institute of Industrial Relations; California Institute of Technology, Pasadena, California —Industrial Relations Section; Cambridge University, 200 Euston Road, London, W.1, England—Business Administration School; Carnegie Institute of Technology, Pittsburgh, 13, Pa.—Industrial Relations Section, Industrial Management School:

Graduate School of Industrial Administration, Institute of Management Sciences; Case Institute of Technology, Cleveland, 6, Ohio—Operations Research Section; Catholic University of America, Washington, 17, D. C.—Department of Economics, Graduate School of Social Science; Central Missouri State College, Warrensburg, Missouri—Department of Business Administration; University of Chicago, Chicago, 37, Illinois—Industrial Relations Center: (a) Union Leadership Development Project, (b) Management Leadership Project, Executive Program, Management Services—School of Business Monthly; University of Cincinnati, Cincinnati, 21, Ohio—College of Business Administration; City College of New York, New York, 31, N. Y.—Bernard M. Baruch School of Business and Public Administration; Clark University, Worcester, 3, Mass.—School of Business Administration; Cleary College, Ypsilanti, Michigan—Industrial Relations Section; Colgate University, Hamilton, N. Y.— Psychological Laboratory; University of Colorado, Boulder, Colo.—School of Business; Columbia University, New York, 27, N. Y.—School of Business—Graduate School of Business—Department of Industrial Engineering—Bureau of Applied Social Research—New York School of Social Work; University of Connecticut, Storrs, Conn.—Labor Management Institute—Department of Industrial Administration; Cornell University, Ithaca, N. Y. —Executive Development Institute— Graduate School of Business and Public Administration—School of Industrial Labor Relations: (1) Publishes "Industrial and Labor Relations Review of Cornell University," (2) Research in labor-management relations, labor economics, labor conditions and problems, labor organizations, government and labor, social insurance, industry, personnel, sociology and psychology in industry; Creighton University, Omaha, 2, Nebraska—College of Commerce; Dalhousie University, Halifax, Nova Scotia—Maritime Bureau of Industrial Relations; Dartmouth College, Hanover, N. H.—The Amos Tuck School of Business Administration: publishes "A Reading List on Business Administration"; University of Dayton, Dayton, Ohio—Department of Industrial Engineering; University of Denver, Denver, 10, Colorado—College of Business Administration; De Paul University, Chicago, Illinois—Institute of Industrial Psychology; University of Detroit, Detroit, 21, Michigan—Industrial Management Section; Drake University, Des Moines, 11, Iowa—College of Business Administration; Duquesne University, Pittsburgh, Pa.—School of Business Administration; Duke University, Durham, N. C.—School of Business Administration; Emory University, Emory University, Georgia— School of Business Administration; Fenn College, Cleveland, 15, Ohio—Personnel Development Dept.; University of Florida, Gainesville, Florida—Division of Industrial Relations; Fordham University, New York, 7, N. Y.—School of Business; University of Georgia, Athens, Ga.—College of Business Administration; Harvard University, Boston, 63, Mass.—Graduate School of Business Administration—Harvard Business School: publishes "Harvard Business Review"; University of Hawaii, Honolulu, Hawaii—Industrial Relations Center; Hoffstra College, Hempstead, L. I., N. Y. Human Relations Conferences Section; University of Houston, Houston, 4, Texas—Personnel Psychology Service Center; University of Illinois, Urbana, Illinois—Institute of Labor and Industrial Relations, College of Commerce and Business Administration—Bu-

reau of Business Research and Service, publishes "Business Management Service"; Illinois Institute of Technology, Chicago, Illinois—The Armour Research Foundation; Indiana University, Bloomington, Indiana—Department of Management and Bureau of Personnel Relations and Placement—Department of Economics: Division of Economic Research— School of Business: Executive Development Program; The State University of Iowa, Iowa City, Iowa—Bureau of Management and Labor Relations—College of Commerce; Johns Hopkins University, Chevy Chase, Maryland—Operations Research Section—Dept. of Political Economy, publishes Economics Library Selections; University of Kansas, Lawrence, Kansas—School of Business; Kent State University, Kent, Ohio—College of Business Administration; University of Kentucky, Lexington, 29, Kentucky—College of Commerce; Lehigh University, Bethlehem, Pa.—College of Business Administration; Louisiana State University, Baton Rouge, Louisiana—College of Commerce; University of London, London, England —Business Administration School; Loyola University, Chicago, Illinois—Departments of Psychology and Economics—Institute of Social and Industrial Relations —School of Social Work—Profit Sharing Research Foundation; Marquette University, Milwaukee, 3, Wisconsin—Management Center—College of Business Administration—Bureau of Business and Economic Research; University of Maryland, College Park, Maryland—Department of Business Organization; Massachusetts Institute of Technology, Cambridge, Mass.—Department of Economics and Social Science—Industrial Relations Section: School of Management—The Executive Development Program was established under a grant from the Alfred P.

Sloan Foundation, Inc. Publishes: Library Accessions Bulletin of the Industrial Relations Library. Research in industrial relations focuses on five broad areas: (1) labor market and the process of wage determination, (2) labor-management relations, including public policy aspects, (3) patterns of communication in groups, (4) personnel policies and methods, (5) comparative studies of industrial relations in other countries; University of Massachusetts, Amherst, Mass.—Humanities Center; McGill University, Montreal, 2, Canada—Applied Psychology Laboratory; McMurry College, Abilene, Texas—School of Business Administration; Miami University, Oxford, Ohio—Industrial Management Section; Michigan State University, East Lansing, Michigan—Labor and Industrial Relations Center—Department of Business and Economics—Department of Psychology; University of Michigan, Ann Arbor, Michigan—Bureau of Industrial Relations—Institute for Social Research: Survey Research Center, Institute for Social Research—Department of Economics —Department of Psychology—Institute of Labor and Industrial Relations jointly sponsored with Wayne State University; University of Minnesota, Minneapolis, 14, Minn.—Industrial Relations Center; University of Mississippi, University, Mississippi—School of Business Administration; Mississippi State College, State College, Mississippi—School of Business and Industry; University of Missouri, Columbia, Missouri—School of Business Administration; Montana State University, Missoula, Montana—School of Business Administration; University of Montreal, Montreal, P.Q. Canada—Industrial Relations Section; University of Nebraska, Lincoln, 8, Nebraska—College of Business Administration; University of Ne-

vada, Reno, Nevada—College of Business Administration; University of New Mexico, Albuquerque, N. M.—College of Business Administration; New York University, New York, N. Y.—The Management Institute—Institute of Labor Relations and Social Security— Wallace Clark Center of International Management—Annual Conference on Labor; University of North Carolina, Chapel Hill, N. C.—School of Business Administration; University of North Dakota, Grand Forks, N. Dakota—School of Commerce; Northeastern University, Boston, 15, Mass.—Industrial Management Dept.—Bureau of Business Research; Northwestern University, Evanston, Ill. —School of Commerce—Institute for Management; University of Notre Dame, Notre Dame, Indiana—Bureau of Economic Research; Ohio University, Athens, Ohio—College of Commerce; Ohio State University, Columbus, 10, Ohio—College of Commerce and Administration—Bureau of Business Research—Personnel Research Board; University of Oklahoma, Norman, Oklahoma—Department of Business Management; Oklahoma City University, Oklahoma City, Okla.—School of Business;—University of Oregon, Eugene, Oregon—School of Business Administration; University of Ottawa, Ottawa, Ontario, Canada—Institute of Psychology; Pennsylvania State University, University City, Pa.—College of Business Administration: Economics Department, Bureau of Business Research—Personnel Service Division; University of Pennsylvania, Philadelphia, Pa.—Wharton School of Finance and Commerce: Labor Relations Council, Industrial Research Department; University of Pittsburgh, Pittsburgh 13, Pa.—American Institute for Research, Inc.—School of Business Administration; Princeton University, Princeton, N. J.—

Department of Economics and Sociology —Industrial Relations Section: Publishes monthly "Selected References"; Purdue University, Lafayette, Indiana—Department of Industrial Education—School of Industrial Engineering and Management —Management Sciences Research Group: Occupational Research Center—Division of Education and Applied Psychology. This unit also conducts an Industrial Personnel Testing Institute and an Industrial Vision Institute; Radcliffe College, Cambridge 38, Mass.—Management Training Program for Women; Rensselaer Polytechnic Institute, Troy, N. Y. —Personnel Testing Institute; University of Richmond, Richmond, Va.—Dept. of Business Management; Rockhurst College, Kansas City 10, Missouri—Personnel Management Department; Roosevelt University, Chicago, Illinois—Department of Economics; Rutgers University, New Brunswick, N. J.—Institute of Management and Labor Relations; St. Louis University, St. Louis 3, Missouri— School of Commerce; St. Peter's College, Jersey City, N. J.—Institute of Industrial Relations; University of San Francisco, San Francisco 17, California— College of Business Administration; Sacramento State College, Sacramento, California—Business Administration; San Jose State College, San Jose, California— Division of Business; University of Santa Clara, Santa Clara, Cal.—College of Business Administration; Simmons College, Boston, Mass.—School of Business; University of South Dakota, Vermillion, S. D.— School of Business Administration; University of Southern California, Los Angeles 7, Cal.—College of Commerce—The Organization Project; Southern Methodist University, Dallas 5, Texas—The Institute of Management, sponsored by Texas Manufacturers Asso-

ciation—Dept. of Personnel Administration; Stanford University, Stanford, Cal. —Graduate School of Business: Division of Industrial Relations—Dept. of Industrial Engineering; Stevens Institute of Technology, Hoboken, N. J.—Laboratory of Psychological Studies; Syracuse University, Syracuse 10, N. Y.—College of Business Administration—Business and Economic Research Center of the Institute of Industrial Research; Temple University, Philadelphia 22, Pa.—School of Business Administration—Bureau of Industrial and Special Services; University of Tennessee, Knoxville 15, Tenn.—College of Business Administration; University of Texas, Austin 12, Texas—Dept. of Managament, College of Business Administration—Bureau of Business Research; Texas Western College, El Paso, Texas—Department of Economics and Business Administration; University of Toronto, Toronto, Canada—Institute of Industrial Relations; Tulane University, New Orleans 18, La.—College of Business Administration; University of Tulsa, Tulsa, Oklahoma—College of Business Administration; University of Utah, Salt Lake City, Utah—School of Business— Institute of Industrial Relations; University of Virginia, Charlottesville, Va.— McIntire School of Commerce—Graduate School of Business Administration; Wake Forest College, Wake Forest, North Carolina—School of Business Administration; Washington and Lee University, Lexington, Virginia—School of Commerce and Administration; State College of Washington, Pullman, Washington— School of Economics and Business; University of Washington, Seattle 5, Washington—College of Business Administration—Institute of Labor Economics; Washington University, St. Louis 5, Missouri—School of Business Administration; Wayne State University, Detroit, Michigan—School of Business Administration—Department of Management: this has superseded both the "Personnel Research Center" and the "Department of Personnel Methods"—Institute of Labor and Industrial Relations jointly sponsored with University of Michigan; Western Michigan College, Kalamazoo, Michigan—School of Business; Western Reserve University, Cleveland 8, Ohio—Personnel Research Institute—Department of Industry; West Texas State College, Canyon, Texas—School of Business Administration; West Virginia University, Morgantown, West Virginia—Institute of Industrial Relations; College of William and Mary, Williamsburg, Virginia—Department of Business Administration; University of Wisconsin, Madison 6, Wisconsin—Industrial Management Institute—Industrial Relations Research Center—Bureau of Industrial Psychology—Bureau of Business Research and Service; Yale University, New Haven, Connecticut—Labor and Management Center—Institute of Human Relations.

industrial revolution. The change occurring when an economy passes from predominantly rural or manual to factory or industrial production. The "Industrial Revolution" came to England when inventions in the textile industry replaced the home looms in the middle of the 18th century. The steam engine was also a contributing factor. Currently, "automation" is said to be causing an "industrial revolution" in manufacturing establishments and offices.

"Industrial Services." A term used by the United States Employment Service. The following services which are provided through local offices to employers and to labor and other organizations to aid them in resolving manpower problems: (1) assistance in analyzing and evaluating the basic causes of in-plant manpower problems in individual establishments; and (2) giving instruction in the application and/or use of those materials, techniques, and related information developed by the employment service, which will aid in resolving these manpower problems.

industrial union. A union which has members engaged in various occupations, both skilled and unskilled, in a particular industry. The industrial union had its origin in the Knights of Labor of the 1870's but with the rise of craft consciousness in the American Federation of Labor industrial unions tended to disappear. Both the International Workers of the World (I.W.W.) and the Communist Party sought to foster industrial unionism to combat the conservative policies of the craft unions. Agitation for the organization of the unskilled workers on an industrial basis began in the A.F. of L. in the 1920's but the indifference of the craft unions and jurisdictional jealousies prevented active organization until 1936 when John L. Lewis, of the United Mine Workers, formed the Committee on Industrial Organization within the A.F. of L. Opposition to the Committee's activities forced the Committee to leave the ranks of the A.F. of L. and form the Congress of Industrial Organizations which soon started to rival the A.F. of L. in numbers and power. Bargaining power of an industrial union is secured by 100 per cent organization of workers rather than by the monopoly power over a few strategic skills.

industrial vision research. A program of sight conversation is in effect at Purdue

University, Lafayette, Indiana. Data from many companies have made it possible to develop "Visual Performance Profiles" for hundreds of different jobs. These profiles, when compared with an individual's visual skills, show immediately whether the employee's visual skills are adequate for the job in question. The profiles thus identify those employees who are working under a visual handicap in terms of their particular job. One study was conducted to see whether minimum or maximum visual skill standards were to be employed in the construction of the visual skill profiles. This study showed that the minimum standards are preferable since there are many jobs that do not show an appreciable increment in performance with a corresponding increase in visual skill after the visual skill has reached a certain magnitude although, in general, the better the visual skill the higher the likelihood of superior performance. Another project was completed which indicated that visual acuity requirements for the job studied are general and relative and not specific and absolute and that the use of standardized (or composite) profiles instead of individual profiles can be used with success in differentiating low- from high-criterion employees.

Industrial Workers of the World. A well known labor organization, described as radical, which once had a reputed peak strength of 100,000 members but has declined through the years to the point where it is now regarded chiefly as a chapter in labor history. Enemies called the organization "wobblies" and "I Won't Workers." The basic ideology of the I.W.W. is expressed in its constitution adopted in Chicago in 1905: "The working class and the employing class have nothing in common," it asserts. "There can be no peace so long as hunger and want are found among millions of working people and the few who make up the employing class have all the good things of life . . . Between these two classes a struggle must go on until the workers of the world organize as a class, take possession of the earth and the machinery of production and abolish the wage system." At the founding convention were "Big Bill" Haywood, head of the Western Federation of Miners, a left-wing labor organization, and Eugene V. Debs, later Presidential candidate of the Socialist party. A strike of Haywood's union in 1903 had led to formation of the I.W.W.

"Industry Code." A term used by the United States Employment Service. The number which identifies an industry or group of industries in the industrial classification system.

"Industry Composition Pattern." A term used by the United States Employment Service. See OCCUPATIONAL COMPOSITION PATTERN.

"Industry Description." A term used by the United States Employment Service. The description of the activities included in an industry which is identified by a code and title in an industrial classification system.

"Industry Title." A term used by the United States Employment Service. The title given to an industry which has been defined and given an industry code in an industrial classification system.

industry-wide bargaining. See BARGAINING, INDUSTRY-WIDE.

industry-wide strike. See STRIKE, INDUSTRY-WIDE.

inequities. Wages and working conditions which are grossly out of line with the remainder of the wage structure in a particular plant, area or industry.

"Information Stations." A term used by the United States Employment Service. Points established on principal highways, commonly traveled by migrant agricultural workers, for the purpose of measuring the composition, volume, timing, and direction of migratory movements, supplying current crop and employment information to migrants, and transmitting advice of the movements to local employment offices in destination areas. *Intrastate Information Station*: A station operated by a State agency which provides service primarily to migrants whose next work area lies within the State. *Interstate Information Station*: A station operated by the Bureau which provides service primarily to migrants enroute to the employment areas within two or more States.

"Initial Claim." A term used by the United States Employment Service. See CLAIM.

"Initial Determination." A term used by the United States Employment Service. See DETERMINATION.

initiation fee. The sum of money required to be paid by an employee who seeks admission to a union.

injunction, labor. A court order issued to restrain one or more persons or corporations—i.e. a party to a labor dispute —from doing some act which they threatened to commit, or from continuing the prosecution of some act which is already in process, for a specified time period. The injunction has been perhaps most frequently used by employers to prevent or check strikes, picketing or boycotting, on the grounds that their business has been or will be affected.

injunctions in special cases, under Anti-Injunction Act (which see). Temporary or permanent injunctions may be issued by Federal courts without regard to the above provisions of the act, even though a labor dispute may exist, in the following instances: (1) Where an injunction is properly sought by the National Labor Relations Board pending the determination of an unfair labor practice proceeding, (2) in cases where the Board seeks to enforce an order issued by it or an aggrieved party desires to contest the Board's order, or (3) where, in the case of a threatened or actual strike affecting an industry engaged in interstate commerce which would imperil the national health or safety, the Attorney General of the United States requests an injunction. The act does not affect the jurisdiction of Federal courts to issue injunctions in labor disputes between the United States and its employees.

inspect. See EXAMINE.

inspect. A THERBLIG (which see) which is defined as: to examine carefully and critically; to investigate, behold, examine for condition, shape, etc.; to direct a gauge toward an object for the purpose of inspecting it; to exercise the sense of sight attentively; to take care, bestow watchful attention, watch. *Inspect* may include whatever movements are necessary to place and remove the part where it can be seen, or mechanically checked, or it may consist entirely of the use of some one or more of the senses, or it may be one of the various possible combinations of both. The movements should be easy, natural, precise, non-fatiguing, easy for alignment, within range of vision, and all within one area of sight.

inspection. Examining an object for identification or checking it for verification of quality or quantity in any of its characteristics.

installation. (1) The execution of the steps or measures necessary to introduce a procedure, proposed course of action or technique into an organization and to get it functioning properly. (2) An equipment arrangement or procedure that is being set up or used by a company.

Institute for Certifying Secretaries. This institute was established in 1950 under the sponsorship of THE NATIONAL SECRETARIES ASSOCIATION (which see) for the purpose of developing an examination for secretaries. The Institute is composed of six educators, six leading management figures, and six members of THE NATIONAL SECRETARIES ASSOCIATION (which see) plus the President and Immediate Past President of that organization. Extensive research was done in order to determine the work actually performed by leading secretaries over the country; and it was found that secretaries have more than 800 separate duties. The research material was sifted and re-sifted to decide what duties more clearly defined actual secretarial work and what fields should be tested. The result was a six-section examination first administered in 1951. A Certified Professional Secretary is one who has satisfactorily completed all six parts of the examination, these parts being Personal Adjustment and Human Relations, covering the fundamentals of mental, emotional, social, and physical adjustment, problems relating to the exercise of judg-

ment by the secretary in the solution of problems in dealing with superiors, colleagues and subordinates; Business Law, which covers contracts and bailments, the law of agency and sales, insurance, negotiable instruments, and real property, plus the interpretation of the legal implications involved in a secretary's daily work; Economics and Business Administration, covering fundamental economic concepts found in the secretary's day-to-day contacts with prices, taxes, labor, social responsibilities of business, government regulation of business, business organization and management, types of ownership, staffing a business and management controls, techniques of supervision and management, preparation and utilization of various means of communication within and outside a business organization; Secretarial Accounting, which covers principles of accounting and business records in relation to government regulations, employer's personal record keeping, payroll, petty cash, interpretation of financial records as they relate to top-level secretarial work; Stenography, the taking and the transcribing of letters and other business materials, composing business letters and reports from memoranda and rough drafts, grammar, spelling, and punctuation problems; and General Secretarial and Office Procedures, covering knowledge of modern methods of handling mail, dictation, and transcription problems, records management, communications media, selection and procurement of materials and equipment, and duplicating processes. The purpose of CPS is (1) to elevate secretarial personnel throughout the country; (2) to define more clearly the status of secretarial work in the business structure; (3) to establish educational standards for secretaries and promote them through an examination; (4) to give secretaries an educational goal; (5) to gain recognition for secretaries by furthering their educational and professional status; (6) to assist employers in selecting secretarial employees; (7) to assure that only qualified persons will be considered for secretarial positions; (8) to assist schools and colleges in determining content for secretarial training programs; and (9) to broaden the scope of secretarial training to meet more nearly the needs for top-level secretarial positions. To be eligible to take the examination, an applicant must be at least 25 years of age and must give references covering secretarial experience. The examination is open to both men and women, and the applicant does NOT have to be a member of The National Secretaries Association nor does the applicant have to be employed as a secretary at the time of taking the examination. If not a high school graduate, an applicant must have at least seven years actual secretarial experience. If a high school graduate, six years secretarial experience is required. If a graduate of a high school and accredited business college, junior college or equivalent, four years secretarial experience is required. If a college graduate, the applicant must have at least three years secretarial experience.

The Institute of Management Sciences. A non-profit society, formed December 1, 1953 by individuals active in research or practical applications of the management sciences. Purpose of the society (abbreviated TIMS) is "to identify, extend, and unify scientific knowledge that contributes to the understanding and practice of management . . . to cooperate with other organizations in the advance-ment of the practice of management; to stimulate research and promote high professional standards in the development of a unified management science; and, in general, to promote the growth of management science and its practice." The membership includes scientists, managers, educators, government officials and labor union representatives. Specifically, the aims are defined as: (1) To bring to TIMS members a well-rounded concept of their profession—putting each member into contact with others who are active in the field, and to supply a better understanding of the opportunities and responsibilities that this work is creating. (2) To bring to management information about successful, proven ideas, methods and techniques. To supply information on newly emerging ideas and methods. To provide management with the means of acquiring informed judgment in appraising its own operations. (3) To bring to management deeper realization of the importance of technological developments and scientific research to reach the highest obtainable levels of productivity and efficiency. (4) To bring to management a keener realization of the need for, and possibility of, better methods of comparative measurement as a basis for establishing standards for progressive advancement. (5) To bring to TIMS members specific methods and procedures—including case histories—to further individual advancement and progress in general. (6) To bring managers and scientists together in meetings, where ideas and experiences in management and in science can be discussed with mutually beneficial results. (7) To bring to educators and their students information on the objectives and progress of TIMS—and to provide a convenient means for acquainting students with recent knowledge and potential progress in research, applications, and current practice. (8) To bring representatives of government ideas that may prove helpful in mobilizing and utilizing our national resources with a proper balance between long run objectives and immediate necessities. (9) To bring to everyone an opportunity for sharing in the fruits of scientific knowledge.

instruction, of employees. See JOB INSTRUCTION.

instruction card. See INSTRUCTION SHEET.

instruction sheet. Written information which contains organized material for the use of a workman or student taking vocational education, apprenticeship, induction or other job training. Common types are: *Operation sheet*—gives directions on how to perform a single manipulative task. *Job sheet*—gives directions on how to do, completely and in proper sequence, a number of operations. In both instances, the sheet specifies method, machines, and, when appropriate, their speeds, feeds, and depth of cut, tools, fixtures, specification limits, and the like to be used in performing a task. *Assignment sheet*—in the case of a trainee, directs the study to be done by the student on the lesson topic, and may include questions to determine how well the lesson has been learned.

insurance, group. See GROUP INSURANCE.

insurance, group annuity. A type of insurance which provides protection by allowing employer to provide employees with added retirement income over and above that which they will receive under the SOCIAL SECURITY ACT.

insurance, health. A general term covering all plans for offering medical care,

hospitalization and cash disability benefits or any one of these separately on a pre-payment basis. The most extensive and controversial of these plans are the government sponsored plans prevalent throughout Europe. While not typical of all such plans English health insurance comes closest to American thought on the subject. The government, the employer and the employee contribute to a pooled fund. In order to receive cash benefits for disability the insured joins a club through which the benefit is paid. Medical care is offered by any one of a panel of doctors in the local community that the patient selects. Doctors are paid by the government a per capita fee for all persons selecting them as attending doctor regardless of the amount of medical service rendered. In the U.S. similar plans are proposed or in operation but they are sponsored through private rather than public agencies.

insured plan. A pension plan arrangement whereby the employer makes payment to an insurance company to cover cost of pension program. The insurance company guarantees benefits to workers. This may be in the form of a GROUP ANNUITY, GROUP PAYMENT or INDIVIDUAL POLICY PENSION PLAN, which see.

"Insured Employment." A term used by the United States Employment Service. Unemployment during a given week for which waiting-period credit or benefits are claimed under the State employment security program, the unemployment compensation for Federal employees program, the unemployed compensation for veterans program, or the railroad unemployment insurance program.

"Insured Status." A term used by the United States Employment Service. See DETERMINATION.

"Insured Work." A term used by the United States Employment Service. Employment as defined in a State employment security law, performed for a subject employer, or Federal employment as defined in title XV of the Social Security Act.

"Insured Worker." A term used by the United States Employment Service. An individual who has had sufficient insured work in his base period to meet the requirements for receipt of benefits under a State employment security law.

intelligence quotient. The numerical ratio between the chronological age of a person and his mental age times 100 in order to give a whole number. If a ten-year-old child makes a score on an intelligence test equal to that of a ten-year-old, his IQ is 100; if it is only equal to a seven-year-old, his IQ is 70; if it is equal to an eleven-year-old, his IQ is 110.

intelligence tests. Tests designed to measure general mental ability. Most generally used in personnel work in testing candidates for employment. Intelligence tests are intended to give information about a person's judgment, memory, type of response to given situations, ability to learn, follow instructions, and maintain attention. They do not purport to test acquired knowledge, education, or efficiency of performance. Among well-known intelligence tests are: American Army, Alpha and Beta Tests; Binet, Thorndike; and the Otis self-administered tests. In "Personnel and Industrial Psychology," Edwin E. Ghiselli and Clarence W. Brown say, "The major characteristic of intelligence tests which is so often overlooked, is that they are intended primarily to give a very general and over-all picture of an individual's abilities. Like tests of any other kind, intelligence tests measure several different abilities. Important differences between intelligence tests and other tests are that intelligence tests tend to measure a large number of different abilities, and the abilities that they do measure tend to be of a more abstract and purely intellectual nature, such as those important in school and academic success. This is best shown by the types of items ordinarily included in an intelligence test. One finds in them questions on vocabulary, sentence completion, arithmetic, analogies, meaning of proverbs, reasoning problems etc. If the purpose and nature of intelligence tests are kept in kind, it will be apparent that these tests will have limited use in business and industry. It cannot be expected that they will be of value for all personnel problems."

intelligence tests, types of. Intelligence tests that are in use in industry are of two types, omnibus and battery. Omnibus tests have an over-all time limit and over-all score. Usually the items of which they are composed are arranged in order of increasing difficulty, and are selected from longer and well-tried tests. Battery tests consist of a number of tests combined together into one group and under one caption. Each subtest usually contains one type of material and attempts to evaluate only one phase of ability, and each subtest has a time limit and specific directions. The result of the combined group is given as an over-all score, and separate norms and critical score ranges are provided for the separate subtests. Well-known intelligence tests include: Adaptability Test— Tiffin and Lawshe—Science Research Associates; Army General Classification Test—Science Research Associates; Purdue Industrial Training Classification Test—Lawshe and Motoux—Science Research Associates; SRA Verbal Classification Form—Thurstone and Thurstone—Science Research Associates; SRA Non-verbal Classification Form—McMurray and Johnson—Science Research Associates. Thurstone Test of Alertness—Science Research Associates; P.T.I. Oral Directions Test—Langmuir—Psychological Corp.; Scoville Classification Test—Psychological Corp.; Otis Self-administering Test of Mental Ability—Psychological Corp.; Wechsler Adult Intelligence Scale—Psychological Corp.; Mooney Problem Check Lists—Mooney and Gordon—Psychological Corp.; Social Intelligence Test—Moss, Hunt and Omwake—Psychological Corp.; Store Personnel Test—Seashore and Orbach—Psychological Corp.; Chicago Non-verbal Examination—Brown—Psychological Corp.; Goodenough Intelligence (Draw-a-Man) —Psychological Corp.; Henmon-Nelson Tests of Mental Ability—Psychological Corp.; Kuhlmann-Anderson Intelligence Tests—Psychological Corp.; Personnel Tests for Industry-Staff—Psychological Corp.; Pintner General Ability Tests—Psychological Corp.; Watson-Glaser Critical Thinking Appraisal—Psychological Corp.; Wesman Personnel Classification —Psychological Corp.; Wechsler-Bellevue Intelligence Scale—Psychological Corp. See PUBLISHERS, PERSONNEL TESTS.

intercity differential. Differences in prevailing wage levels among a group of cities. Usually such differences are measured by rates for comparable occupations and industries from city to city, but more general measures are sometimes employed. In particular negotia-

tions, historical relationship in rates between various cities may be of prime importance. In such instances, the rank of a particular city with respect to other cities may be of more significance than the percentage relationships among the cities over a period of years.

"Interest Check List." A term used by the United States Employment Service. A selected list of jobs tasks, used as an aid in determining vocational interests.

interests tests. The purpose of interest tests is to ascertain: (1) has the person being tested well-established interest in the type of work for which he is being considered? (2) is he interested in different types of work to such an extent that he will easily become dissatisfied with the job to which he is being assigned? (3) does the candidate share common interests with those with whom he will be associated? Interest tests in use are: Vocational Interest Blank for Men, Strong—Psychological Corporation; Vocational Interest Blank for Women, Strong—Psychological Corporation; The Brainard Occupational Preference Inventory—Psychological Corporation; C—R. Opinionaire, T. F. Lentz et al.—Psychological Corporation; Minnesota Inventories of Social Attitudes, Williamson and Darley—Psychological Corporation; Edwards Personal Preference Schedule, Allen L. Edwards—Psychological Corporation; Kuder Preference Record—Personal.—G. F. Kuder—Science Research Associates; Primary Business Interests Test, Cardall—Science Research Associates; Test of Practical Judgment, Cardall —Science Associates. See PUBLISHERS, PERSONNEL TESTS.

interference time. A period of time during which one or more machines are not operating because the workman or workmen assigned to operate them are busy operating other machines in their assignment or are performing necessary duties related to operating such other machines as making repairs, cleaning the machines or inspecting completed work.

intermittent element. In industrial engineering terminology, an element essential to an operation which occurs at less regular intervals than those of the regular or basic cycle of elements.

internal element. In industrial engineering terminology (1) any element performed by a workman while the machine he controls is operating automatically. (2) A short duration element performed by one hand while the other hand is performing a more time-consuming element.

International Federation of Trade Unions. A world labor organization formally reconstituted in 1919 following a Congress held at Amsterdam. It consists of trade unions of various nations, including the American Federation of Labor, for the collection and dissemination of labor information and expression of organized labor's views and objectives. It was dissolved in December 1945, and succeeded by the World Federation of Trade Unions in 1946.

International Labor (Labour) Organization. (ILO). Division of the United National Organization which collects and publishes labor information and formulates minimum international labor standards to be acted upon by national legislatures. The ILO was originally established at the second session of the Peace Conference in 1919 as an integral part of the League of Nations. There are three divisions: (1) the International Labour Conference, (2) the Governing Body and (3) the International Labour Office. The governing body is made up of 32 persons, 16 government representatives, and 8 representatives each from employer and labor groups. See INTERNATIONAL LABOUR REVIEW.

International Labour Review. Published monthly since 1897 in English, French and Spanish. It is the official journal of the International Labour Organization and deals mostly with labor matters of international concern. The Review has an extensive section on industrial and labor information of wide general interest, a statistical section, and a series of valuable book notes or reviews.

international union. The parent organization of affiliated unions in one craft or industry in the United States, Canada, Mexico and other American nations. Examples of international unions with locals in both the United States and Canada are: United Automobile, Aircraft and Agricultural Implement Workers of America (U.A.W.); Textile Workers Union of America (T.W.U.).

"Interstate Arrangements." A term used by the United States Employment Service. *Interstate Benefit Payment Plan*: The plan under which each State acts as an agent for every other State in taking claims for individuals who are not in the State in which they earned their base-period wages. *Interstate Reciprocal Coverage Arrangement*: An administrative interstate arrangement, permitted under most State employment security laws, which provides for the election of coverage of services under specified conditions which may or may not constitute an exception to the mandatory coverage provisions of the State law. *Wage-Combining Arrangements—*

Basic plan: An interstate agreement which allows workers who lack qualifying wages in any one State to combine wages from more than one State, to become eligible for benefits. *Extended plan*: An interstate agreement which allows workers having sufficient base-period wages to qualify for less than maximum benfits in one or more States, and insufficient base-period wages in other States, to increase benefits by combining wages.

"Interstate Claim." A term used by the United States Employment Service. See CLAIM.

"Interstate Claimant." A term used by the United States Employment Service. An individual who files a claim for benefits in an agent State on the basis of employment covered by the employment security law of a liable State.

"Interstate Conference of Employment Security Agencies." A term used by the United States Employment Service. An association of State employment security agencies whose objective is to advance employment security by encouraging the study, development, and acceptance of more efficient methods of administration; in cooperating with the Bureau of Employment Security toward attaining this objective, it represents the collective viewpoint of State agencies.

Interstate Transportation of Migrant Farm Workers. Act of August 3, 1956. This act amends the Interstate Commerce Commission Act of certain transportation in interstate and foreign commerce of migrant farm workers. The amendment defines the term "carrier of migrant workers by motor vehicle" as any person, including any "contract carrier by motor vehicle," but not including any "common carrier by motor vehicle," who transports in interstate or foreign commerce at any one time three or more migrant workers to or from their employment by motor vehicle other than a passenger automobile or station wagon, except migrant workers transporting themselves or their immediate families. A migrant worker is defined as any individual proceeding to or returning from employment in agriculture. The amendment requires the Interstate Commerce Commission to establish for carriers of migrant farm workers by motor vehicle reasonable requirements with respect to the comfort of passengers, qualifications and maximum hours of service of operators of the vehicles, and safety of operation and equipment. Such requirements are to apply to any such carrier only in the case of transportation of migrant workers for a total distance of more than 75 miles, and then only if such transportation is across the boundary line of any State, the District of Columbia, or Territory of the United States, or a foreign country. For further information write to the Director, Bureau of Motor Carriers, Interstate Commerce Commission, Washington 25, D. C.

"Interview." A term used by the United States Employment Service. *Application Interview*: A face-to-face discussion between an employment service interviewer and an applicant for the purpose of (1) obtaining information about the applicant's qualifications for work ;(2) ascertaining any need he may have for employment counseling; and (3) providing him with information which may increase his opportunities for placement. *Counseling Interview*: An interview (1) in which a face-to-face discussion occurs between a counselor (or a staff member designated and trained to provide the counseling services offered by the local office) and an applicant who needs assistance regarding problems of vocational choice or vocational adjustment; and (2) which results in obtaining and recording on the application card one or more of the following: (a) a summary statement to establish the existence of a problem of vocational adjustment, (b) additional information contributing to a sharper definition of the problem or to its solution, (c) a statement of a vocational plan or recommendaton for the solution of the problem, (d) a statement concerning the outcome and effectiveness of the counseling service elicited in the course of follow up. *Eligibility-Benefit Rights Interview*: A detailed interview with a claimant for the purposes of (1) explaining his monetary determination, (2) exploring his eligibility for benefits, and (3) explaining his rights and responsibilities under the law; or alternately, an interview with a claimant, who has been determined to be monetarily ineligible for purposes of (1) explaining his monetary determination, (2) ascertaining the possibility of missing wage credits, and (3) advising him as to possible future rights. *Employment Counseling Interview*: A face-to-face discussion between a counselor and an applicant who needs assistance in solving problems of vocational choice or vocational adjustment. *Periodic Interview*: An extended interview of preselected claimants to re-examine more thoroughly their continuing eligibility. *Pre-Referral Interview*: A face-to-face discussion between an employment service interviewer and an applicant to determine the applicant's qualifications for and interest in specific job openings. *Selection Interview*: An interview in which (1) the qualifications of an applicant or groups of applicants represented by a leader are reviewed in relation to specific job openings which are available in the local office and for which the applicant or applicants may be qualified, and (2) the applicant or representative of a group of applicants and a staff member, responsible for deciding whether to refer or reject the applicant or applicants for available job openings, participate. *Based on Selection Notice*: An interview with an Applicant whose application card was selected from the file for purposes of filling a specific job opening available in the local office, and who was notified of such selection. *Self-Application Interview*: A face-to-face discussion between an employment service interviewer and an applicant to review the applicant's self-application card to insure that it contains information sufficient for purposes of selection. *Subsequent Application Interview*: An interview during which (1) information is obtained to bring up to date an application card by adding to or changing the recorded information so as to include new or additional work experience or educational qualifications, or a change in physical qualifications which affects the occupational qualifications of the applicant, and (2) counseling, selection interviewing, or testing does not occur.

interview, employment, evaluation of. Proper evaluation of the employment interview serves to promote its general usefulness. Points to remember are: (1) The interview should be intelligently limited to elicit certain required facts and to appraise important personal characteristics. The interview should not be

(155)

used to secure estimates about those aptitudes, skills, or other attributes for which sound and practical measuring devices exist or can be readily developed. (2) The interview should be made more reliable and more valid. Many companies report amazing improvement in the reliability and objectivity of judgment if interviewers are given appropriate training both before handling applicants and on a continuing basis on the job.

interview, employment, nature of. The employment interview is characterized: (1) by an exchange of ideas and information and (2) by an exchange of attitudes to enable the interviewer to determine whether the applicant is suitable for the job. The interviewer must appraise the qualifications of individuals in respect to differences in intelligence, dexterities, coordination, aptitudes, trade knowledge and proficiency, education, experience, stability, interests, and ability to cooperate with others. Some additional criteria of evaluation may also be demanded by various jobs. In some instances, the applicant may not be suited in the job for which he is being interviewed, but the alert interviewer may place him in another opening for which he has qualifications.

interview, employment, objectives of. The general objective of the interview is described under the heading, INTERVIEW, EMPLOYMENT, NATURE OF. Specific objectives include: (1) To afford the opportunity to judge an applicant's qualifications as a basis for sound selection and placement. (2) To give the applicant essential facts about the job and the company (nature of the work, hours, medical requirements, opportunities for advancement, special hazards,

employee benefits and services, company policies, etc.) to enable him to decide intelligently as to the acceptability of the employment. (3) To initiate a feeling of mutual understanding and confidence—between the personnel department and the applicant who is employed. (4) To promote good will toward the company, whether or not the interview culminates in employment.

interview, employment, physical setting of. The physical setting is determined by such factors as: (a) the volume of applicants handled; (b) the type of jobs for which hiring is done; (c) the need for nearness to other sections of the employment of personnel departments; (d) whether the volume of employees handled in the future will tend to increase or decrease. Some criteria are: (1) Sufficient permanent space should be provided to accommodate three-quarters of the peak load of applicants. Advance arrangements should also be made for handling peak loads. Cafeterias and other large rooms can often be temporarily used. (2) Furniture and equipment should be tasteful and functionally be arranged. (3) Light, heat and ventilation should be adequate. (4) Reading material, particularly facts about the company, should be available. (5) Provision should be made for hanging coats and hats. (6) Such cheerful notes as a bowl of flowers, a mirror, or a wall picture are helpful. (7) Washroom and toilet facilities should be in close proximity to the waiting room. (8) If possible, smoking should be permitted. (9) Arrangements should be made to have an exit from the interview room direct to the street or outer hall so rejected or accepted applicants will not influence those who are waiting.

interview, employment, techniques of. Three broad phases of interviewing include: (A) Arranging the circumstances of the interview. (1) Schedule appointments; (2) Prepare to give sufficient time to each interview; (3) Insure a maximum of privacy. (B) Planning the course of the interview. (1) Are the applicant's qualifications to be considered in relation to a particular job, or several? In either case, is the interviewer familiar with job requirements? (2) Has the interviewer carefully examined the application? Number of positions and length of time held, breaks in service, progression in past employment, etc.? (3) Does the way in which the application has been filed out—legibility, neatness, completeness of information, agreement in dates —tell anything significant about the applicant? (4) When practicable, has the interviewer already gathered required information about the applicant from reliable sources (e.g., previous employers, etc.) so interview time may be used to obtain data which only the applicant can give and to observe personality characteristics? (5) In the available information, are there clues to establish rapport with the applicant? Is there anything about his education, family, previous employment, which would furnish good material for opening remarks. (6) Is the interviewer conscious of prejudice arising out of race, color, creed, previous experience or other factors which he must be prepared to discount? (7) What information should the interview yield? (8) Has the interviewer on hand all the material and equipment needed (job specifications, rating scale, other forms?) (C) Conducting the Interview. (1) Opening the Conversation (2) Observing— good observation includes a) alertness, b) the ability to make reasonably accu-

rate estimates without the use of special instruments, c) the capacity to make fine distinctions, d) freedom from various pathological states, e) making an immediate and accurate record, f) the ability to perceive accurately, g) freedom from prejudice or from habits of interpretation, h) freedom from excitement. (3) Questioning. a) Clarity of meaning— words connecting with the applicant's experience, b) suggestiveness—avoiding suggestive questions that bring negative answers. (4) Evaluating and interpreting interview data. (5) Terminating the interview when: a) The interviewer has discovered a definite basis for disqualification, b) he has obtained the pertinent information required for a final decision, c) he has collected as much information as is customary at this stage and wishes to send the applicant on to the next step in selection.

interview, employment, type of. Three types of interviews which can usually be differentiated are: (1) preliminary interviews—the first screening device utilized in the personnel department. (2) final interviews, which may consist of: a) additional personnel department interviews, b) line department interviews. (3) follow-up interviews or reports—continuing the liaison between the personnel department, the supervisor and the new employee.

interview, exit. See EXIT INTERVIEW.

"Interviewing Aid." A term used by the United States Employment Service. "A card which lists aspects of the job in which significant variations may occur. It serves as the basis for asking questions that assist the interviewer in obtaining information regarding applicant's qualifications and employer's requirements for a specific job."

interviewing, pitfalls in. Preconceived habits of thought and action are detrimental to sound interviewing. Some pitfalls are: (1) Personal bias, both favorable and unfavorable. Some interviewers hesitate to hire a man who avoids looking them in the eye, doodle, are jittery, or whose dress prejudices them. (2) A pseudo-scientific attitude such as identifying certain physical characteristics with personality traits and specific talents. (3) Stereotyped interviewing, or asking the same questions in exactly the same way and in the same sequence. (4) Placing too great reliance on previous experience of the same type as that required on the job. (5) Tactlessness, in respect to questions about age, handicaps, or other personal characteristics.

Iota Rho Chi. First professional fraternity in field of industrial relations, organized in 1957 at University of Minnesota. Purpose: to further professional status and encourage competent practice of industrial relations. Membership is open to men and women taking graduate training in field and to practitioners who have demonstrated professional competence.

inventory. (1) All the materials, parts, supplies, expense tools, and in-process or finished products recorded on the books by an organization and kept in its storerooms, warehouses, or plants. (2) A list of the names and/or quantities, and/or monetary values of all or any group or classification of the items specified in (1). Used as a verb to inventory means to identify, count, weigh, or measure; i.e. to evaluate the worth of all or any group or classification of items specified in (1) and to record this information.

irregular element. An industrial engineering term. See INTERMITTENT ELEMENT.

"Itinerant Point." A term used by the United States Employment Service. "A location at which employment security services are provided on a scheduled part-time basis by staff from a local office operated at another location." See also LOCAL OFFICE.

J

jig. A device which holds a piece of work in a desired position and guides the tool or tools which perform the necessary operations.

Jim Crow laws. Any legislative measure which tends to discriminate or segregate colored from white people, especially in drawing a sharp line of demarcation between these races as to the type of work in which they may make their living.

job. (1) A position or post of employment. (2) A specific task, or group of tasks, assigned to an employee.

"Job Analysis." A definition used by the United States Employment Service is: "The process of determining, by observation, interview, and study, pertinent information relating to a specific job, including factors such as duties, responsibilities, purpose, qualifications for employment, relations to other jobs, equipment and material used, and training and physical demands data."

job analysis. A detailed study of the component parts of a job to discover duties, operations and skills necessary to perform a clearly defined, specific job; physical and mental requirements, tools and equipment used, lines or promotion, experience and abilities, require- ments, wage rates, working hours and conditions and relationships to other jobs, organized and listed in a logical sequence. Also see JOB CLASSIFICATION.

"Job Breakdown." A definition used by the United States Employment Service is: "The division of a complex job, requiring extensive training for mastery, into a number of work units, any one of which can be mastered by less skilled workers."

job characteristic. See JOB FACTOR.

job class. (1) A group of jobs or positions having approximately the same relative worth as determined by a job evaluation plan. (2) A group of jobs or positions with duties and responsibilities so similar that individuals with approximately equivalent education, experience, skills, and the like are required for their satisfactory performance.

job classification. An arrangement of jobs in an establishment or industry into a series of categories, each of which is based on progressively higher requirements in terms of skill, experience, training, and similar considerations. Essentially, this process results in a rough grouping of occupations where distinctions between jobs are clear and sharp.

Usually job descriptions are used as a basis for classification. See also JOB EVALUATION and LABOR GRADE.

job comparison scale. A listing of job factors and the points or money assigned to key jobs under each factor.

job content. The duties, functions, and responsibilities comprising a given job.

job descriptions, supervisory. See SUPERVISORY JOB DESCRIPTIONS.

job description. A summary of the most important features of a job, in terms of the general nature of the work involved and the types of workers required to perform it in an efficient manner. The job description usually includes the job title, the classification number, a brief statement of tools or equipment used, the usual physical position of the worker, a description of the material used, the training required, the amounts and types of compensation, the usual working hours and special conditions under which the employee will have to work. Also, the requirements of the worker such as physical characteristics required, as to weight, appearance, height, visual demand; and mental qualifications as responsibility for work of others; responsibility for safety. The *job description* is a description of a job, and *not* of the individual who fills it. See also JOB EVALUATION.

"Job Description." A definition used by the United States Employment Service is: "A detailed description of a complete job which highlights such significant factors as the purpose, duties, equipment, working conditions, qualifications, relation to other jobs, training information, physical demands, and employment factors. *Local Job Description.* A job description based on analysis of a job in a

given local area and representative only of the local characteristics of that job. *National Job Description.* A composite of a complete job, based on analyses made in a number of representative communities throughout the country. See also OCCUPATIONAL GUIDE. *Pamphlet Job Description.* A National Job Description, published in pamphlet form, which describes a single job. *Volume Job Desription.* A volume of National Job Descriptions which describes the jobs found in a specific industry."

"Job Development." A term used by the United States Employment Service to designate the process of soliciting an employer's order for a specific applicant for whom the local office has no suitable opening currently on file.

job enlargement. A specific program of adding more and varied operations to a job and giving an employee more responsibility, so that he finds some intrinsic meaning in his work. Four basic requisites of job enlargement defined by management consultant Peter Drucker are: a worker must understand what he is doing and be interested; he must understand what is going on around him; he must feel that he is a real member of the working community; he must get recognition, prestige and a chance to participate.

"Job Evaluation." The term, as used by the United States Employment Service in its *Employment Security Manual* is defined as the process of determining the relative values of individual jobs in an organization so as to establish a wage classification system for that organization.

job evaluation. A systematic procedure for maintaining proper differentials between basic compensation rates within an organization by the use of some sound and defensible measuring stick. The first serious movement toward the use of formal job evaluation as an analytical approach to setting wage differentials began around 1930. Since then an ever-increasing number of companies have adopted the procedure. Job evaluation is always applied to jobs rather than the qualities of individuals in the jobs. The evaluation may be achieved through the assignment of points or the use of some other systematic rating method for essential job requirements or job factors. Many successful evaluation plans consider from ten to twenty-five job factors; others employ only a few. A characteristic plan (11 job factors) (included in "Job Evaluation," Studies in Personnel Policy No. 25, National Industrial Conference Board), follows:

Skill	Relative Weight
Education required	14
Experience required	22
Initiative and ingenuity required	14
Effort	
Physical demand	10
Mental or visual demand	5
Responsibility	
Responsibility for equipment or process required	5
Responsibility for material or product required	5
Responsibility for safety of others required	5
Responsibility for work of others required	5
Job Conditions	
Working conditions involved	10
Unavoidable hazards involved	5

See also, *Manual of Job Evaluation,* by Benge, Burk and Hay, Harper & Brothers.

job evaluation manual. A handbook explaining a job evaluation plan and how it is to be installed and administered.

job factor. Any characteristic of a job which influences its relative worth or value and provides a basis for the selection, training, placement and compensation of employees. Major job characteristics or factors are skill required, responsibility exercised, physical and mental effort involved, working conditions, and experience and education required.

"Job Family." A term used by the United States Employment Service to designate a grouping of jobs which have varying degrees of the following elements in common: work done; tools, machines, or other work aids used; materials worked with; knowledge and skill required; and worker characteristics needed for successful performance. The service has three types of job families: *Industrial Job Family ("I" Series).* Groups of jobs related to the jobs in a selected industry or industrial process. Related jobs given may be in other industries or in the same industry. *Occupational Job Family ("O" Series).* Groups of jobs related to a specific base job or a small group of base jobs. *Special Job Family ("S" Series).* An occupational industrial, or special type job family for use in a particular region, or office and not usually printed for general distribution.

job family. See JOB CLASS.

job grading. That phase of a systematic program of wage and salary administration which involves job evaluation for the purpose of arranging all jobs into a series of grades according to relative difficulty, responsibilities required, and working conditions.

job hierarchies. A system of groupings whereby job families are classified in ranks or orders.

job instruction. The formal approach to job instruction is generally credited to the late Charles R. Allen, author of "The Instructor, the Man and the Job," J. B. Lippincott Co., 1919. Allen divided the teaching of any lesson into four steps: Preparation, Presentation, Application and Test. The Preparation (Step I) embraces those preliminary questions put to the learner by the instructor to prepare his mind for the new ideas to put over in Presentation (Step II). These questions must lead up to a smooth transition from Step I to Step II, which Allen calls the j.o.p. or "jumping off place." It is here that the instructor begins his presentation of new ideas by lecture, demonstration, illustration or any combination of these methods. Step III, Application, gives the learner an opportunity to apply immediately any new ideas he has received in Step II; Step IV, Test, may occur immediately at the close of Step III, or it may occur later, on the job. In either case, in this step the learner, without assistance from anyone, must perform the newly taught operations one or more times successfully.

"Job Instruction." A ten-hour Training Within Industry (which see) program, based on the principle that "if the learner hasn't learned, the teacher hasn't taught." To get ready to instruct: Break Down the Job—list important steps; pick out the key points. (Safety is always a key point.) Have Everything Ready—the right equipment, materials and supplies. Have the Workplace Properly Arranged

—just as the worker will be expected to keep it. The four steps on how to instruct are: (1) Prepare the Worker; put him at ease; state the job and find out what he already knows about it; get him interested in learning job; place in correct position. (2) Present the Operation; tell, show, and illustrate one IMPORTANT STEP at a time; stress each KEY POINT; instruct clearly, completely, and patiently, but no more than he can master. (3) Try Out Performance; have him do the job—correct errors; have him explain each KEY POINT to you as he does the job again; make sure he understands; continue until YOU know HE knows. (4) Follow Up; put him on his own; designate to whom he goes for help; check frequently; encourage questions; taper off extra coaching and close follow-up.

"Job Inventory." A term used by the United States Employment Service. See PERSONNEL RECORDS. See also STATE INVENTORY OF JOB OPENINGS.

job lot. A relatively small number of a specific type or part of a product that is produced at one time. The part or product may be a standard item that has been and will again be produced, or it may be a special item destined for a specific customer who has not ordered it before and may not order it again.

job lot layout. An arrangement of machines, equipment, and facilities specially set up or arranged to handle job lot production.

job lot production. The manufacturing of parts or products to customer or stock orders in small quantities.

"Job Methods." A ten-hour Training Within Industry (which see) program,—a practical plan to help produce greater quantities of quality products in less time by making the best use of manpower, machines and materials available. It is based on four steps: (1) Break Down the job: list all details of the job exactly as done by the present method; be sure details include all material handling—machine work—hand work. (2) Question every detail. Use these types of questions: WHY is it necessary? WHAT is its purpose? WHERE should it be done? WHEN should it be done? WHO is best qualified to do it? HOW is the best way to do it? Also question the: Materials, Machines, Equipment, Tools, Product Design, Layout, Work-place, Safety, Housekeeping. (3) Develop the new method: ELIMINATE unnecessary details; COMBINE details when practical; REARRANGE for better sequence; SIMPLIFY all necessary details; To make the work easier and safer: Pre-position materials, tools, and equipment at the best places in the proper work area; use gravity-feed hoppers and drop-delivery chutes; let both hands do useful work; use jigs and fixtures, instead of hands, for holding work; WORK OUT your idea with others; WRITE UP your proposed new method. (4) Apply the new method: sell your proposal to your "boss"; sell the new method to the operators; get final approval of all concerned on Safety, Quality, Quantity, Cost; put the new method to work; use it until a better way is developed; give credit where credit is due.

"Job Opening." See OPENING.

"Job Opening for Inventory." A term used by the United States Employment Service to designate a form used by an order-holding office for submitting clearance job openings for inclusion in the State Inventory of Job Openings.

job rate. See MINIMUM JOB RATE and STANDARD RATE.

Job Rating. Title of a procedures manual presenting definitions of the factors used in rating hourly paid jobs, description of each level of each factor and a table of points assigned to the factors. Originally published by the National Metal Trades Association, Chicago, Ill., and widely adapted.

joint rate setting. The process of establishing rates jointly by representatives of management and labor. The extent of labor participation in the actual process of rate setting varies from industry to industry and from establishment to establishment. In some of the apparel industries, the unions have achieved a relatively high degree of participation through formal joint organizational machinery. At the other extreme are situations where management alone sets rates, but labor through its grievance machinery has the right to "protest" specific rates, and to adjust them in conference with management if the grievance is found to have validity.

job reclassification. Changing the rate for any occupation without involving related occupations.

"Job Relations." A ten-hour Training Within Industry (which see) program. It is based on four steps showing how to handle a problem: (1) Get the Facts: review the record; find out what rules and plant customs apply; talk with individuals concerned; get opinions and feelings; be sure you have the whole story. (2) Weigh and Decide: fit the facts together; consider their bearing on each other; ask what possible actions are there?; check practices and policies; consider objective and effect on individual, group and production; don't jump at conclusions. (3) Take action: Are you going to handle this yourself? Do you need help in handling? Should you refer this to your supervisor? Watch the timing of your action. Don't pass the buck. (4) Check Results: How soon will you follow up? How often will you need to check? Watch for changes in output, attitudes and relationships. Did your action help production? The principles of "Job Relations" training are that a supervisor gets results through people and people must be treated as individuals. "Foundations for Good Relations" are: Let each worker know how he is getting along. Give credit when due. Tell people in advance about changes that will affect them. Make best use of each person's ability.

"Job Requirements." A term used by the United States Employment Service. See PERFORMANCE REQUIREMENTS.

job rotation. A term designating a schedule or plan to permit an employee to move about different jobs; (1) it applies to learners or trainees who move from job to job or even among departments to gain diversified experiences in several operations or phases of the work; also it applies to a schedule whereby employees work at different job assignments of the same or similar classifications, so that the same employees do not always get desirable or undesirable duties.

job safety. See ACCIDENT PREVENTION. Foundations for establishing job safety are: (1) Make a Regular, Systematic Check-Up of Hazards: Locate unsafe mechanical or physical conditions. Observe unsafe acts. Keep devices and safety equipment in good order. Fit personal protective clothing individually.

Recommend corrective measures. Detect and correct. (2) Welcome Safety Suggestions: Give credit for ideas. Watch people's attitudes, traits and habits. Investigate all complaints and suggestions thoroughly. (3) Explain New Rules or Changes: Hold occasional group meetings on safety subjects. Remind people of hazards often. Give reasons, not arbitrary decisions. Never make a rule that can't be enforced. (4) Teach the Job Fully and Logically: Break down every job. List principal steps. Stress safety key points. Don't talk safety as a separate subject.

job satisfaction. A constructive wholesome attitude on the part of employees. Robert Hoppock, in "Job Satisfaction," (Harper & Brothers, 1935) has published the results of an interesting investigation into the problem of job satisfaction and the conditions that favor it. He reached the conclusion that job satisfaction is related to a good many things besides financial return, such as relative status of the individual within the social and economic group with which he identifies himself, relations with superiors and associates on the job, nature of the work, earnings, hours of work, opportunities for advancement, variety, freedom from close supervision, visible results, the satisfaction of doing good work, opportunities for service to others, environment, freedom to live where one pleases, responsibility, vacations, excitement, opportunity for self-expression, competition, religion, opportunity for or necessity of traveling, fatigue, appreciation or criticisms, security, and ability to adjust oneself to unpleasant conditions. The "Personnel and Guidance Journal," published by the American Personnel and Guidance Association, Inc., publishes an annual series of "Job Satisfaction Researches," listing all studies on this subject. See also "Job Satisfaction," by Robert Hoppock (Harper & Bros.).

job seeking. Much help is available through the United States Employment Service, scores of private agencies, and books and publications for those seeking jobs. The American Management Association puts out a "Guide to Job Seekers." Other books on the subject include: "Blueprint Your Career," by Robert F. Moore (Stackpole and Heck); "How to Get and Hold the Job You Want," by Ruth H. Larison (Longmans, Green and Co.); "How You Can Get a Job," by Glenn L. Gardiner (Harper & Bros.); "6 Ways to Get a Job," by Paul W. Boynton (Harper & Bros.); and many others.

job shop. A manufacturing enterprise devoted to producing special or custom-made parts or products usually in small quantities for specific customers.

"Job Solicitation." A term used by the United States Employment Service. The process of soliciting employers' orders for workers seeking employment through the local office, except that solicitation for a specific applicant is defined as job development. See JOB DEVELOPMENT.

job specialization. A term used to denote a highly simplified, repetitive job. The fundamentals are: separate the planning from the doing, break the job down into mechanical sequence of simple motions, each of which an employee could repeat over and over at a rate determined by the entire production machinery. The idea of specialization—of every man for his trade—was supported by Greek statesmen and philosophers. "More is done, and done better," according to Plato, "when one man does one thing according to his capacity and at the right moment." See ASSEMBLY LINE.

"Job Specification, Employer-Prepared." A term used by the United States Employment Service. A statement, prepared by an employer for his own use, which contains information about the content of a job in his establishment.

Job Specification, Employment Service. A term used by the United States Employment Service. A continuing record of a specific job prepared by an employment service staff member on the basis of observation of the job in the employer's establishment. This record (1) specifies those facts about the job which are essential in order to locate and select workers for it; and (2) expresses agreement as to the requirements to be used by the Employment Service in selecting applicants for referral and by the employer in hiring workers for the job.

job specification. A detailed written statement of the physical and mental attributes required of a person to perform a specific job competently.

job standardization. The establishment of a prescribed method for performing an operation or procedure and the specifying of its minimum requirements.

"Job Vacancy." A term used by the United States Employment Service. A job for which the employer's hiring schedule calls for recruitment of a new worker currently or during the next week, excluding short-time jobs (those expected to last for not more than three days). A job vacated, or expected to be vacated in the next week, as a result of turnover is considered to be a job vacancy if the employer has scheduled a new hire for replacement purposes; scheduled call-backs of workers on temporary lay-off are not job vacancies. If it is not known whether recruitment will be for new workers or call-backs, the scheduled hires are considered to be job vacancies. The time period of reference for vacancy data is the date on which the information is furnished by the establishment.

joint apprenticeship council. A group of representatives of employers and labor, organized to cooperate with vocational schools in setting up, conducting and maintaining standards for apprenticeship programs.

Joint Congressional Committee on the Economic Report. Committee established following a provision for its formation by the Employment Act of 1946 (which see). It is made up of seven Senators and seven Representatives. It is required by law to evaluate the President's annual Economic Report. It has the responsibility of preparing committee recommendations on the proposals contained in the Report.

joint time study. (1) A time-study technique that utilizes more than one observer and is often used to study large, complex operations performed by more than one employee. (2) A time study made by both company and union representatives in order to prevent or to resolve disagreements over time standards.

journeyman. A worker who has satisfactorily completed his apprenticeship and is classified as a skilled worker in his trade.

journeyman rate. The rate of pay for a journeyman or a fully qualified worker in a skilled trade or craft, who has com-

pleted an apprenticeship or equivalent training. Typically, such rate is a minimum rate for the trade in a particular area of a union scale; some journeymen, however, may receive rates above or below the union scale. The latter are generally paid to certain employees (superannuated or handicapped) by special arrangement with the respective unions.

Junior Achievement. The national headquarters of this organization are Junior Achievement Incorporated, 345 Madison Avenue, New York 17, N. Y. The Achievement movement, incorporated since 1926, got its start when the late Horace A. Moses, chairman of the Strathmore Paper Company, argued that American high school students should have the chance to learn the principles of our free enterprise system along with their formal education. In the beginning the program was limited to New England, but in 1942 the group set up headquarters in New York and operations have been enlarged to the extent that there are now over 1,800 companies throughout the United States. In each community the program is developed by local community leaders who organize a local Junior Achievement committee which assumes the responsibility for guiding and financing the program. Anyone between the ages of 15 and 21, regardless of race, color or creed, is eligible to join the program. Achievers meet one night a week during the school year (September to June) and are assisted in the various phases of running their companies by adult advisors. The Junior Achievement miniature businesses follow the same pattern as any company. The young people assigned, under the direction of three advisors, meet for the first time. The first order of business is to decide upon a company product or service they wish to sell. Products range from ash trays to lamps, from toys to shampoo; services include banking, advertising, and many others. Here, at the first meeting, the students learn that they have to consider markets in selecting the type of product or service they would like to sell. A name must be chosen for the firm, and the students elect their own officers and apply for a charter. Now that the company has been formed, the only thing missing is capital to buy raw materials, machinery, and pay wages. So another lesson is learned —capitalization. Stock is sold by the students at 50c a share, and usually around two hundred shares are sold. Every Achiever must be a share owner in his or her company, but no one may purchase more than five shares of stock in ony one company and the stock is non-transferable. The Achievers sell stock to their parents, friends, and neighbors who in turn also get a keen insight into this important phase of operating a business. Each company then opens a bank account, and signs a lease for the use of the room in which it will operate and for the machinery needed. With the capital raised, each company purchases raw materials and sets up production lines. Production methods are explored and short-cuts developed to improve efficiency and to keep costs and prices down. All students in the company are members of their board of directors and do all the work themselves under the guidance of their advisors. They set their own pay scales, selling prices, sales commissions, and discounts. Products are sold door-to-door, by mail order and through local retailers. At times, members of the production force double as salesmen. During the year the treasurer

and secretary keep books which are equal to those which you would find in any well-organized business. They file reports and pay all applicable federal, state and local taxes. At the end of the business year, each Achievement company deliberately goes out of business. Inventory and raw materials are liquidated and all bills are paid. The board of directors decides whether dividends can be paid to share owners, whether bonuses can be paid to workers. Share owners' notices are sent out along with proxy cards, and an annual report is presented to all share owners. All of the necessary business forms, instructions, guides and pamphlets, needed in the complete organization and operation of Junior Achievement companies are furnished by Junior Achievement national headquarters. Near the end of the year, Junior Achievement companies compete for national awards in various fields of business, which are provided by various national business associations. In addition, each Achiever can compete for scholarships provided by schools, organizations, and individuals. Progress recognition certificates are awarded which correspond to the individual Achiever's development in the program.

jurisdictional dispute, under National Labor Relations Act (which see). The act forbids jurisdictional strikes and boycotts as an unfair labor practice and provides special machinery for deciding disputes over the assignment of work. Section 8 (b) (4) makes it an unfair labor practice for a labor organization or its agents *to engage in, or to induce or encourage the employees of any employer to engage in, a strike or concerted refusal in the course of their employment to use, manufacture, process, transport, or otherwise* *handle or work on any goods, articles, materials, or commodities or to perform any services, where an object thereof is: . . . (D) forcing or requiring any employer to assign particular work to employees in a particular labor organization or in a particular trade, craft, or class rather than to employees in another trade, craft, or class, unless such employer is failing to conform to an order or certification of the Board determining the bargaining representative for employees performing such work . . .* Section 10 (k) gives the Board authority to hear and decide cases involving jurisdiction of work. This section states that *Whenever it is charged that any person has engaged in an unfair labor practice within the meaning of paragraph (4) (D) of section 8 (b), the Board is empowered and directed to hear and determine the dispute out of which such unfair labor practice shall have arisen, unless, within ten days after notice that such charge has been filed, the parties to such dispute submit to the Board satisfactory evidence that they have adjusted, or agreed upon methods for the* *voluntary adjustment of the dispute. Upon compliance by the parties to the dispute with the decision of the Board or upon such voluntary adjustment of the dispute, such charge shall be dismissed.* Should the parties fail to reach agreement, the procedure before the Board is the same as in any other unfair labor practice case.

jurisdictional dispute. (1) A disagreement between members of two or more different trade unions as to who should perform a particular type of work; i.e. the allocation of particular job functions to specific jobs. (2) Disputes between or among rival or different unions competing for members in a given craft, plant or industry.

jurisdictional strike. Strike due to a disagreement between two or more unions over the right to represent a certain group of workers.

jurisdiction, union. Exclusive right to represent certain workers within specified occupations, industries, or geographical boundaries.

K

Keays-Weaver Plan. A wage incentive system similar to DYER SYSTEM, which see.

key job. A job used in job evaluation systems as a guide or bench mark when evaluating other jobs. It is selected because its duties and responsibilities are known and are relatively stable, and because both management and labor agree that the evaluation of, and the wage paid for, the job are fair and equitable. The wage paid for key jobs serves as a basis for setting wage rates for other jobs.

key personnel. Personnel which is essential to an organization or which cannot be replaced without causing a reduction in efficiency or in output. Examples of key personnel are: top management executives, foremen, scientists, engineers, designers, financiers—all those who possess special skills, knowledge or experience which cannot be acquired quickly and where persons cannot be replaced without delay.

kick-back. A practice by which an employer or his representative arranges with his workers for a return of a part of their wages, established by union contract or by law, as a condition of employment. The FEDERAL ANTI-KICKBACK LAW was enacted in 1934 (which see) prohibiting kick-backs by workers employed on public construction work or on any work financed wholly or in part by Federal funds.

K. I. M. System. A wage incentive system evolved by King, Irvin and MacLachan. Similar to Dyer System.

Knoeppel System. A wage incentive system, the provisions of which are almost the same as in the Emerson Graduated Bonus Plan.

Korean GI Bill of Rights (Veterans Readjustment Assistance Act of 1952. Act of July 16, 1952), as amended. The Veterans Readjustment Assistance Act of 1952, otherwise known as the Korean GI bill, permits eligible veterans who have had active service in the U.S. Armed Forces any place in the world between June 27, 1950, and January 31, 1955, inclusive, to receive an education and training allowance while pursuing a program of education or training at an approved educational institution or job training establishment. It also provides loan credit assistance to veterans for the purchase, construction, or improvement of homes, farms, and business property, and provides for mustering-out payments and unemployment compensation. Title IV of the act, establishing unemployment compensation and the provision of Title II dealing with on-the-job training are summarized as follows: *Unemployment Compensation for Veterans*: Qualified veterans may receive unemployment compensation benefits under Title IV of the Veterans Readjustment Assistance Act of 1952 as amended. These benefits are paid by the State employment security agencies under agreements with the Secretary of Labor. *Qualifications for Receiving Unemployment Compensation*: To be eligible for unemployment compensation, the veteran must: (a) Have had military service between June 27, 1950 and January 31, 1955, inclusive. (b) Be discharged under conditions other than dishonorable. (c) Have at least 90 days service or be released because of actual service-incurred disability or injury. *Benefit Payments*: The veteran is entitled to receive $26 for each week of total employment until a maximum of $676 has been paid. If he has benefit rights under a State unemployment compensation law or the Federal Railroad Unemployment Insurance Act, of $26 a week or more, he must exhaust these benefits before being eligible to receive Title IV payments. If his weekly benefit amount under the State or railroad unemployment insurance law is less than $26 per week, he is entitled to a supplement to make up the difference between his State or railroad benefit and $26. After he has exhausted his State or railroad benefits he may be eligible for $26 a week until the total of $676 has been paid. No benefits are payable for weeks of unemployment during the period for which a veteran receives mustering-out pay and generally no benefits are payable to a veteran receiving educational or subsistence allowances under the act. Under the 1955 amendments to the Veterans Readjustment Assistance Act of 1952, no compensation is payable for weeks of unemployment occurring after 3 years from the date of discharge or from July 26, 1955, whichever is later, and in no event for any period after January 31, 1960. For further information go to the nearest local public employment office or write to the State Employment Security Agency of your State, in the capital city, or to the Bureau of Employment Security, U. S. Department of Labor, Washington 25, D. C.

kymograph. An electrical recording device, used chiefly in laboratory micromotion studies, developed by Dr. Ralph M. Barnes, to measure extremely short (.0001 minute) time intervals. Solenoid operated pencils, when actuated by pushbuttons, photocells, or other contacting devices, make jog marks on a motor driven tape which moves at a constant velocity. The distance between the jogs indicates the elapsed time interval.

L

labor. (1) The mental and/or physical effort and energy expended by humans to produce and distribute materials, goods, and services. (2) Employees with little or no supervisory responsibilities whose sole or main task is to aid in the production of materials, goods, or services. (3) To work or toil.

labor class. See JOB CLASS.

labor, common. The workers engaged in the manual occupations. They generally perform the simple types of duties and tasks which may be quickly learned and which require little or no exercise of independent judgment.

labor cost. That part of the cost of goods, services, and the like attributable to wages. It commonly refers only to direct workers, but may include indirect workers also.

labor court. In certain foreign countries, a permanent court of industrial arbitration to which labor disputes are referred for settlement.

labor dilution. A term used to describe when labor performs at a lower level than normal level of efficiency. It may result in the decline of the performance of wage earners under any circumstances in which the intrinsic value of their services is not commensurate with wages paid or normal standards. Such labor dilution may stem from low morale, inadequate training or the necessity for using marginal workers in a period of labor scarcity.

labor dispute. A controversy involving persons who have actual or alleged employer-employee relationships and who are in disagreement growing out of the terms and conditions of the employment, representation of persons negotiating terms, interpretation of the contract, etc.

laborer. The "Dictionary of Occupational Titles," defines laborer as a grouping title for a number of jobs that may occur in any of a large number of industries (workers should be classified as laborer in the industries in which they have had experience). Some general categories include operator, cleaner, labeler, packer, loader, driver, stamper, cutter, order filler, wrapper, and many others.

labor force. According to the U.S. Census Bureau, the civilian labor force includes those of civilian noninstitutional population fourteen years of age and over who are classified as employed or unemployed in accordance with the fol-

(171)

lowing definitions: *Employed*—those who in the survey week did any work for pay or for profit or worked without pay for fifteen hours or more on a family farm or business, and those with a job but not at work. *Unemployed*—those who did not work during the survey period, and who were looking for work. Also included as unemployed are persons who would have been looking for work except that they were ill, they were temporarily laid off, or they believed no work was available in their line of work or in the community. Figures issued by the Bureau of the Census and those issued by Bureau of Labor Statistics have a tendency to disagree. Census estimates are obtained from interviews with a national sample of households. The Bureau of Labor Statistics uses payroll reports from a sample of establishments. The two samples are projected mathematically to give a national employment picture.

labor grade. One of a series of rate steps (single rate or rate ranges) in the wage rate structure of an establishment. Labor grades are an outcome typically of some form of job evaluation in which various occupational classifications are rated on the basis of such labor requirements as skill, experience, training, working conditions, etc. The occupations are then grouped into a limited number of steps or grades, so that occupations of approximately equal "value" or "worth" fall into the same grade. See also JOB CLASSIFICATION and JOB EVALUATION.

labor law, background of. The background of labor law is stated in "Cases and Statutes on Labor Law," by Dr. Walter H. E. Jaeger, Director of Graduate Research, Georgetown Law School. "The history of the rules governing con-

tests between employer and employed in the several English-speaking countries illustrates both the susceptibility of such rules to change and the variety of contemporary opinion as to what rules will best serve the public interest. . . . In the United States the rules of the common law governing the struggle between employer and employee have been subjected to modifications. These have been made mainly through judicial decisions. The legal right of workingmen to combine and to strike in order to secure for themselves higher wages, shorter hours, and better working conditions, received early recognition. But there developed a great diversity of opinion as to the means by which, and also as the person through whom, and upon whom pressure might permissibly be exerted in order to induce the emloyer to yield to the demands of the workingmen. Courts were required, in the absence of legislation, to determine what the public welfare demanded; whether it would not be best subserved by leaving the contestants free to resort to any means not involving a breach of the peace or injury to tangible property; whether it was consistent with the public interest that the contestants should be permitted to invoke the aid of others not directly interested in the matter in controversy; and to what extent incidental injury to persons not parties to the controversy should be held justifiable. . . . The right of employees, through their unions, to negotiate with employers—the right of collective bargaining—as fought for by workmen during many years, and its recognition and vindication are comparatively recent matters. Once achieved, such a right imports reciprocal obligation."

labor-management committee. A group of employee and management representatives concerned with methods of making the best use of manpower and materials.

Labor Management Relations Act of 1947 (Taft-Hartley Act). The Labor Management Relations Act, passed June 23, 1947, guarantees the right of workers to organize and to bargain collectively with their employers, or to refrain from all such activities. To enable employees to exercise these rights and to prevent labor disputes which may burden and obstruct commerce, it places certain limits on the activities of employers and labor organizations. The act applies to all employees and employers engaged in industries affecting commerce between the States. The following employees are not subject to the act: (a) Those employed by an employer subject to the Railway Labor Act. (b) Agricultural laborers (as defined by the Fair Labor Standards Act), domestic servants, or any individual employed by his parent or spouse. (c) Supervisors having authority, in the interest of the employer, to hire, transfer, suspend, lay off, recall, promote, discharge, assign, reward, or discipline other employees, or responsibility to direct them, or to adjust their grievances, or effectively to recommend such action, if in connection with the foregoing the exercise of such authority is not a merely routine or clerical nature, but requires the use of independent judgment. (d) Government employees. (e) Those employed by Government corporations, Federal Reserve Banks or any entirely nonprofit hospital. (f) Independent contractors who depend upon profits, rather than commission or wages, for their income. Title I of the act is administered by the National Labor Relations Board, composed of five members, and the General Counsel, all appointed by the President. The principal office of the Board is in Washington, D. C. *General Statement of the Rights of Employees*: Section 7 of the act contains a general summary of the rights guaranteed to workers. It states that: Employees shall have the right to self-organization, to form, join, or assist labor organizations, to bargain collectively through representatives of their own choosing, and to engage in other concerted activities for the purpose of collective bargaining or other mutual aid *or protection, and also have the right to refrain from any or all of such activities except to the extent that such right may be affected by an agreement requiring membership in a labor organization as a condition of employment as authorized in section 8 (a) (3).* In addition to the usual activities of organizing and maintaining a union, the Board has found protected concerted activities to include the circulation of a petition asking for a wage increase, and meetings of employees to draft a letter of complaint to management. In order to protect employees in the exercise of these rights, the act gives the Board authority to: (1) Remedy or prevent unfair labor practices of either employers or labor organizations (section 8). (2) Conduct elections to determine whether or not employees wish to have a representative bargain for them as a group (section 9). (3) Conduct polls to determine whether or not employees who have been under a union-shop agreement want to revoke the authority of their bargaining agent to make such agreements (section 9). The right of employees to strike, except as specifically modified by the act, is preserved (section 13). However, the

Board and the courts have ruled that "sitdown" strikes are not activities protected by the law because they involve the unlawful seizure of property. The Board has held also that the law does not protect slowdowns by employees who remain on the job, or partial strikes, such as a refusal to work on a certain day each week. See also: NONCOMMUNIST AFFIDAVITS, FILING OF; UNFAIR LABOR PRACTICES OF EMPLOYERS, PREVENTION OF; UNFAIR LABOR PRACTICES OF UNION, PREVENTION OF; "FREE SPEECH"; COLLECTIVE BARGAINING; BARGAINING STEPS TO CHANGE OR TERMINATE A CONTRACT UNDER L.M.R.A., PROCEDURE IN UNFAIR LABOR PRACTICE CASES; JURISDICTIONAL DISPUTES; EMPLOYEE ELECTIONS; COLLECTIVE BARGAINING REPRESENTATIVE, DETERMINATION OF; BARGAINING REPRESENTATIVES, RIGHTS OF; UNIT APPROPRIATE FOR BARGAINING; UNION SHOP; PROCEDURE IN REPRESENTATION CASES; NATIONAL EMERGENCIES; RESTRICTIONS TO PAYMENTS TO EMPLOYEE REPRESENTATIVES; POLITICAL CONTRIBUTIONS.

labor market. An abstract term referring to the processes in which services of labor are marketed and jobs are filled.

labor market area. An area within which buyers and sellers of the services of a specified type of labor fill demands for those services. Sometimes defined by reference to the wage structure common to that area, or to the residence of employes.

"Labor Market Area." A term used by the United States Employment Service. A geographic area consisting of a central city (or cities) and the surrounding territory, within a reasonable commuting distance.

labor market, free. The condition of the labor market which exists when labor is plentiful and the number of job applicants exceeds the openings.

labor market, tight. The condition of the labor market which exists when job openings are plentiful and applicants scarce and difficult to attract.

labor movement. Groups of wage earners with common interests who organize into federations or unions of various types for the purpose of improving the status of the several groups and their members in regard to dealing with employers concerning conditions of work.

labor movement, theories of. Various writers have tried to define the theories of the labor movement, or the goals that labor has in mind, taking into consideration political, economic, psychological, institutional and technological factors. Orme W. Phelps, in "Introduction to Labor Economics," (McGraw-Hill Book Company, 1955) says, "There will be no absolute agreement by students of the labor movement as to which theories should be included in the first 10, but there would probably be unanimity on at least half of them . . . The complete list includes one German, Karl Marx (and his coauthor Friedrich Engels); two Englishmen, (Sidney Webb [and his wife and coauthor Beatrice Potter Webb], and G. D. H. Cole); and six Americans, John R. Commons, Robert F. Hoxie, John Mitchell, Selig Perlman, Frank Tannenbaum, and Henry C. Simmons. In background, they range from active revolutionaries (Marx and Engels) through the academic ranks (Cole, Commons, Hoxie, Perlman, Simmons and Tannenbaum) to high public office through politics, the civil service (Webb), and active labor leadership (Mitchell). In theory, they run the gamut from the revolutionary design of Marx to the influence of technology cited by Tannenbaum." See entries under these names.

labor organization. A group of employees organized principally to deal with employers concerning conditions of work.

labor pirating. A practice, condemned as unethical, of enticing employees from another company, particularly during periods of labor shortages. See LABOR SCOUT.

labor policy, company. The principles or objectives established by a company for the guidance of management in its relations with employees.

labor productivity. The rate of output of an employee or group of employees per unit of time, usually compared to an established standard or expected rate of output.

labor racketeering. A term used to indicate unethical and dishonest methods used by certain groups or leaders. Labor leaders who are "racketeers" may use violence or blackmail to force non-union men to join the union. Business agents may use threats and bribery in attempts to achieve their ends. Labor racketeering is not approved or practiced by the great majority of ethical unions today.

labor relations. The relationship between management and organized labor, including negotiations for contracts with unions, as well as the daily relations with union stewards and business agents, in respect to the handling of differences growing out of interpretations and applications of labor agreements, arbitration, and governmental regulations. It

has been said that "the foreman and the steward are at the very cutting edge of the labor relations tool."

labor saving ratio. The relation of the unit labor cost of an improved method to the unit labor cost of another method.

labor scout. An agent employed by a company, who tries to secure workers, especially in times of labor shortage. Constant vigilance must be exerted so that the labor scout does not entice workers from other companies, a practice known as "labor pirating." See LABOR PIRATING.

labor scouting. A method of recruiting workers which consists in making a widespread personal canvas for persons who have the required abilities. Scouting may be done among persons already employed, in which case it may result in "labor pirating"; it also may be done among colleges, as in recruiting engineers, etc.; or other schools.

labor turnover. See TURNOVER, LABOR.

"Labor Turnover." A term used by the United States Employment Service. The ebb and flow of workers out of or into the workforce of an establishment. See also ACCESSIONS; SEPARATIONS.

"Labor Turnover Rates." A term used by the United States Employment Service. The relationship, expressed as a percentage, between any class of labor turnover (e.g., accessions, separations, quits) during a given time period (usually a month) and average employment during that period.

labor union. In the popularly accepted sense a group consisting of wage earners, or wage and salary earners, organized along formal lines, for the purpose of improving their status and conditions. Technically, an association of employees, generally unskilled or semi-skilled, but frequently including representatives of several trades, organized for collective bargaining. Also, a general term applied to any association of employees organized for the purpose of bargaining as a group with respect to conditions of employment. The Bureau of Labor Statistics of the U.S. Department of Labor publishes "A Directory of National and International Labor Unions in the United States," Bulletin No. 1185. This provides general information about the structure and activities of the American labor movement and gives details about all known national and international unions and State labor bodies. The bulletin analyzes the interrelationship of union levels as well as the size and composition of membership.

Labor, U.S. Department of. The United States Department of Labor was created by Congress in 1913 to foster, promote, and develop the welfare of the wage earners of the United States, to improve their working conditions, and to advance their opportunities for profitable employment. One of the primary functions of the Department is to provide informational services to labor and management and to assist them in the improvement of labor standards and working conditions. Requests for assistance of publications can be made to the U.S. Department of Labor in Washington, D. C. See UNITED STATES DEPARTMENT OF LABOR.

"Lag Quarter." A term used by the United States Employment Service. The quarter between a claimant's base period and the quarter which includes the beginning date of his benefit year.

laissez faire. A French term, meaning "let alone." It describes the concept that the maximum welfare of society is best achieved by the competitive pursuits of enlightened self-interest. Those who believe in this principle maintain that in a competitive society every factor of production is eventually used in those ways in which the rewards are the greatest and that in this manner each factor makes its greatest contribution to social welfare. Consequently, it is held that government should not interfere with individual enterprise and should not place restrictions on private industry.

laws setting wage standards for construction. The laws described below provide for minimum wages on construction work, based on wage determinations by the Secretary of Labor. With the exception of the Federal Airport Act, which requires the payment of *minimum* wages as determined by the Secretary of Labor, each of the following laws is a "prevailing wage law." This means that wages paid to laborers and mechanics must not be less than the wage rates determined by the Secretary of Labor to be *prevailing* for these classifications of workers on similar construction in the locality. *Wage Rates Incorporated in Contracts*: The wage rates determined by the Secretary of Labor under the following described laws for each class of laborer or mechanic are made part of the contract specifications and the contractors and sub-contractors have to agree that their workers will not be paid at lower rates, although higher rates can be paid. The schedule of wage rates determined by the Secretary of Labor must be posted by the contractor on the construction site and all laborers and mechanics working at the site must be paid their wages in full without any unlawful deductions at least once each week. *Enforcement*: Enforcement of the following laws is the duty of the Federal agency that makes the contract or furnishes Federal aid for the project. Under Reorganization Plan No. 14 of 1950, the Department of Labor has the legal duty to see that there is a coordinated and consistent enforcement of these laws by the responsible Federal agencies. Labor Department regulations provide what the contractors, subcontractors, and Federal agencies have to do. *Penalties*: Regulations, Part 5, issued by the Secretary of Labor (29 CFR [1955 Supp.] 5; as amended, 21 F. R. 7936, 8319) provide that if the contractor or subcontractor fails to live up to any one of the contract provisions under the following laws, he has broken the contract and it may be canceled and the work given to another contractor for completion. In addition, if a contractor has failed to pay required wages under these laws, the Federal Government may withhold or have withheld the full amount of any back wages due, from money that would otherwise be made available for payments to the contractor. Also, on written notice further payments or guarantees of funds may be suspended until violations have been corrected. Contractors and subcontractors who disregard their obligations under any of these laws may be barred for a period of 3 years from receiving any further contracts to which the laws apply.

layoff. Termination of employment without prejudice to the employee. See also DISCHARGE, QUIT, SEPARATION. Union agreements usually set up the procedures to follow when layoffs must take place.

Companies without unions may set up their own programs.

"Lay-offs." A term used by the United States Employment Service. See SEPARATIONS.

layout. The arrangement of items within an area. The items may include roads, railroads, buildings, offices, departments, warehouses, equipment, machinery, furniture, facilities, parts, aisles, and so on. See also PLANT LAYOUT and WORK STATION LAYOUT.

lay out. To draw lines on material as guides for subsequent operations.

Lea Act. See UNLAWFUL PRACTICES IN RADIO BROADCASTING.

leader, autocratic. See also LEADER, DEMOCRATIC. An extensive study of autocratic vs. democratic leadership is in progress at the Institute for Social Research at the University of Michigan. Briefly, the autocratic leader is a person who retains his hold over a group of employees through domination and the power of his position in the organization.

leader, democratic. See LEADER, AUTOCRATIC. A person who maintains his position in a group through his personal abilities and capabilities, his ability to represent his employees, persuade them, guide them, express their wishes, and who considers the values of others as possibly being as important as his own. In one experiment at the Institute for Social Research at the University of Michigan, it was found that the conference leader can increase the quality of solutions by protecting persons who hold minority opinions. In protecting such individuals the leaders permit them to make a positive contribution without running the risk that they will have an undesirable effect on others.

leadership. The art of leadership is best defined by Dr. Ordway Tead, as in his book "The Art of Leadership" (Whittlesey House). He says, "Leadership is the activity of influencing people to cooperate toward some goal which they come to find desirable. Obviously, there have been other conceptions in other times, which gave the name of leader to those who could dominate and command, to those in positions of headship who bore titles of authority. The unique emphasis in the idea of leading (today) is upon the satisfaction and sense of self-fulfillment secured by the followers of the true leader. Today, a psychologically and democratically adequate idea of leadership centers as much attention upon the results within the led as on the attributes or tangible methods of the leader."

learner rate. The rate or, more frequently, the schedule of rates applicable to workers inexperienced in the job for which they are employed, during their period of training. The schedule of rates is usually established in such a manner as to permit the gradual achievement of the minimum job rate as the learner develops competence on the job. Under the Fair Labor Standards Act, an employer may be permitted to employ learners in a specified plant at a wage lower than the legal minimum, whenever employment of learners at such lower rate is believed necessary to prevent curtailment of employment opportunities. Hearings are held by the Administrator to determine under what limitations as to wages, time, number, proportion, and length of service, special certificates authorizing the employment

of learners at subminimum rates may be issued to an employer for certain occupations in his plant.

learners, apprentices and handicapped workers, employment of, under Walsh-Healey Public Contracts Act. Under specified conditions, wage determinations of the Secretary for some industries permit payment of less than the established minimum wage to learners and apprentices. When employed in accordance with special regulations, handicapped workers may be employed at less than the prevailing minimum wage. For further information on this subect consult the nearest office of the Wage and Hour and Public Contracts Divisions.

lecture method. Perhaps the oldest method of instruction used both in employee and supervisory training. It should especially be considered as a tool if: (1) time is short; (2) the group is accustomed to it; (3) the group is competent in verbal situations; (4) the material is new and completely outside the experience of the group; (5) the purpose is to inspire; (6) the purpose is to impart new information. When the lecture method is used it is more likely to be effective if the following points are kept in mind: (1) it requires a particular kind of instructor; (2) "telling" is not always "teaching"; (3) the trainee's participation is unseen. There is no participation unless the trainee is actively thinking through the lecture material; (4) it is instructor-centered; (5) it is difficult to gauge its communication while it is in progress; (6) it may become tiresome and dull. However, it may be used well with top management groups who appreciate its economy of time. These groups may be more accustomed to reasoning quickly from principle to facts and back. Perhaps they are at home in verbal situations. The lecture method may do well with orientation groups which are set up to receive a great out-pouring of information scaled carefully for easy consumption. This method may be suited to trades training groups if the lecture material is short, succinct, and limited to one or two points. ("Establishing A Training Program," Institute of Management and Labor Relations, Rutgers University.)

legal aid services. A type of employee service which provides arrangements through which employees may obtain free legal advice.

level annual premium funding method. A method of figuring actuarially the annual pension costs for an individual employee depending on his age when he becomes a member of a pension plan. The contributions, or premiums, are paid into a fund or to the insurance company, in equal installments during the employee's participation in the plan so that upon retirement the benefit is fully funded.

level, occupational. A class of occupations defined in terms of the skill required or in some cases of the functions performed. For example, skilled, semiskilled or unskilled levels, or in census classification, proprietary, professional or skilled labor levels.

leveled elemental time. See RATED AVERAGE ELEMENTAL TIME.

leveled time. The average time adjusted to account for differences in skill, effort, conditions, and consistency between workmen and the factors surrounding an operation. See NORMAL TIME.

leveling. A method of performance rating in which the causes for the observed performance, considered to be skill, effort, conditions, and consistency are evaluated. The algebraic sum of the point values assigned to each factor is used in adjusting the time taken by the workman working at the average performance level under the usually prevailing conditions.

"Liability Report." A term used by the United States Employment Service. See STATUS REPORT.

"Liable State." A term used by the United States Employment Service. Any State against which a worker claims benefits through the facilities of the employment security agency of another (agent) State. See also AGENT STATE.

libraries, industrial. More than 3,000 libraries exist in American industrial plants. They are usually staffed by trained industrial librarians. The science-technology division of the Special Libraries Association is helpful in connection with the organization and maintenance of such libraries.

Library, use of. Persons interested in personnel, will find the library a source of much information. Most libraries use the Dewey decimal system. By this system, books are divided into ten classes, according to the subjects that the books deal with. These ten classes with their numbers are as follows: 000 to 099 General works (periodicals, encyclopedias, etc.); 100 to 199 Philosophy, psychology, etc.; 200 to 299 Religion (and mythology); 300 to 399 Sociology, (government, economics, etc.); 400 to 499 Language (dictionaries, grammars, etc.); 500 to 599 Natural science (chemistry, biology, etc.); 600 to 699 Useful arts (home economics, engineering, etc.); 700 to 799 Fine arts (painting, architecture, music, etc.); 800 to 899 Literature; 900 to 999 History (including geography, biography). Each of these ten classes is again divided into ten groups. Science, for example, is divided as follows: 500 General science; 510 Mathematics; 520 Astronomy; 530 Physics; 540 Chemistry, etc. These groups in turn may be subdivided by decimal fractions as far as necessary. The following are common to most libraries: 000 *General Works*: 016 Bibliographies; 020 Library work; 030 Encyclopedias; 100-199 *Philosophy*: 170 Conduct of life; 200-299 *Religion*: 220 Bible; 290 Myths; 300-399 *Sociology*: 325 Immigration; 330 Economics; 350 Government; 370 Education; 398 Folk-lore, legends, fairy tales; 400-499 *Language*: 500-599 *Natural Science*: 500 General Science; 510 Mathematics; 520 Astronomy; 530 Physics; 540 Chemistry; 550 Geology; 570 Biology; 580 Botany; 590 Animals and animal stories; 595 Insects; 598 Birds; 600-699 *Useful Arts*: 608 *Inventions*; 614 Health. Public Health; 620 Engineering; 630 Gardening, Agriculture; 640 Home economics; 645 House furnishing and decoration; 646 Clothing; 650 Business methods; 680 Manual training; 700-799 *Fine Arts*: 730 Sculpture; 750 Painting; 780 Music; 790 Amusements, Sports; 800-899 *Literature*: 810 History of American Literature; 811 American poetry; 812 American drama; 814 American essays; 820 History of English literature; 821 English poetry; 822 English drama; 822.3 Shakespeare: 824 English essays; 900-999 *History*: 910 Geography. Travel; 920 Biography—Collective; 921 Biography—Individual (Sometimes B or 92 is used instead of 921); 930 Ancient and

general history; 940 Medieval and modern history; 942 England—History; 943 Germany—History; 944 France—History 970.1 Indian life; 973 United States—History; 973.1 Discovery—Explorations; 973.2 Colonial times; 973.3 Revolution; 973.4 Middle period; 973.7 Civil war; 973.8 Recent times; 974 to 979 Individual states—U. S. History; 980 South America—History. Many personnel books are found under *Philosophy* which includes some books in psychology; *Sociology*, including education; and *Useful Arts*, including business methods.

life expectancy. The average number of years an employee can expect to live. More than 18 years have been added to the average American life span since 1900. Today a man of 65 has, on the average, around 13 more years to live, a woman, 15 years. See also MORTALITY TABLE.

line-and-staff organization. A type of organizational set-up which combines the principles of both types of organization. Authority and responsibility are vested in the line organization, the staff departments give the line executives specialized advice and assistance, and perform service functions. In actual practice, line-and-staff organization prevails in most companies. Disadvantages are that lines of authority are easily overstepped. See also LINE ORGANIZATION, STAFF ORGANIZATION.

line balance. See BALANCED LINE.

line layout. See LINE PRODUCTION.

line organization. A type of organizational set-up in a company where authority flows from the president or head of the concern through his "lieutenants" departmentally to the department heads, group heads and foremen or supervisors, and finally to the rank-and-file. Advantages are it is economical, definite, and insures specialization. Disadvantages are it is inflexible, makes it necessary for specialists to perform additional duties, particularly of administrative nature, for which they may not have adequate training. Straight line organization is better suited to smaller companies than to large concerns. See also LINE-AND-STAFF ORGANIZATION; STAFF ORGANIZATION.

line production. A method of plant layout in which the machines and other equipment required, regardless of the operations they perform, are arranged in the order in which they are used in the process.

"listening." White collar workers, on the average, receive 40% of their salaries for listening. Studies show that every person spends about 70% of his time in verbal communication, of which about 45% is spent listening, but tests show that most people absorb only about 25% of what they hear. Studies have been made at University of Minnesota. Suggestions are: (1) Think ahead and try to anticipate what the speaker is going to say. (2) Relate own experiences to what speaker is saying, and mentally go back every 3 or 4 minutes to recapitulate what has already been heard. Some serious mistakes made by listeners: (1) listening only for facts and evaluating too quickly; (2) faking attention to speaker; (3) avoiding difficult material, and calling the subject uninteresting.

"List Report." A term used by the United States Employment Service. See WAGE REPORT.

Little Steel. This term refers to American steel companies other than the U. S.

Steel Company. It was first used in 1937 in connection with the strike for union recognition launched by the workers of the steel companies other than the U. S. Steel.

Little Steel Formula. A decision laid down by the National War Labor Board of the United States government in July, 1942, governing wages and union recognition of the workers of the little steel companies, including Bethlehem Steel, Republic Steel, Inland Steel, and Youngstown Sheet and Tube. In its decision, the Board ordered a pay increase of 44 cents a day, union recognition, and the check-off, basing itself on the rise of 15 percent in the cost of living between January 1941 and May, 1942, according to the Bureau of Labor Statistics' cost-of-living index. According to the Board's policy, which came to be known as the "Little Steel formula," a maximum wage increase of 15 percent was permissible between Jan. 1, 1941 and May 1, 1942. If employees had received that much already, they were not in line for more. If they had received part of it, they could receive the remainder. If they had received no increase at all since January, 1940, they were eligible to receive the whole 15 percent. The idea was to hold real wages at the January, 1941 level, relying upon the Office of Price Administration to keep prices at a constant level, thereby stabilizing the civilian economy.

LMRA. See LABOR MANAGEMENT RELATIONS ACT.

lobster shift. The third, or midnight shift. Same as GRAVEYARD SHIFT or NIGHT SHIFT.

local director of vocational education. The school administrator appointed to take charge of the total activities of a vocational education program in a school district.

Local industrial union. Local union composed of workers representing numerous occupations in an industry.

"Local Job Description." A term used by the United States Employment Service. See JOB DESCRIPTION.

"Local Office." A term used by the United States Employment Service to designate a full-time office of a State agency (or an office operated by the USES, as in the District of Columbia), maintained for the purpose of providing the placement and other services of the public employment service system, and/or the claims-taking and related unemployment insurance services. See also ITINERANT POINT.

"Local Office Administrative Area." A term used by the United States Employment Service to designate the total geographical area in which a local office has the responsibility for performing the functions assigned to that office. See also AREA ACTIVELY SERVED.

"Local Placement." A term used by the United States Employment Service. See PLACEMENT.

"Local Referral." A term used by the United States Employment Service. See REFERRAL.

lock-out. An employer-employee relationship in which the employer, or group of employers, during a labor dispute withholds work from employees or closes the place of business and refuses to admit any workman pending the settlement of the dispute, in order to coerce them into accepting the employer's terms.

Longshoremen's and Harbor Workers' Compensation Act. Act of March 4, 1927, as amended. The Longshoremen's and Harbor Workers' Compensation Act provides workmen's compensation benefits for certain private employments subject to Federal jurisdiction. *Persons and Employments Covered:* The law covers substantially all maritime employment on the navigable waters of the United States (including drydocks), except the master or members of the crew of a vessel. The principal employments covered are longshoremen and ship repairmen while on board a vessel. The law has been extended to other employments, including all private employment in the District of Columbia, the outer Continental Shelf lands, and employment outside the United States at military, air, or naval bases or on public works. *Injuries and Diseases Covered:* The law provides workmen's compensation benefits for accidental injuries arising out of and in the course of the employment, and occupational disease arising naturally out of the employment. *Amount of Benefits:* Compensation for disability and death is based on the average weekly wage of the injured worker. There is a statutory limit of $54 on the weekly compensation. The minimum weekly wage for computing compensation is $27 but the award cannot exceed the average weekly wage. *Temporary Total Disability:* The compensation rate is two-thirds of the average weekly wage, subject to a maximum of $54 a week, and a minimum of $18, or average weekly wages, if less. There is a 3-day waiting period, but if the disability lasts more than 28 days, compensation is paid for the waiting period. Compensation, up to the aggregate maximum of $17,280, continues during the period of disability. *Permanent Partial*

Disability: Compensation for permanent partial disability is paid under a statutory schedule and for nonscheduled injuries on a loss in wage earning capacity. The aggregate compensation is $17,280, exclusive of medical care. *Permanent Total Disability*: Compensation is payable for life at two-thirds of the weekly wage up to the maximum of $54 per week, and a minimum of $18, or average weekly wages, if less. *Death*: Burial expenses are provided up to a maximum of $400. Persons eligible for death compensation include a widow, children under 18 years, and those over 18 if incapable of self-support, and dependent parents, brothers and sisters, grandparents, and grandchildren. The aggregate award to all beneficiaries may not exceed two-thirds of the average weekly wage. The average weekly wage shall be considered not to be more than $81, nor less than $27, but the total weekly compensation shall not exceed the weekly wage. The maximum compensation in any case may not exceed $54. Compensation to a widow is payable for life, or until remarriage, and to children until they reach 18, or marry. Upon remarriage, the widow receives 2 years' compensation. *Medical Treatment*: All necessary medical care is authorized for the effects of an injury. The employer is required to arrange for such care. There is no limit on the cost or period of treatment. *Vocational Rehabilitation*: Provision is made for furnishing prosthetic appliances and for the payment of not to exceed $25 per week for maintenance while undergoing vocational training. *Second Injuries*: The law sets up a special fund for payment of compensation in certain cases in which the employee suffers a permanent partial disability which, combined with a previous disability, causes permanent total disability. *Administration*: This law is administered by the Bureau of Employees' Compensation of the U. S. Department of Labor, through Deputy Commissioners appointed to 13 Compensation Districts. The Deputy Commissioner is responsible for the decision in respect to claims arising in his District. *Appeals*: The decision of a Deputy Commissioner is subject to review on questions of law by the Federal District Court for the District in which the injury occurred.

loose rate. See RUNAWAY RATE.

loose standard. A colloquial term, used in an industrial engineering reference, to denote allowed or standard time greater than that required by a qualified employee performing his job with normal skill and effort and following the prescribed method.

local union. Organization of employees in one locality, generally affiliated with a national or international union.

"Low Earnings Report." A term used by the United States Employment Service to designate a report from an employing unit with respect to the earnings of a worker whose hours of work and earnings have been reduced to the extent that he may be eligible for benefits or waiting-period credit.

M

machine attention time. That portion of a machining operation during which the workman performs no physical work yet must watch the progress of the work and be available to make necessary adjustments, initiate subsequent steps or stages of the operation at the proper time, and the like.

machine controlled time. That part of a work cycle that is entirely controlled by a machine and, therefore, is not influenced by the skill or effort of the workman.

machine downtime. Any time during a regular working period that a machine cannot be operated.

machine element. A work cycle subdivision that is distinct, describable, and measurable, the time for which is entirely controlled by a machine, and therefore, not influenced by the skill or effort of the workman.

machine flow diagram. See FLOW DIAGRAM.

machine hour. A unit for measuring the availability or utilization of machines. It is equivalent to one machine working for 60 minutes, two machines working for 30 minutes, or an equivalent combination of machines and working time.

machine idle time. That portion of a regular working period during which a machine that is capable of operating is not being used.

machine layout. See PLANT LAYOUT.

machine time. See MACHINE CONTROLLED TIME.

made work. A job that fulfills no productive requirements, the purpose of the work being merely to create more employment.

"Mail Claim." A term used by the United States Employment Service. See CLAIM.

"Mail Referral." A term used by the United States Employment Service. See REFERRAL.

maintenance of membership clause. A union contract clause which states that all members of the union must remain members of the union in good standing during the existing life of the contract as a condition of employment. New employees are not required to join the union, but if they voluntarily do join, they must remain members during the life of the contract.

"Major Market." A term used by the United States Employment Service to designate those relatively few employing units which, when ranked according to size from the largest downward, account for approximately 75% of the non-agricultural employment in the area actively served. See AREA ACTIVELY SERVED.

"Major Market Establishments." A term used by the United States Employment Service to designate the employing units which comprise the major market. See MAJOR MARKET.

make-up pay. Allowances given by employers to piece workers to make up differences between actual piece-work earnings and earnings at guaranteed rates or statutory minimum rates. At times, the term is also associated with the practice of permitting employees to earn a full week's wages by making up for lost time.

make-up time. The difference between the standard time earned by an employee failing to attain the established standard output and the actual time taken.

management. (1) the art and science of directing and controlling human effort so that the established objectives of an enterprise may be attained in accordance with accepted policies. (2) The group of people who direct and control human effort toward the attainment of the objectives of an enterprise.

management associations. See PERSONNEL ASSOCIATIONS.

management audit. A systematic appraisal or evaluation of the worth or quality of the various management functions and/or activities or procedures in an organization made by comparing them to established normals for good management or theoretical measures of management perfection.

management consultant. One who counsels or advises on a professional basis in an organization, administrative or operational activity, such as production, marketing, research, individual relations, and accounting. See CONSULTANT.

management counselor. See MANAGEMENT CONSULTANT.

management engineer. One who has the necessary education, training and experience to perform the functions of management engineering (which see).

management engineering. The application of engineering principles to all phases of planning, organizing, and controlling a project or enterprise.

management, foreman as a member of. The status of the foreman as a member of management has been the subject of considerable study. "The Foreman as a Member of Management" is the title of a survey on this subject by Foremanship Foundation. The Opinion Research Corporation of Princeton, N. J. makes periodic studies. Many of the industrial relations centers of colleges and universities are concerned. Among this research is that done at the Graduate School of Business Administration, Harvard University; also by associations such as the American Management Association and Society for Advancement of Management.

management publications. See PERSONNEL PUBLICATIONS.

Management Training Program for Women in Business. Offered at Radcliffe College, Cambridge, Mass. The Management Training Program offers a professional education of the highest quality. Designed to equip women with the skills and attitudes necessary for effective ad-

(185)

ministration, it has a unique combination of classroom work and actual job experience. Throughout the year, each individual is trained to think for herself in a variety of situations involving responsible decision and action. The program provides an educational experience which will be useful to a woman in her domestic and community life as well. The close association of Radcliffe College with Harvard University makes possible the extensive use of the facilities of the Harvard Business School.

manager, department. (1) A general term applied to anyone who directs the work within a particular department of an establishment, such as the marking department of a laundry. May be specifically designated according to departments supervised, as marking-department head. (2) A general term applied to anyone whose duties are more administrative than supervisory.

manager, employment. Also known as director, employment; employment supervisor; superintendent, employment. Interviews applicants and hires or refers those possessing satisfactory qualifications, to departmental managers for hiring; maintains harmony among establishment personnel by the adjustment of disputes and grievances, review of transfers, promotions, and discharges; conducts research in wages, hours, and working conditions.

manager, industrial organization. According to the Dictionary of Occupational Titles, (which see) is also known as general manager, or superintendent. Is responsible for the efficient management of an industrial corporation; coordinates the operation of production, distribution and selling departments; de-

termines administrative policies, and executes them through subordinate managers.

manager, personnel; also director, personnel. According to the Dictionary of Occupational Titles (which see) formulates policies relating to the selection, training, promotion, welfare, compensation, recreation, and discharge of employees and other employer-employee relationships, supervising subordinates engaged in executing the policies or performing duties himself, directs the hiring of employees.

man and machine chart. A synchronized graphic representation of operations performed simultaneously by two or more men, two or more machines, or a combination of men and machines.

man-hour. A unit for measuring work. It is equivalent to one man working at normal pace for 60 minutes, two men working at normal pace for 30 minutes, or some proportionate and similar combination of men working at normal pace for a period of time.

manit. A contraction for man-minute. Originally used in the Haynes incentive plan.

man-hours, total. The sum of the hours worked by all employees. On a weekly basis, equivalent to average number of employees multiplied by average weekly hours.

man-minute. A unit used for measuring work. It is equivalent to one man working at a normal pace for one minute, two men working at normal pace for thirty seconds, or an equivalent combination of men working at normal pace for a period of time.

(186)

manning table. Classification of employees in an organization, indicating age, job, sex, marital status, experience, handicaps and other characteristics which provides a useful source of reference information on manpower requirements. Sometimes called "personnel inventory."

manpower inventory. A record or file of all personnel in an organization including education, abilities, traits. Frequently includes extracurricular activities, hobbies, and record of skills not currently used in job, but which may at some time be desirable.

Mansfield plan. See ROWAN VARIABLE SHARING PLAN. An adaptation of the Rowan plan used by Westinghouse.

man-to-man scale. A type of rating scale in which each rater ranks the person being rated for each quality specified by the scale. The individuals are then ranked with respect to each other.

manual dexterity. See SKILL.

manual element. A distinct, describable and measurable subdivision of a work cycle or operation performed by one or more human motions that are not controlled by process or machine.

marginal worker. A worker the value of whose production just equals his wage; the last worker among a number of equally efficient workers who can be employed at profit to the company.

marstochron. An instrument used in time-study work to measure and record short (.01 minute) time intervals. Two or more finger-controlled type bars make instantaneous marks on a motor driven tape which moves at a constant velocity.

The distance between the marks indicates the elapsed time interval.

Marx, Heinrich Karl. (1818-1883), social philosopher, revolutionary leader, and founder of "scientific" socialism, or present-day communism. He was the son of a Jewish lawyer who was converted to Christianity. He studied law, history, and philosophy at the universities of Bonn and Berlin, taking his Ph.D. degree at the latter in 1841. Shortly after his marriage in 1843 to the daughter of a high government official, he went to Paris. Before the year was out, he had formally announced the fundamental conclusion around which his life work was built, namely, the "class struggle" and the necessity of the emancipation of the proletariat through the dissolution of all constituted society and its replacement by the classless community. In Paris, Marx met Friedrich Engels, (which see) and the two collaborated in perfect agreement and in closest friendship. From Paris, Marx moved to Brussels, where he and Engels wrote the *Communist Manifesto* in 1847, on the eve of the French and German revolutions. Returning to Germany, Marx took an active part in the revolt, was tried for high treason and acquitted, but was expelled from Prussia and subsequently from France. He moved to London and lived there until his death. He did most of the research work for his great work *Das Kapital*, in the British Museum.

"Mass Partial Employment." A term used by the United States Employment Service to designate partial unemployment of a large number of workers in a given employing unit occurring at approximately the same time and arising from a reason common to all such workers.

mass picketing. Assembling large numbers of pickets at the entrance to an employer's establishment.

mass production. A method of quantity production in which a high degree of planning, specialization of equipment and labor, and integrated utilization of all productive factors are the outstanding characteristics.

"Mass Referral." A term used by the United States Employment Service to designate referral of a group of workers to an employer who has requested workers on a group rather than on individual basis.

"Mass Separation." A term used by the United States Employment Service to designate the separation from a given employing unit of a large number of workers at approximately the same time and for the same reason common to all such workers.

"Mass Separation Notice." A term used by the United States Employment Service to designate a report of a mass separation sent to the State employment security agency by an employer, stating the number of workers separated and listing their names and other required data. Such a notice serves as a substitute for individual separation notices. See also SEPARATION NOTICE.

"Mass Total Unemployment." A term used by the United States Employment Service to designate the total unemployment of a large number of workers occurring as the result of a separation of such workers from a given employing unit at approximately the same time and for a reason common to all such workers.

master. A skilled workman in a trade, who is qualified to train apprentices and carry on his own business.

master agreement. See AGREEMENT, MASTER.

master contract. Same as AGREEMENT, MASTER.

"Master Order." A term used by the United States Employment Service. See ORDER.

master table of detail time studies. A master record of time-study data arranged so that times for the same elements can be compared. It is used to collect, analyze, and develop standard time data.

material flow. The progressive movement of materials, parts, or products, toward the completion of a production process between work stations, storage areas, machines, departments, and the like. See FLOW PROCESS CHART, FLOW DIAGRAM, and ROUTING.

material handling. The movement of materials, parts, subassemblies, or assemblies either manually or through the use of powered equipment.

maternal and child welfare. The Children's Bureau in the Social Security Administration administers grants to State agencies for three programs authorized under Title V of the Social Security Act, for extending and strengthening services for children, especially in rural areas. *Maternal and Child-Health Services*: State health departments administer this program and provide services directly or through local health departments. Among the services offered are maternity clinics, child-health conferences for infants and preschool children, public-health nursing services, health services for school-age children, through which medical, nursing, dental, and nutrition services are given. *Services for Crippled Children*: State crippled children's agencies, with the assistance of local health and welfare agencies and other groups locate crippled children and provide medical, surgical, corrective, and other services for children who are crippled or suffering from conditions that may lead to crippling. Facilities and services for diagnosis, hospitalization, and after-care for these children are also provided. *Child-Welfare Services*: State public welfare agencies provide directly or through local public welfare agencies child-welfare services for the protection and care of homeless, dependent, and neglected children, and children in danger of becoming delinquent. Child-welfare workers in local communities provide these social services to children in their own homes and to children who need foster care away from their own homes. Under a 1912 act, the Bureau is also responsible for research relating to the welfare of children and child life. The Bureau gives advisory services to public and voluntary agencies through its medical, nursing, nutrition, medical-social, child welfare, juvenile delinquency and other technical consultants to help States and local communities in developing services for the health and welfare of children and youth.

"Maximum Annual Benefits." A term used by the United States Employment Service. See BENEFITS.

"Maximum Benefit Amount." A term used by the United States Employment Service. Same as MAXIMUM ANNUAL BENEFITS. See BENEFITS.

"Maximum Potential Benefits." A term used by the United States Employment Service. See BENEFITS.

"Maximum Weekly Benefit Amount." A term used by the United States Employment Service. See BENEFIT AMOUNT.

maximum working area. (1) Horizontal plane. The area at the work place which is bounded by the imaginary arc drawn by the workman's finger tips moving in the horizontal plane with the arm fully extended and moving about the shoulder as a pivot. The section where the maximum areas of the right and left hands overlap constitutes the maximum working area for the two hands. (2) Vertical plane. The space on the surface of the imaginary sphere which would be generated by rotating, about the workman's body as an axis, the arc traced by the workman's finger tips of the right or the left hand when the arm is fully extended and is moved vertically about the shoulder as pivot. (3) Three dimensional. The space within reach of a workman's finger tips as they develop arcs of revolution when the workman's hands are extended and moving about the shoulder as a pivot.

measured day work. (1) The establishment of standard or allowed times for operations without providing the opportunity for incentive earnings. (2) A type of wage incentive plan in which each employee's performance record is reviewed periodically and his base wage rate is adjusted upward or downward from his base wage rate for the previous period as warranted by his average performance over the previous period but never below his guaranteed base wage rate.

mechanical tests. The chief use that is made of mechanical tests is the selection of apprentices for trades, and the selection of routine workers for elementary factory positions. Two types of tests are used by employment offices: (1) Selection of those who will absorb job demands of a simple nature in a very short time, and who will be content to stay on similar jobs. (2) Selection of those who are to be part of a training program over a period of months or several years, with the end view of developing fine skills and possibly executive ability. Some of the more widely-used mechanical tests include: Purdue Mechanical Assembly Test—Graney & Tiffin—Division of Applied Psychology, Purdue University; Purdue Mechanical Adaptability Test—Lawshe & Tiffin—Division of Applied Psychology, Purdue University; Purdue Hand Precision Test —Tiffin—Division of Applied Psychology, Purdue University; Hand Tool Dexterity Test—Bennett—Psychological Corporation; Crawford Small Parts Dexterity Test—Psychological Corporation; Pennsylvania Bi-Manual Worksample—Roberts—Psychological Corporation; Stromberg Dexterity Test—Psychological Corporation; D.A.T. Mechanical Reasoning Test—Bennett, Seashore and Wesman—Psychological Corporation; Engineering and Physical Science Aptitude Test—Moore, Lapp and Griffin—Psychological Corporation; Mechanical Comprehension Test — Bennett — Psychological Corporation; D.A.T. Space Relations Test—Bennett, Seashore and Wesman—Psychological Corporation; Purdue Pegboard—Purdue Research Foundation—Science Research Associates; SRA Test of Mechanical Aptitude—Richardson & al.—Science Research Associates; Purdue Tests for Machinists and Machine Operators—Owen, Stevason, McComb & Hume—Science Research Associates; McQuarrie Test for Mechanical Ability—California

Test Bureau. See PUBLISHERS, PERSONNEL TESTS.

mediation. Attempts by a person or group of persons to bring together, or exchange information between, the parties in a labor dispute so that an agreement can be reached.

mediator. An individual who undertakes mediation of a labor dispute.

memo-motion study. A motion study technique that utilizes a motion picture camera operating at slower than normal speeds such as one frame per second or one frame per one hundredth minute.

Menninger Foundation. Located in Topeka, Kansas. A non-profit center for research, professional education, treatment and prevention in psychiatry. Among its activities are the Menninger Foundation Survey of Industrial Mental Health. Publication: The Menninger Quarterly.

merit increase. An increase in the wage rate of an individual worker on the basis of performance or service. This is widely used as a method of advancing workers within established rate ranges, sometimes in conjunction with a provision for automatic increases over part of the range. Merit increases may be administered informally at the discretion of the employer, or provision may exist for the periodic review of the performance of employees for granting of merit increases. See also WAGE REVIEW.

"Merit Rating." When used by the United States Employment Service, the definition is given under EXPERIENCE RATING which see.

merit rating. An organized and systematic method of appraising an employee's ability and job performance, usually for a specified period of time. Factors such as quality and quantity of work, knowledge, initiative, and dependability are considered. Ratings are made periodically usually for the purpose of determining promotions, transfers, layoffs, or pay increases. Among the various rating plans used are graphic scales, check lists, paired comparisons and over-all ranking. Frederick H. Harbison, in "Seniority Policies and Procedures as Developed through Collective Bargaining," Princeton University, Industrial Relations Section, says: "Whether a formal rating plan is adopted or not, management is constantly rating employees . . In the absence of precise records of performance and ability, management must rely solely on the supervisor's opinion of the relative worth of an employee . . . Haphazard, careless, or biased decisions on matters of layoff and promotion may be more injurious to employee morale and efficiency than are rigid seniority rules. For this reason, progressive employers have introduced formal ability rating plans as an aid in reaching more objective and unbiased judgments respecting the relative competency of individual employees."

"Merit Rating Account." A term used by the United States Employment Service. Same as EXPERIENCE-RATING ACCOUNTS. See ACCOUNTS.

merit rating plans. These can generally be classified into: (1) Ranking—Employees are ranked on an overall basis, usually by the supervisor, ranking from best or most satisfactory worker, to worst, or least satisfactory employee. Sometimes employees are ranked by traits instead of an overall basis, thus giving several sets of results showing each employee's standing with respect to each trait. (2) Man-to-man comparisons—The plan uses five basic factors: (a) physical qualities, (b) intelligence, (c) leadership, (d) personal qualities, (e) general use to the service. Numerical values are set for each of 5 degrees of each factor, ranging from highest, high, middle, low, lowest. (3) Check lists—Such lists are made up of a series of statements, questions, or phrases concerning the employee's performance on the job. The rating process usually consists simply of checking statements with "yes" or "no." (4) Scales—Plans involving scales consist of a list of traits or attributes, accompanied by a scale on which the person who does the rating indicates the degree to which the employee possesses that trait or attribute and displays it in his work. Scale forms usually are: (a) Continuous. A simple line placed to the right of the factor under consideration, the instructions being to regard one end of the line as the minimum amount of the trait and the other end as the maximum amount, thus:

Alphabetical Scale
Initiative

A	B	C	D	E	F	G	H

Numerical Scale
Initiative

100	90	80	70	60	50	40	30	20	10	0

Descriptive Scale
Initiative

	excellent		Good		Average		Poor	

(b) Discontinuous. Modifications in the scales so that the fine discrimination demanded of continuous scales is not required.

Merrick Differential Bonus Plan. A piece-rate type incentive plan whereby one large step is broken into two smaller steps, put one of them at task and the other at some point a little below task where it would be more in reach of the developing employee. He felt that the best point for this first step was about 83% of task. He took as the whole amount of bonus 20% and divided this equally, 10% bonus at 83% of task and 10% at task. Formula for Earning:

Earning up to 83%

task=Number of Pieces x Basic Piece Rate

$$E = N_p \ (R_p)_1$$

Earning from 83% to

100% task=Number of Pieces x Intermediate Piece Rate

$$E = N_p \ (R_p)_2$$

Earning at and above

task=Number of Pieces x High Piece Rate

$$E = N_p \ (R_p)_3$$

Where $(R_p)_2 = 110 \ R_1$

$(R_p)_3 = 120 \ R_1$ or

Where $(R_p)_2 = 108 \ (R_p)_1$

$(R_p)_3 = 120 \ (R_p)_1$

An $(R_p)_4 = 133\frac{1}{3} \ (R_p)_1$

might be used from 110% task and on up.

Merrick Multiple Piece-Rate Plan. See MERRICK DIFFERENTIAL BONUS PLAN.

method. (1) The procedure or sequence of motions used by one or more individuals to accomplish a given operation or work task. (2) The sequence of operations and/or processes used to produce a given product or accomplish a given job. (3) A specific combination of layout and working conditions; materials, equipment, and tools; and motion pattern, involved in accomplishing a given operation or task.

methods engineer. The title given a member of that sub-classification of industrial engineering comprised of persons qualified by training, education, or experience to establish methods and the means by which they can be made most effective.

methods engineering. The technique that subjects each operation of a given piece of work to close analysis in order to eliminate every unnecessary element or operation and in order to approach the quickest and best method of performing each necessary element or operation. It includes the improvement and standardization of methods, equipment and working conditions; operator training; the determination of standard times; and occasionally devising and administering various incentive plans.

methods study. The analysis of the sequence of motions used or proposed for use in performing an operation and of the tools, equipment and work station layout used or proposed for use.

methods-time measurement. A system of predetermined motion time standards. It is a procedure which analyses any operation into certain classifications of human motions required to perform it and assigns to each motion controlled only by the individual performing it a predetermined time standard which is determined by the nature of the motion and the conditions under which it is made. Abbreviated as MTM.

methods training. (1) Detailed instruction and guided practice given employees to insure that they use the proper methods to perform their jobs. (2) Courses or programs of instruction given in the techniques of scientific management as related to methods engineering. See also "JOB METHODS."

Mexican farm labor. The Federal government has in effect a program of services for in-migrant Mexican farm laborers. Under the 2-nation agreement of 1951, the United States Department of Labor operates reception centers for these Mexican laborers, assists in negotiating contracts, guarantees employer performance of wages and transportation expenses, generally supervises living and working conditions, and assumes other responsibilities. A new treaty, applying to 1954 and 1955, was concluded as of March 10, 1954.

microchronometer. (1) A two-handed clock, whose dial is divided into 100 divisions, the large hand of the clock usually geared to make 20 revolutions in one minute and the small hand to make two revolutions each minute. (2) A clock devised by Frank B. Gilbreth, which is used in micro-motion study by placing it in the foreground when photographing an operation so that the time is recorded on the film. (3) An accurate time piece which measures time in units of 1/2000 part of a minute and fractions thereof.

micromotion study. (1) That phase of motion study which divides manual work into fundamental elements, often called therbligs or Gilbreth basic elements, analyzes these elements separately and relatively, and, from this analysis, establishes more efficient methods. (2) The analysis of elements of motions too short or rapid for the eye to distinguish, by the

use of motion pictures, sometimes in combination with an adequate time-indicating device. (Since the motion picture camera itself can indicate time-intervals, an additional timing device is often dispensed with in micromotion study.)

"Migratory Labor." When used by the United States Employment Service, this term is defined as workers who occasionally or habitually leave their established place of residence to accept seasonal or temporary employment in another locality where they reside during the period of employment.

"Military Separations." A term used by the United States Employment Service. See SEPARATIONS.

Miller Act. Act of August 24, 1935. *Persons and Employments Covered*: The Miller Act applies to every contract of over $2,000 for the construction, alteration, or repair of any public building or public work of the United States and provides that, before any contract covered by its provisions is awarded, the contractor must execute a payment bond with a surety or sureties to protect the wages of all persons supplying labor. This law, while not a prevailing wage law or overtime pay law, is particularly important to laborers and mechanics who work on construction covered by the Davis-Bacon Act—that is, on construction contracts made directly by the Federal Government. Although the law does not apply to Federal-aid projects but only to direct Federal contracts, it is usual for Federal agencies administering grant-in-aid, loan, mortgage guarantee, and similar Federal-aid programs to require by regulation that contractors on construction under these programs execute a performance bond. Generally, the term of such bonds extends to 1 year after completion of the project. *Right to Sue*: The Miller Act gives the worker a right to sue on the contractor's bond if he does not receive payment in full within 90 days after the day on which the last labor was performed. If the worker was employed by a subcontractor, he can sue the prime contractor and sureties on the bond for his unpaid wages, if the first gives written notice to the prime contractor within 90 days after the last labor was performed. This notice must be sent by registered mail, postage prepaid, in an envelope addressed to the contractor at any place he maintains an office or conducts a business; or it may be served in any other way that the U.S. marshal or the Federal district court for the district where the job is located is authorized to serve a summons. *Time and Manner for Bringing Suit*: Suits to recover under the Miller Act must be commenced within 1 year after the date of final settlement of the contract and must be brought in the name of the United States, for the use of the person suing, in the United States District Court in any district in which the contract was to be performed and executed. Suit is brought and prosecuted by the worker's own attorney. For further information write to the office of the Solicitor, U.S. Department of Labor, Washington 25, D. C.

mind reaction. A THERBLIG (which see) which is defined as: to translate the messages received from the five senses and transferred by means of the NERVE REACTION (which see) into conclusions and definite policies of movements, inactivity, or sense organ use, and vice versa.

minimum pension. If the pension provided by a pension formula is less than a specified amount, the employer will provide an additional amount to bring the pension up to this level.

"Minimum Potential Benefits." A term used by the United States Employment Service. See BENEFITS.

minimum rate. There are several kinds of minimum rates, those that are applicable to specific jobs and those that are applicable to entire establishments. Normally, those that are applicable to specific jobs are called *minimum job rates* and those applicable to entire establishments are called minimum plant rates. In addition, there are several varieties of guaranteed minimum rates, usually applicable to individual jobs under wage incentive systems. *Minimum job rate*: The minimum rate of pay for experienced workers on a given job. The minimum rate may be either a single rate or the minimum of a rate range. Union rates or union scales are usually minimum job rates. Normally, entrance rates, probationary rates, or learners' rates fall below the minimum job rates. *Minimum plant rate*: Normally the minimum rate of pay for experienced workers in the lowest-paid job in the establishment. The term may, however, mean different things in plants with differently organized wage structures. In some plants, the term refers to the rate for the lowest-paid production job, although lower rates may exist for such jobs as common laborer or janitor. In some plants, there are different minimum rates for men and women workers, or for white and Negro workers. In some plants, the so-called minimum rate may actually be a hiring or probationary rate. See also ENTRANCE RATE.

minimum time. The shortest elapsed time recorded for a particular element of a time study excepting those known to be incorrect.

minimum wage. Rates of wages established legally or through collective bargaining, below which workers cannot be employed. The Fair Labor Standards Act establishes the legal minimum wage to be paid to workers engaged in interstate commerce, unless such workers are covered by State laws which provide for higher minimum wages. Minimum rates are also established through collective bargaining and are applicable to individual plants, or to groupings of plants within an area or an industry.

minimum wage rates, under Walsh-Healey Public Contracts Act. The Secretary of Labor is authorized to determine prevailing minimum wages in an industry on the basis of standards provided in the Act. Such minimum-wage determinations generally are issued by the Secretary after a public hearing of the interested parties. All workers engaged in performance of a contract let under the Act must be paid not less than the minimum so set by the Secretary. For information as to which industries are covered by public contracts minimum-wage determinations, communicate with the nearest office of the Wage and Hour and Public Contracts Divisions or write to the Wage and Hour and Public Contracts Divisions, U. S. Department of Labor, Washington 25, D. C.

"Minimum Weekly Benefit Amount." A term used by the United States Employment Service. See BENEFIT AMOUNT.

"Minority Groups." As defined by the United States Employment Service, any group of people, regardless of numerical size or ethnological grouping, whose members are denied or limited in job opportunities as a result of local hiring practices or the practices of a given employer for the following non-occupational reasons: race, creed, color, religion, national origin, or citizenship, except where citizenship as a condition of employment is required by law.

"Minor Market." A term used by the United States Employment Service to designate those nonagricultural employing units in the area actively served which are not included in the major market. See MAJOR MARKET.

misfits. See PROBLEM EMPLOYEES.

Mitchell, John. (1870-1919), American labor leader. John Mitchell was an orphan at an early age, started to work when he was 9, went into the mines at the age of 10, and joined the Knights of Labor when he was 15. Upon the subsequent collapse of that Order, he took out membership in the United Mine Workers of America, becoming national president of that union in 1899. He retired from the presidency in 1908 on account of ill health and became a freelance writer and lecturer on labor problems. In 1914 he was appointed Commissioner of Labor for the State of New York, and, later, chairman of the State Industrial Commission. Mitchell was active in the AFL, serving as vice-president from 1899 to 1914. He fought the craft principle as the exclusive basis of organization and established the right of the mine workers to organize on an industrial basis in 1901. His principal written works were *Organized Labor* (1903) and *The Wage Earner and His Problems* (1913). The explanation of trade unionism, according to Mitchell, who was one of its most successful practitioners in this country, lies in the economic protection it affords to workingmen. The essence of trade unionism is the collective bargain, which gives the worker economic equality with the employer, rids him of fear, raises his efficiency and establishes his citizenship in the industrial order.

Molly Maguires. A secret society organized in Ireland whose purpose was to obtain advantages by intimidation of officials and citizens. In 1867 branch organizations were set up in the coal districts of Pennsylvania. For 10 years they committed many murders and outrages, until broken up by the conviction and execution of several of their ringleaders. Their warning and threatening letters were signed "Molly Maguire."

money purchase benefit. A pension which is dependent entirely upon the contributions made to the individual's account. The contributions may be either a percentage of pay or a fixed amount, such as six cents per man-hour worked. The accumulated funds in the individual account are used to provide a pension. If the plan is insured under a group annuity contract the annual contributions are used to purchase annual deferred annuities, the amount of which decreases each year as the employee grows older.

Monthly Labor Review. Official publication of the Bureau of Labor Statistics of the U.S. Department of Labor.

modal selection. The elapsed time that appears most frequently for an element in a time study.

"moonlighting." A term in personnel literature meaning double employment.

Moonlighting is paid work done after hours (day, night, or weekends) that is entirely separate from a man's regular job and which takes ten hours or more of his time per week.

morale. Four approaches to morale are generally accepted: (1) Morale and the individual employee—his personal adjustment and job satisfaction. (2) Morale and acceptance of the company and identification with the company goals. (3) Morale in terms of the work group and its integration. (4) Morale and the organization as a whole. See MORALE, INDIVIDUAL EMPLOYEE; MORALE OF ORGANIZATION AS A WHOLE; MORALE, OF WORK GROUP.

morale, individual employee. The concept of morale in terms of the individual employee, as defined by Dr. Robert K. Burns, Professor of Industrial Relations at the University of Chicago, stems in part from needs psychology and from the ideas of personal adjustment, individual orientation, job satisfaction of the employee in the work situation.

morale, of organization as a whole. Morale in respect to the organization as a whole has included: (1) Technology, the work flow, and working conditions. (2) Financial and non-financial incentives and remarks. (3) Communications and the flow of ideas in the organization. (4) The relation of the hierarchy of authority to teamwork and cooperation. (5) Job roles in terms of what the individual does to carry out his work. (6) Personal roles in terms of what the individual seeks to get from his work situation. (7) The determinants of status within and between departments of an organization. (8) The inter-personal and informal relations that develop between individuals, work groups, and leadership within the organization.

morale, of work group. This refers to integration of the individual and the group, the element of social cohesion and cooperation, goal-oriented activity, ability to stick together in the face of danger, and the like. These point to inter-dependent relationships between the group and individual elements of morale. In this connection, morale has been defined as: (1) A positive goal; (2) A feeling of "togetherness"; (3) an awareness of danger to a group; (4) A conviction that conditions can be improved; (5) A sense of advance toward group goals.

morale surveys. An employee morale, or attitude survey, is a device for finding out how a worker feels about his job, his supervisor, the management of the company and its policies. Morale surveys are frequently in the form of questionnaires, conducted through the cooperation of colleges and universities, to which the answers (anonymous) may be sent direct, giving employees a feeling of freedom. See section, "Employee Attitude or Opinion Surveys," in Personnel Handbook (Ronald Press). Widely used is the SRA Employee Inventory (Science Research Associates—See PUB-LISHERS, PERSONNEL TESTS). This test has been prepared by Robert K. Burns, *Executive Officer, Industrial Relations Center, The University of Chicago*; L. L. Thurstone, *Director of the Psychometric Laboratory, University of North Carolina*; Melany E. Baehr, *Research Associate, Industrial Relations Center, The University of Chicago*; and David G. Moore, *Industrial Consultant.* The *Employee Inventory*, a 78-item questionnaire, measures how all types of em-

ployees feel about their jobs, their pay, and the company they work for. It combines the techniques of psychological test construction with those of public opinion polling. Unlike questionnaires prepared especially for one company, the *Employee Inventory* is a standardized instrument. Through the use of the *Inventory*, management can compare its employees' attitudes with those of more than 250,000 employees in over 850 different companies, large and small, across the nation. The *Employee Inventory* uses easy-to-understand language. Since it requires only a few minutes to administer, it can be given during working hours with little disruption or loss of production time. The brief time required for answering the questions is equally important where the *Inventory* is given to employees on their own time. Because employees are asked not to sign their names, they are willing to answer frankly. Management can use the *Employee Inventory* to: (1) Measure morale for a company as a whole. (2) Compare morale between departments or plants in an organization. (3) Compare morale in a company with the average of others, particularly in the same industry. With it, companies can find out what employees really think, can pin-point weak departments, increase the effectiveness of supervision, learn if communication is adequate, discover training needs, improve employee relations, build community goodwill, and cut employee turnover. Items in the questionnaire fall in 15 categories: *Job Demands, Working Conditions, Pay, Employee Benefits, Friendliness and Cooperation of Fellow Employees, Supervisor-Employee Interpersonal Relations, Confidence in Management, Technical Competence of Supervision, Effective-*

ness of Administration, Adequacy of Communication, Security of Job and Work Relations, Status and Recognition, Identification with the Company, Opportunity for Growth and Advancement, and Reactions to the Inventory. A special form of this questionnaire, designed for use in municipal, state, and federal offices is now available.

mortality experience. The rate at which employees have died in the past projected for the future. This rate affects the cost of a pension plan for a particular plant or industry.

mortality table. Table, computed by life insurance companies, which shows the death rate for various age groups by sex. Also shows how long a worker at a particular age can expect to live. Such tables are used in setting up pension plans as costs vary with age and life expectancy and sex of workers.

motion. A movement of the human body or any of the body members.

motion cycle. A complete series of motion elements involved in performing an operation, beginning with a motion connected with the production of the unit and ending when the same motion is about to be repeated with the next unit.

motion study. A detailed analysis of the individual manual body and eye movements of a worker occurring in an operation or work cycle of a given piece of work for the purpose of eliminating wasted movements and establishing a a better sequence and coordination of movements.

motion-time analysis. A system of predetermined motion time standards used for describing and recording an operation in terms of its motions. The value of each motion is predetermined both as to utility and time allowance. Abbreviated as MTA.

motivation. To motivate is to cause a release of energy in relation to a desired goal. Dr. Herbert Moore, in "Psychology for Business and Industry," (McGraw-Hill Book Company, Inc.) describes motivation as follows: "Effective motivation is determined by three factors: the goal that is to be realized, the energy that is to be released, and the tools that are to be used to direct and control that energy. The released energy depends upon the capacity and the will to work of the individual employee. The goal that business and industry hope to reach through the use of that energy varies in different organizations and expresses itself in a number of forms. At one time it may be a willingness to work at increased pace for a long period of time; at another, it may be a voluntary cut in pay; at another, a sacrificing of one's promotional possibilities in the interests of the welfare of the organization; and at yet another, apparently excessive supplementary responsibilities without any promise of immediate reward. The nature of goal is of minor importance; the desirable state is that the attitude of the employee toward the organization be such as to make possible his carrying on these supplementary efforts as spontaneously and as willingly as if they were being made in the interests of his own home. To reach that stage in an employee's relations with an organization in which loyalty to the firm and consideration for its welfare are of more importance than temporary personal sacrifices is the goal of motivational endeavors. The whole problem of motivation is the problem of the development of attitudes, loyalties, and capacities for making sacrifices toward an entity that is of greater consequence to the individual worker than his own job or his personal welfare."

move. An industrial engineering term meaning the basic element employed when the predominant purpose is to transport an object to a destination. See THERBLIG; TRANSPORT LOADED.

MRLF. Monthly Report of the Labor Force, released by the United States Bureau of the Census, giving civilian employment status for persons fourteen years of age and over.

multi-employer bargaining. Employers may create a formal association for purposes of negotiation. Member firms may retain authority to reject a contract, or they may grant the association complete power. It may have either a craft or industry base. Most commonly operates on a local level; less frequently regionally and nationally.

multiple activity chart. See MAN and MACHINE chart.

multiple activity process chart. See MAN and MACHINE chart.

"Multiple Management." A term created by Charles P. McCormick, president and Chairman of the Board, McCormick & Co., Inc. "Multiple Management" is a democratic method of government for business. The active management is carried on through groups of more than fifty persons instead of a few executive officers. These groups are (1) the Factory Board, chosen by board members themselves at elections held semi-annually, which represents factory employees in respect to working conditions, employees' suggestions, improving relationships be-

tween company and employees; (2) the Sales Board, composed of fifteen men active in positions in outside selling; (3) the Junior Board, chosen in the same manner as the Factory Board, which represents the office employees and those concerned with personnel and administration; (4) the Institutional Sales Board, representing the sales force concerned with sales to the bulk and institutional trade; (5) the Senior Board, elected annually by the stockholders. Each member of a Board is paid an extra fee for the time spent on board business. All suggestions of subordinate boards must be approved unanimously before being forwarded to the Senior Board. The Senior Board, in turn, must give unanimous approval before suggestions are passed along to the line organization for action. A number of companies have adopted the basic "Multiple Management" concept and have adapted it to best serve their needs.

multiple time plan. A type of wage incentive plan that provides for the payment of higher base rates at progressively higher levels of production. For example, a workman may be paid $2.00 per hour at an output of 60-65 pieces per hour, $2.20 per hour at an output of 66-71 pieces per hour, $2.42 at an output of 72-77 pieces per hour and so on.

multiple watch timing. See ACCUMULATIVE TIMING.

"Multistate Worker." A term used by the United States Employment Service to designate an individual who performs service for one employer in more than one State.

music. Music has proved to be one way to reduce employee fatigue. Music in the plant or in the office must vary radically depending upon the audience and environment, if it is to serve its best purpose. Surveys show it is best to have bright and peppy tunes to start off the day, followed by steady, rhythmic accompaniment to work until mid-morning. At this point, to meet the slump, quick rhythms should be programmed. The pattern is about the same in the afternoon. In arranging for music, it must be remembered that people do not actually "listen" to the music, just as they do not look at walls which are painted in colors designed to create a mood, or consciously feel the effects of air conditioning. Lyrics, for example, are undesirable and so are staccato songs which invite time keeping.

Mutual Benefit Association. An association organized by a group of employees, usually of one company for the purpose of providing financial aid, death and sickness benefits to members. Membership is usually voluntary; some associations exclude employees of advanced age and some require very young employees to wait until they are of age before joining. The benefits are financed by funds accumulated through regular membership contributions or by assessments. Most employers cooperate by deducting association membership dues from employees' pay checks and remitting these funds to the officers of the association. Membership in the benefit association may be a condition of employment for all new workers where companies do not provide insurance programs or other financial aids for employees. In most instances employers prefer to have employees manage the associations, with all officers elected from the employee group. A member of management, however, is frequently found on the executive board and provides counsel and advice.

N

National Association of Manufacturers.
Founded in 1895 in Cincinnati, Ohio.
One of the two largest over-all organizations representing American business.
Some 20,000 companies are members.
Its programs include educational, public
relations, legislative and research activities. It publishes numerous pamphlets
and booklets, obtainable through its national headquarters at 2 East 48th Street,
New York, N. Y. The NAM's "basic
tenets" for management's approach to
industrial relations is as follows: (1) Industry exists for the individual—not the
individual for industry. The human personality, not the organization or any institution, is the paramount and supreme
consideration. (2) The individual business
enterprise, in its operation, must take full
account of the social, spiritual, and economic needs of the individual as an employee, as a stockholder, as a consumer,
and as a member of society. (3) Sound
company personnel policy and practices
must be designed to safeguard and promote the rights, interests, and welfare of
employees as persons. (4) The relationship of the individual to the enterprise
is the basic one—irrespective of whether
there is or is not a union in the plant.
Policies and activities of government, labor unions, or management in the field

of industrial relations must be judged in
the light of whether they promote or
jeopardize, this basic relationship. (5)
Loyalty is not an "either-or" proposition.
There is no basic inconsistency or in-
compatibility between an employee's interest in his company and his acceptance
of a union. (6) Cooperation of the individual in the productive process must be
won and deserved. It cannot be forced.
(7) Employers should, so far as lies within their control, work for and provide a
maximum degree of economic security
for employees. (8) The individual employee, in respect to his status, rights,
prospects for advancement, and his economic well-being is inescapably linked
to the success of the enterprise in which
he is employed. (9) No policy or institution, whether it be of management or
of labor, which violates or affronts the
rights and freedom of the individual can
long survive in a free society. (10) Our
free society has an obligation and responsibility to uphold and safeguard the
rights and privileges of the individual
and to see to it that this principle receives effective expression in national labor policy.

**national emergencies, under Labor Man-
agement Relations Act of 1947.** The La-

bor Management Relations Act of 1947 places special restrictions on actual or threatened strikes or lockouts which may result in a national emergency. In order for such a work stoppage or threatened stoppage to be subject to these restrictions it must affect an entire industry or a substantial part of an industry that is engaged in trade, commerce, transportation, or communication in interstate or foreign commerce, or in the production of goods for such commerce provided that in each case the national health or safety would be imperiled. If the President is of the opinion that such an actual or threatened strike or lockout will imperil the national health or safety, he is authorized to appoint a board of inquiry to investigate and report on the issues involved without making any recommendations. One copy of the report is to be filed with the Federal Mediation and Conciliation Service and the contents made public. After receiving the report of the Board, the President may direct the Attorney General to ask for an injunction from a Federal district court having jurisdiction of the parties to the dispute. If the court finds that the threatened strike or lockout in such an industry will imperil the national health or safety, it may grant an injunction without regard to the provisions of the Norris-LaGuardia Act. In addition the court may issue whatever orders are deemed appropriate. After the injunction is issued the parties to the dispute are required, during the next 60 days, to try to settle their differences with the assistance of the Federal Mediation and Conciliation Service. During the same time the President is authorized to reconvene the Board of Inquiry. At the end of the 60-day period, a further report is required to be made by the Board to the

President which he must make available to the public. The report must include a statement of the employer's last offer of settlement. Within 15 days, following the end of the 60-day period, the National Labor Relations Board must hold an election to determine whether the employees involved in the dispute wish to accept the final offer of settlement made by their employer. The results of the election are then certified to the Attorney General who must request the court to discharge the injunction. After the court has granted this request, a report of the entire proceedings must be made to Congress by the President with such recommendations as he desires to make. For further information write to the U. S. Department of Justice, Washington 25, D. C.

National Industrial Conference Board. This organization, located at 460 Park Avenue, New York, N. Y. is an independent and nonprofit institution for business and industrial fact finding through scientific research. In terms of every-day usefulness, the Board is a source of facts and figures bearing on all aspects of economic life and business operation. By charter, the organization is specifically prohibited from attempting to influence legislation of any kind. The Board conducts unbiased research in the fields of economics, business management and human relations. Facts, experiences and opinions relating to these fields are collected and appraised. The results of these inquiries are then issued as published reports, press releases, conferences and correspondence. The work of The Conference Board is made possible through the support of more than 3,000 Subscribing Associates. These include: Business Organizations; Trade Associations;

Government Bureaus; Labor Unions; Libraries; Individuals; Colleges and Universities. The Board is continuously examining various aspects of the nation's economy, business practices, human relations, and other practical problems which must be met intelligently by having the facts at hand. The Board's research program is carried on by its four major divisions: Division of Business Economics; Division of Business Practices; Division of Personnel Administration; Statistical Division. Studies, surveys, and analyses are periodically issued in the following publications: *Studies in Personnel Policy; Studies in Business Policy; Studies in Labor Statistics; Studies in Business Economics; The Management Record; The Business Record.* Other surveys and statistical series that the Board maintains include: Consumers' Price Index in major cities, Clerical Salaries and Occupational Wage Data in a cross-section of U.S. industrial cities, and Executive Compensation Data. *Conferences*: During each year, The Conference Board brings together business, labor and industrial executives in monthly conferences in order to provide them the opportunity to participate in discussions led by speakers of national and international prominence. In smaller, technical sessions, experts appraise timely subjects as a prelude to a period of questions and general discussion. *Education*: Studies prepared by The Conference Board often serve as textbook material and collateral reading in leading colleges and universities. The Board, as a public service to educators, has made its weekly "Road Maps of Industry" charts available without charge upon request to teachers at the secondary school level, staff members of teachers colleges and administrators at these levels.

National Housing Act (FHA), As Amended. This law covers construction which is financed with assistance by the Federal Government through mortgage insurance by FHA. Its prevailing wage provisions apply to laborers and mechanics working on construction of multi-type dwellings for rental purposes (walk-up and elevator apartments) and do not apply to building of individual homes under FHA mortgages unless done by cooperatives or unless the mortgage insured by FHA covers a project of 12 or more family homes. Under a 1956 amendment to the law, the requirement for the payment of not less than the prevailing wage scales determined by the Secretary of Labor continues to apply to projects approved through June 30, 1958, on rental housing built with FHA financing for military personnel on or near Federal military installations. (The Davis-Bacon Act applies to military housing built by the Federal Government on its military installations.)

"National Job Description." A term used by the United States Employment Service. See JOB DESCRIPTION.

National Labor Relations Board. Administration of the National Labor Management Relations Act of 1947, (Taft-Hartley Law) rests primarily with the National Labor Relations Board, which is composed of five members, and the General Counsel of the Board. Members of the Board are appointed by the President, with consent of the Senate, for terms of 5 years. The term of one board member expires each year. The General Counsel is appointed by the President, with consent of the Senate, for a term of 4 years. Headquarters of the Board and the General Counsel are in Washington, D. C. *Place To File Charges or Petitions.* Charges of unfair practices or petitions for elections should be filed with the Board's regional offices serving the area where the case arises. These offices are located in various cities throughout the United States and the Territories. *Businesses and Industries in Which the Board Takes Cases.* The Board, as a matter of policy, does not take cases in all businesses or industries which affect interstate commerce within the meaning of the act. For its own guidance and the guidance of employees, employers, unions, and others concerned with Board proceedings, the Board has established certain standards by which it ordinarily will determine whether or not to take a case. The standards are based upon the character or the amount of the business of the employer or employees involved in the case.

National Management Association. (formerly National Association of Foremen) has its headquarters in Dayton, Ohio. It started shortly after World War I when Louis Ruthenberg, then with Domestic Engineering Laboratories Co. (Delco) began teaching a class of 80 Delco foremen on fundamentals of supervision. In 1919 he was asked to instruct a city-wide class of 100 foremen on the same subject. This class, in 1921, expressed a desire to perpetuate itself by organizing the Dayton Foremen's Club, with A. L. Freedlander president. Similar clubs were organized in many Ohio cities and in 1923 the Ohio Federation of Foremen's Clubs came into being. On October 8, 1925, the National Association of Foremen was founded by delegates from foremen's clubs in five states, with Thomas B. Fordham its president. In January 1956 the member clubs voted to change the name of the Association to The National Management Association. Official publication is *Manage* (magazine).

National Mediation Board. Functions under the Railway Labor Act. The Railway Labor Act was passed in 1926, (which see) and under it the former United States Board of Mediation operated until 1934. On June 21, 1934, the Act was amended by adding the adjustment board machinery provided in Section 3, and also by the addition of Section 2, under which this Board has certain duties in the handling of representation disputes among carrier employees. The Board of Mediation ceased to exist with the passage of the 1934 amendments, being replaced by the present National Mediation Board. The nation's commercial airlines were placed under the Railway Labor Act by an amendment approved April 10, 1936. The handling of representation disputes among the various groups of airline employees and the mediation of controversies between air carriers and the various labor organizations representing their employees now consumes approximately one-third of the time of the Board and its staff of mediators. An amendment to the law approved August 13, 1940, eliminated from the definitions of "carrier" and "employee" as used in the Act, any company and its employees engaged in the mining of coal, the supplying of coal to a carrier where delivery is not beyond the tipple, and the operation of equipment and facilities therefor. An amendment to the Railway Labor Act known as Public Law 914 of the 81st Congress, approved in 1951, legalized the negotiation of union shop agreements covering carrier employees and the checkoff of union dues and assessments. The general purposes of the Act are described as follows: (1) To avoid any interruption to commerce or to the operation of any carrier engaged therein; (2) to forbid any limitation upon freedom of association among employees or any denial, as a condition of employment or otherwise, of the right of employees to join a labor organization; (3) to provide for the complete independence of carriers and of employees in the matter of self-organization; (4) to provide for the prompt and orderly settlement of all disputes concerning rates of pay, rules, or working conditions; (5) to provide for the prompt and orderly settlement of all disputes growing out of grievances or out of the interpretation or application of agreements covering rates of pay, rules, or working conditions. To promote the fulfillment of these general purposes, the National Mediation Board is charged with two major duties, viz: (1) The mediation of disputes between carriers and the labor organizations representing their employees having to do with changes in rates of pay, rules and working conditions. (2) The duty of ascertaining the representation desires of the majority of any craft or class of carrier employees by conducting secret ballot box elections, or by other appropriate methods. In addition, the Board has the duty of appointing referees to sit with the various divisions of the National Railroad Adjustment Board, when requested to do so; the Board also appoints neutral members of arbitration boards created under the provisions of Section 7 of the Act; and it has the duty of reporting to the President situations which, in its judgment, threaten to interrupt interstate commerce to a degree which would deprive any section of the country of essential transportation service. In such situations, the President may, in his discretion, create an emergency board to hear the dispute and report thereon to him. This procedure provides a "cooling off" period of 60 days, in which the dispute may be settled by acceptance of the recommendations of the emergency board, or by agreement between the parties. The National Mediation Board also has certain functions in connection with claims of labor organizations of the right to participate in the selection of labor members of the National Railroad Adjustment Board. The Board also has the power to direct the air carriers and the labor organizations representing their employees to constitute a National Air Transport Adjustment Board. Furthermore, it is the duty of the National Mediation Board to interpret the provisions of the agreements made in mediation upon request of one or both parties to such an agreement. Thus the Board is charged with many and varied duties in connection with the administration of the Railway Labor Act, and in the exercise of its primary function of assisting the rail and air transport carriers and their employees to maintain industrial peace and assure the minimum of interruption to the flow of interstate commerce.

"National Physical Demands Information Series." A term used by the United States Employment Service. Volumes of composite descriptions of the physical demands of occupations. Because the physical demands of specific jobs in an occupation vary considerably from plant to plant, these composite descriptions are presented in such a manner that they can readily be adapted to those specific jobs.

National Records Management Council. Located at 50 E. 42nd St. New York, 17, N. Y. Deals in archives administration; business history, correspondence control; disposal and preservation of records; filing, indexing and classifying; forms control; office machines and equipment; office manuals; office systems; procedures; photo-reproduction processes; rehabilitation and repair of records; testing and training for records operations and work standards for offices.

National Secretaries Association. This organization started in 1942. In 1946 it held its first National Convention in Kansas City, Missouri and elected first national officers, adopted a national constitution and by-laws, and set the pattern for a national education program—the Certified Professional Secretary program. In 1953 the first chapter outside continental United States was established with the formation of a San Juan, Puerto Rico, chapter. In 1954, the organization became international with the installation of a Canadian chapter. The U. S. Secretary of Commerce annually issues a proclamation designating Secretaries Week, of which one specific day is known as Secretaries Day. The symbol of the organization is a red rose, and many bosses give their secretaries such a flower on that occasion. The emblem is stamped with the letters B-L, which stands for Better Learning, Better Letters, Better Living. See INSTITUTE FOR CERTIFYING SECRETARIES.

National Training Laboratory in Group Development. 1201 Sixteenth Street, N.W., Washington, D. C. The need for training and research in human relations led to the establishment of the First National Training Laboratory in Group Development in the summer of 1947. In succeeding summers the success of the Laboratory in producing research and in developing training methods and teaching skills applicable to a wide range of settings led to a demand for an expansion of activities. As a result, four years ago the Laboratory established a year-round service which provides training opportunities to selected participants and organizations. There are full-time consultants on the Washington headquarters staff for this purpose, extended, by special arrangement, by summer staff members. This consultation function is on a self-sustaining basis. In addition, in 1954 the organization became officially the National Training Laboratories, which will continue to sponsor, as one of its activities, the NTLGD at Bethel, Maine. Additionally, the National Training Laboratories, as an organization, will sponsor throughout the year: (1) one-week training laboratories in special vocational areas; (2) field service consultation; (3) inter-university center cooperation in human relations activities; (4) inter-laboratory cooperation; (5) continuous program of training of trainers; (6) applied research; (7) publications and films. The National Training Laboratory in Group Development is sponsored by the National Training Laboratories of the Division of Adult Education Service, National Education Association of the United States. A number of universities and institutions cooperate in providing staff members.

nepotism. The practice of hiring and retaining relatives in employment. Nepotism may create problems when relationships result in favoritism, promotions, or other inequalities. See "Would You Hire Your Son?" by Perrin Stryker, March, 1957 issue of *Fortune* magazine.

nerve reaction. A THERBLIG (which see) which is defined as: a message passing through the nervous system from the sense organ to the mind or from the mind to the sense organ.

net labor turnover rate, adjusted formula. The prescribed form for computing the net labor turnover adjusted to compensate for unavoidable separations. It is customarily expressed as follows:

$$T= \frac{100\ (R-U)}{W}$$

where: T= Turnover; R=Replacements; U=Unavoidable separations; W=Work force.

net labor turnover rate. The number of replacements monthly per one hundred workers in the average working force. See also AVERAGE WORKING FORCE; REPLACEMENT.

net labor turnover formula. The prescribed form for computing the net labor turnover. It is customarily expressed as:

$$T= \frac{100\ R}{W}$$

where: T=Turnover; R=Replacements; W=Work force.

neurosis. A functional disorder of the nervous system. The incidence of neurosis in industrial production is undoubtedly great enough to be significant from a personnel standpoint. In writing on "The Significance of Neurosis in Production," R. F. Tredgold, in *Human Relations in Modern Industry* (International Universities Press, Inc.), says that the effect which neurosis has can be regarded under several heads: (1) The direct

amount of work lost through absence from neurosis. (2) The wastage caused by the inefficiency of those people who remain at work at less than their maximum efficiency. (3) The effect on the rest of the firm; that is, on the excellent steady worker and on the reliable supervisor. In a study made by Dr. Russell Frazer for the Medical Research Council (1947) neuroses showed a significant increase in people: (a) who worked more than 75 hours a week (perhaps a point of now merely academic interest); (b) who had had frequent changes of work; (c) who lived alone or who were overcrowded; (d) who had been separated or widowed, or (e) who had heavy domestic responsibilities, or severe domestic stress; (f) who had poor social contact, i.e. spent leisure mostly at home; (g) who disliked their job or found it boring; (h) who were on assembly, bench, inspection or toolroom work requiring close attention; (i) who were on jobs too high or too low for their intelligence; (j) who were on jobs inadequately lighted. To counteract neurosis: (1) The worker's intelligence must match his job; (2) There must be some scope for initiative; (3) Supervision must be prepared to recognize some of the minor disorders and to cope with them.

"New Application Card." A term used by the United States Employment Service. See APPLICATION CARD.

"New Claim." A term used by the United States Employment Service. See CLAIM.

new hire. A person taken into the employment of an organization for the first time; one who has never worked for the company at any previous time.

"New Hires." A term used by the United States Employment Service. All permanent and temporary additions to the employment roll, other than those of former employees who have been recalled to work on the initiative of the employer.

nominal hours. See HOURS, NOMINAL.

nominal wages. An expression sometimes used to denote money wages.

nominal work week. The total number of scheduled operation hours of a plant, shift, or department for a one-week period, including overtime.

"Nonagricultural Placement." A term used by the United States Employment Service. See PLACEMENT.

"Nonagricultural Referral." A term used by the United States Employment Service. See REFERRAL.

noncommunist affidavits, filing of, and other data. Under NATIONAL LABOR MANAGEMENT RELATIONS ACT (which see) to use the facilities of the National Labor Relations Board, a labor organization must file the following: (1) Copies of its constitution and bylaws. (2) An annual report of its finances. (3) Certain information about its organization and operation. (4) A list of its officers. (5) An affidavit by each officer that he is not a Communist or a supporter of the Communist Party or any other subversive organization. These must be filed or the Board or its regional offices will not proceed with any case filed by the labor organization. The Board has ruled that a labor organization which has not complied with these filing requirements may participate in only one type of election —an election to determine whether the employees wish to revoke the union's authority to represent them. A noncomplying union is not entitled to certifica-

tion by the Board. Forms for these filings are available at the Board's regional offices, where the affidavits of local officers should be filed along with copies of the organization's constitution and bylaws. National and international unions must file the affidavits with the Board in Washington, D. C. The financial statements and organizational data and additional copies of the union's constitution and bylaws must be filed with the Bureau of Labor Standards, U. S. Department of Labor, Washington, D. C. Each officer of a labor organization must state under oath: *That he is not a member of the Communist Party or affiliated with such party, and that he does not believe in, and is not a member of or supports any organization that believes in or teaches, the overthrow of the United States Government by force or by any illegal constitutional methods.* It is specifically provided that Section 35A of the U. S. Criminal Code (18 U. S. C. 1001) shall apply to such affidavits. This section provides a maximum penalty of $10,000 fine and 5 years in prison for giving false statements to a Government agency. In order for a local union to have a case processed by the Board, any national, or international union or federation with which it is affiliated, also must comply with all the affidavit and filing requirements. The information filed with the Department of Labor must show: (1) Name of the organization and address of its principal place of business. (2) Names, titles, and compensation and allowances of its three principal officers, and the total amount of compensation and allowances paid them. The same information must be given on any other officials who received more than $5,000 in the preceding year. (3) The manner in which the officers mentioned above

are elected, appointed, or otherwise selected. (4) The initiation fee or fees
which new members are required to pay
on becoming members. (5) The regular
dues or fees which members are required
to pay in order to remain in good standing. (6) A detailed statement, or reference to provisions of its constitution and
bylaws, showing the procedure followed
with respect to: qualifications for or restrictions on membership; election of officers and stewards; calling of regular and
special meetings; levying of assessments;
imposition of fines; authorization for bargaining demands; ratification of contract
terms; authorization for strikes; authorization for disbursement of union funds;
audit of union financial transactions; participation in insurance or other benefit
plans, and; expulsion of members and
the grounds therefor. (7) A report showing (a) all of its receipts of any kind
and the sources of such receipts; (b) its
total assets and liabilities as of the end
of its last fiscal year; (c) the amounts
paid out during this fiscal year and the
purposes of the payments. (8) A statement that it has furnished copies of the
financial statement mentioned above to
all of its members, detailing the method
by which it was distributed.

non-contributory pension plan. A pension plan for the benefit of an employee
under which the entire cost is borne by
the employer.

"Noncovered Employment." A term used
by the United States Employment Service. Excluded employment, or employment for an employer below the size-of-
firm coverage requirements of the State
employment security law.

**Non-Federal Employees Engaged in
Work on Federal Property.** Act of June
25, 1936. This act grants to the States
jurisdiction and authority to apply their
workmen's compensation laws to non-
Federal employees engaged in work on
Federal property within the exterior
boundaries of any State. For further information write the Bureau of Employees' Compensation, U. S. Department of
Labor, Washington 25, D. C.

non-financial incentive plan. Any program designed to stimulate employees
to greater effort by providing a reward
other than financial, such as praise, recognition, training, or social symbols denoting prestige.

non-financial incentives. All influences,
other than financial, which tend to stimulate employees to greater exertion, such
as promotion, training, competition with
others, recognition, praise or factors
growing out of high morale or motivation.

"Nonperformance Specifications." A term
used by the United States Employment
Service. Factors included in employers'
requirements to which work applicants
are expected to conform, yet which have
no relationship to satisfactory job performance.

nonproduction bonus. A bonus that depends on factors other than the output
of an individual worker or a group of
workers. Profit-sharing, safety, attendance, waste elimination, and Christmas
bonuses are examples of nonproduction
bonuses. See also BONUS AND PRODUCTION
BONUSES.

non-productive labor. See INDIRECT LA-
BOR.

non-qualified plan. A pension plan which
does not meet the requirements of the
Internal Revenue Code Section 165 (a).

This type of plan is disadvantageous tax-wise.

non-repetitive. A descriptive term applied to a type of work, operation, part, or the like that does not recur frequently or in any reasonably regular sequence.

"Non-White." A term used by the United States Employment Service to designate a person who is not a member of the Caucasian or white race.

norm. A term used in employment testing. A rule or authoritative standard, model, type or criterion against which an applicant's test scores may be compared and evaluated.

"Normal Credit Allowance." A term used by the United States Employment Service. See CREDIT ALLOWANCE.

norms. As used in psychological testing, norms are tables of performance scores covering large numbers of personnel who have taken a test.

normal elemental time. An industrial engineering term, signifying the selected or average elemental time adjusted by leveling and/or other methods of adjustment to obtain the time required by a qualified workman to perform a single element of an operation.

normal operator. An employee who is sufficiently trained and qualified to perform his job operations with the average amount of effort, minimum amount of errors, and normally high quality of work.

normal worker. See NORMAL OPERATOR.

normal pace. The work rate usually used by workmen performing under capable supervision but without the stimulus of an incentive wage payment plan. This pace can easily be maintained day in and day out without undue physical or mental fatigue and is characterized by the fairly steady exertion of reasonable effort.

normal time. (1) The time required by a qualified workman, working at a pace which is ordinarily used by workmen when capably supervised to complete an element, cycle, or operation when following the prescribed method. (2) The sum of all the normal elemental times which constitute a cycle or operation.

normal working area. (1) Horizontal plane. The area at the workplace which is bounded by the imaginary arc drawn by the workman's finger tips moving in the horizontal plane with the elbow as a pivot when the workman is standing or is seated in the normal working position and when the upper arm is hanging from the shoulder in a relaxed position. The section where the normal areas of the right and left hands overlap in front of the workman constitutes the optimum normal working area for the two hands. (2) Vertical plane. The space on the surface of the imaginary sphere which would be generated by rotating, about the workman's body as an axis, the arc traced by the workman's finger tips of the right or the left hand when the fore arm is moved vertically about the elbow as a pivot. (3) Three dimensional. The space within reach of a workman's finger tips as they develop arcs of revolution, the elbow acting as a pivot when the workman is standing or is seated in the normal working position and when the upper arm is hanging from the shoulder in a relaxed position.

normalize. To adjust the actual, selected, representative, or average time taken to perform a task to the normal time to perform the task by employing a performance rating technique such as leveling or speed training.

normal labor force. The number of persons regularly at work or seeking work as estimated on the basis of previous trends. No allowance is made for the temporary entrance and withdrawal of students and other occasional workers into or out of the labor market or for persons drawn into the labor force during periods of increased labor demand. See LABOR FORCE.

Norris-La Guardia Act. See ANTI-INJUNCTION ACT.

"Notice of Employment." A term used by the United States Employment Service. A notice filed by an individual with a State employment security agency that he is unemployed, necessary to initiate a claim series for total unemployment.

O

observation. (1) In time study the act of noting and recording the time taken by a workman performing an operation or an element of an operation. (2) In motion study the act of noting and recording the motions used by an employee to perform an operation or an element of an operation. (3) In work sampling the act of noting and recording what a workman is doing at a specific instant.

observation board. A portable, flat rigid backing designed to be held by one hand and to support observation forms while information is written on them. Usually a spring clip attached to the board holds the forms firmly in place. A device for holding a stop watch may or may not be attached.

observation form. A sheet of paper used to record data taken during time studies, methods studies, or work sampling studies, specifically ruled into titled lines, columns, and spaces to suit the specific requirements of the study.

observation period. See ELAPSED TIME.

observer. An individual who makes an observation or collects data.

"Occupational Analysis." A term used by the United States Employment Service.

The collection, organization, processing, adapting, or issuing of information about the duties, responsibilities, and performance requirements of jobs, and the relationships that exist among jobs.

"Occupational Aptitude Pattern." A term used by the United States Employment Service. The combination or pattern of aptitudes that is required for probable success in learning to perform the major tasks of the fields of work from Part IV of the *Dictionary of Occupational Titles* which have been identified with each pattern.

"Occupational Classification." A term used by the United States Employment Service. (a) A systematic grouping of jobs according to significant factors involved in the job or group of jobs; (b) the process of determining a title and code number to be assigned to an application or job order; (3) the title or code of a job or group of jobs for which an applicant is qualified, as contained in the *Dictionary of Occupational Titles. Additional Occupational Classification*: The occupational classification in any occupation for which an applicant is fully qualified, other than the occupation designated as his primary occupational classification. *Entry Occupational Classification*: A classification that is assigned to an applicant on the basis of his potential qualifications (aptitudes, interests, personality, etc.). *Primary Occupational Classification*: The first title and code in the list of occupations or fields of work for which an applicant is considered qualified and which represents the one for which he is considered best suited, if such a distinction is possible.

occupational information. Systematically organized data used by guidance personnel about the nature of the work, duties and responsibilities, and compensations involved in the several vocations, including information about employment outlook, promotional opportunities and entrance requirements for the purpose of helping persons make a vocational choice.

"Occupational Code." A term used by the United States Employment Service to designate a symbol used to represent a given occupation or group of occupations.

"Occupational Composition Pattern." A term used by the United States Employment Service. A publication which provides information on the occupations and activities occurring in a single industry. Each pattern describes the industrial processes in the industry, presents a list of the occupations found, and shows which jobs occur in significant numbers as well as the percentage distribution of workers by occupational fields of work and by departments or other organizational units peculiar to the industry. See FIELDS-OF-WORK GROUPING.

"Occupational Composition Study." A term used by the United States Employment Service. See STAFFING SCHEDULE.

"Occupational Guide." A term used by the United States Employment Service. A pamphlet covering a single occupation or group of closely related occupations which contains (1) information describing the occupation (similar to that contained in a National Job Description), and (2) labor market information which describes the importance of the occupation in the economy, the industries in which it is important, the current and near-future employment prospects, wages, hours, hiring practices, and channels of entry into the occupation. See also NATIONAL JOB DESCRIPTION under JOB DESCRIPTION.

"Occupational Job Family." A term used by the United States Employment Service. See JOB FAMILY.

occupational rate. Rates (single or ranges) that are designated for particular occupations in an establishment, area, or industry. Generally, these rates are formal rates, and are paid to any worker who is qualified to perform the work of the occupation.

occupational standard. An established measure for judging the quality of work performed in a trade or occupation.

occupational wage. See OCCUPATIONAL RATE.

occupational wage relationship. The relationship of wage rates among occupations representative of a range of duties, skills, and responsibilities. Relationships may be analyzed within an individual plant, a community or region, or on an industry basis.

occupations, description of. For descriptions of thousands of specific occupations, see *Dictionary of Occupational Ti-*

tles, published by the Department of Labor, U.S. Government.

"Odd-Job Earnings." A term used by the United States Employment Service. Any earnings which a claimant may have during a week of unemployment as a result of temporary work with an employing unit other than his regular employing unit.

office management. The field of office management has several distinct, though sometimes overlapping, components: (1) standardization—forms, methods, equipment, records, systems, procedures, routines; (2) physical properties—layout, working conditions, office machinery, supplies; (3) personnel selection—scientific selection procedures, psychological, aptitude and intelligence testing, placement, induction orientation, training; (4) performance—job evaluation, merit rating, incentives, production control, quality, advancement, wages; (5) human relations—motivation, morale, maintaining loyalty, good will, cooperation.

Office of International Affairs. An agency of the U. S. Department of Labor which directs and coordinates the Department's international activities. It advises the Secretary of Labor on the impact of foreign labor developments on domestic policy, advises the Department of State on the implications of domestic labor policy on foreign policy, and recommends to the Department of State international labor policy as a part of total U. S. foreign policy. Specific functions and responsibilities of the Office include: Primary responsibility, under the over-all foreign policy guidance of the Department of State, for U. S. participation in the International Labor Organization; statutory membership on the Board of

Foreign Service, including responsibility for the labor attache program; representation and formulation of labor policy in connection with U. S. participation in the United Nations Economic and Social Council and its Commissions; membership on the Interdepartmental Committee on Trade Agreements program; and direction and coordination of the Department's programs of technical cooperation with other countries, including the training and servicing of foreign visitors, providing experts for assistance to various countries, and furnishing technical materials and information with respect to labor matters. The activities of the Office also include servicing the Secretary of Labor's Trade Union Advisory Committee on International Affairs, composed of top officials of the AFL-CIO and Railroad Brotherhoods.

Office of Vocational Rehabilitation. The Office of Vocational Rehabilitation is a constituent of the Department of Health, Education, and Welfare. Its responsibilities and objectives are defined by a series of laws going back to 1920, the most recent being the act of August 3, 1954. Known as the "Vocational Rehabilitation Amendments of 1954," this law provides for a progressive expansion of the State-Federal Vocational Rehabilitation program over the next 5 years. Services are available to civilian men and women of working age whose ability to get or hold a job or to secure a better job has been impaired through mental or physical handicap, no matter what the cause. The Office of Vocational Rehabilitation distributes grants for such services to 88 State and Territorial agencies which have approved vocational rehabilitation plans. It also extends technical assistance and consultation to the States, makes studies and investigations, and disseminates information on the utilization of disabled persons in gainful employment. Services available to the disabled worker include physical examination, medical, surgical, and psychiatric treatment, hospitalization, occupational and physical therapy, vocational counseling and training, financial help during rehabilitation, and placement on jobs. Services to management include retraining injured workers, assistance in plant surveys to determine suitable jobs for disabled persons, and referral of trained skilled workers. The Vocational Rehabilitation Amendments of 1954 provide for a stronger financial structure and improved administration for the State-Federal vocational rehabilitation program. They are designed to reach an increasing number of disabled people annually. The 1954 amendments authorize increased Federal appropriations to help the State vocational rehabilitation agencies serve more disabled persons. They also provide for training grants to institutions and traineeships to individuals to increase the number of rehabilitation personnel needed to carry on an expanded vocational rehabilitation proram—therapists, social workers, psychologists, rehabilitation counselors and others. This law provides that Federal funds made available to State agencies may, in turn, be used for grants to private, nonprofit organizations for the establishment or expansion of such centers and workshops. The Medical Facilities Survey and Construction Act of 1954—a collateral law—provides Federal grants for the *construction* of comprehensive facilities, chronic disease hospitals, nursing homes, and diagnostic and treatment centers. The 1954 amendments also open the road to rehabilitation for an increased number of Americans through the encouragement of special projects for research and demonstration which hold promise of making a substantial contribution to the solution of vocational rehabilitation problems that are common to several States. The Office of Vocational Rehabilitation makes grants to State agencies and to public and private nonprofit groups to pay part of the cost of such projects of a research or demonstration nature or for the establishment of special facilities and services. The Office of Vocational Rehabilitation also administers the Randolph-Sheppard Act (U.S. Code 1952, Title 20, Sections 107-107f), which was amended by the Vocational Rehabilitation Amendments of 1954. The Randolph-Sheppard Act originally provided for the licensing of qualified blind persons to operate vending stands in Federal and other buildings. As amended, the act permits stands to be operated on Federal *property* as well as in Federal buildings and also gives preference for the establishment of vending stands to licensed blind vending-stand operators. For further information contact your State vocational rehabilitation agency, your State agency for the blind, or write to the Office of Vocational Rehabilitation, Department of Health, Education, and Welfare, Washington 25, D. C.

office practice. A term generally applied to courses designed primarily as terminal courses to prepare students to enter the nonstenographic and nonbookkeeping office occupations, including office machine training, clerical, filing instruction, and typing. See SECRETARIAL PRACTICE.

"Offices of Direct Clearance." A term used by the United States Employment Service. Offices within a State or in ad-

joining States which have been authorized by the appropriate State administrative office or offices to negotiate directly
on clearance matters.

"Okies." A term used to describe migratory workers from Oklahoma. Popularized through John Steinbeck's "Grapes
of Wrath."

Old-Age and Survivors Insurance. See
also *Social Security Act.* Old-age and
survivors insurance is a nationwide social
insurance system. It provides old-age
benefits to an insured worker and his
family after the wage earner reaches 65
and is no longer substantially employed
(after age 72 there is no disqualification
because of employment), and survivors
benefits to his family when an insured
worker dies, whatever his age. It provides benefits to disabled workers between the ages of 50 and 65 who meet
specified work requirements.

older women. The problems of employment for older women are especially
acute. In 1954, the Commission on the
Status of Women presented to the
United Nations Economic and Social
Council a study on "Economic Opportunities for Women: Older Women
Workers." The Women's Bureau, U. S.
Department of Labor issues numerous
publications directed both to employers
and to help women secure jobs.

older workers. Much interest centers in
helping older people find jobs. The
problem is aggravated by the fact that
pensions, and other fringe benefits, become expensive when employees enter
a company at a relatively late date. The
U. S. Department of Labor, Federal and
state governments, universities, and private groups make surveys and foster
activities encouraging the hiring of older

people. A survey of 3,313,000 employees
made by the National Association of
Manufacturers shows that in work performance 93 percent of the older workers
were equal to younger workers. A more
detailed study by the University of Illinois revealed that rates of absenteeism
and lateness are actually lower among
older employees, and that their loyalty,
sense of responsibility and morale are
higher. They are also less prone to accidents. See Forty-Plus Clubs; Careers
Unlimited, publications of the U. S. Department of Labor, National Industrial
Conference Board.

one best way. (1) A term originally used
by Frank and Lillian Gilbreth to describe
a method of performing an operation
that cannot be economically improved at
the moment by those attempting to do
so. (2) The ideal method of performing
an operation that is the goal of all methods engineering work. (3) A figure of
speech which denotes the optimum
method of performing an operation under present conditions, at the present
time, and in the opinion of this particular
analyst.

one-man car differential. In the transportation industry, a premium paid to
streetcar operators who operate vehicles
without the assistance of conductors.

on-the-job training. Instruction in the
performance of a job given to an employed worker by the employer, during
the usual working hours of the occupation, for which wages are paid.

"On-the-Job Training." When used by
the United States Employment Service,
the term designates training given to an
employed worker, while he is engaged
in productive work, which provides him
with knowledge or skills essential to the

full and adequate performance of his job. Includes training of the same nature for veterans which has been approved under the Servicemen's Readjustment Act of 1944, as amended.

On-The-Job Training, for veterans. Qualified veterans who served in the U. S. Armed Forces between June 27, 1950, and January 31, 1955, inclusive, are entitled to an education and training allowance to supplement their wages while receiving on-the-job training at an approved industrial or business establishment. Veterans may be eligible to receive educational and training benefits for up to 3 years, depending on their length of service in the Armed Forces. The veteran's program of training must be initiated on or before August 20, 1954, or within 3 years after discharge or release from active military service, whichever is later, and no training may be afforded beyond 8 years after either his discharge or release from active service or at the end of his basic service period, whichever is earlier. In no event may training be afforded under this law after January 31, 1965. The Veterans Administration administers the payment of education and training allowances for on-the-job training programs which have been approved by the appropriate State agency. *Qualifications for Receiving Allowances*: To be eligible for on-the-job training allowances the veteran must: (a) Have had active military service some time between June 27, 1950 and January 31, 1955, inclusive. (b) Be discharged under conditions other than dishonorable. (c) Have at least 90 days active service or be discharged by reason of an actual service-incurred disability. *Allowance Payments*: When a program of training on the job is initiated, monthly educa-

tion and training allowances up to $70 are paid to veterans without dependents, $85 per month to veterans with one dependent, and $105 per month to veterans with more than one dependent. However, the law requires these rates to be reduced at 4-month intervals as training progresses. The law restricts the education and training allowance payable to an amount which, when added to the income to be paid to the veteran for productive labor, performed as a part of his course, would not exceed $310. Tools, equipment, and training supplies will be furnished by the veteran since the Government will not pay for them as separate items of expense. *Standards for Approving on-the-Job Programs*: Standards to be used by State agencies in approving on-the-job training establishments are set forth in the Veterans Readjustment Assistance Act of 1952. These include that: (a) The training content of the course is adequate to qualify the veteran for appointment to the job for which he is to be trained. (b) There is reasonable certainty that the job for which the veteran is to be trained will be available to him at the end of the training period. (c) The job is one in which progression and appointment to the next higher classification are based upon skills learned through organized training on-the-job and not on such factors as length of service and normal turnover. (d) The wages to be paid the veterans for each successive period of training are not less than those customarily paid in the training establishment and in the community to a learner in the same job who is not a veteran. (e) The job customarily requires a period of training of not less than 3 months and not more than 2 years of full-time training, except that this provision shall not apply to apprentice training. (f) The length of the training period is no longer than that customarily required by the training establishment and other training establishments in the community, to provide a veteran with the required skills, arrange for the acquiring of job knowledge, technical information, and other facts which the veteran will need to learn in order to become competent on the job for which he is being trained. (g) Provision is made for related instruction for the individual veteran who may need it. (h) There is in the training establishment adequate space, equipment, instructional material, and instructor personnel to provide satisfactory training on the job. (i) Adequate records are kept to show the progress made by each veteran toward his job objective. (j) Appropriate credit is given the veteran for previous training and job experience, whether in the military service or elsewhere, his beginning wage adjusted to the level to which such credit advances him and his training period shortened accordingly, and provision is made for certification by the training establishment that such credit has been granted and the beginning wage adjusted accordingly. No course of training can be considered bona fide if given to a veteran who is already qualified by training and experience for the job objective. (k) A signed copy of the training agreement for each veteran, including the training program and wage scale as approved by the State Approving Agency by the employer. (l) Upon completion of the course of training furnished by the training establishment, the veteran is given a certificate by the employer indicating the length and type of training provided and that the veteran has completed the course of training on the job

satisfactorily. (m) That the course meets such other criteria as may be established by the State Approving Agency. *Steps in Securing On-the-Job Training*: There are two essential steps: (a) The employer must be approved and certified by the appropriate State agency to the Veterans Administration as being equipped to provide training in the occupation for which the veteran is being trained. The appropriate State agency may be the State Labor Department, State Department of Education, or any other agency designated by the Governor for that purpose. (b) The veteran must file an application, VA Form 7-1990, with the Veterans Administration and secure a certificate for education and training. For further information contact the nearest regional office of the Veterans Administration.

open ended payroll deduction. A union dues deduction authorization in which no amount is specified. The company is informed by the union what amount to deduct, and this amount is subject to change at the discretion of the union.

"Opening." A term used by the United States Employment Service to designate a single job for which the local office has on file a request to select and refer an applicant or applicants. *Active Opening.* A job opening which has not yet been filled. *Cancelled Opening.* A job opening on which action by the local office has formally ceased for any reason other than placement. *Clearance Job Opening.* An opening which cannot be filled locally and which has been extended to other local offices by means of a clearance order, and/or which has been listed on a State Inventory of Job Openings. *Filled Opening.* A job opening for which an applicant referred by a local office has been hired by an employer and has entered on the job. *Unfilled Opening.* An active opening.

"Open Order." A term used by the United States Employment Service. See ORDER.

open shop. A situation in which no individual has to be a union member in order to secure or retain employment in a company, even though there may be collective bargaining relationships between the employer and employees.

operation analysis. (1) A study of the factors which affect the performance of an operation such as purpose of the operation, other operations on the part, inspection requirements, materials used, manner of handling material, setup and tool equipment, existing working conditions, and methods employed. (2) A procedure employed in studying the major factors which affect the general method of performing a given operation.

operation analysis chart. A form that lists all the important factors affecting the effectiveness of an operation and is used to guide the progress and insure the completeness of an operation analysis.

operation breakdown. See JOB BREAKDOWN.

operation element. See ELEMENT.

operation instruction card. See INSTRUCTION CARD.

operation instruction sheet. See INSTRUCTION CARD.

operation process chart. A motion study aid used to chart the time relationship of the movements made by the body members of a workman performing an

operation. See RIGHT- AND LEFT-HAND CHART; SIMO CHART, FULL; and SIMO CHART, SIMPLE. It is a graphic representation of the points at which materials are introduced into the process and of the sequence of inspections and all operations except those involved in material handling. It may include other information considered desirable for analysis such as time required and location.

operations research. "Operations Research" (O.R.) began in England during World War II when the government asked a group of scientists to help decide the most effective use of the small amount of personnel and equipment available. Successful reports prompted American military people to organize some operations research teams. With the end of the war, O.R. has been defined as a scientific method of providing executives with a quantitative basis for decisions regarding the operations under their control. An "operation" is a system of interrelated machines and/or men and/or materials. O.R. emphasizes: (1) team-work in the investigation and solution of problems; (2) use of scientific methods; (3) constructing a working model; (4) defining a criterion; (5) elevation of intangible factors; (6) consideration of the total system in relation to its parts; (7) making a choice; (8) taking action.

"Oral Trade Questions." A term used by the United States Employment Service. See TRADE QUESTIONS UNDER TESTS.

"Order," as used by the United States Employment Service means a single request for referral of one or more applicants to fill one or more job openings in a single occupational classification; also, the record of such a request. *Canceled*

Order. An order on which action by a local office has formally ceased for any reason other than placement. *Clearance Order.* An order on which clearance has been initiated. *Closed Order.* An order on which local office action has ceased because all openings have been filled or canceled. *Discriminatory Order.* An order on which an employer or his representative includes nonperformance specifications based on race, creed, color, religion, citizenship (except where citizenship is required by law), or national origin. *Master Order.* A form which contains order information compiled from previous orders of a relatively unchanging nature about a specific job in an employer's establishment. *Open Order.* An order which has not been filled or cancelled.

"Order File." A term used by the United States Employment Service. A file containing employer orders which is maintained by the local office. See also ORDER.

"Order-Holding Office." A term used by the United States Employment Service. A local office with an order for which it is unable to locate an adequate supply of qualified applicants from its local office administrative area and for which the assistance of other local offices is requested to locate and refer applicants.

organization. (1) The process of determining the necessary activities and positions within an enterprise, department, or group arranging them into the best functional relationships; clearly defining the authority, responsibilities, and duties of each; and assigning them to individuals so that the available effort can be effectively and systematically applied and coordinated. (2) The group of people which has been brought together to conduct a business or enterprise.

organization chart. A graphical representation of the formal organizational structure of an enterprise showing lines of authority, responsibility and coordination.

orientation. A planned and guided adjustment of an employee to his company, his job and his associates in that job. Orientation training usually occurs when an employee is hired by a company. It can also be applied effectively when transfers occur, or when older employees must adapt themselves to changing policies and conditions. The objectives of orientation are: (1) Inform workers about rules, regulations and policies so as to enable them to understand the conditions under which they are to work. This information will: (a) reduce wasted time on employee's part; (b) reduce ill will, disciplinary action and dismissals caused where employees did not know rules or consequences of violating them; (c) reduce supervisor's burdens in teaching and explaining company's rules and policies; (d) reduce fear of the unknown. (2) Instruct employees as to company history, personalities, products in order to show the stability of the company, its reputation, its future. (3) Show how the company depends upon the workers by explaining how the workers are the company, illustrating each worker's contribution to the finished article or the service being rendered. (4) Provide a permanent channel for presenting information to employees and influencing their reaction to it. See "Orientation Training Today," by Earl Planty, in *Personnel Journal*, June, 1944.

orientation check list. A chart for checking off in orderly sequence the items about which a new employee should be informed or which otherwise apply, in inducting a new worker. Such a check list might include: First Day (or Week) (1) Personal Welcome; (2) Supervisor's Name and Position; (3) Departmental Organization; (4) Employee's Name; (5) Nickname or first name employee wishes used; (6) Why supervisor is concerned about employee's welfare; (7) Safety Rules; (8) Specific hazards in connection with job; (9) Fire regulations; (10) First aid facilities; (11) Plant rules—absenteeism, tardiness; (12) Privileges—smoking, snacks; (13) Weekly work schedule; (14) Shifts; (15) Method of pay; (16) Uniforms or work clothes; (17) Introduction to fellow worker who is "sponsor"; (18) Dressing and restrooms, carpools; (19) Identification badge; (20) Good housekeeping practices; (21) Training program; (22) Introduction to instructor or operator; (23) Announcements on bulletin boards; (24) Amount of work he will possibly be able to produce first week; (25) Pensions, insurance, benefits. Second Week. (1) Importance of job in respect to quality, total production, production of other employees; (2) Shift rotation; (3) Seniority; (4) Changes in job duties. Third Week. (1) Suggestions system; (2) Vacation and holiday policy (specific dates of interest to employee); (3) Analysis of his scrap, rejects, etc.; (4) Participation in employee recreational activities, etc.

orientation procedure. A term applied to the formal or informal program for starting a new employee on the job. Some suggestions, given in "Orienting the New Worker," Metropolitan Life Insurance Company bulletin, outline the procedure as: (1) Reception and interview, (2) Acceptance and rejection; (3) Initial contact with supervisor; (4) Induction; (5) Reporting for work.

operation. The intentional changing of an object in any of its physical or chemical characteristics; the assembly or disassembly of parts or objects; the preparation of an object for another operation, transportation, inspection or storage; planning, calculating, or the giving or receiving of information.

opportunity school. A school providing specialized courses to meet widely varied adult needs; such as those of illiterates, applicants for naturalization, workers needing retraining, or adults seeking various types of vocational training.

ordinary life pension trust. Trust fund set up to buy life insurance for employees until retirement age. At retirement, the life insurance is converted to annuity benefits. Usually a separate trust is set up for annuity payments.

out-of-line rate. See RUNAWAY RATE.

output. The quantity of goods produced or manufactured.

output standard. See PERFORMANCE STANDARD.

overhead. Costs or expenses which are not directly identifiable with or chargeable to the manufacture of a particular part or product. For example, items such as taxes, insurance, supplies, supervisory and clerical charges, and the like, are overhead. Synonyms for overhead are burden, indirect manufacturing expense.

overseer. See FOREMAN.

overtime, calculation of, under Fair Labor Standards Act. *Calculation of Overtime:* Compensation for overtime—work after 40 hours in a workweek—ordinarily is due when the employee customarily receives his pay. Such overtime payments must be at the rate of not less than one and one-half times the "regular rate" at which the employee is actually employed and paid, except as otherwise specifically provided . . . The employee's "regular rate" of pay includes all remuneration for employment, with the exception of certain special payments excluded under section 7 (d) of the act, such as premium payments of at least time and one-half for work on Saturdays, Sundays, or holidays. Alternative methods of computing overtime compensation are provided under certain conditions for (1) employees employed at piece rates, (2) employees performing two or more kinds of work for which different hourly or piece rates have been established, and (3) for employees whose overtime compensation is based on an established rate substantially equivalent to their average hourly straight-time earnings. For employees whose duties necessitate irregular hours of work, section 7 (e) of the act permits that payment may be made pursuant to a certain specified contract arrangement. *Piecework Basis of Computation.*—For the employee who is employed on a piecework basis, the regular hourly rate of pay is computed for each workweek by dividing the total piecework earnings by the total number of hours worked. For overtime work, the pieceworker is entitled to be paid, in addition to piecework earnings for the entire period, a sum equivalent to one-half the regular hourly rate of pay multiplied by the number of hours worked in excess of 40 in the week. *Weekly or Monthly Pay Basis of Computation.*— When a salary is paid for a specified number of hours worked in a workweek, the regular hourly rate is the weekly salary (or monthly salary reduced to a weekly basis) divided by the specified weekly number of hours. When a salary is paid for whatever number of hours is worked in the workweek, the weekly salary is divided by the number of hours actually worked each week, to obtain the "regular rate" of pay. *What the "Workweek" Is.*—Under the Fair Labor Standards Act, an employee's workweek is a fixed and regularly recurring period of 168 hours—7 consecutive 24-hour periods. A workweek need not coincide with the calendar week—it may begin on any day of the week and at any hour of the day. The beginning of an employee's workweek may be changed if the change is intended to be permanent and not to evade the overtime provisions of the act. *Each Workweek Stands Alone.*—Each workweek stands alone under the act. There may be no averaging of hours of work over 2 or more workweeks for determining overtime hours; that is, overtime must be paid for all hours worked over 40 in *each* workweek. *Deductions From Wages.*—Deductions which bring the employee's *free and clear* cash wages below one dollar an hour are permitted only when the employer makes the deductions for employee facilities as discussed below. The employer may deduct the reasonable cost of furnishing his employees with board, lodging, or other facilities which are primarily of benefit to the employee if they are customarily furnished by the employer to his employees. *Reasonable cost* does not include a profit to the employer or to any affiliated person. The cost of furnishing facilities which are primarily for the benefit or convenience of the employer (such as tools of the trade, required safety equipment, required uniforms or their laundering) may not be included in figuring the minimum wage and may be deducted only if the actual cash wage paid after such deductions is at least one dollar an hour. Deductions for union dues, charitable contributions, and other payments to someone other than the employer, which bring the cash wage below one dollar an hour, are allowable provided they are made with the consent of the employee and the employer does not derive any profit or benefit from the deduction.

overtime pay for supervisors. Although companies are not legally obligated to pay supervisors exempt from the Fair Labor Standards Act any additional pay for working overtime, many have elected to do so. For example, 35 of 40 large companies surveyed by the National Industrial Conference Board have some formal plan for compensating their first-line supervisors for overtime work. The company's primary concern in paying for such work is to maintain the basic differential between the supervisor and those working under him. For this rea-son, even the companies that pay their supervisors the same premium that goes to the nonexempt workers—time and one-half—usually apply some form of restriction on the overtime pay for the supervisory group. In some cases, overtime pay does not begin immediately after eight hours in the day or forty in the week. Casual and emergency overtime are rarely recognized with pay. Many companies require that paid overtime work must be scheduled in advance. Eligibility for overtime pay may also be limited on a salary basis.

overtime premium pay. Payment of wages at a premium rate for time worked beyond the regular hours of employment established by union agreement, employer or industry practice, or law. In the United States, payment is typically made at one and a half times the regular rate of pay. Higher premium rates are found to a limited extent. See also PRE-MIUM RATE.

P

pace setter. A worker who is better than average on a particular job, and whose production is used by the employer as a standard for measuring the amount of work which can be done in a given period of time.

pace setting. See SPEED RATING.

package. A term used to describe a combination of benefits received by workers as a result of collective bargaining. A package may include wage increases and other benefits of monetary value, such as insurance, paid holidays, paid vacations, and sick leave. The term generally implies that during the bargaining process the parties agreed that a specified amount of increase was to be applied partly to rate of pay and partly to the financing of the related benefits.

"paper local." A local union that has no real members to start with—only a legal charter and a few names on paper. A "racketeer" with a paper local may make a deal with an employer to profit the two of them—at the expense of the worker. In these "sweetheart contracts" (which see) the racketeer agrees to keep a legitimate union out, and the employer agrees to recognize the paper local, with a contract providing substandard wages.

The racketeer collects initiation fees and dues, and sometimes kicks back part of the take to the employer.

Parkhurst System. An incentive wage plan which provides for gain sharing by employees, the amount received fluctuating with the amount of gain earned by the group of which the employee is a member. An employee thus may be a member of the group which receives twice as much as another group because his group earned more gain, etc.

"Partial Benefits." A term used by the United States Employment Service. See BENEFITS.

"Partial Earnings Allowance." A term used by the United States Employment Service. The amount of earnings that are disregarded in calculating a claimant's benefit for a week.

"Partial Unemployment." A term used by the United States Employment Service. See WEEK OF UNEMPLOYMENT.

"Partially Pooled Account." A term used by the United States Employment Service. See ACCOUNTS.

part-time programs, vocational. Programs conducted for workers during the usual working hours of the occupations in

(224)

which they are employed. There are three general kinds, as follows: (1) Part-time trade extension classes—instruction given to employed workers for the purpose of increasing or extending their skill and knowledge in the trade or occupation in which they are or have been engaged. (2) Part-time trade preparatory classes—instruction given to workers who have left the full-time school for the purpose of fitting themselves for useful employment in trades, occupations, or fields of industry other than those in which they are or have been employed. (3) Part-time general continuation classes —instruction given to employed persons for the purpose of enlarging their civic or vocational intelligence. Instruction is not confined to trade or industrial pursuits but may cover any subject relative to civic or vocational needs, offered to workers who return to the school during their usual working hours.

"Part-Time Work." A term used by the United States Employment Service. Employment in which a worker is regularly scheduled to work substantially fewer hours per week than is customary for the occupation or department within the establishment or for the occupation within the community.

part-time worker rate. A rate paid to a part-time, temporary, or contingent worker, as distinguished from that paid to a regular or full-time worker. Part-time rates may be equal to, or lower or higher than, regular or full-time rates. During periods of ample labor supply, part-time rates are usually lower, but may become equivalent or higher when the labor market is tight because of keen competition for such help. Retail trade establishments and restaurants are among the industries dependent on part-time or

temporary help to carry on their normal functions.

"Part-Time Workers." A term used by the United States Employment Service. A person engaged in, or available only for, part-time work.

"Part-Total Benefits." A term used by the United States Employment Service. See BENEFITS.

"Part-Total Unemployment." A term used by the United States Employment Service. See WEEK OF UNEMPLOYMENT.

past (prior) service benefit. Pension credits, provided by the employer, for all or part of the individual's years of service with the company prior to the adoption of the plan.

past service funding. Method of funding the past service liability. This cost may be amortized over a period of years. The Internal Revenue Code specifies that the employer may not deduct more than one-tenth of the original liability in any one year for income-tax purposes.

past service liability. The cost of providing pensions for service rendered prior to the adoption of the pension plan. The cost, which is determined actuarially, will depend upon the age, sex, and years of service of the working force and upon the number of years of past service which are credited under the plan.

pattern-following bargaining. Also known as area-wide or industry-wide bargaining. Bargains made elsewhere determine or influence the negotiations. The union acts as spokesman for employees in the industry. Employers may consult among themselves prior to taking action, thereby creating an informal association. Pattern-following bargaining may be local, regional, or national; it may be on a craft, industry, or interindustry basis.

pay-as-you-go plan. Employer pays for pensions out of current income as they become due. No advance funding.

payment by results. A term applied to financial incentive plans (which see). According to *Payment By Results*, published in 1951 by the International Labor Office, Geneva, such systems, which relate directly to some measurement of the work done either by the worker or by the group or working unit to which he belongs, can be classified in four main groups according to whether the worker's earnings vary: (1) in the same proportion as output—Straight Piece-Work System, Standard Hour System; (2) proportionately less than output—The Halsey System, The Rowan System, The Barth Variable Sharing System, The Bedaux System; (3) proportionately more than output—High Piece-Rate and Standard Hour Systems where the worker also shares the savings in overhead costs which result from increased output; (4) in proportions which differ at various levels of output—The Taylor Differential Piece-Rate System, The Merrick Differential Piece-Rate System, The Gantt Task System, The Emerson Empiric or Efficiency System, and Similar Systems as Wennerlund, Knoeppel, Bigelow, Bigelow-Knoeppel, Atkinson and Allingham systems. C. W. Lytle in *Wage Incentive Methods*, uses a slightly different grouping as will be noted. Individual systems are described under their alphabetic listing.

payments in kind. (Income in Kind) Noncash payments for labor, received by individuals in the form of lodging, meals and other services or commodities. (Such income is particularly important in agriculture, domestic service, hotels and restaurants and military service.)

"Pay Roll, Annual" (Experience-Rating). A term used by the United States Employment Service to designate the total amount of taxable wages payable (or paid) by a subject employer for insured work during a calendar year or period of twelve consecutive months.

pay-roll deduction. A deduction from an employee's gross earnings made by his employer for social security, unemployment insurance, Federal income tax, local government pay-roll tax, union dues, special union assessments, group insurance premiums, etc.

pay-roll period. The established frequency with which workers are paid in a particular industry, regardless of the time to which the rate applies. Thus, hourly rated workers may be paid weekly, biweekly, semi-monthly, or monthly. Similarly, workers on an annual or monthly rate basis may be paid weekly; the pay-roll period in this case is a week. The minimum frequency of pay-roll periods is often specified in State legislation.

"Pay-Roll Period." A term used by the United States Employment Service. A work period established by an employer for which earnings of employees are computed for payment (e.g., day, week, two-weeks, half-month, month).

pay-roll tax. Taxes levied by the Government and paid by employers, employees, or both, creating funds from which employees receive retirement, unemployment, or other benefits. Also may refer to employer contributions, based on fixed percentages of total pay roll, to union or other private health and welfare and vacation funds, and to pay-roll taxes levied by cities.

peak load. A term used chiefly in financial houses, or establishments doing clerical work, where the work piles up during a certain period of the day and must be finished by a certain time. Often this results in hiring people who are not completely utilized the balance of the day. "Staffing for peak load," may become uneconomical office management.

peg point. An occupational rate for a key unskilled, semiskilled, or skilled job, establishing differentials within the wage structure. Term first used by the National War Labor Board in its decision on wages in the cotton textile industry in 1945 (see 21 W. L. B. 882), and thereafter applied to the wage structure through collective bargaining.

penalties, under Fair Labor Standards Act. The Federal Government may prosecute criminally for willful violations of the Fair Labor Standards Act. Upon conviction, the employer may be fined up to $10,000, and, in the case of a second conviction, imprisoned for up to six months. The Secretary of Labor may ask a Federal district court to restrain violations of the Act by injunction. Under certain conditions, an employer may have a "good faith" defense against liability or punishment for failing to pay minimum wages or overtime compensation due under the Fair Labor Standards Act. The Act prohibits discharging or discriminating against an employee because he has filed a complaint or started or participated in a proceeding under the Act. Complaints, records, and other information obtained by the De-

partment of Labor from employees and employers are treated confidentially.

penalties under the Railway Labor Act. (which see) Violation by a carrier of the provisions of the Railway Labor Act regarding rights of employees, determination of collective bargaining representatives, giving notice of intended change of agreements, and posting notices, is a misdemeanor, punishable by fine up to $20,000, imprisonment, or both. Claims of violations should be filed with the United States district attorney in the area where the violation occurred.

penalties, under the Walsh-Healey Public Contracts Act. Violation of the Act may result in cancellation of the contract by the awarding agency, with any additional costs charged to the original contractor. Sums due the United States may be recovered by withholding payment of monies due or by court action. No award of Government contracts may be made to the responsible person or firm within 3 years from the date on which the Secretary of Labor determines that a breach of contract occurred, unless the Secretary specifically recommends otherwise.

penalty rate. An extra rate which is paid for hazardous jobs, late shift work, Sunday and holiday work, or for overtime. See also PREMIUM RATE.

"Penetration Ratio." A term used by the United States Employment Service. See PLACEMENT PENETRATION RATIO.

pension plan. In business and industry, a plan established and maintained by an employer alone, or by a union alone, or by both together in collective bargaining, primarily to provide systematically for the payment of definitely determinable benefits to employees in regular payments, usually monthly, over a period of years, usually for life, from the time they retire until they die. Pension plans are contributory or non-contributory, which see.

pension committee. A committee in a company set up to administer the pension plan. Keeps track of changes in beneficiaries, checks on retirements, prepares statistics, particularly at times when union negotiations involving pensions are in progress, and may perform a variety of other duties. May be composed of management representatives, or have union representation on the committee.

pension plan, approved. See APPROVED PENSION PLAN.

periodic review. Periodic appraisal of the employment status and impact of the personnel program upon the individual employee.

performance. The degree with which a workman applies his skill and effort to an operation under the conditions prevailing. This degree is expressed in terms of a performance efficiency or defined bench marks such as good, average and poor.

performance efficiency. A ratio—usually expressed as a percentage—of actual output to a bench mark or standard output when both are measured on the same basis.

performance rating. The act of comparing an actual performance by a workman against a defined concept of a normal performance. Various methods of performance rating are in use differing primarily as to the bases on which comparison is made.

performance rating factor. (1) A numerical index that relates an observed performance to a defined normal performance. (2) Any of the terms or elements used for the comparison of performance.

performance rating scale. (1) A series of descriptive graduated statements and/or numbers serving as a guide by which an observed performance may be estimated and its worth more objectively determined. (2) A series of graduated statements and/or numbers that describe a specific characteristic and serve as a guide for making more objective estimates of the degree to which that characteristic is exhibited in any specific instance.

"Performance Requirements." A term used by the United States Employment Service to designate the basic skills, knowledges, abilities, and responsibilities of a worker for successful job performance.

performance standard. A criterion or bench mark with which actual performance is compared.

performance trade test. A trade or proficiency test designed as a replica of the work situation, in which the applicant actually demonstrates his skill by doing a work sample. Examples: Typing and dictation tests.

"Performance Trade Test." A term used by the United States Employment Service. See TESTS.

Perlman, Selig. (1888-   ) Professor emeritus of economics at the University of Wisconsin. He is the chief disciple and inheritor of Common's intellectual leadership in labor economics at that school. Two of his more important books are: *A History of Trade Unionism in the*

United States (1922) and *A Theory of the Labor Movement* (1928). His doctrine is the dominating influence of a consciousness of scarcity of opportunity on the part of the workingman as opposed to the consciousness of an abundance of opportunity which characterizes the self-confident businessman. The ultimate aim is "communism of opportunity." It is reached by solidarity and job control, through which there is a "rationing" of the existing job opportunities among the members of the group. The answer apparently lies through exclusion of "outsiders," presentation of a solid bargaining front to both employers and customers—in a word, in combination and collective unity.

permanent piece rate. A rate established for a piecework job calculated to yield an appropriate level of earnings and based, generally, on experience with trial rates for the job assignment; such rates are expected to persist until basic conditions change.

permits, work. See EMPLOYMENT CERTIFICATES.

perquisite. Relates to the furnishing by employers of food, lodging, and other payments in kind to workers in addition to monetary compensation. Thus, waitresses are generally allowed a certain number of meals, depending upon the length of the shift; board and lodging are usually supplied to workers in lumber camps and in some cases to farm labor.

personal allowance. Time included in the production standard to permit the workman to attend to personal necessities; as, obtaining drinks of water, making trips to the rest room, and the like.

(Usually applied as a percentage of the leveled, normal, or adjusted time.)

personal time. See PERSONAL ALLOWANCE.

personality tests. Personality tests are intended to supplement those of intelligence, special aptitudes, interest, etc. in order to give a more complete picture of the vocational potentialities of the individual. Successful accomplishment is determined, in part, by the personal characteristics of the individual, by his ability to adjust to the job, and by his ability to maintain the social relationships required of him. Personality tests include: Specimen Packet C.P.F. (Short Personality Test)—Industrial Psychology, Inc.; Personal Inventory I. Guilford and Martin—Sheridan Supply Co.; Inventory of Factors—Sheridan Supply Co.; Personal Audit, Adams and Lepley—Science Research Associates; Thurstone Temperament Schedule—Science Research Associates; Ascendance-Submission Test—Allport—Psychological Corporation; Minnesota Multiphasic Personality Inventory—Hathaway and McKinley—Psychological Corporation; Social Adjustment Inventory — Washburne — Psychological Corporation; The Adjustment Inventory —Bell—Psychological Corporation; Revision of A-S Reaction Study for Business Use—Beckman—Psychological Corporation; Attitude-Interest Analysis Test —Terman and Miles—Psychological Corporation; Gordon Personal Profile—Psychological Corporation; Heston Personal Adjustment Inventory — Psychological Corporation; Minnesota Personality Scale —Darley and McNamara—Psychological Corporation; Psycho-Somatic Inventory— McFarland and Seitz—Psychological Corporation; A Study of Values—Allport, Vernon and Lindzet—Psychological Corporation; The Guilford-Zimmerman Temperament Survey—Guilford and Zimmerman — Sheridan Supply Company; Humm-Wadsworth Temperament Scale—Humm Wadsworth Personnel Service.

personnel. The people comprising an organization.

personnel audit. Systematic survey and evaluation of the entire body of personnel policies and practices of an organization in terms of established objectives.

personnel administration. A term describing the personnel rather than the material phase of promotion, emphasizing human relations; includes hiring, classifying, training, promotion, transfer, wage rates, bonus systems, discharges, health, recreation sometimes also public relations and arbitration. The word itself has come into general use only since about 1930. Its content derives from early English progressive employers like Robert Owen, was stimulated by Frederick Winslow Taylor and other protagonists of "scientific management," and during World War I by use in civilian production and in the United States Army. Dr. Ordway Tead, in "Personnel Administration," (McGraw-Hill Book Company, 1933) says, "Personnel Administration is the planning, supervision, direction, and coordination of those activities of an organization which contribute to realizing the defined purposes of that organization with a minimum of human effort and friction, with an animating spirit of cooperation, and with proper regard for the genuine well-being of all members of the organization." The phrase *personnel department* indicates the staff department which is charged with the advisory, executive, and operating duties which are agreed to fall under the personnel function. The personnel manager is, if properly termed, the staff executive possessed of equal rank with other staff officials in handling matters of general administrative policy, who is looked to for the initial formulation of sound policies in employee relations and under whom the operating work of employment, health and safety, training, and other activities are carried on.

personnel associations. The following list includes only national organizations. An asterisk (*) indicates there is a separate entry for the organization named. Addresses are subject to change in those instances where associations have no permanent headquarters, and the secretaryship revolves. In addition, *Personnel,* published by the American Management Association, annually presents a *"Directory of Local Personnel Groups"* giving officers, addresses and other details.

*American Accounting Association, Ann Arbor, Michigan.

*American Arbitration Association, 477 Madison Avenue, New York, 20, N. Y.

American Association for the Advancement of Science, 1515 Massachusetts Ave., Washington 5, D. C.

American Association of Industrial Editors, 1728 Cherry Street, Philadelphia 3, Pa.

*American Bankers Association, 12 E. 36th Street, New York, N. Y.

American Chemical Society, 1155-16th St., N.W., Washington, D. C.

American Economic Association, Northwestern University, Evanston, Ill.

*American Economic Foundation, 295 Madison Ave., New York 17, N. Y.

American Gas Association, 420 Lexington Ave., New York, N. Y.

American Institute of Accountants, 270 Madison Avenue, New York, N. Y.

American Institute for Economic Research, Great Barrington, Mass.

* American Institute of Industrial Engineers, 145 North High St., Columbus 15, Ohio.

*American Institute of Management, 125 E. 38th Street, New York 16, N. Y.

American Institute for Research, 410 Amberson Ave, Pittsburgh 12, Pa.

American Library Association, 50 E. Huron Street, Chicago, Illinois.

*American Management Association, 1515 Broadway, New York 36, N. Y.

*American Marketing Association, 1525 E. 53d Street, Chicago 15, Ill.

*American Medical Association, 535 N. Dearborn St., Chicago 10, Ill.

*American Personnel and Guidance Association, 1534 "O" St., N. W. Washington 5, D. C.

American Psychiatric Association, 1270 6th Avenue, New York 20, N. Y.

American Psychological Association, 1133 Sixteenth St., N.W., Washington 6, D. C.

American Society of Mechanical Engineers, 29 West 39th St., New York 18, N. Y.

American Society for Personnel Administration, Kellogg Center, East Lansing, Mich.

American Society for Public Administration, 1313 E. 60th St., Chicago 37, Illinois.

American Society for Quality Control, 50 Church Street, New York, N. Y.

American Society of Tool Engineers, 10700 Puritan Avenue, Detroit 38, Michigan

*American Society of Training Directors, 202 University Ave., Madison 5, Wisconsin

American Standards Asociation, 70 E. 45th Street, New York 17, N. Y.

American Statistical Association, 1108-16th St. N.W., Washington, D. C.

*Association of Consulting Management Engineers, 347 Madison Avenue, New York 17, N. Y.

Association of Iron and Steel Engineering, 1010 Empire Building, Pittsburgh, Pa.

British Institute of Personnel Management, 8 Hill St., London W 1., Eng.

*The Brookings Institution, 722 Jackson Place, N.W., Washington, D. C.

California Personnel Management Association, 2180 Milvia St., Berkeley 4, California

Canadian Industrial Trainer's Association, 35 Notre Dame St., W., Montreal, Canada

*Chamber of Commerce of the United States, 1615 H St., N.W., Washington 6, D. C.

Civil Service Assembly, 1313 E. 60th Street, Chicago 37, Illinois

Commerce and Industry Association of New York, 99 Church St., N. Y. 7, N. Y.

Committee for Economic Development, 444 Madison Avenue, New York 22, N. Y.

Conference Board of Associated Research Councils, 2101 Constitution Avenue, N.W., Washington, D. C.

Controllers Institute of America, 1 East 42nd St., New York, N. Y.

Council of Profit Sharing Industries, First National Tower, Akron 8, Ohio.

Econometric Society, Box 1264, Yale University, New Haven, Conn.

Edison Electric Institute, 420 Lexington Avenue, New York, N. Y.

Employers Labor Relations Information Committee, Inc., 33 E. 48th St., New York, N. Y.

Foreman's Association of America, 515 Barium Tower, Detroit 26, Mich.

Foremanship Foundation, 512 Harries Bldg., Dayton 2, Ohio.

Foundation for Economic Education, Irvington on Hudson, N. Y.

Foundation on Employee Health, Medical Care and Welfare, 477 Madison Ave., New York, N. Y.

Industrial Hygiene Foundation of America, 4400 Fifth Avenue, Pittsburgh 13, Pa.

Industrial Management Society, 35 E. Wacker Drive, Chicago 1, Ill.

Industrial Medical Association, 366 Madison Avenue, New York 17, N. Y.

*Industrial Relations Research Association, Sterling Hall, Madison 6, Wisconsin

*The Institute of Management Sciences, Mt. Royal and Guilford Avenues, Baltimore 2, Maryland

International Association of Personnel Women, c/o Employers Mutual, Wausau, Wisconsin (subject to change)

International Labour Organization, 734 Jackson Place, Washington 6, D. C.

*Junior Achievement, Inc., 345 Madison Ave., New York 17, N. Y.

Kiwanis International, 520 N. Michigan Ave., Chicago 11, Ill.

Life Office Management Association, 110 E. 42nd Street, New York, N. Y.

Lions International, 209 North Michigan Avenue, Chicago 1, Ill.

Machinery and Allied Products Institute, 1200-18th Street, N.W., Washington, D. C. (Affiliate for Council for Technological Advancement.)

Mellon Institute of Industrial Research, 4400 Fifth Ave., Pittsburgh 13, Pa.

Merchants and Manufacturers Associa-

tion, 725 S. Spring St., Los Angeles 14, Cal.

National Association and Council of Business Schools, 601-13th St., N.W., Washington, D. C.

National Association of Cost Accountants, 505 Park Avenue, New York, N. Y.

*National Association of Manufacturers, 14 W. 49th St., New York 20, N. Y.

National Association for Mental Health, 1790 Broadway, New York 19, N. Y.

National Association of Personnel Consultants, LeVeque Lincoln Tower, Columbus, Ohio

National Association of Suggestion Systems, 122 S. Michigan Ave., Chicago 3, Ill.

National Bureau of Economic Research, 261 Madison Avenue, New York 16, N. Y.

*National Council of Industrial Management Clubs, 291 Broadway, New York 7, N. Y.

*National Industrial Conference Board, 460 Park Avenue, New York 22, N. Y.

National Industrial Recreation Association, 203 N. Wabash, Chicago 1, Illinois

National Institute of Industrial Psychology, 14 Welbach St., London, W. 1, England

*National Management Association, 321 W. 1st Street, Dayton, Ohio

National Office Management Association, Willow Grove, Pa.

National Metal Trades Association, 337 W. Madison St., Chicago 6, Illinois

National Planning Association, 1606 N. Hampshire Ave., N.W., Washington 6, D. C.

*National Records Management Council, 50 E. 42nd St., New York 17, N. Y.

National Research Council, 2101 Constitution Avenue, Washington 25, D. C.

National Safety Council, 425 N. Michigan Avenue, Chicago, Ill.

National Sales Executives, Inc., 136 E. 57th Street, New York 22, N. Y.

National Secretaries Association, 222 West 11th St., Kansas City 5, Mo.

*National Training Laboratories, 1201-16th St., N.W., Washington 6, D. C.

Operations Research Society of America, Mt. Royal and Guilford Aves., Baltimore, Maryland

Personnel Research Institute, 11800 Shaker Blvd., Cleveland 20, Ohio

Public Affairs Committee, Inc., 22 E. 38th St., New York, N. Y.

Public Affairs Information Service, 11 West 49th St., New York 18, N. Y.

Research Council for Economic Security, 111 W. Jackson Blvd., Chicago 4, Ill.

Rotary International, 35 E. Wacker Drive, Chicago 1, Ill.

Social Science Research Council, 230 Park Avenue, New York 17, N. Y.

*Society for the Advancement of Management, 74 Fifth Avenue, New York 11, N. Y.

Society for Applied Anthropology, 150 E. 35th Street, New York, N. Y.

Society for Personnel Administration, 5506 Connecticut Ave., N.W., Washington, D. C.

Special Libraries Association, 31 E. 10th Street, New York 3, N. Y.

Tavistock Institute of Human Relations, London, England

Transcription Supervisors Association (Address rotates.)

*The Twentieth Century Fund, 330 West 42nd Street, New York 36, N. Y.

"Personnel Functional Time Distribution System." A term used by the United States Employment Service. A system of reporting the time spent by State employment security personnel on the various functions of their operations, for use as management and budgetary tool. See also STANDARD FUNCTIONAL TIME DISTRIBUTION CODE.

personnel groups, local. Progress in personnel administration and industrial relations has been accelerated by the growing activities of local personnel groups. These are known by such titles as personnel association, personnel club, personnel women, personnel management association, etc., almost always preceded by the name of the city or the area where they are located, as "Bay Area Personnel Women," or Phoenix Personnel Club. *Personnel*, published by the American Management Association, includes an annual listing of these groups, usually in its November issue.

personnel information, general sources. Among sources helpful in securing personnel information, are: "The Office Library of the Industrial Relations Executive," published by Department of Economics and Social Institutions, Princeton University, Princeton, N. J. "The Management Index," published annually by American Management Association. Index of the National Industrial Conference Board. "Library Accessions Bulletin," Industrial Relations Library, Massachusetts Institute of Technology. "Business Information—How to Find and Use It," by Marian C. Manley, Harper & Brothers.

personnel management. That part of management which is primarily concerned with the human relationship within an organization. Its aim is the maintenance of these relationships on a basis which, by consideration of the well-being of the individual, enables all those engaged in the undertaking to make their maximum personal contribution to the effective working of that undertaking. The primary task of the personnel function is to assist production or business management in the effective discharge of their responsibilities to enable them to carry out more fully their task of "managing personnel" in the finest sense of the term. Essentially, the personnel function is a service function which has as its aim to secure such conditions of employment as will enable every member of the undertaking to obtain the utmost personal satisfaction and to make the greatest possible contribution to the success and effectiveness of the organization. It is only in the careful balance between personal satisfactions of employees and their material contributions to the company that a successful personnel policy can be developed and harmonious relations between management and employees can be achieved. At the same time personnel management must be specialized. Modern personnel management attempts to apply scientific methods to its special range of problems. But correct use of the various underlying sciences, on which the correct handling of individuals working in groups must be based, involves some knowledge of individual and group psychology, medicine, economics, law, sociology and statistics as a start. To this must be added experience in trade union organization and relations, unemployment and health insurance, methods of selection, employee rating, training, etc. Such knowledge and experience needs to be interpreted in the light of a practical understanding of the organization and technical processes of the particular undertaking involved.

personnel publications. Following are the major publications in the field of personnel: *Abstracts and Annotations,* New York State School of Industrial and Labor Relations, Cornell University, Ithaca, N. Y.; *Acme Reporter,* Association of Consulting Management Engineers, 347 Madison Avenue, New York, 17, N. Y.; *Administrative Science Quarterly,* Cornell Univ., Graduate School of Business Administration; *Advanced Management,* Society for Advancement of Management, 74 Fifth Avenue, New York 11, N. Y.; *Adult Leadership,* Adult Educ. Association of U. S., 743 Wabash Avenue, Chicago, 11, Illinois; *A.F.L.-C.I.O. News,* Washington, D. C.; *American Business,* Dartnell Corporation, 4600 Ravenswood Avenue, Chicago, 40, Illinois; *American Economic Security,* Chamber of Commerce of U. S., 1615 H. St., N.W., Washington, D. C.; *American Journal of Psychology,* Mezes Hall, University of Texas, Austin, Texas; *American Journal of Sociology,* University of Chicago, 5750 Ellis Avenue, Chicago, 37, Ill.; *American Machinist,* McGraw-Hill Publishing Co., 330 West 42nd St., New York, 36, N. Y.; *American Psychologist,* American Psychological Association, 1333-16th St., N.W., Washington, 5, D. C.; *Annals of the Academy of Political and Social Science,* 3837 Chestnut Street, Philadelphia, 4, Pa.; *Arbitration Journal,* American Arbitration Association, 477 Madison Avenue, New York, 20, N. Y.; *Armed Forces Management,* Professional Service Publ. Co., 208 South Second Street, Rockford, Illinois; *Barron's National Business and Financial Weekly,* 40 New Street, New

York, 4, N. Y.; *Best's Insurance News*, 75 Fulton Street, New York, 38, N. Y.; *Business*, Business Publications Ltd., 180 Fleet Street, London, E.C. 4, England; *Business Education World*, 330 West 42nd Street, New York, 36, N. Y.; *Business Management*, 100 Simcoe Street, Toronto, 1, Canada; *Business Management Service Bulletin*, University of Illinois, Urbana, Illinois; *Business Record*, National Industrial Conference Board, 460 Park Avenue, New York, 22, N. Y.; *Business Week*, 330 West 42nd Street, New York, 36, N. Y.; *Canadian Business*, 524 Board of Trade Bldg., Montreal, P.Q. Canada; *Canadian Personnel and Industrial Relations Journal*, Personnel Associations (Canada), 143 Yonge Street, Toronto, Canada; *Challenge Magazine*, Institute of Economic Affairs, 32 Broadway, New York, 4, N. Y.; *Changing Times*, Kiplinger Magazine, 1729 H. St., N.W., Washington, 6, D. C.; *Clarkson Letter*, Clarkson Institute of Technology, Potsdam, N. Y.; *Commerce*, Chicago Association of Commerce and Industry, 1 N. LaSalle Street, Chicago, 2, Illinois; *Contemporary Psychology*, American Psychological Association; *The Controller*, 73 Main Street, Brattleboro, Vermont; *Cost and Management*, 66 King Street, East, Hamilton, Ont., Canada. *Dun's Review and Modern Industry*, 99 Church Street, New York, 8, N. Y.; *Economic Intelligence*, Chamber of Commerce of the U. S., Washington, D. C.; *Economics and Business Bulletin*, Bureau of Eco. and Business Research, Temple University, Phila., 22, Pa.; *Educational and Psychological Measurement*, Duke University, Durham, N. C.; *Employee Relations Bulletin*, National Foremen's Institute, New London, Conn.; *Employment Security Review*, U. S. Government Printing Office, Washington, D. C.; *Executive Service Bulletin*, Metropolitan Policy Holders Service Bureau, 1 Madison Avenue, New York, 10, N. Y.; *Factory Management and Maintenance Magazine*, 330 West 42nd Street, New York, 36, N. Y.; *Flow*, 1230 Ontario Street, Cleveland, 13, Ohio; *For the Informed Executive*, Associated Industries of Cleveland, NBC Building, Cleveland, Ohio; *For Your Information*, Edwin Shields Hewitt and Associates, Libertyville, Illinois; *Forbes Magazine*, 80 Fifth Avenue, New York, 11, N. Y.; *Foreman's Digest*, 2000 P St. N. W. Washington, D. C.; *Foreman Facts*, Labor Relations Institute, 11 Hill Street, Newark, N. J.; *Fortune*, Time-Life Publishing Co., 9 Rockefeller Plaza, New York, 20, N. Y.; *The Freeman*, Foundation for Economic Education, Irvington-on-Hudson, New York; *Harper's Magazine*, 49 E. 33d Street, New York, 16, N. Y.; *Harvard Business Review*, Soldiers Field Station, Boston, 63, Mass.; *Human Factor*, National Institute of Industrial Psychology, 14 Welbeck St., London W.1., England; *Human Organization*, Society for Applied Anthropology, 61 W. 55th Street, New York, 19, N. Y.; *Human Relations*, Research Center for Group Dynamics, University of Michigan, Ann Arbor, Mich.; *Idea Clinic*, National Industrial Recreation Association, 203 N. Wabash, Chicago, 1, Illinois; *Industrial Bulletin*, Arthur D. Little, Inc., 30 Memorial Drive, Cambridge, 42, Mass.; *Industrial Canada*, 1404 Montreal Trust Bldg., Toronto, 1, Canada; *Industrial and Labor Relations Review*, Cornell University, Ithaca, N. Y.; *Industrial Marketing*, 200 E. Illinois Street, Chicago, 11, Ill.; *Industrial Medicine and Surgery*, 605 North Michigan Avenue, Chicago, 11, Ill.; *Industrial Relations Counselors*, 1270-6th Avenue, New York, 20, N. Y.; *Industrial Relations News*, 230 West 41st

(235)

St., New York, 36, N. Y.; *Industrial Welfare and Personnel Management*, Industrial Welfare Society, Inc., 48 Bryanstan Square, London, W. 1, England; *International Labour Review*, 1825 Jefferson Place, Washington, 6, D. C.; *Iron Age*, 100 E. 42nd Street, New York, 17, N. Y.; *Items*, Social Science Research Council, 230 Park Avenue, New York, 17, N. Y.; *Journal of American Society of Training Directors*, 2020 University Ave., Madison, 5, Wisconsin; *Journal of American Trade Ass'n. Executives*, American Trade Association Executives, Associations Building, Washington, 6, D. C.; *Journal of Applied Psychology*, American Psychological Association; *Journal of Business Education*, 512 Brooks Bldg., Wilkes Barre, Pa.; *Journal of Business Monthly*, University of Chicago, Chicago, Illinois; *Journal of College Placement*, 123 S. Broad Street, Phila., 9, Pa.; *Journal of Commerce*, 88 Varick St., New York, N. Y., *Journal of Counseling Psychology*, Room 2, Old Armory, Ohio State University, Columbus, Ohio; *Journal of Industrial Engineering*, A. French Bldg., 225 North Ave., N. W., Atlanta, Ga.; *Journal of the Institute of Industrial Administration*, Management Publications, Ltd., Management House, 8 Hill St., London, W 1, Eng.; *Journal of Personnel Administration and Industrial Relations*, Box 662, Benjamin Franklin Station, Washington, D. C.; *Journal of Public Administration*, The Treasury, Wellington, New Zealand; *Labor and Nation*, Inter-Union Institute, Inc., Box 18, Ansonia Station, New York, 23, N. Y.; *Labor Coordinator*, Research Institute of America, Inc., 292 Madison Avenue, New York, 17, N. Y.; *Labor Information Bulletin*, U. S. Government Printing Office, Washington, 25, D. C.; *Labor Law Journal*, Commerce Clearing House, 214 N. Michigan Avenue, Chicago, 1, Illinois; *Labor-Personnel Index*, Information Research Service, Inc., 10 Warren Street, Detroit, 1, Michigan; *Labor Policy and Practice*, Bureau of National Affairs, Inc., 1231-24th Street, N.W., Washington 6, D. C.; *Labor Relations Advisory Letter*, Labor Relations Advisors, 10 E. 43 Street, New York, N. Y.; *Labor Reports*, Research Institute of America, Inc., 292 Madison Avenue, New York, 17, N. Y.; *L.O.M.A. Bulletin*, Life Office Management Association, 110 E. 42nd Street, New York 17, *Manage*, National Management Association, 321 W. 1st St., Dayton, Ohio; *Management*, Kelly Read & Co., Inc., Rochester, N. Y.; *Management Abstracts*, British Institute of Management, 8 Hill St., London, W. 1, England *Management Aids for Small Business*, Small Business Administration, Washington, 25, D. C.; *Management Briefs*, Rogers, Slade and Hill, 342 Madison Avenue, New York, 17, N. Y.; *Management Digest*, Prudential Ins. Co., Box 594, Newark, 1, N. Y.; *Management Guide*, 516 Fifth Avenue, New York 36, N. Y.; *Management Information*, Elliott Service Company, 30 North MacQuestion Parkway, Mt. Vernon, N. Y.; *Management Methods*, 22 West Putnam Avenue, Greenwich, Conn.; *Management Newsletter*, National Foreman's Institute, New London, Conn.; *Management Record*, National Industrial Conference Board, 460 Park Avenue, New York, 22, N. Y.; *Management Review*, American Management Association, 1515 Broadway, New York, 36, N. Y.; *Management Science*, Mt. Royal and Guilford Avenues, Baltimore, 2, Md.; *Manufacturing and Industrial Engineering*, 73 Richmond St., West, Toronto, 1, Canada; *Mechanical Engineering*, 29 W. 39th Street, New

York, 18, N. Y.; *Michigan Business Review*, School of Business Administration, University of Michigan, Ann Arbor, Mich.; *Mill and Factory*, 205 E. 42nd Street, New York, 17, N. Y.; *Modern Management*, Bureau of National Affairs, Inc., Washington, 7, D. C.; *Modern Office Procedures*, 812 Huron Road, Cleveland, 15, Ohio; *Monthly Labor Review*, U. S. Government Printing Office,, Washington, 25, D. C.; *N.A.C.A. Bulletin*, National Association of Cost Accountants, 505 Park Avenue, New York, 22, N. Y.; *National Safety News*, National Safety Council, 425 N. Michigan Ave., Chicago, 11, Ill.; *National Sales Executive Digest*, 136 E. 57th Street, New York, 22, N. Y.; *Nation's Business*, U. S. Chamber of Commerce Building, Washington, 6, D. C.; *New York Times Magazine*, 229 W. 43d Street, New York, N. Y.; *N.O.M.A. Forum, National Office Management Association*, 1927 Old York Road, Willow Grove, Pa.; *Notes and Quotes*, Connecticut General Life Insurance Company, 55 Elm St., Hartford, Conn.; *Occupational Hazards*, 1240 Ontario St., Cleveland, 13, Ohio; *Occupational Health*, U. S. Government Printing Office, Washington, 25, D. C.; *Occupational Psychology*, National Institute of Industrial Psychology, 14 Welbeck St., London, W.1., England; *The Office*, 232 Madison Ave., New York 16, N. Y. *Office Economist*, Jameston, New York; *Office Executive*, National Office Management Association, Willow Grove, Pa; *Office Management*, 212 Fifth Avenue, New York 10, N. Y.; *Operations Report*, Research Institute of America, Inc., 292 Madison Ave., New York, 17, N. Y.; *Pacific Factory*, 709 Mission St., San Francisco, California; *Paperwork Simplification*, Standard Register Company, Dayton 1, Ohio; *Personnel*, American Management Association, 1515 Broadway, New York, 36, New York; *Personnel Administration*, Society for Personnel Administration, 5506 Connecticut Avenue, N. W., Washington, 16, D. C.; *Personnel Administration Service*, Dartnell Corporation, 4660 Ravenswood Ave., Chicago, 40, Ill.; *The Personnel Administrator*, American Society for Personnel Administration, P. O. Box 18413, Milwaukee, Wisconsin; *Personnel and Guidance Journal*, American Personnel and Guidance Association, 1534 "O" St., N.W. Washington, 5, D. C. *Personnel Journal*, Swarthmore, Pa.; *Personnel Management Abstracts*, P. O. Box 71, Benjamin Franklin Station, Washington, 4, D. C.; *Personnel Management*, Commerce and Industry Association of New York, Inc., 99 Church Street, New York, 7, N. Y.; *Personnel Management*, Institute of Personnel Management, Hill St., London, W.1., England; *Personnel Management, and Methods*, Shaw Publications, Ltd., 180 Fleet Street, London, E.C. 4, England; *Personnel News*, American Society for Personnel Administration, 2041 Beverly Road, Brooklyn, 26, N. Y.; *Personnel News*, Civil Service Assembly, 1313 E. 60th Street, Chicago, 37, Ill.; *Personnel Panorama*, Pacific Northwest Personnel Assn., 8711 N. E. 4th Place, Bellevue, Washington; *Personnel Pointers*, Air Training Command, Scott Air Force Base, Illinois; *Personnel Policies Forum*, Bureau of National Affairs, 1231-24th St., N.W., Washington, 7, D. C.; *Personnel Practice Bulletin*, Century Building, 129 Swanston Street, Melbourne C.1, Australia; *Personnel Psychology*, Personnel Research Institute, 11800 Shaker Boulevard, Cleveland, 20, Ohio; *Plant Administration*, 522 Fifth Avenue, New York, 36, N. Y.; *Plant Administration*, 481 University Avenue, Toronto, Ontario,

Canada; *Prentice-Hall Labor Report*, 70 Fifth Avenue, New York, 11, N. Y.; *Printers' Ink*, 205 E. 42nd Street, New York, 17, N. Y.; *Production Engineering and Management*, Birmingham, Michigan; *Profit Sharing Newsletter*, Council of Profit Sharing Industries, First National Tower, Akron, 8, Ohio; *Psychological Abstracts*, American Psychological Association, 1333 Sixteenth St., N.W., Washington, 6, D. C.; *Public Administration Review*, American Society for Public Administration, 1913 E. 60th Street, Chicago, 37, Ill.; *Quotes Ending*, American Association of Industrial Editors, 1728 Cherry St., Philadelphia, 3, Pa.; *Record Trends*, Record Controls, Inc., 209 S. La Salle St., Chicago 4, Ill.; *Safety Maintenance and Production*, 75 Fulton St., New York, 38, N. Y.; *Safety Review*, Office of Industrial Relations, Department of the Navy, Washington, 25, D. C.; *Safety Standards*, Government Printing Office, Washington, D.C.; *Sales Management*, 386 Fourth Ave., New York, 16, N. Y.; *Saturday Review*, 25 W. 45th Street, New York, 36, N. Y.; *The Score*, Newcomb and Sammons, 224 E. Ontario St., Chicago, 11, Ill.; *The Secretary*, National Secretaries Association, 222 West 11th Street, Kansas City, 5, Missouri; *Service for Employee Publications*, National Association of Manufacturers, 14 W. 49th St., New York, 20, N. Y.; *Social Science Reporter*, 365 Guida St., Palo Alto, California; *Steel*, Penton Building, Cleveland, 13, Ohio; *Supervision*, Madison, N. J.; *The Supervisor*, Foreman's Association of America, 515 Barium Tower, Detroit, 26, Mich.; *The Supervisor*, Labor Relations Advisors, 10 E. 43 St., New York, N. Y.; *Supervisor's Personnel Newsletter*, Bureau of Business Practice, New London, Conn. *Supervisory Management*, American Management Association, 1515 Broadway, New York, 36, N. Y.; *Survey of Current Business*, U. S. Government Printing Office, Washington, 25, D. C.; *Systems Magazine*, 315 Fourth Avenue, New York, 10, N. Y.; *Systems and Procedures Quarterly*, Box 96, Madison Square Station, New York, 19, N. Y.; *Tide*, 232 Madison Avenue, New York, 16, N. Y.; *Today's Secretary*, 330 West 42nd Street, New York, 36, N. Y.; *Trained Men*, International Correspondence Schools, 1001 Wyoming Avenue, Scranton, Pa.; *Vital Speeches*, 33 West 42nd St., New York 36, N. Y.; *Wall Street Journal*, 44 Broad Street, New York, N. Y.; *Western Industry*, 609 Mission St., San Francisco, 5, California.

personnel records. About 150 different types of personnel records are required in the modern business or industry—from the time a person is hired, until he retires, or leaves the company under other circumstances. Many companies have more; this is occasioned by international set-ups, mergers, etc. Three sources of the form and functions of personnel records that are comprehensive are: *Studies in Personnel Policy No. 145*, "Personnel Practices in Factory and Office," published by the National Industrial Conference Board, (fifth edition) and containing information gathered from more than 3,000 companies. *Handbook of Personnel Forms and Records, Research Report Number 16*, published by American Management Association. *Personnel Handbook*, Ronald Press.

"Personnel Records." A term used by the United States Employment Service. Data kept by an employer pertaining to the workers in the establishment, their jobs, performance, work history, attendance, vacancies and other information necessary for effective personnel management. Of particular interest to employment security operations are the following types of personnel records: *Employer-Prepared Job Specification.* See JOB SPECIFICATION, EMPLOYER-PREPARED. *Job Inventory.* A continuing or periodic record of the jobs, workers, and vacancies in a plant or establishment. *Turnover and Absenteeism Records.* Continuing or periodic records which provide data on the number of employees separating or taking leave.

personnel review. See MERIT RATING.

personnel work, training for. The undergraduate training for personnel work should not overspecialize. On the graduate level, the combination of actual experience in personnel work along with academic training is invaluable. College-employer cooperative personnel training programs are found effective. *Professional Standards for Personnel Work*, published by Society for Personnel Administration, gives details.

"Physical Capacities Appraisal." A term used by the United States Employment Service. A procedure whereby a determination is made of the physical activities which a person is capable of performing and the working conditions under which he can safely be employed.

"Physical Demands Analysis." A term used by the United States Employment Service. That phase of job analysis by which the physical activities and working conditions involved in jobs are determined.

"Physically Handicapped Worker." A term used by the United States Employment Service. See APPLICANT.

picket. A person who is stationed outside a place of business during a labor dis-

pute to inform the public of the existence of a disagreement. Often pickets wear placards, carry banners, or use other visible means of telling their story.

picketing. The act of a person or persons who station themselves outside of a place of business during a labor dispute. The purpose is to observe, to coerce or to threaten, to intimidate, to halt or to turn aside against their will those who would go to work, or to seek work therein, or in some other way to hamper, hinder, or interfere with the free conduct of business by the employer.

picketing, mass. See MASS PICKETING.

"Picture Trade Questions." A term used by the United States Employment Service. See TRADE QUESTIONS, under TESTS.

Piece Rate. Under an incentive wage system, the predetermined amount paid to a worker for each unit of output. Rates may be based on individual or group output. See also INCENTIVE RATE.

piece rate plan. See PIECE WORK.

piece work. A wage incentive plan which pays a definite sum of money for each unit of production.

piece scale. See PRICE LIST.

pilot lot. An experimental or preliminary order for a product. Such an order is relatively small and is produced to correlate the product design with the development of an efficient manufacturing process. It may also be used to establish time standards for the operations that comprise the developed process.

pilot order. See PILOT LOT.

pilot plant. A plant devoted to the production of pilot lots or to the continuous production of small quantities of a product for the purpose of experimenting with its design and production methods.

"Placement." A term used by the United States Employment Service. *Placement.* An acceptance by an employer of a person for a job as a direct result of employment office activities, provided the employment office has completed all of the following four steps: (a) Receipt of an order, prior to referral; (b) selection of the person to be referred without designation by the employer of any particular individual or group of individuals; (c) referral; and (d) verification from a reliable source, preferably the employer, that a person referred has been hired by the employer and has entered on the job. *Agricultural Placement.* A placement in an establishment primarily engaged in farming (major industry group 01), or agricultural and similar services (major industry group 07). *Clearance Placement.* A placement resulting from the joint action of an order-holding office and an applicant-holding office. *Local Placement.* A placement made by a local office which does not involve cooperation with another office. *Nonagricultural Placement.* A placement in an establishment primarily engaged in activities classifiable in one of major industry groups 08 through 99. *Short-Time Placement.* A placement in a job which the employer expects to involve work in each of three days or less, whether or not consecutive. *Spot Placement.* A placement resulting from referral of an applicant who happens to be in the office at the time of selection, rather than one whose selection results from a search of the files or other sources.

"Placement Follow-Up." A term used by the United States Employment Service. A contact or communication with an applicant or employer to determine the suitability and success of the placement or to assure the resolution of an applicant's vocational problem.

"Placement Penetration Ratio." A term used by the United States Employment Service. The ratio between placements made by the local employment office with the major market employer during a given period of time and the potential placement opportunities which existed with those employers during the same period of time.

placement service. Assistance given through a private or public agency to help persons to locate work, either part-time or full-time, in the field for which they are trained, which is consistent with their abilities, experiences, and backgrounds. See UNITED STATES EMPLOYMENT SERVICE.

plan. A THERBLIG (which see) which is defined as: to form a scheme or method for the doing of. In industry, every possible need for the operator to make decisions, to devise means of handling or controlling the work, or to determine the next step in his activity is carefully avoided. Tools, jigs and fixtures often help in reducing these decision items. The part may have prepositioned delivery; the conveyor speed may be synchronized with the operator's cycle time; mechanical contrivances may be used to move the part or the scrap, to stop the process at a definitive point, to inform the operator when the process is completed, or when a desired situation or condition is about to occur.

planning. A method of handling work. Steps in effective planning include: (1) Analyze the Job: Find out its purpose. Is it necessary? What are quality specifications? Break it into elements. (2) Determine How to do the Job: Can it be combined? How has it been done before? Check facilities, costs, arrangements. (3) Decide When to do the Job: First things first. Use a schedule. Arrange for machines. Keep work flowing. (4) Delegate when Possible: Distinguish between work to perform and work to delegate. Determine when to delegate: when you have authority; when more important work takes priority. Decide whether to delegate to a procedure, machine, person.

planning center. The area in a shop or laboratory where mechanical drawing equipment, magazines, reference and textbooks are available for use when developing shop jobs or projects.

planning sheet. A prepared form to aid in organizing work effectively.

plant flow diagram. See FLOW DIAGRAM.

plant layout. The physical arrangement, either existing or in the shape of plans, of industrial facilities.

plant training. Any type of instruction given by the employer on working hours, in his own establishment.

P.M. An incentive payment to sales personnel in retail trade to push and sell items on which the margin of profit is large, to dispose of slow moving items, or to clear out old stock. Also referred to as "premium money," and "push money."

point method. See POINT SYSTEM.

point of make-out. The performance level where calculated earnings are ex-

actly equal to the guaranteed base wage rate earnings.

point plan. See POINT SYSTEM.

point system. A method of job evaluation (which see) in which a range of point values is assigned to each of several job factors. The wage rates for specific jobs are then determined by comparing the total points each receives with the point values and wage rates of key jobs.

political contributions, under Labor Management Relations Act (which see). Corporations and labor organizations are forbidden to make any contribution or expenditure in connection with an election to Federal office. This includes primary elections, political conventions, or caucuses held to select candidates for a political office. It also applies to Presidential and Congressional elections and to elections for delegates and resident commissioners to Congress from the Territories. The U. S. Department of Justice is charged with prosecuting violators. Corporations of labor unions are subject to a fine of not more than $5,000, and labor and corporation officials may be punished by a fine of not more than $1,000 and imprisonment for not more than 1 year, or both.

policy manuals. See SUPERVISORS' POLICY MANUAL.

"Pooled Fund." A term used by the United States Employment Service. See FUNDS.

portal-to-portal pay. In mining, the computation of hours worked and paid for so as to include travel time between the mine entry and the place of work at the start and completion of the work shift. Also applies to payments made by other industries for time spent on company premises in traveling between factory gate, or time clock and work place at the start and finish of the work shift, or to dressing-up time.

position. This word has various meanings in personnel and industrial engineering terminology. (1) Place, office or employment, as, he has a position in a bank. (2) Attitude or point of view, as his position on the labor question. (3) The element (in time study usage) which consists of aligning, orienting, or locating one object in relation to another. (4) The basic element (in motion study usage) which consists of aligning, orienting, and engaging one object with another where the motions used are so minor that they do not justify classification as other basic elements.

position. A THERBLIG (which see) which is defined as: to place in position, give a fixed place to; to locate, to obtain suitable alignment or relationship; the motion with which a thing is placed. A form may be provided to support a tool in a preposition location and relationship, or a hollow in the bench of table top may accomplish the same purpose. A rack or recess may be the means of always holding and aligning the tool for a quick and usable position to grasp. Guides or stops can sometimes be designed or devised to assist in locating the part or tool or assembly into its correct position for further use or completion of the activity. Reasonable use may also be made of pins, stop shoulders or edges, burr clearances or recesses, lubrication, and mechanical means or devices to decrease the number of movements necessary to complete the *position* movement. Indexing fixtures, or notches in a slide, may be used to assist in positioning.

position class. See JOB CLASS.

"Positive Recruitment." A term used by the United States Employment Service. See REFERRAL.

posting notices, under the Railway Labor Act (which see). All carriers covered by the Railway Labor Act are required to post notices specified by the National Mediation Board stating that all disputes will be handled in accordance with the act, and reprinting sections of the act relating to the rights of employees.

"Potential Benefits." A term used by the United States Employment Service. Same as Maximum Annual Benefits—See BENEFITS.

potential earnings. The earnings considered possible for a qualified employee to attain with a given time or money allowance under a specified incentive wage payment plan.

practical arts education. A type of functional education predominantly manipulative in nature which provides learning experiences in leisure-time interests, consumer knowledge, creative expression, family living, manual skills, technological development, and similar outcomes of value to all. It includes those phases of agriculture, business, education, fine arts, homemaking, and industrial arts in which occupational efficiency is not a major goal.

praise. The expression in any manner, of the approval of others in sincere and appropriate terms, as contrasted with flattery which is insincere and uses extravagant terms. Praise flows downward from super-ordinates to subordinates, whereas flattery flows upward.

precedent. A reference to previous decisions, used particularly in connection with the settling of grievances. Often the steward and foreman will be able to agree on settlements in line with the procedure established previously when similar issues were involved. Precedents, especially important arbitration awards, may develop over a period of years into a body of industrial common law supplementing the basic contract. Having in mind the best interests of both labor and management, however, Sumner Slichter, Professor of Industrial Relations, Harvard University, warns, "Precedents should be established slowly and previous decisions should be regarded as *guides* to future decisions rather than binding precedents. The process of interpreting an agreement is an experimental one, and should be regarded as such by both sides. Experience under one interpretation may be the reason for changing the interpretation."

"Predetermination." A term used by the United States Employment Service. See DETERMINATION.

predetermined motion time system. A procedure in which (a) all manual motions are analytically subdivided into the basic elements required for their performance and (b) predetermined time values are assigned to the basic elements.

pre-employment training. Organized, brief, intensive instruction for entrance into employment in a specific industrial job or retraining for workers leading to new duties or a new position.

preferential shop. An establishment where a preferential hiring agreement exists to the effect that an employer must hire union workers in a specific bargaining unit as long as qualified union people are available. After the lists of capable union people are exhausted, the

employer may hire nonunion people. During lay-offs, the employer must dismiss nonunion people first. Thus, union workers get preferential treatment in hiring and firing.

"Preferential Treatment." A term used by the United States Employment Service. The service provided to disabled veterans. Veterans entitled to preferential treatment are served ahead of other applicants and are offered referral to jobs for which they qualify before other qualified applicants, including other veterans.

preferential union shop. See PREFERENTIAL SHOP.

premium. See BONUS.

premium money. See P. M.

premium rate. An extra rate paid for overtime, work on late shifts, holiday and Sunday work, or for work in particularly dangerous or unpleasant occupations. The term is also used in reference to extra rates paid to employees, usually because of exceptional ability or skill in the occupation. See also OVERTIME PREMIUM PAY, PENALTY RATE, and SKILL DIFFERENTIAL.

preparatory training subsequent to employment. In training programs which fall within this classification, the general objective is to train new employees in the duties which they will be expected to perform and to supply them with the information which they will need as employees, including special rules and regulations under which they will work.

pre-position. The basic element employed when the transporting device or the object transported is prepared for the next basic element which is usually position.

(243)

preposition. A THERBLIG (which see) which is defined as: the previous placing of a part in position to prevent further positioning; to obtain in advance a suitable alignment or relationship; to align previously the body or body members for further service. The *preposition* action places the part or tool so that the hand can grasp without positioning, or the part or tool can be used without further positioning, or both. Hoppers, stackers, chutes, mechanical movements of the guiding equipment, or the manipulation of a mechanical device may aid or eliminate preposition.

"Pre-Referral Interview." A term used by the United States Employment Service. See INTERVIEW.

President's Committee on National Employ the Physically Handicapped Week. See BUREAU OF LABOR STANDARDS.

President's Conference on Industrial Safety. See BUREAU OF LABOR STANDARDS.

Prevailing Rate. Typically, the predominant or more common rate paid to a group of workers, usually with reference to specific occupations in an industry or labor market area. In actual application, the term "prevailing rate" is used in a variety of ways. Some of the variations arise from differences in the concept of the geographic unit or industry that is pertinent to a particular situation. For example, where comparable occupations are found in an area in numerous establishments, the geographic unit may be narrow as, for example, the metropolitan area. If labor has to be induced to migrate to the area where the prevailing rate is to be set, and no local labor is available, the geographic unit upon which determination is made may be a

locality far removed from the site under consideration; at times, additional pay may be provided to induce labor to move. Such situations frequently arise under Davis-Bacon Act determinations. Under Public Contracts Act determinations, prevailing minimum wage determinations usually refer to an industry in the United States as a whole. Another set of variations in the application of the term "prevailing rate" arises from differences in industry limits used as a reference. Thus, certain occupations are found only in metalworking establishments, and prevailing rates for engine lathe operators in an area, for example, are in effect rates found in that portion of industry that employs such workers, whether or not the limits are specified in the determination. Other occupations, on the other hand, may be found in all industries in an area. Frequently, variation in the concept of prevailing rate arises from differences in rate structure in particular occupations and in bargaining conditions. Thus, in the building trades and in some of the metal trades, there is a tendency toward single rate formation in an area, even though bargaining is conducted with reference to a minimum rate only, or a union scale. Another source of variation in the use of prevailing rate concept arises from the use of quantitative or statistical descriptions of prevailing rates. Some of these terms are rather loosely conceived as, for example, "going rate," when reference is made to the rate received by a substantial number of workers, possibly the modal rate. In some situations, notably locality wage surveys, measures of prevailing rates relate to the arithmetic mean or to the median. In view of these variations, the use of the term "prevailing rate" requires specific mention of the area, occupation, industry, rate, and type of quantitative measure involved to have definite meaning.

Prevailing Wage Law (Bacon-Davis Act). Passed in March, 1931 and subsequently amended. This act covers direct Federal construction, alteration, or repair of public buildings or public works, including painting and decorating, where the contract is more than $2,000, and applies to all agencies of the Federal Government and of the District of Columbia that directly make construction contracts. The act provides for withholding money from the contractor to pay workers who have not been paid the required wages and gives the Comptroller General the authority to pay out the money for back wages. To obtain payment of unpaid wages from the money withheld, the employee has to file a claim with the Comptroller General. If enough money has not been withheld to cover all underpayments to laborers or mechanics, a worker who does not receive all that is due him has the right to sue the contractor and the sureties on his bond under the Miller Act. It is no defense for the contractor that the worker has accepted or agreed to accept wages at rates less than the rates determined by the Secretary, or has refunded any of the wages voluntarily.

price list. A listing of piece prices or rates to be paid by a company or a group of companies making similar products. In unionized establishments, price lists are established typically upon agreement between the union and the employer.

"Primary Application Card." A term used by the United States Employment Service. See APPLICATION CARD.

"Primary Occupational Classification." A term used by the United States Employ-

ment Service. See OCCUPATIONAL CLASSIFICATION.

principles of motion economy. The rules and their corollaries applying to human motions, which guide toward development of the optimum way of accomplishing a given job.

"Priority in Referral." A term used by the United States Employment Service. The process of offering referral to qualified disabled veterans, other qualified veterans, and other qualified applicants in that order.

private vocational school. A school established and operated by an agency other than the state or its subdivisions and supported by other than public funds, which has as its purpose the preparation of students for entrance into or progress in trades or skills occupations.

probationary rate. The rate of pay for an experienced and otherwise qualified worker during the initial period of his employment on a new job or in a new plant. The probationary rate is usually lower than the minimum rate for the job (in which case it is usually indistinguishable from the hiring rate for the job), although it may sometimes be the minimum rate applicable to the individual job. See also ENTRANCE RATE.

problem employees. About 80 percent of people in business and industry do their work well and lose little time through tardiness, sickness, or other similar causes. The other 20 percent create the "problem employees," or "misfits." The term "misfit" as it applies to any job in industry, describes only the end result in a series of circumstances, the vast and intricate network composed of sociological, physical, mental, and psychological factors originating with management as well as with the individual employee, in relationship to the interdependence of job and living. Dr. Lydia G. Giberson, Personnel Advisor, Metropolitan Life Insurance Company, describes these factors as: *Physical Conditions*: (1) Individual handicaps—poor eyesight, defective hearing, chronic diseases such as tuberculosis, diabetes, etc. (2) Working condition and occupational hazards. *Mental Conditions* are included largely in the term "nervous disorders" (epileptic fits, sleeping sickness, manic depressive psychoses, etc.). *Psychological Conditions* are readily discernible as insecurity, anxiety, worry and fears.

problem-solving. See "BRAINSTORMING."

procedure in disputes arising out of existing agreements on air lines, under Railway Labor Act (which see). Air line carriers and their employees are required by the Railway Labor Act to establish machinery for the adjustment of grievances as a part of their collective agreements.

procedure in disputes arising out of existing agreements on railroads, under Railway Labor Act (which see). The National Mediation Board, on request of either party, will give interpretations of agreements reached through mediation. The following procedure is prescribed for all other instances of disputes arising out of agreements. (a) When disputes arise growing out of grievances or out of the interpretation or application of agreements, they shall be handled through the regular grievance procedure in the contact, up to and including the chief operating officer of the carrier. (b) If no adjustment is reached, either or both parties may petition the appropriate

division of the National Railroad Adjustment Board, submitting a full statement of the facts and supporting data. The Board is divided into four divisions, each representing the carriers and the labor organizations equally. Divisional jurisdictions are: First Division—train, engine, and yard service employees. Second Division—shop crafts. Third Division—station, tower, telegraph, dispatching, clerical, store maintenance-of-way, sleeping car, and dining car employees, and signalmen. Fourth Division—Marine service employees, and all other employees not included in the first three divisions. (c) The appropriate Division may hold hearings if requested by either party and make an award. (d) If the Division fails to agree and cannot itself agree on a referee, the National Mediation Board is required to appoint a referee to sit with the Division and make an award. (e) Awards of the Adjustment Board are final and binding. If a carrier fails to comply with a money award, such as the payment of back pay, the employee or labor organization in whose favor it is made may apply to a United States district court for enforcement.

procedure in making and revising agreements, under Railway Labor Act (which see). The act provides for the following procedure in making and revising agreements: (a) *Notice.*—Carriers and employees alike are required to give at least 30 days' notice of any intended change in their collective bargaining agreements regarding rates of pay, rules, or working conditions, and within 10 days the time and place for a conference shall be agreed upon. (b) *Mediation.*—In case of a dispute not settled in conference, either party may request the mediation services of the National Mediation Board. The

Board, at its discretion, may also proffer its services without a request. (c) *Arbitration.*—If mediation is unsuccessful, the Board shall endeavor to induce the parties to submit their controversy to arbitration. However, the act does not compel the parties to arbitrate. Arbitration boards, when agreed upon, may consist of three to six members, one-third of the number being appointed by each party to the dispute, who must then choose the remaining members. If they fail to do so within a time limit specified in the act, the Board appoints the neutral members. At the request of either or both parties, any arbitration board so established shall also have authority to pass on any dispute over the meaning or application of its award. (d) *Emergency Boards.*—Should arbitration be refused by either party and the dispute remain unsettled, and should it, in the judgment of the National Mediation Board, *threaten substantially to interrupt interstate commerce to a degree such as to deprive any section of the country of essential transportation service* [sec. 10], the National Mediation Board is required to notify the President. The President may then at his discretion appoint an Emergency Board to investigate and report within 30 days. During this period, and for 30 days after the Board has made its report to the President, no change may be made in the conditions which gave rise to the dispute except by mutual agreement of the parties.

procedure in representation cases, under Labor Management Relations Act of 1947, (which see). Petitions for the holding of any type of election should be filed with the nearest NLRB regional office, which will provide the required forms. In cases where the employer and the representative of the employees are unable to agree on conduct of the election, the regional director may order a public hearing. If the regional director declines to order such a hearing or dismiss the petition for election, any party may appeal directly to the Board in Washington, D. C.

procedure in unfair labor practice cases, under Labor Management Relations Act, (which see). If an employee believes that the employer or a union is engaged in one or more of the unfair labor practices outlined in the Act, he may file charges with the appropriate regional office of the National Labor Relations Board on forms supplied by that office. A union which has complied with the filing requirements also may file charges against an employer or another union. An employer also may file charges. Charges may be filed against a union even if it has not met the filing requirements. After the charges are filed, the procedure followed by the regional office and the Board is: (1) Charges are investigated by field examiners. During this investigation, charges may be adjusted, withdrawn, dismissed, or otherwise closed without formal action. (2) A formal complaint is issued if charges are found to be well grounded and the case is not settled by adjustment. (3) Public hearing is held before a trial examiner. (4) The trial examiner's findings and recommendations are served upon the parties and sent to the Board in Washington in the form of an intermediate report. At this point the case is transferred to the Board in Washington. Unless either of the parties files a statement of exceptions to the trial examiner's findings within 20 days, his order takes the full effect of an order by the Board. Parties who except to the examiner's findings also may file a brief to support their exceptions and may request oral argument before the Board. Exceptions are in effect an appeal from the intermediate report. (5) The Board reviews the case and makes a decision. (6) In case a union or employer fails to comply with a Board order, the Board may ask the appropriate U. S. Court of Appeals for a decree enforcing its order. Also, any party to the case who is aggrieved by the Board's order may appeal the Board's order to an appropriate U. S. Court of Appeals. (7) The Board or an aggrieved party may petition the Supreme Court of the United States to review the decision of the Court of Appeals. Failure to obey a final court decree is punishable as either civil or criminal contempt of court, or both. The regional director issues the complaint which begins formal proceedings in an unfair labor practice case. This complaint is issued after investigation of the charges filed by the party which alleges that an unfair labor practice has been committed. If, however, the regional director refuses to issue a complaint, the charging party may appeal to the General Counsel in Washington, D. C., who has final authority over the issuance of complaints. Ordinarily, 10 days are allowed for making such an appeal, which should be accompanied by a full statement of the facts in the case and the reasons why it is believed that the regional director erred.

process. (1) A planned series of actions or operations which advances a material or procedure from one stage of completion to another. (2) A planned and controlled treatment that subjects materials to the influence of one or more types of energy for the time required to bring about the desired reactions or results. Examples include heat treating of metals, mixing of chemicals, curing of rubber.

process chart. A graphic presentation of events occurring during a series of actions or operations and of information pertaining to those events.

process chart symbols. Graphical symbols or signs used on process charts to depict the type of events that occur during a process. Five such symbols have been defined and approved by the American Society of Mechanical Engineers. Their names and symbols are:

Operation ◯ Delay D
Inspection ☐
Transportation ◯ Storage ▽

process engineer. An individual who is qualified by education, training, and experience to prescribe efficient production processes to produce a product as designed and who specializes in this work. This may include specifying all the equipment, tools, fixtures, etc. which are to be used. The job of the process engineer may include estimating the cost of producing the product by the method he prescribes.

process layout. A method of plant layout in which the machines, equipment and areas for performing the same or similar operations are grouped together. For example, all welding is done in one area or department, all painting in another, and so on. It is layout by function.

process symbols. See PROCESS CHART SYMBOLS.

process time. (1) The time required to complete a specified series of progressive actions or operations on one unit of production. (2) That portion of a work cycle during which the material or part is being machined or treated according to a specification or recipe designed to produce the desired reaction or result. The time required is controlled by the machine, specification or recipe, and not by the workman.

processing. (1) The act of prescribing the production process to produce a product as designed. This may include specifying the equipment, tools, fixtures, machines, and the like required, the methods to be used, the workmen necessary, and the estimated or allowed time. (2) The carrying out of a production process.

product layout. See LINE PRODUCTION.

production. (1) The manufacturing of goods. (2) The act of changing the shape, composition, or combination of materials, parts, or subassemblies in order to increase their value. (3) The quantity of goods manufactured.

"Production and Related Workers." A term used by the United States Employment Service. *Includes* working foremen and all non-supervisory workers (including leadmen and trainees) engaged in fabricating, processing, assembling, inspection, receiving, storing, handling, packing, warehousing, shipping, maintenance, repair, janitorial services, watchman services, product development, auxiliary production for plant's own use (e.g., power plant), and record-keeping, and other services closely associated with the above production operations. *Excludes* employees engaged in the following activities: Executive, purchasing, finance, accounting, legal, personnel, cafeterias, medical, professional and technical activities, sales, sales-delivery (e.g., routemen), advertising, credit, collection,

and in the installation and servicing of own products, routine office function, factory supervision (above the working foremen level), and force-amount construction-employees on plant's own payroll engaged in construction of major additions or alterations to the plant who are utilized as a separate workforce.

production bonus. A bonus payment directly related to the output of an individual worker or a group of workers. Usually paid for production in excess of a quota or for the completion of a job in less than standard time. The bonus may be a flat amount paid for all production above standard or it may increase in various proportions as production increases. See also BONUS and NON-PRODUCTION BONUS.

production center. (1) A group of productive facilities (machines, auxiliary tools, and the like) which, for administrative and accounting purposes are considered a unit. (2) The area containing the machine or machines operated by a workman or workmen as well as the space required for the storage of materials at the machine and for loading and unloading it; auxiliary tools, benches, jigs, and the like; and the free and safe movement of the workman while working.

production center layout. The arrangement of the machines, processing equipment, work benches, storage areas, aisles, stationary material handling equipment, and offices within a production center. See PRODUCTION CENTER.

production control. The procedure of planning, routing, scheduling, dispatching, and expediting the flow of materials parts, subassemblies, and assemblies within the plant from the raw state to the finished product in an orderly and efficient manner.

production department. (1) That part of a manufacturing organization responsible for the actual processing of materials or parts. (2) That subdivision of management responsible for planning how, where, and at what cost to manufacture or assemble a product. See PRODUCTION ENGINEERING.

production engineer. An individual qualified by training, education and experience to perform production engineering functions and who specializes in this work. See PRODUCTION ENGINEERING.

production engineering. (1) The function of planning where and when to perform work necessary to produce a product and of coordinating internal and external orders, delivery dates, workmen, machines, and the like thereby promoting efficient operation. (2) A term used as a synonym for industrial engineering, manufacturing engineering, or methods engineering. (3) Designing products to be manufactured utilizing materials, equipment, methods, processes, and skills that are available.

production load. The demand for output established by scheduling based on consumer orders or sales forecasts. Usually it is stated in terms of the time required to produce the demanded output or as a percent of capacity output, normal output, available machine-hours, or the like.

production, nature of. The nature of production can be defined under five main headings: (1) Continuous processes, exemplified in paper making, steel production, chemical manufacture, electricity generation, etc. and where the process is continuous, complex and involving the use of expensive plant. (2) Mass production, exemplified in the manufacture of cigarettes, electric lamps, bricks, etc., where the quantity is high, complication and variety comparatively low, and where mechanization should be highly developed. (3) Line production, exemplified in the production of motor vehicles, radio and television sets, etc. where the quantity is high and the comparatively complicated products progress through a series of processes which, while consistent in nature over fairly long periods, must be adaptable to changes or modifications. (4) Batch production, exemplified in the production of the bulk of domestic and office appliances, clothes, furniture, machine tools, etc., where specific quantities of component parts and assemblies are progressed to a completion or final assembly stage. (5) Jobbing, exemplified in engineering development work and small quantity manufacture of specification products where the product is subject to infinite variety, but the manufacture may be grouped by such qualifications as trade or degree of precision.

production planning. (1) The systematic scheduling of men, materials, and machines by using lead times, time standards, delivery dates, work loads, and similar data for the purpose of producing products efficiently and economically and meeting desired delivery dates. (2) Routing and scheduling.

production report. A formal written statement giving information on the output of an organization or one or more of its subdivisions for a specified period. The information normally includes the type and quantity of output; workmen's efficiencies; departmental efficiencies;

cost of direct labor, direct material, and the like; overtime worked; and machine downtime.

production standard. See PERFORMANCE STANDARD.

production study. A detailed record, often in the form of a time study or work sampling study, kept of an activity, operation, or group of activities or operations, for a period of time in order to obtain reliable data concerning working time, idle time, downtime, personal time, machine breakdowns, amounts produced, and so on.

production, types of. The general types of production may be classified as: (1) self-contained production, where all the processes are carried out from raw material to finished product, with the exception of relatively few partly-finished or finished items purchased outside; (2) Aided production, where a great many items are purchased outside; (3) Short-cycle production, where the process time from material to finished product is comparatively short; (4) Long-cycle production, where the process time from material to finished product is comparatively long.

production unit. (1) The workmen, equipment, and areas involved in performing a given task. (2) A measure of a product expressed in terms of weight, volume, quantity, dollar value or the like.

productive labor. See DIRECT LABOR.

productive time. (1) Elapsed time during which useful work is performed in a manufacturing process. (2) That portion of an operation cycle during which the workman's time is utilized effectively.

The balance of his time is considered idle or unproductive.

productivity. The actual rate of output or production per unit of time worked.

products, type of. In broad terms, products can be classified as (1) Stable products, where the product is firmly established with a minimum of variety and is slow in development; (2) Progressive products, where the product is fairly new, subject to rapid development and with considerable variety; (3) Specification products, where the product is made to measure and subject to more than considerable variety.

proficiency. A term used in employment tests. The skill or knowledge acquired by an applicant in an occupation or training course.

proficiency test. A term used in employment testing. See TRADE TEST.

"Proficiency Tests." A term used by the United States Employment Service. See TESTS.

profit and loss statement. See INCOME STATEMENT.

profitgraph. See BREAK-EVEN CHART.

profit sharing. One of a number of practices introduced by employers to stabilize employer-employee relationships. It is a plan to share the earnings of business with employees on the theory that they will work harder and more efficiently and will be less likely to change jobs if they are rewarded for such services. Public opinion has been widely divided on the plan. Employers said it allowed workers to share in profits without sharing in losses. Employees claimed it was meaningless since the worker's profit came out of wages anyway.

profit-sharing retirement benefit plan. The employer's contributions to the plan are based on a percentage of the company's profits, according to a predetermined formula. The funds are deposited in a trust to the account of the participants according to a formula. The employee's retirement benefit is dependent upon the funds to his credit.

"Program Development." An institute developed by Training Within Industry (which see) to help meet production problems through training. It is based on four steps: (1) Spot a production problem. Tackle one specific need at a time. (2) Develop a specific plan. Watch for relation of this plan to other current training plans and programs. (3) Get into action. Be sure management participates. (4) Check results. Ask, is the plan helping production?

progress chart. A running record showing the operations, jobs, projects or other assignments, completed, particularly by those taking vocational education, apprenticeship, induction or other job training. A graphical representation of the status or extent of completion of work in progress.

progress report. See MERIT RATING.

promotion. The advancement of a person into a job usually carrying a different level of responsibility, or with different requirements than the previous job. Although the two sometimes coincide, a promotion does not necessarily carry with it an increase in salary; in fact, less salary (but perhaps more opportunity and better working conditions) may be involved in the new job. Pro-motions of unionized employees are generally determined by seniority according to contract. This may, or may not, be a determining factor if a unionized employee becomes a supervisor and leaves the bargaining unit, depending upon the labor agreement, as such a selection of an employee to be promoted may be a management prerogative. Typical promotional situations are: (1) A change of grade or classification involving higher salary or wage rate. (2) A merit increase to a person continuing in the same work in recognition of proficiency. (3) An hourly employee becoming a supervisor with one or more people under him; any subsequent progression, as supervisor becoming a general foreman or overseer, etc. (4) A person is taken out of a group to work in an individual capacity, as an operator becoming a production clerk, or a stenographer becoming a secretary. (5) Conversely, a person working for an individual joins a group, as a secretary becomes an advertising copy-writer, or junior accountant, or buyer, etc. (6) A person is transferred from a branch to the home office, or vice versa from the home office to a branch. (7) An entirely new job is created in which a person can utilize some special ability, as one person in an accounting group may be designated to do all the tabulating. (8) A person is transferred to a different type of work such as using machines that require added skills. (9) A person moves up automatically with his or her supervisor, as a secretary or assistant goes along with the boss who is promoted.

promotion, horizontal. Advancement of an employee in which there is no deviation from the major job classification. It may, or may not, include an increase of the pay rate. A promotion from a junior to a senior stenographer is considered a horizontal promotion, since both are in the stenographer classification.

promotion, systematic. An established procedure whereby employees are advanced in accordance with clearly defined schedules. This may include point systems, merit rating, seniority plus ability, the completion of specified training, passing of tests, personnel audits.

promotion, vertical. Advancement involving the crossing of classification boundaries. Such promotion usually involves increased opportunities, more training and experience, greater responsibilities. A distinct change occurs, for example, when a girl moves from stenographer to secretary.

promotional chart. A visual or graphic presentation giving information about job descriptions, transfers, policies determining promotion, etc. so employees can see by what avenues they can advance to higher positions.

"Promotional Telephone Contact." A term used by the United States Employment Service. A telephone call to an employer's establishment or site of operation, or to a union or employer organization which is itself either an employer or serves as a hiring agent for employers, to promote the use of the Employment Service and to solicit orders.

"Proof of Credit." A term used by the United States Employment Service. A report submitted by the State employment security agency to the Bureau of Internal Revenue certifying the amount of contributions paid to the unemployment fund of such State by an employer

with respect to wages paid during a given calendar year of employment.

protective labor legislation. Laws designed to lessen the dangers threatening the safety or general welfare of workers. Such laws include measures providing for unemployment insurance, unemployment relief, accident prevention. Much protective labor legislation originated in the 1930's during the "New Deal" administration. See also "Principles of Labor Legislation," by John R. Commons and John B. Andrews.

protest price. In some industries, notably pottery and women's dresses, piece rates on new work are determined on the basis of previously developed time elements. A worker may not be able to earn an appropriate amount under such estimated time allowances and piece rates. If he does not earn enough, he enters a protest but continues to work at these rates until a review is made and new rates are set. Any adjustment in rates is usually retroactive to the time of protest or to the time the worker was started on the new work. See also TEMPORARY RATE.

Public Assistance. A Social Security Program. The public assistance program provides monthly cash payments to or payments for medical care on behalf of four types of needy people who have not had an opportunity to build up social insurance rights or whose needs are different or greater than can be met by present social insurance benefits. The programs are: *Old-Age Assistance*—for men and women 65 and over who are in need and living outside of a public domiciliary institution; *Aid to Dependent Children*—for needy children under 18 who have lost the support or care of a parent and are living with a parent or with some other close relative; *Aid to the Needy Blind*—for those who cannot see well enough to provide for themselves, who are not living in a public domiciliary institution, and are not receiving old-age assistance; *Aid to the Permanently and Totally Disabled*—for those seriously disabled who are 18 years of age and over, are in need, live outside a public domiciliary institution, and who do not receive either aid to the blind or old-age assistance. Unlike old-age and survivors insurance, which is financed from employer-employee contributions, public assistance funds are obtained from general taxation. *Federal Standards*: Public assistance is a Federal-State program. The Federal Government sets up certain standards for the four programs and shares the cost of public assistance with every State that maintains these standards. These include, among others: (a) Statewide operation of an assistance program. (b) The distribution of public assistance on the basis of need. (c) No citizenship requirement, such as length of citizenship, which would exclude a United States citizen. (d) The right to a fair hearing before a State agency if claimant is not satisfied with action taken or with undue delay in taking action. (e) Safeguards to keep confidential names and other information about people applying for or receiving assistance; and (f) Selecting on the basis of merit the personnel needed to administer a State agency's program. *Wide Variety in Actual Provisions*: It is the State however—not the Federal Government—that decides who shall get aid and how much shall be paid each person. Wide variation exists from State to State in regard to eligibility and amount of payments.

Public Contracts Act. See WALSH-HEALEY PUBLIC CONTRACTS ACT.

public relations training. Many department stores, public utility corporations, banks, and manufacturing corporations have in effect programs for training employees in contact with the public. Alfred M. Cooper in "Employee Training," (McGraw-Hill Book Company, Inc.), says that in public contact training programs all instructions should center around the five elements of personal service, which are: (1) The *interest* shown by the employee in the customer's problem. (2) The *quality of information* given by the employee. (3) The employee's *speech*. (4) The employee's *politeness*. (5) The employee's *appearance*.

public service training. Vocational courses organized to train persons employed in state or municipal departments, such as firemen or policemen.

public speaking. A skill useful in personnel work. The ability to speak well gives increased poise, courage and self-confidence; develops personality; enables people to think more clearly and logically on their feet; aids memory; gives a better command of English; makes it easier to approach people; trains people to talk more convincingly in private as well as in public. It is helpful in a financial way since increased self-confidence and ability to influence others are almost certain to be reflected in earning capacity. To get action through public speaking, the following steps are suggested by Dale Carnegie, in "Public Speaking and Influencing Men in Business," (Association Press, 1935): (1) Get interested attention. (2) Win confidence by deserving it, by sincerity, by being properly introduced, by being qualified to speak on your subject, by telling the things that your experience has taught you. (3) State your facts, educate your audience regarding the merits of your proposal, answer their objections. (4) Appeal to the motives that make men act: the desire for gain, self-protection, pride, pleasures, sentiments, affections, ideals such as justice, mercy, forgiveness, love.

public vocational school. A secondary school under public supervision and control and supported by public funds which provides instruction that will enable high school youth and adults to progress in a skilled trade or occupation of their choice.

publications, personnel and management. See PERSONNEL PUBLICATIONS.

Public Opinion Index for Industry. A confidential monthly index prepared by Opinion Research Corporation, Princeton, N. J., which deals with problem-solving research centered on management's major publics: employees, supervision, stockholders, plant communities and the nation's voters. The Public Opinion Index, through the sponsorship of some 80 large companies, makes possible large scale research investigations that individual companies would find difficult to tackle by themselves.

publishers, personnel tests. Many colleges and universities publish personnel tests, and some tests are published by industrial, business, insurance and other concerns. Well known commercial publishers include: Acorn Publishing Company, Inc., Rockville Centre, N. Y.; American Optical Company, Southbridge, Mass.; Aptitude Test Service, Box 239, Swarthmore, Pa.; California Test Bureau, 5916 Hollywood Boule-

vard, Hollywood 28, Cal.; Education Test Bureau, 720 Washington Avenue, S.E. Minneapolis 14, Minn.; Educational Testing Service, Princeton, N. J.; Houghton Mifflin Company, 2 Park Street, Boston 7, Mass.; Industrial Psychology, Inc., Tucson 6, Arizona; Institute for Personality and Ability Testing, 1608 Coronado Drive, Champaign, Illinois; Martin Publishing Company, 690 Market Street, San Francisco, Cal.; Robert N. McMurry and Company, Chicago, Illinois; Psychological Corporation, 522 Fifth Avenue, New York 36, N. Y.; Division of Applied Psychology, Purdue University, Lafayette, Indiana; Remington Rand, Inc., 315 Fourth Avenue, New York, N. Y.; Science Research Associates, 57 W. Grand Avenue, Chicago 10, Ill.; Sheridan Supply Company, Box 837, Beverly Hills, California; Johnson O'-Connor Research Foundation, 11 E. 62nd Street, New York, N. Y.; Stanford University Press, Stanford, Cal.; C. H. Stoelting Company, 424 N. Homan Avenue, Chicago 24, Ill.; United States Employment Service, Washington 25, D. C.; Western Psychological Services, Box 775, Beverly Hills, Cal.; World Book Company, 313 Park Hill Avenue, Yonkers 5, N. Y.; Humm-Wadsworth Personnel Service, Los Angeles, California.

purchasing power of the dollar. Determination of the quantity of commodities and services that can be purchased with a dollar in a given period as compared with another index. It is usually shown statistically as the reciprocal of a price index. Purchasing power of the dollar determines the real wage.

push money. See P. M.

pyramiding. The accumulation, multiplication and doubling up of wages for the same job.

Q

qualified operator. A person who has the mental and physical characteristics, the job knowledge, and experience required by the work he is to perform and who should be able to meet or exceed the performance level expected on that work without undue mental or physical fatigue.

qualified pension plan. See APPROVED PENSION PLAN.

"Qualifying Employment." A term used by the United States Employment Service. The amount of insured work which an individual must have had within a specified period in order to be an insured worker. See also BENEFIT ELIGIBILITY CONDITIONS.

"Qualifying Wages." A term used by the United States Employment Service. See WAGES.

quality bonus. A reward paid by certain employers to their employees on the basis of the quality of the work they turn out.

quantity bonus. A reward paid by certain employers to their workers for the work performed by them over an established standard of minimum.

quality control. The procedure of establishing acceptable limits of variation in size, weight, finish, and so forth for products or services and of maintaining the resulting goods or services within these limits.

quarters of coverage. A term used in the Social Security Act. A person is fully insured if he has at least one quarter of coverage for each two calendar quarters that have passed since Dec. 31, 1950. At least six quarters are necessary in every case. Once anyone has 40 quarters, he is fully insured for life. The calendar quarters are January-March, April-June, July-September, and October-December. A person gets credit for a calendar quarter if he earns at least $50 in wages in that quarter. If self-employed, he gets credit for four quarters if he has at least $400 of net earnings in a year.

Quarters Needed To Be Fully Insured

Year of Birth	Quarters Needed	
	If Born in:	
	First Half Of Year	*Second Half Of Year*
1888 or before	6	6
1889	6	7
1890	8	9

Quarters Needed To Be Fully Insured (continued)

Year of Birth	Quarters Needed	
	If Born in:	
	First Half Of Year	Second Half Of Year
1891	10	11
1892	12	13
1893	14	15
1894	16	17
1895	18	19
1896	20	21
1897	22	23
1898	24	25
1899	26	27
1900	28	29
1901	30	31
1902	32	33
1903	34	35
1904	36	37
1905	38	39
1906 or later	40	40

A special temporary provision gives recently-covered older persons a chance to catch up to those who had earlier had opportunities for coverage. A person who reaches 65 before Oct. 1, 1958 will be entitled to old-age payments if he has a quarter of coverage for every calendar quarter after 1954 and until he reaches 65. For example, a man who will be 65 in the first half of 1957 needs twelve quarters under the usual rule. But under the temporary special provision, he can qualify as soon as he reaches 65 in 1957, even though he may have only eight or nine quarters, as long as he does have coverage in all quarters after 1954.

questionnaire. A form or schedule used for collecting data, usually referring to forms submitted by mail or filled out by the informant without the assistance of an interviewer.

quickie strike. A short-term, suddenly called and possibly repeated strike in sympathy with workers of another employer or in protest against labor conditions in their own establishment. The main difference between the quickie and the ordinary strike is the fact that the former, unlike the latter, is not a continuous cessation of work but a brief stoppage of work, repeated at intervals if necessary to have the employer accede to labor's demands.

quit. Termination of employment initiated by an employee. See DISCHARGE, LAYOFF, SEPARATION.

"Quits." A term used by the United States Employment Service. See SEPARATIONS.

R

race differential. Differentials in rates paid to workers of different races in the same occupation for similar or identical duties and responsibilities.

radius clause. An agreement signed by an employee in a company training program which provides that he will not seek employment with another firm within a specified area for a stated period.

Railway Labor Act. The Railway Labor Act passed on May 20, 1926, and subsequently amended governs the labor relations of railroads and airlines and their employees. The act makes it the mutual duty of carriers and employees to make and maintain agreements, guarantees and provides for the exercise of labor's collective bargaining rights, and prescribes methods for the settlement of various types of disputes. The act applies to all railroads, express companies and sleeping-car companies engaged in interstate commerce and their subsidiaries (such as refrigerator car companies, bridge companies, and others engaged in transport, transfer, or storage services), and to airlines engaged in interstate and foreign commerce and transportation of mail. Two agencies administer the act: *The National Mediation Board* in Washington, D. C., composed of three members appointed by the President, handles disputes concerning (1) designation of representatives for collective bargaining purposes, (2) negotiation of changes in rates of pay and new or revised collective bargaining agreements, and (3) interpretation of agreements reached through mediation. *The National Railroad Adjustment Board* in Chicago, Ill., is composed of 36 members, 18 of whom represent and are paid by the carriers, and 18 by the national railway labor organizations. Unlike the National Mediation Board, it has jurisdiction only over railway carriers and employees. It makes final and binding decisions in disputes growing out of grievances or the application and interpretation of existing agreements. *Rights of Employees*: Section 2 of the act states that *Employees shall have the right to organize and bargain collectively through representatives of their own choosing.* Section 2 (3), (4), and (5) of the act, outlined below, which protect this right, are made a part of every collective agreement. In order to protect workers in exercising this right, carriers are forbidden to do any of the following acts: (a) To deny or question the right of their employees to organize or to interfere with their organization [sec. 2 (4)]. (b) To use funds of the carrier in maintaining any labor organization or to pay any employee representative [sec. 2 (4)]. (c) To influence employees to join or not to join any labor organization [sec. 2 (4)]. (d) To require employees to sign any agreement promising to join or not to join any labor organization [sec. 2 (5)]. See also: DE-TERMINATION OF COLLECTIVE BARGAINING REPRESENTATIVES, under Railway Labor Act; DUTIES OF CARRIERS AND EMPLOYEES TO BARGAIN COLLECTIVELY, under Railway Labor Act; PROCEDURE IN MAKING AND REVISING AGREEMENTS, under Railway Labor Act; PROCEDURE IN DISPUTES ARISING OUT OF EXISTING AGREEMENTS ON RAILROADS, under Railway Labor Act; PROCEDURE IN DISPUTES ARISING OUT OF EXISTING AGREEMENTS ON AIR LINES, under Railway Labor Act; STATUS QUO, MAINTENANCE OF, under Railway Labor Act; POSTING NOTICES, under Railway Labor Act; PENALTIES, under Railway Labor Act.

Railroad Retirement Act. Act of August 29, 1935, as amended. The Railroad Retirement Act provides retirement benefits which were running as high as $166.64 a month at the end of 1955. The top retirement benefit is gradually rising and eventually will be $250 or more a month. Under the act, wives of retired employees get as much as $54.30 a month and the families of deceased employees, as much as $200 a month. The act is administered by the Railroad Retirement Board, composed of 3 members appointed by the President, with 1 member recommended by the carriers and 1 by the railway labor organizations. The act applies to employees of rail-

roads, sleeping car and express companies, other companies performing services in connection with railroad transportation, and certain railway labor organizations. *Retirement Benefits*: There are two kinds of retirement benefits under the act—old age and permanent disability. Workers in covered employment are eligible for retirement annuities if they are: (a) Sixty-five years of age or over, and have 10 years of service, or (b) between 60 and 65 years and have completed 30 years of service, except that if the worker is a man the benefit is reduced for each month that he is under age 65, or (c) permanently disabled for all regular work and have completed 10 years of service, regardless of age, or (d) permanently disabled for work at regular railroad occupation, currently connected with the railroad industry, and have completed 20 years of service, regardless of age, or (e) permanently disabled for work at regular railroad occupation, currently connected with the railroad industry, between 60 and 65 years of age, and have completed 10 years of service. (An employee is "currently connected with the railroad industry" if he worked in at least 12 out of the last 30 months before his annuity begins. Any other 30-month period may be used, if the employee had no regular non-railroad employment after such 30-month period.) If a railroad worker is at least 65 years of age and is receiving a railroad retirement annuity, his wife (or dependent husband, in the case of a woman employee) may be eligible for an annuity as follows: (1) A wife may receive an annuity at age 65, or before that age if she is caring for a child of the employee who would be eligible for a monthly benefit if the employee should die. (Although a child would receive a benefit as such, the amount of such benefit would be included in the minimum guaranteed to the employee and his family.) (2) A husband may receive an annuity at age 65 if he was dependent upon his wife for at least half of his support when she retired. No person may receive benefits while working in employment covered by the act, or, in the case of disability retirement, if he recovers from disability before age 65. Also, a disabled annuitant under 65 who earns more than $100 outside the railroad industry in any month cannot receive his annuity for that month. The amount of a retirement annuity is based upon the employee's average monthly compensation and years of railroad service. The average monthly compensation is computed by dividing the employee's total creditable railroad earnings by the number of months of service counted toward his annuity, except that the average for the years 1924 through 1931 is in the ordinary case considered to be the average for all creditable service before 1937. Not more than $300 may be counted for any one month through June 1954, and not more than $350 for any month thereafter. Months in which the employee was in creditable military service are added to his total railroad service, and he will be deemed to have earned $160 compensation for each such month after 1936. All service after 1936 is credited; in most cases, service before 1937 is also counted, but only enough to bring the total up to 30 years. The annuity formula is applied by taking 3.04 percent of the first $50 of average monthly compensation, 2.28 percent of the next $100, and 1.52 percent of the remainder, then multiplying the sum of these three months by the number of years of service. The result is the monthly annuity, subject to minimum provisions mentioned below and the reduction made in the annuity to a nondisabled male employee retiring before age 65. When a man is awarded an old-age annuity at ages 60 to 64 with 30 years of service, the amount must be reduced by 1/180 for each month that he is under 65 on the date the annuity begins. This reduction does not apply to women, nor does it apply to disability annuitants even though they have less than 30 years of service or are less than 60 years of age, or both. If an employee has a "current connection" with the railroad industry, the minimum annuity formula may be used. (An employee has a current connection if he worked in at least 12 out of the last 30 months before his annuity begins. Any other 30-month period may be used, if the employee had no regular non-railroad employment after the 30-month period.) This means that the amount may not be less than the lowest of the following: (a) $75.90; (b) $4.55 times his years of service; or (c) his average monthly compensation. A retired employee is guaranteed that the total monthly benefits to him and his wife (including social security benefits, if any) will not be less than the amount that would have been payable under the Social Security Act to him and his family had his railroad employment been creditable under that act. This guarantee applies to male annuitants aged 65 or older (since the social security system does not pay male employees old-age benefits before that age) and to women annuitants at age 62, except that beginning with July 1957 it may also apply to a disability annuitant, male or female, after attaining age of 50. When the wife (or dependent husband) of a retired employee is entitled to an annuity, that benefit is equal to half of the employee's annuity, or $54.30, whichever is less. A wife's (or dependent's husband's) annuity is reduced by the amount of any railroad retirement annuity for which she qualifies on the basis of her own service, or by the amount of any benefit, other than a wife's (or dependent husband's) benefit under the Social Security Act. A wife's (or dependent husband's) annuity is suspended for any month in which either she or her annuitant husband works for a railroad or for the last non-railroad employer. An employee who has less than 10 years of railroad service at retirement will not qualify for an annuity under the Railroad Retirement Act. His railroad credits, however, are transferred to the Social Security Administration for the payment to him of benefits under that system on the basis of his combined railroad and social security credits. *Survivor Benefits*: A) If an employee dies "completely insured," monthly benefits are payable to his survivors as follows: (1) A widow (or dependent widower) at age 60, if she has not remarried. (2) Dependent unmarried children who are under age 18, or who became totally and permanently disabled before that age. (3) A widow having in her care unmarried children who can qualify for a child's annuity. (4) Dependent parents at age 60, if the employee is not survived by a widow, widower, or eligible child. If the employee dies leaving no survivor entitled to immediate monthly benefits, an insurance lump-sum benefit is payable to the widow, widower, children, parents, or persons who paid the funeral expenses. B) If an employee dies only "partly insured," the monthly benefits described under 2 and 3 above, and the insurance lump-sum, are payable. To be "completely insured" at death, an employee must have been receiving a retirement annuity or a pension under the Railroad Retirement Act (if receiving an annuity, it must have begun before 1948 and have been based on at least 10 years of service); or must have had a specified amount of service after 1936. In general, he must have a current connection with the railroad industry and have worked under the Railroad Retirement Act or Social Security Act, or both, approximately one-half the time from 1937 until he dies, retires, or becomes 65, but not less than the minimum of 1½ years (6 quarters of coverage). If he became 21 after 1936, he must have worked one-half the time after he reached that age, but not less than the minimum of 1½ years (6 quarters of coverage). To be "partly insured," an employee must have had 10 years of railroad service, must have a current connection with the railroad industry, and must have worked about 1½ years in the period beginning with the third calendar year before the year of his death. If an employee is not insured under the Railroad Retirement Act when he dies, his railroad credits after 1936 will be transferred to the Social Security Administration, and any benefits, other than a residual payment (described in C below), due his family, will be paid by that agency on the basis of his combined railroad and social security credits. The amount of monthly survivor benefits is computed by determining first the deceased employee's "basic amount," which is the sum of the following three amounts: (1) 44 per cent of the first $75 of his average monthly remuneration; (2) 11 percent of the remainder; and (3) 1 percent of the sum in (1) and (2) for as many years after 1936 as he earned $200. In general, the average monthly remuneration is the total of the employee's taxable railroad and social security earnings after 1936 (or after the year in which the employee reached age 22, if later) and before the quarter of death, divided by the number of months in that period. In counting railroad earnings, no more than $300 a month may be included for any month before July 1954, nor more than $350 for any month after June 1954. In counting combined railroad and social security service, not more than $3,600 may be included for any year through 1954, nor more than $4,200 for any year after 1954. A widow or widower receives the full "basic amount" each month and a child or parent, two-thirds. The maximum family benefit is 2⅔ times the basic amount up to $176. The minimum is $15.40. The act guarantees, however, that the total monthly survivor benefit to a family shall not be less than it would be under the Social Security Act. Under that law, the maximum family benefit is $200 and the minimum, $30. The monthly annuity of a widow, widower, or parent is payable (without reduction) in addition to any retirement annuity under the Railroad Retirement Act or any "insurance" benefit under the Social Security Act. When an insurance lump sum is payable, it is equal to 10 times the basic amount. C) A *residual* lump sum may also be payable to the widow (or widower), children, or parents, in that order, regardless of the employee's insured status. It is equal to 4 percent of the employee's taxable railroad compensation from January 1937 through December 1946, and 7 percent thereafter, minus any retirement benefits paid to the employee on the basis of railroad service and any benefits paid with respect to his death under the Railroad Retirement Act or the Social Security Act. The residual payment can be made only when no other benefits will ever be payable with respect to the employee's death. However, a widow, widower, or parent entitled to a monthly survivor annuity at some time in the future may waive rights to that annuity at any time before it could become payable and thereby make the residual payment available immediately. If an employee wishes to name someone other than those listed above to receive any residual lump sum which may be due, or if he wishes to change the order of precedence, he must file a designation of beneficiary with the Railroad Retirement Board. *The Cost of Benefits*: Railroad workers and their employers share equally the cost of this insurance by paying a special payroll tax. The tax rate is 6¼ percent for each, on earnings up to $350 a month. *Claiming Benefits*: A worker or his survivor may file a claim for benefits at the Railroad Retirement Board in Chicago, or at any field office of the Board. Any decision of the initial adjudicating unit of the Board may be appealed by the person aggrieved thereby to an Appeals Council, then directly to the Board members themselves, and finally to a United States Circuit Court of Appeals. *For Further Information*: The Railroad Retirement Board has issued a series of pamphlets describing the provisions of the act in detail. For copies or for any further information write to the Railroad Retirement Board, 844 Rush Street, Chicago 11, Illinois.

"Railroad Unemployment Insurance Account." A term used by the United States Employment Service. An account, established pursuant to the Railroad Unemployment Insurance Act, maintained in the Unemployment Trust Fund for the payment of benefits provided in that Act.

Railroad Unemployment Insurance Act. Act of June 25, 1938, as amended. The Railroad Unemployment Insurance Act provides for the payments of unemployment and sickness benefits (including maternity benefits) to qualified railroad workers under a uniform nationwide system. This act also authorizes the operation of free employment offices in which the activities are primarily directed toward the re-employment of claimants for unemployment benefits. The act is administered by the Railroad Retirement Board. The act applies to employees of railroads, sleeping cars and express companies, other companies performing services in connection with railroad transportation, and certain railway labor organizations. In order to qualify for benefits under the act in any benefit year (July 1 to June 30), a worker must have earned at least $400 from covered employers during the preceding calendar year (base year). He may be paid benefits when he is unemployed, as, for example, furloughed, discharged, or suspended from employment, or when he is sick and unable to work. Unemployment and sickness benefits for railroad workers are paid for by a payroll tax on the carriers. No part of the employer's contribution can be deducted from wages. The contribution rate varies from ½ to 3 percent, depending upon the balance in the railroad unemployment insurance account. *Benefit Payments*: Benefit payments are based on earnings in the base year in accordance with the following schedule, subject to the minimum described below:

Base-year earnings	Daily benefit rate
$400 to $499.99	$3.50
$500 to $749.99	4.00
$750 to $999.99	4.50
$1,000 to $1,299.99	5.00
$1,300 to $1,599.99	5.50
$1,600 to $1,999.99	6.00
$2,000 to $2,499.99	6.50
$2,500 to $2,999.99	7.00
$3,000 to $3,499.99	7.50
$3,500 to $3,999.99	8.00
$4,000 and over	8.50

In addition, an employee is guaranteed that his daily benefit rate in any benefit year will be no less than half of his regular rate of pay for his last railroad job in the base year, up to a maximum daily benefit rate of $8.50. In the first 14-day registration period in a benefit year in which an employee is unemployed for 7 or more days, he is paid for all days over 7. In all later 14 day registration periods in that year, he is paid for all days over 4. Benefits for sickness are computed similarly. The maximum amounts of benefits which may be paid to an employee in a benefit year for either unemployment or sickness is 130 times the employee's daily benefit rate or the amount of earnings credited to him in the base year, whichever is less. *Disqualifications*: A worker may be disqualified for unemployment benefits: (a) For any day he receives unemployment benefits under any other law, sickness benefits under the Railroad Unemployment Insurance Act or any similar act, or social insurance benefits under any other law, State or Federal; (b) For any day he is unemployed due to a strike in violation of the Railway Labor Act or the established rules and practices of his labor union; (c) For 30 days if, without good cause, he leaves work voluntarily, refuses suitable work, or fails to comply with instruction from the Board to apply for work or to report to an employment office; (d) For 57 days if he knowingly makes false or fraudulent statements or claims to get benefits. The worker may be disqualified for sickness benefits: (a) If he does not take medical examinations required by the Board; (b) If he receives sickness benefits for the same time under any other law; (c) If he receives unemployment benefits under the Railroad Unemployment Insurance Act or any similar act, or social insurance benefits under any other law, State or Federal; (d) For 75 days if he knowingly makes false or fraudulent statements or claims to get benefits. *Claiming Benefits*: To claim unemployment benefits, a railroad worker must register with an unemployment claims agent, who is usually a railroad employee, such as a foreman or supervisor. He must register for each day that he considers a day of unemployment, but generally need not appear at the claims agent's office oftener than once a week. Sickness benefits must be claimed on the basis of a *statement of sickness* signed by an authorized person and filed within the time prescribed by the law. If not filed within 10 days, beginning with the first day claimed as a day of sickness, one or more days' benefits may be lost. The worker may appeal the decision of the initial adjudicating unit of the Rail-

road Retirement Board on his claim; first to a referee or other reviewing body assigned by the board; second to the Board itself; and finally, to a United States Circuit Court of Appeals. *For Further Information*: The Railroad Retirement Board has issued a booklet containing information on the Railroad Unemployment Insurance Act. For copies or for any further information on the law write to the Railroad Retirement Board, 844 Rush Street, Chicago 11, Ill.

rapport. An existing relationship which includes the established confidence, understanding, trust; usually a term used in employment interviewing.

rate. A verb meaning to estimate the worth or value of anything by comparing it with a standard or scale, as, for instance, in performance rating.

rate change. (1) An upward or downward adjustment of a production standard generally made because of a revision in product design, quality requirements, production methods, materials, or conditions. (2) An upward or downward adjustment in wages paid per unit of time or unit of output.

rate cutting. Term generally refers to reduction by employers of established incentive or time rates in the absence of changes affecting job content. May also refer to rate reductions in cases in which technological or other changes have altered job content and methods, or in which incentive rates were set "too high" in terms of earnings levels for similar work in the industry or area.

rated average elemental time. The result of adjusting by a performance rating factor the mathematical average of the times obtained for one element of a time-studied operation. Usually any abnormal time values are excluded in calculating the mathematical average.

rated selected elemental time. See NORMAL ELEMENTAL TIME.

rate for the job, the. The policy and practice of paying workers the regular wage rate for certain jobs or occupations regardless of sex, age or racial origin of the worker or of other factors having no bearing on the employee's output or efficiency.

rate range. A range of rates for the same job, with the specific rates of individual workers within the range determined by merit, length of service, or a combination of various concepts of merit and length of service. Rate ranges may be set up with various degrees of formality and more or less rigid rules respecting the position within the range at which new workers are hired and the rules concerning their automatic or nonautomatic advancement to the maximum rate. The range may be expressed as a spread from a set minimum to a set maximum rate (e.g., a spread of $1.40 to $1.60) or as a series of specific rates between a set minimum and a set maximum rate ($1.60—A rate, $1.55—B rate, $1.50—C rate, $1.45—D rate, $1.40—E rate). In the latter case, the individual A-B-C-D-E points within the range may actually represent different jobs or classes or grades within jobs rather than parts of the same range. This would be the case, for instance, if the requirements for the rates related to job content rather than to the merit and ability of the individual worker. A rate range, like a single rate, is usually established for experienced workers, and the minimum rate of the range is not intended for workers who are not at all experienced in the job. A complete and separate rate structure below the minimum rate of the range, including learner or apprenticeship schedules, is frequently established for workers not fully qualified for the full job rates. Automatic progression from the minimum to the maximum of the range after specified periods of service is common.

rate setting. The process of establishing rates through joint union-management action or by management alone. May involve use of job evaluation and, in the case of incentive plans, time and motion study. Job evaluation is used primarily for setting time rates or incentive base rates in proper relation to each other, taking into account for each job such factors as skill, responsibility, and working conditions. Incentive rate-setting involves the establishment of a production standard by time or other study methods. Rate setting may also involve comparison with rates for similar work in the industry or local labor market.

rate, single. A wage rate established as the same for all workers employed on the same job or in the same job classification; the rate remains at the same level for the entire period during which the workers hold the job.

rates, subminimum, under Fair Labor Standards Act. The minimum wage of $1 per hour applies to all covered workers, irrespective of age. Under certificates issued by the Wage-Hour Administrator, subminimum rates may be paid to certain learners, messengers, apprentices, and handicapped workers, subject to regulations issued under Section 14 of the Act, which provides for subminimum rates in some instances, "to the extent necessary in order to prevent curtailment of opportunities for employment."

rating, experience merit. Method used to determine (1) an employer's rate of taxation under the unemployment compensation laws on the basis of past employment, or (2) an insurance premium under the workmen's compensation laws on the basis of safety record.

rating sheet. A form used in the rating of personnel. To be satisfactory the sheet must be well planned and adapted to the type of worker being rated. In the rating sheet for shopworkers, provision must be made for the rating of such traits as: quantity and quality of work, ability to progress, safety record, attendance, attitudes towards work, length of service, loyalty to get along with fellow workers. The rating sheet for supervisory personnel should include factors as personality, character, ability to make decisions, leadership qualities, initiative, cooperative attitude, ability to communicate, willingness to take responsibility for work and safety of others.

rating, supervisory. See SUPERVISORY RATING.

ratio delay study. See WORK SAMPLING STUDY.

reach. An industrial engineering term meaning the basic element employed when the predominant purpose is to move the hand to a destination or general location. See THERBLIG; TRANSPORT, EMPTY.

reading racks. Also known as information racks. Used to distribute literature to employees on subjects that range from sports schedules, cooking, hobbies, housekeeping, home budgeting, retirement planning, health, taxation, economics, free enterprise, and information about the company itself. Information racks have a built-in check on their effectiveness. A count of what is picked up will show whether the plan meets over-all employee approval; what booklets should go into the racks, and how much on each subject is wanted. Unlike many other forms of communication, reading racks don't carry the burden of requiring "captive audiences," because the system is completely voluntary. Questionnaires to test the efficacy of reading racks are available through Employee Relations, Inc., 13 E. 53d Street, New York 22, N. Y. One of the largest suppliers of reading rack material is Good Reading Rack Service, Inc., 76 Ninth Avenue, New York 11, N. Y. Also National Research Bureau, Chicago, Illinois.

reading, skill in. Personnel executives are interested in reading better and faster. Business reading in general takes up about five hours daily—four in the office and one at home. A study of the reading habits, "How Much Is Too Much?" by the American Management Association, breaks down the executive's reading habits. Rapid reading courses are given at many colleges, including specifically "The Reading Institute," New York University. Commercially, the Foundation for Better Reading, 20 W. Jackson Blvd., Chicago 4, Illinois, puts out a kit. Numerous books are also available.

"Readjustment Allowance." A term used by the United States Employment Servince. See SERVICEMEN'S READJUSTMENT ALLOWANCE.

real earnings. See REAL WAGES.

"Reallotted Administrative Funds." A term used by the United States Employment Service. See FUNDS, REALLOTTED ADMINISTRATIVE.

real wages. Real wages are represented by the goods and services typically consumed by workers that can be purchased with money wages; i.e., real wages are an expression of the purchasing power of money wages. Over periods of time, changes in real wages are obtained by dividing indexes of money wages by an appropriate index of consumers' prices. Thus, if wages increase by 5 percent and consumers' prices by 10 percent, real wages have declined by 4.5 percent ($105 \div 110 \times 100 = 95.5$, the new level of real wages). The Bureau of Labor Statistics maintains a series on Gross Average Weekly Earnings in Current and 1939 Dollars, which indicate changes in the level of weekly earnings prior to and after adjustment for changes in purchasing power as determined from the Bureau's Consumers' Price Index, the year 1939 having been selected for the base period.

recall. The calling back of laid-off employees. In companies with unions, the labor contract usually will have specific clauses on recall. In companies without unions, the management sets up plans for the recalling of employees to their jobs. Seniority in most cases will have a bearing on recall, although obviously the workers most needed will be called back first.

"Reciprocal Coverage Arrangement." A term used by the United States Employ-

ment Service. See INTERSTATE ARRANGEMENTS.

"Reconsidered Determination." A term used by the United States Employment Service. Same as Redetermination—See DETERMINATION.

records and posting notices, required by Walsh-Healey Public Contracts Act. Contractors are required to display a copy of the Public Contracts Act poster, with applicable attachment, wherever work is being performed under the Act. Contractors also are required to keep specified records which are open for inspection by representatives of the Wage and Hour and Public Contracts Divisions, and to maintain records of injury frequency rates.

records management. A scientific system of file administration. Includes archives administration; business history; correspondence control; disposal and preservation of records; filing; indexing; classifying; forms control; office machines and equipment; office manuals; office systems and procedures; photo-reproduction processes; rehabilitation and repair of records; microfiling; testing and training for records operations and work standards for offices. See "Selected Readings in Records Management," put out by National Records Management Council, 50 E. 42nd Street, New York 17, N. Y.

records, required by Fair Labor Standards Act. No particular order or form is prescribed by regulations of the Department of Labor for employees generally. It is required only that an employer make and keep clear, accurate, and complete records which shall reflect the information and data required by the regulations with respect to the persons employed by him and of the wages, hours, and other conditions and practices of employment maintained by him.

recovery of back wages, under Fair Labor Standards Act. The act provides three methods for the recovery of unpaid minimum and/or overtime wages due an employee. (1) The employee may bring suit against the employer to recover the wages withheld, together with liquidated damages equal in amount to the back wages due, plus a reasonable fee for an attorney and suit costs. Under specified conditions, the court may limit or eliminate the recovery of liquidated damages from employers, found to have acted in good faith. (2) The Secretary of Labor on the written request of affected employees, may under certain conditions bring suit against the employer to recover back wages due. Employees consenting to the bringing of such suits waive their independent right to sue for such back pay and for liquidated damages. (Suits to recover such back wages must be commenced within 2 years from the time when the minimum and/or overtime wages became due and the employer failed to pay them.) In August 1956, the act was amended to provide that no action could be brought and no penalties would apply for noncompliance with provisions respecting work performed in American Samoa, prior to the establishment by the Secretary of a minimum wage applicable to such work. (3) The Wage and Hour Division may supervise the payment of back wages for employees. Employees who agree to accept such payment and are paid in full the unpaid minimum wages or the unpaid overtime compensation owing to them under the

act waive their independent statutory rights to sue for wages due and liquidated damages.

recreation programs. Recreation programs sponsored wholly or partially by companies have been on the increase. They range from chess and photography classes to golf clubs. Some are tied in with preparing people for retirement. The National Industrial Recreation Association has details how such programs operate.

"Recruitment." A term used by the United States Employment Service. Active solicitation of applicants for specific openings, using mail, radio, newspaper, and other promotional devices.

"Redetermination." A term used by the United States Employment Service. See DETERMINATION.

"Reduced Contribution Rates." A term used by the United States Employment Service. See CONTRIBUTION RATES, REDUCED.

"Referee, Appeals." A term used by the United States Employment Service. See APPEAL, ADMINISTRATIVE.

"Referral." A term used by the United States Employment Service. The act of arranging to bring to the attention of an employer (or another local office) the qualifications of an applicant who is available for a job opening on file for which he has been selected by a local office. *Agricultural Referral*: A referral of a worker to a job opening in an establishment primarily engaged in farming (major industry group 01) or agricultural and similar services (major industry group 07). *Clearance Referral*: The referral of an applicant, selected by an applicant-holding office, to a job opening on file in an order-holding office. *Delegated Hiring Authority*: A clearance referral in which the Employment Service, having been designated as hiring agent by an employer makes actual hiring commitments which are binding on the employer. *Direct Referral*: A clearance referral of a qualified applicant by an applicant-holding office to an order-holding office, or to an employer in another local office administrative area, for an employment interview. *Local Referral*: Referral of an applicant to a job opening by a local office which holds the order and also selects the applicant. *Mail Referral*: A clearance referral in which an applicant holding office transmits an applicant's clearance application to an order-holding office for referral to a definite job opening. *Nonagricultural Referral*: A referral of a worker to a job opening in an establishment engaged in activities classifiable in one of the major industry groups 08 through 99. *Positive Recruitment*: A clearance referral in which a qualified applicant is referred for an employment interview with an employer or his representative in an applicant-holding office. *Telephone Referral*: A clearance referral in which a telephone interview occurs between an applicant and an employer.

regional differential. Differences in wage levels among several broad geographic sub-divisions. In the United States, attention has tended to focus on differentials that prevail between the South and the North. Such differences have particular significance in individual industries that are found in the South and in other parts of the United States. Important examples are: hosiery, textiles, lumber, furniture, and cotton garments. There are also significant differences in wage levels among other regions in the United States (New England, Pacific Coast, Middle West, etc.).

regular element. Any element of an operation or process that occurs either every cycle of that operation or process or occurs frequently and in a fixed pattern with the cycles of that operation or process as, for example, once every third cycle.

regular rate. The rate of pay received by a worker for all hours of work performed at straight-time rates. Also refers to the rate of pay at which a worker is predominantly engaged when he is subject to assignments at varying rates.

rehabilitation, vocational. The service of preparing disabled persons for remunerative employment through diagnosis, guidance, physical restoration, training and placement.

reimbursable vocational program. A class or curriculum offered through a public school or teacher-training institution which is organized and conducted in accordance with the provisions of the state plan for vocational education approved by the U.S. Office of Education. Such programs are eligible to receive funds from the state (from state and federal vocational education appropriations) to cover in part certain costs already incurred.

release. A THERBLIG (which see) which is defined as: to free from restraint, liberate; to put into circulation; to relinquish control, to lose control.

reliability. As used in psychological testing, reliability refers to the consistency of the test in yielding similar results when administered on different occasions.

reliability. A term used in employment tests, which see. A measure which provides an indication of how well a test is providing a consistent measure of an individual's aptitude or skill. This may be shown by the extent to which a test gives the same score when re-administered to the same applicant at a later date.

remedies in unfair labor practice cases, under Labor Management Relations Act of 1947. When the Board finds that an employer or union or the agents of either have engaged in unfair labor practices, the Board is empowered by Section 10 (c) to issue an order requiring such person or organization to "cease and desist from such unfair labor practice, and to take such affirmative action including reinstatement of employees with or without back pay, as will effectuate the policies of this Act: . . ." The purpose of the Board's orders is remedial—to undo the effect of the unfair labor practices and to direct such action as will dissipate the effect of violations of the act. The means to remedy such unfair labor practices is a matter in which the Board has broad discretion. The Board ordinarily frames its orders on patterns generally appropriate to each general type of unfair labor practice, but the Board may vary the remedy in order to fit it more precisely to the needs of a particular case. There are no penalties or fines as such under the Title I of the act. It is only after a court has upheld a Board order and an employer or union has refused to comply that either may be held in contempt of court

and subject to penalties. Typical affirmative action ordered by the Board may include orders to the employer to: (a) Disestablish a company-dominated union. (b) Reinstate immediately all persons discharged, laid off, or demoted, to their former positions without prejudice to seniority rights or other privileges enjoyed before the unfair labor practices, and if necessary discharge any person hired in place of those discriminated against. (c) Pay back-pay for time lost since the employee was discharged. The amount of back-pay awarded an employee is usually the difference between his net earnings since discharge and what he would have earned had he not been discharged, ascertained on a quarterly basis. A discharged employee must try to find a new job while awaiting reinstatement. Affirmative action required of a union may include orders to: (a) Notify the employer and the employee that it withdraws any objection to reinstatement or employment of an employee who has been subjected to illegal discrimination. (b) Reimburse the employee for any wages he has lost as a result of the discrimination. (c) Refund dues or fees illegally collected. Employers or unions also are usually ordered to post notices in their offices or plants notifying the employees that they will cease the unfair labor practices and announcing the action being taken to remedy the violations. An employer and a union also may be held jointly and severally liable for back pay due an employee suffering unlawful discrimination. *Injunction Procedure:* Sections 10 (j) and (l) of the act enable the Board or the General Counsel to petition the appropriate United States district court for an injunction to stop any conduct alleged to constitute an unfair labor practice. Section 10 (j) confers discretion on the Board to petition for an injunction against any type of conduct, of either an employer or a union, which is alleged to constitute an unfair labor practice forbidden by the act. Such a restraining order may be sought upon issuance of a formal complaint in the case by the General Counsel. The court may grant "such temporary relief or restraining order as it deems just and proper." Section 10 (1) makes it mandatory for the General Counsel to seek an injunction whenever charges are filed alleging that certain unfair labor practices are being committed by a union, if the General Counsel's investigation reveals "reasonable cause to believe such charge is true and that a complaint should issue . . ." The unfair labor practices subject to this provision are strikes or picketing to—(1) compel an employer to recognize one union when another has been certified by the Board as bargaining agent for the employees; (2) enforce a secondary boycott aimed at compelling one employer to stop doing business with another; (3) force an employer other than the employer of the employees engaging in a strike or boycott to bargain with a union which has not been certified by the Board, or (4) force an employer or self-employed person to join any labor or employer organization.

"Renewal." A term used by the United States Employment Service. The transfer from the inactive file of the application of an applicant who is again considered to be available for referral to job openings.

re-operation. (1) The term applied to an operation when it is performed on the same material or item more than once in order to correct the result of performing it the first time. (2) Any work done on material or an item in order to correct work done improperly or to comply with revisions in design or specifications.

repetitive. The general term used when referring to processes, operations, elements of operations, or the products resulting therefrom that occur or are produced over and over again with negligible variation. The term must be qualified or explained when it is used in order to have a concrete meaning.

replacement. An employee hired to fill a position left vacant due to separation. In computing net labor turnover rate: the lesser of either accessions or separations.

replacement rate. The number of replacements per one hundred members of the labor force; hence the separation rate or accession rate, whichever is smaller. See also ACCESSION RATE; SEPARATION RATE.

reporting pay. The amount of pay guaranteed to a worker who reports for work at the usual hour, without notification to the contrary, and finds no work available or is not given a full shift's employment. Typically, pay for a minimum number of hours at regular rate is provided for in union agreements. See also CALL-IN PAY.

"Report to Determine Liability." A term used by the United States Employment Service. Same as STATUS REPORT.

"Request for Determination of Insured Status." A term used by the United States Employment Service. A request

(271)

by an individual for a determination of his insured status.

required idle time. See UNAVOIDABLE DELAY.

"Reserve Account." A term used by the United States Employment Service. See ACCOUNTS.

resignation, involuntary. A termination of employment initiated by the employer and resulting in a break in employment service. The term, "resignation" is generally used in connection with salaried employees, while "quit" is more commonly used in connection with hourly-rated employees.

resignation, voluntary. A type of employment termination which results in a break in employment service, but which is initiated by the employee's voluntary action.

rest delay. A THERBLIG (which see) which is defined as: a temporary act or state of resting. *Rest delay* may become necessary because of excessive exertion; condition of heat, cold, wet, light, sound; physical discomfort caused by maintaining a straining position of the body members; or by poor health, low vitality, or individual aggressiveness.

rest to overcome fatigue. An allowance or delay allowed workmen for the purpose of recovering from the effects of exertion or sustained mental or visual attention. It is usually included in the general allowance, but on work of a particularly exhausting nature it may be included in the job time standard as a separate allowance or element.

restricted element. An operation element for which the performance time is not completely under the control of the workman but is instead governed or paced by a machine, process, or other element. See PROCESS TIME and MACHINE CONTROLLED TIME.

restricted job. A job for which the performance time is not completely under the control of the workman but is instead governed or paced by a machine, process, other job, or the nature of the job itself.

restrictions on payments to employee representatives, under Labor Management Relations Act (which see). Payments to employee representatives by an employer and the receipt of such payments by employee representatives are prohibited in industries affecting interstate commerce except that certain payments are recognized as proper and legitimate. The permitted payments are limited to (a) compensation paid to a union representative for work as an employee, (b) payment in satisfaction of a court judgment, arbitration award, or settlement of a claim, (c) the purchase price of an article or commodity sold in the regular course of business at prevailing market prices, (d) money deducted from wages for union dues (checkoff), and (e) payments to a welfare fund. The last two types of payment are subject to restrictions as indicated below. Checkoff of union dues is permitted if the employer has received the employee's written consent. The consent must not be irrevocable for more than 1 year or beyond the termination of a collective agreement establishing the checkoff, whichever occurs sooner. Payments made to welfare funds are subject to the following conditions: The fund must be established as a trust under a written agreement and administered jointly by employers and employees. It must provide for medical or hospital care, pensions, workmen's compensation, insurance of any of the foregoing, unemployment benefits, life insurance, disability and sickness insurance, or accident insurance. Contributions to funds established after January 1, 1947, providing for pooled vacation benefits are prohibited. Pension funds must be kept separately. The restrictions on the administration of the funds do not apply to funds established by collective agreements prior to January 1, 1946. The Department of Justice is charged with prosecuting violators, who are subject to a fine of not more than $10,000 or imprisonment for not more than 1 year, or both. The Federal courts may also enjoin violations of these provisions.

restudy. See CHECK STUDY.

retail training. A term often used synonymously with distributive education but properly referring to education for work in places of business where commodities are sold directly to the consumer.

retime. To make a time study of an operation in order to check the validity or application of a previous time study.

retirement. A withdrawing from active employment. Although people retire at all ages, the fact that employees qualify for monthly payments under the Social Security Law at 65 if they are in covered employment, has made age 65 more or less the accepted retirement age. Recent years have seen more and more people retire at 65. In 1890 two out of every three men who were 65 or older were still in full-time employment. In 1940 less than half in this age group were so employed. Many business organizations

are offering counselling service, booklets, or are initiating projects to help employees plan for pleasant retirement years.

retirement benefits, under Social Security Act. The term "retirement age" means: (1) in the case of a man, age sixty-five, or (2) in the case of a woman, age sixty-two. Retirement benefits may be claimed by a fully insured worker when he retires at retirement age or later. The family of a retired worker may also be entitled to receive monthly benefits. Family benefits are based on primary benefits. The retired worker's wife (who has reached age 62 or at an earlier age if she has a child of the worker in her care) and each child under 18 are entitled to receive amounts equal to one-half of the worker's primary benefit. However, there is a limit on the amount the family can receive. Altogether, (if the wife is 65) they cannot get more than 80 percent of his average monthly pay, or $200, whichever is least. If the wife takes her benefits at age 62, or anytime between 62 and the time she reaches 65, the amount will be smaller, as explained below. Retired individuals, 65 up to 72 years of age, will be permitted up to $1,200 a year in earnings without loss of benefits. In addition, from age 72 no maximum will be applied to current earnings for the purpose of determining benefit amounts. Some special provisions applying to women are: (1) A working woman may become entitled to social security benefits after she reaches age 62 instead of having to wait until she reaches 65. However, if she chooses to take the payments before she reaches 65, the amount of the monthly benefit she will receive will be permanently reduced. The amount of the reduction depends on the number of months it will be after she starts getting benefits before she reaches 65. If she chooses to start getting payments as soon as she reaches 62, the amount of her payment each month will be 80 percent of what she would get if she were 65. If she waited until her 63d birthday, the amount of the payments would be 86⅔ percent of what she would receive if she were 65, and if she waited until she reached 64, the amount would be 93⅓ percent. The reduction is permanent; her payments after 65 would also be reduced. (2) If she is the wife of a man who is getting social security retirement payments, she may be entitled to wife's insurance benefits in a reduced amount when she reaches 62, or she may wait until she reaches 65 and get the entire amount of the wife's benefit. If she chooses to start getting the payments as soon as she reaches 62, the amount of her payment each month as a wife will be 75 percent of what she would get if she were 65. If she waited until her 63d birthday, the amount of the payments would be 83⅓ percent of what she would receive if she were 65, and if she waited until she reached 64, the amount would be 91⅔ percent. The reduction is permanent; her payments after 65 would also be reduced. (3) If a woman has a child under 18 or a disabled child in her care, and the child is entitled to benefits based on her husband's earnings, she may be entitled to monthly payments as a mother regardless of her age. Her payments as a mother would not be reduced. See also: BENEFITS, SOCIAL SECURITY, TABLE OF.

retirement, compulsory (automatic). The employee must retire when he reaches the normal retirement age.

retirement, early. Voluntarily initiated retirement before normal retirement date, usually with smaller benefits. Generally an employee must have a minimum number of years of service and must have reached the minimum age required under the plan. When early retirement is necessitated by a disability, it is known as DISABILITY RETIREMENT, which see. The employer also may request early retirement, with the consent of the employee.

retirement, deferred. The employee is permitted to work after the normal retirement date on a year-to-year basis. If the employee works beyond the age of normal retirement, he does not normally receive a larger pension.

retirement, normal date. The normal retirement date is the age at which retirement occurs, except under unusual circumstances, and is the basis of all retirement benefits.

retirement, preparation for. Much interest centers in helping people make the transition to retirement. The U. S. Department of Health, Education and Welfare has set up a Committee on Aging; a number of state governments have set up local groups to deal with the problem. Numerous companies have extensive educational programs to prepare employees for retirement. The Mutual Benefit Life Insurance Company publishes a booklet, "Begin Now to Enjoy Tomorrow," and similar publications are issued by other groups. The National Industrial Conference Board and American Management Association are among national organizations devoting literature to this subject.

retraining programs. Courses which provide an occupational changing type of instruction, serving to prepare persons for entrance into a new occupation or to instruct workers in new, different skills demanded by technological changes in their trades.

retroactive pay. Delayed payment of part of the wages for a particular period, resulting from a retroactive application of wage increases arising from wage negotiations. See also BACK PAY.

right and left hand chart. A form of operator process chart on which the motions made by one hand in relation to those made by the other hand are recorded, using standard process chart symbols or basic therblig abbreviations or symbols.

right-to-work laws. State laws which forbid employers and labor unions to sign contracts requiring workers to join a union in order to keep their jobs. Most of these laws owe their birth to the Taft Hartley Law, as far as formal legislation is concerned, although the evolution of the principle underlying these laws dates back many years. The Taft-Hartley Law specifically outlawed the closed shop, but the union shop was allowed as it was permitted under the Wagner Act. However, within the framework of the Taft-Hartley Law there was one section 14B which took the compulsion out of union shop clauses if the individual states legislated to this effect. Section 14B of the Taft-Hartley Law (which see) reads: "Nothing in this act shall be construed as authorizing the execution or application of agreements requiring membership in a labor organization as a condition of employment in any State or Territory in which such

execution or application is prohibited by state or territorial law." Proponents of the "right to work" laws argue that union shop agreements violate the rights of workers who object in principle to joining unions. The National Right to Work Committee argues that "Americans must have the right, but not be compelled," to join. The unions reply that workers have a right to refuse to work beside non-unionists. In May, 1956, the Supreme Court limited the field in which these controversial statutes—at that time in effect in 18 states—can apply. The decision arose from a conflict between the state laws and the National Railway Labor Act, which sanctions the union shop in the railway industry and asserts precedence over state legislation. The court unanimously upheld the Federal act on the ground that Article VI of the Constitution declares the laws of the United States to be "the supreme law of the land." The unanimous decision applied only to the railroads; there was no broad ruling on the legality of the "right-to-work" laws in other industries.

role-playing. A training technique usually used in supervisory training, based on the principles of "learning by doing." By dramatizing a situation, enacting the roles of different people involved, those participating gain a better understanding of each others' viewpoints and feelings. It "puts the shoe on the other foot." Advantages of role-playing are: (1) role-playing situations can be repeated. If one conclusion seems unsatisfactory, the group can try for another; (2) those who participate in the role-playing can be asked how they "feel" or react, which often cannot be determined in real life situations; (3) it is possible to see how

(275)

different personalities affect the solution; (4) role-playing broadens viewpoints. The acting out of actual situations shows that when disagreements arise between supervision and the employee, neither one is necessarily wrong. The customary steps in role-playing include: (1) The leader designates the general area of the problem (grievance, delegating authority, unequal work distribution, work not ready on time, poor quality, overlapping functions). (2) A sample case can be cited, either by the leader or the group, that illustrates the same general problem. This shows the group how to develop the principles that should be used in handling the case that is to be acted out. This will provide them with a solid basis for constructive discussion. (3) Two or three of the members of the group are sent out of the room. These usually are the people who take the part of the various supervisors. (4) The leader describes the background of the case which will be played out. He briefs them on events leading up to the introductory statement of the employee. (5) One member of the group is selected to play the employee. (6) The leader asks the group if they have any questions. He also tries to draw from the group possible lines of action that the supervisors should take. They set up recommendations on how the case should be handled. The audience acts as experts. (7) The stage is set with whatever makeshift properties are available—desk, table, chair, etc. (8) The supervisors are called in one at a time. Each one handles the case as he sees fit. As soon as he finishes, a discussion takes place and he learns the recommendation of the group. (9) The leader outlines the events of the first presentation on the blackboard. Thus it will be possible later to compare how each supervisor handled the situation. (10) The second supervisor is called in, handles the situation. He learns the recommendations of the group. His presentation is summarized on the blackboard. (11) This procedure is repeated. (12) The leader opens the meeting for general discussion. The group arrives at conclusions on how the case should be handled. These conclusions are placed on the blackboard side by side with the outlines made at the end of each presentation. (13) One member of the group is now asked to "play the role" according to the final recommendations made by the group; i.e. the role of the "good" or "ideal" supervisor. (14) If the group is "stumped" by a problem, the leader may offer some suggestions on how the situation could be handled. But role-playing is not intended to come up with any one perfect answer. In some training meetings, problems arise which permit several almost equally acceptable solutions. In other meetings, problems are discussed which cannot be solved in any final sense. Role-playing merely points up some better approaches to such problems. Complete role-playing sessions are sometimes difficult to handle. Various adaptations are frequently used.

rotating shift. The system of rotating the crews where two or more shifts are worked in an establishment. This system is designed to distribute day and night work on an equal basis among the various workers. In some industries, where 7-day operations are common, the work schedules may be arranged so that workers are given different days off in each week. See also FIXED SHIFT, SHIFT, SPLIT SHIFT, and SWING SHIFT.

round of wage increases. A term widely used after the end of World War II to describe broad wage movements affecting large segments of the economy. Thus, the "first round" of postwar wage increases is identified largely with the period between VJ-day and the autumn of 1946; the "second round" with 1947, etc. Actually, these wage movements exhibited great internal diversity and were in no sense uniform among industries or occupational groups or even, in many cases, among establishments in the same industry.

route. (1) The path followed by a man, material, part or the like in a particular production process. (2) To describe the above path.

routing. (1) A form listing for the manufacture of a particular item the sequence of operations, transportations, storages and inspections to be used, and usually also the standard times applicable, and the machines, equipment, tools, work stations, number of workmen, materials, parts, and the like that are to be used. (2) Establishing the sequence of processes, operations, transportations and miscellaneous equipment that will be used in producing a particular product, part, or job lot.

Rowan Premium Plan. An incentive system which has an established day rate, which is guaranteed, plus a premium representing an increase by a percentage equal to that percentage the worker saved on the standard time allowed for the job. The premium is a percentage of the time worked, rather than of the time saved.

Rowan Premium Plan Formula. The for-

mula for figuring an employee's wage under the Rowan Plan is generally computed to compensate: Earnings up to low task:

$$E = H_a R_h \text{ or } RT$$

Earnings at and above low task:

$$E = H_a R_h + (H_s - H_a)/H_s \times H_a R_h = H_a R_h [2 - H_a/H_s]$$

in the form $y + mx + b$

$$E/H_a R_h = [2 H_a H_s - H_a{}^2/H_s{}^2] H_s/H_a$$

See symbols, wage formula

Rowan Variable Sharing Plan. See ROWAN PREMIUM PLAN FORMULA.

royalty. In relation to wages, the payments to union health and welfare funds, such as those benefiting members of the United Mine Workers and the American Federation of Musicians, although the term is not the official designation for such payments. In these cases, the application of the term stems, at least in part, from the fact that employer contributions are based on tons of coal mined and number of musical records produced. For some types of professional workers, such as musicians, singers, and writers, payment for work is frequently based on a percentage on sales of the final product (book, article, or song). Such payments are referred to as royalties.

rule of three. The practice followed in the U. S. Civil Service of certifying the three candidates with the highest ratings for certain positions. The ratings are based on examination results, experience qualifications, and results of interviews with candidates. The purpose of the practice is to give a choice to the government official requisitioning the employees.

runaway rate. A piece rate or other incentive rate which results in earnings that are out of line with earnings in other jobs of similar requirements. This situation may occur because of changed technology or from faulty rate setting and may cause earnings to reach levels beyond normal expectations.

run-off election. A second balloting by employees, directed by a labor board when a first election fails to show that a total of more than half of the votes recorded were in favor of any one particular union of those presented on the ballot to determine the union which would represent the employees.

S

sabotage. A policy advocated by revolutionary or militant labor unions with the immediate aim of paralyzing an individual plant, and the ultimate aim of establishing an economy controlled by organized labor. Peaceful sabotage consists of soldiering on the job and other slowdown tactics. Violent sabotage may include such practices as dismantling or breaking of machinery, spoiling raw materials or finished goods. Other forms of sabotage are spreading false rumors, or publicly revealing unfavorable truths about goods (open-mouthed sabotage) or increasing costs through waste or using expensive materials. Soldiering on the job is known in Scotland as "ca'canny." The word "sabotage" traces to the sabots worn by French peasants, who, it is said, threw their wooden shoes into the machinery to slow it down.

safety and health requirements, under Walsh-Healey Public Contracts Act. The contract may not be performed nor the materials, supplies, articles, or equipment manufactured or furnished under working conditions which are unsanitary or hazardous or dangerous to the health and safety of employees engaged in the performance of the contract. Compliance with the safety, sanitary, and factory inspection laws of the State in which the work is performed is prima facie but not conclusive evidence of compliance with this provision of the Act.

salary rate. For workers hired on a weekly, monthly, or annual basis, the rate of pay is normally expressed in terms of dollars per week, month, or year. Workers employed on a monthly or annual salary basis may actually be paid monthly, semi-monthly, or more frequently. Usually, the length of the workweek is specified and a policy is established for compensation in the event that longer or shorter hours than a full week are worked.

salaried employee. An employee whose income is computed on the basis of a period of one week or longer.

salary and commission. See COMMISSION EARNINGS.

salary. Fixed compensation paid weekly, monthly, or yearly for services rendered, usually based on a certain minimum number of hours per day or week.

sampling. The practice of selecting a small portion (usually determined statistically) of the total group under consideration for the purpose of inferring the value of one or several characteristics of the group.

sandhogs. The workmen who dig tunnels or otherwise work underground on subway or tunnel construction.

scab. A worker who accepts employment or continues working in a plant where a strike is in progress. Compare FINK; STRIKEBREAKER.

scale, sliding wage. A wage rate established in accord with a definite formula and in which changes are automatically adjusted to the changes in the selling price of commodities. The automatic adjusting of wages to conform with changes of price, profit, sales volume.

scheduling. (1) The prescribing of when and where each operation necessary to the manufacture of a product is to be performed. (2) The establishing of times at which to begin and/or complete each event or operation comprising a procedure.

School Survey and Construction Act. This law requires the payment of wages not less than the prevailing rates determined by the Secretary of Labor for work on the construction, alteration, remodeling, or improving of schools in federally affected areas, where financial assistance is furnished by a Federal grant-in-aid program.

scientific management. A technique of plant organization and employee-employer relationship first introduced by Frederick Winslow Taylor, hence often called "Taylorism." The plan calls for hiring the most efficient workmen available, the payment of wages high enough to hold these men, the standardization of work practices, and detailed planning of operations. Modern large-scale production methods are an outgrowth of Taylor's ideas. Taylor interpreted his plan as the application of engineering techniques to management. He himself said, "Scientific Management is not any efficiency device . . . new system of figuring costs . . . not time study . . . not functional foremanship. . . . In its essence, scientific management involves a complete mental revolution . . . the substitution of exact scientific investigation and knowledge for the old individual judgment or opinion."

screening. A process whereby eliminations are effected, or "screened out." In employment procedures, applicants are eliminated who do not fit job requirements. Screening is sometimes done in advance in the employment office, while final selection of an employee may be left to the supervisor, office manager, or other executive.

search. A THERBLIG (which see) which is defined as: to explore thoroughly, to find something concealed or lost. Search may be reduced by convenient and precise arrangement of the work place so that the operator will have assurance of where a part, object, or tool is to be found or to be placed. Prepositioning, the use of stackers or chutes, partitioned trays, symmetrical arrangements of the parts may reduce *search*, or a change in sequence within the operation may eliminate or reduce it. More than one size of a part or tool, or poor workmanship or materials, may increase *search*.

"Seasonal Determination." A term used by the United States Employment Service. See DETERMINATION.

seasonal employment. Employment available only certain times during the year, due to climatic or other factors. Fruit picking, canning of vegetables and fruits, rice harvesting, logging, are examples of agricultural types of seasonal employment. The term also applies to employment created by economic pressures, such as sales clerk in department stores before the Christmas season, hotel and resort work in the summer, work in the garment and textile industries.

seasonal industry. See SEASONAL EMPLOYMENT. An industry or division or branch of an industry whose employment or activity is affected by climatic and temperature changes or economic fluctuations associated with the seasons.

secretarial practice. An advanced vocational course designed for prospective stenographers and secretaries who have acquired basic stenographic skills and need experience in performing the various office duties expected on the job.

secretary. According to the *Dictionary of Occupational Titles*, (which see) performs general office work in relieving executive and other company officials of minor executive and clerical duties; takes dictation, using shorthand or uses a stenotype machine; transcribes dictation or the recorded information reproduced on a transcribing machine; makes appointments for executive and reminds him of them; interviews people coming into office, directing to other workers those who do not warrant seeing the executive; answers and makes phone calls; handles personal and important mail; writing routine correspondence on own initiative.

sedentary occupation. An occupation in which the person is customarily in a sitting position or physically inactive on the job. Statistical work or typing are frequently sedentary.

select. A THERBLIG (which see) which is defined as: to take in preference to another or other, choose; take as being most fit and desirable; to decide after judicial investigation. *Select* may be reduced or eliminated by prepositioning the parts. Proper separation or placing when the parts are made or handled in an operation may reduce *select* in a later operation. Any case of decision, whether the part is to be chosen, or to be picked up in a definite position, increases *select*. *Select* may be repeated two or three times, if the first or second part under observation does not meet the requirements. The parts may fall in many positions, relative one to another. The number of possible positions the part can take is a factor in determining the number of times *select* must be allowed for in the work cycle. The part may have different aspects which cause *select*. It may be upside down, end for end, on edge, partly buried in a mass of similar parts, may require a particular shade of color, have no obvious defects, have a definite characteristic, as a number or decoration or trade mark, have certain definite location in its assembly, be dirty, oily, not oily, unpolished, unplated, not completely machined, scratched, dented, be a scrap part, or a piece of scrap or foreign part. *Select* may be accomplished by mechanical means. A hopper with a mechanical delivery device performs the *select* duty and also prepositions the part. Mechanical deliveries after gauging a part may perform the *select* duty in regard to the part size.

selected average time. See AVERAGE TIME and AVERAGE ELEMENTAL TIME.

selected elemental time. The raw or unadjusted time which is chosen as being representative of the actual time taken to perform a single element of an operation.

selected time. That time value chosen by the time-study observer from those obtained for an element of a time-studied operation as being representative of the time used by the workman when he performed the element correctly.

"Selection." A term used by the United States Employment Service. The process of choosing a qualified applicant for referral to a job by carefully analyzing and comparing employer requirements with applicant interests and abilities.

selection, of executives and supervisors. Studies of the criteria for successful selection have been made by numerous colleges and associations. Kiplinger's *Changing Times* lists ten important qualities: judgment, planning, decisiveness, leadership, expression, responsibility, originality, knowledge, follow-through, and openmindedness. See *Selection of Management Personnel*, in 2 volumes, published by American Management Association; Selecting Company Executives, Studies in Personnel Policy, No. 161, National Industrial Conference Board; Bulletins 6, 7, 8 and 9 on selecting supervisors published by Industrial Relations Section, California Institute of Technology.

selection, supervisory. See SUPERVISORY SELECTION.

"Selective Placement." A term used by the United States Employment Service. The specialized technique used in placing handicapped applicants in jobs suited to their physical capacities, which includes individual appraisal, job analysis, and selective matching of the physical capacities and other qualifications of the applicant with the physical and other requirements of a job.

self-administered pension plan. Under this arrangement a trust fund is created into which the employer pays the money to provide for pension benefits. The trustee of the fund invests the money in securities or other property and uses the proceeds of the fund to make the pension payments. Administrative details are handled by the employer or pension committee, rather than by an insurance company. See TRUST FUND PLAN.

"Self-Application." A term used by the United States Employment Service. See "APPLICATION."

"Self-Application Interview." A term used by the United States Employment Service. See INTERVIEW.

"Self-Filing" (of claim). A term used by the United States Employment Service. The partial or complete filling out of a claim form or request for determination of insured status by the claimant.

Semi-skilled labor. Persons engaged in an occupation requiring the exercise of a manipulative ability of a high order, but limited to a well-defined work routine; or work in which lapses in performance would cause extensive damage to product or equipment; or, to a limited extent, work requiring the exercise of independent judgment to meet variables in the work situation.

seniority. The principle that an employee's relative length of service in an enterprise is a factor in determining priority in his employment rights and job opportunities in that enterprise. There are two general types of seniority: "straight seniority" which means that length of service alone determines employment preference, and "qualified seniority" under which length of service is merely one of a number of specified factors used for determining preference. Seniority is considered in transfers, promotions, layoffs, rehirings, and other employment relations.

seniority, super. The modification of seniority rights in order to give greater weight to some individuals or groups, so they will have greater, or "super" rights than others in the same group or in the department. Such a privilege may be accorded to union shop stewards, or members of the grievance committee.

separation. Termination of employment as a result of a quit, layoff or discharge.

"Separation Notice." A term used by the United States Employment Service. *Separation Notice*: An employer's report of the separation of one or more of his workers showing the date and reason for the separation and such other information as may be required by the State employment security agency. See also WAGE AND SEPARATION REPORT.

separation rate. The ratio of the number of separations per month per hundred employees.

"Separations." A term used by the United States Employment Service. All terminations of employment, generally classifiable as layoffs, quits, discharges, military

separations, or miscellaneous separations. Transfers from one plant or department, or shifts within the establishment, or from regular activities to force-account construction activities, or vice-versa, or from one establishment to another operated by the same employer, are not to be considered as separations. Also a termination of employment with definite instructions to return to work within 7 consecutive days is not to be considered as a separation. *Layoffs*: Terminations of employment (lasting or expected to last more than 7 consecutive calendar days) initiated by the employer, *without* prejudice to the workers, for such reasons as lack of orders, shortages of materials, conversion of plant, release of temporary help, plant shut-down for inventory, plant shutdown for vacation, or introduction of labor-saving machinery or processes. *Quits*: Terminations of employment initiated by employees for such reasons as acceptance of a job elsewhere, return to school, ill health, marriage, maternity, dissatisfaction, or retirement (except on company pension plan). Unauthorized absences lasting more than 7 consecutive calendar days (the 7th day of absence falling within the calendar month reported) should be considered as quits. Also considered as a quit is the failure to report to work after being hired if the person hired has been counted as an accession. *Discharges*: Terminations of employment initiated by the employer for such reasons as inability to meet the organization's physical standards, incompetence, violation of rules, dishonesty, insubordination, laziness, and absenteeism. *Military Separations*: Terminations of employment for military duty lasting or expected to last more than 30 consecutive calendar days, whether or not the employees' names are retained on the payroll. *Miscellaneous Separations*: Terminations of employment due to death, permanent disability, or retirement on company pension, whether or not the employees' names are retained on the payroll.

service. The period during which the employee works for an organization. Also, the work performed during such period, as, a discharge results in a break in service.

"Service-Connected Disability." A term used by the United States Employment Service. A disability recognized by the Veterans Administration or any branch of the armed services as having been incurred in or aggravated by active military or naval service.

service rating. See MERIT RATING.

service trades. Those occupations which have as their primary purpose the rendering of personal service to the customer or maintenance of existing equipment.

"Serviceman's Readjustment Allowance." A term used by the United States Employment Service. A temporary program of Federal unemployment benefits, for ex-members of the armed forces, established by the Servicemen's Readjustment Act of 1944.

services. When work is done by one person or group of persons designed to satisfy the wants or desires of other persons, no goods or commodities being transferred, the persons or enterprises so engaged are said to be providing "services." Typical service industries are the utilities supplying electricity, gas and telephone service. Professionals such as physicians, lawyers and dentists are engaged in providing services. Barbers and auto repair shops are other examples.

setup. Making ready or preparing for the performance of a job or operation. Machine setup involves equipping a machine with the appropriate accessories, tools, and fixtures, setting the proper feed, speed, and depth of cut, and so forth. In manual work setup is the arrangement prior to commencing the work, of the tools, accessories, component parts, and details involved. It also includes the tear-down to return the machine or work area to its original or normal condition.

severance benefits. Benefits collected by employee when he leaves the company before retirement. Special cases include when a company moves to another location and gives employees choice between coming along or severance pay; technological displacement pay, when a worker's job and skill are made obsolete by new machines and no suitable and mutually acceptable job can be found for him; in a pension plan where the employee does not lose if he leaves the company's employ before retirement age. See VESTING RIGHTS.

severance pay. See DISMISSAL COMPENSATION. "Severance Pay Plans," are the subject of *Studies in Personnel Policy No. 41*, published by National Industrial Conference Board.

sex differential. Differences in rates paid to men and women in the same occupation for work of comparable quality and quantity. Where quality of output differs as between men and women, differences in pay are not necessarily differentials based on sex.

Shanley Point Plan. A wage incentive system similar to DYER SYSTEM, which see.

shape-up. The policy and practice of having unemployed longshoremen line up in special formation each day at the docks, in order that potential employers or their representatives may look them over and select the workers they want.

share-the-work plan. A process of spreading employment wherein a larger number of employees are retained on the payroll than work needs require, those employees working shorter hours to spread the work through the entire group, thereby cutting down layoff rates.

Sherman Individual Group Plan. This is a high task (50-50) constant sharing plan to which is added a secondary premium. The latter is the net remainder between the employer's 50% share and any time lost by the employee on the below task productions which he has performed. Half of this net amount of saving goes to the employee and half to the supervisors, so that the employee may get as much as three-quarters of his whole saving if he has not fallen below the task point. The supervisor's half of the secondary premium is divided equally between foremen and higher supervisors. Indirect labor is sometimes grouped with direct labor and rewarded similarly. It is a "balance sheet" method of doing what Taylor did with two piece rates, that is accounting for good and poor productions separately, rather than merging them into a single efficiency for the pay period. Sherman Individual Group Plan Formula:

Earning up to high task=Hours Actual × Rate per Hour

$$E=H_a \qquad R_h$$

Earning at and above high task=Time/Wages+Wages Saved/2+[Hours Saved/2−Hours Lost] × Half Rate per Hour

$$E=H_a R_h+(H_s-H_a)R_h/2+\frac{[(H_s-H_a/2)-(h_a-h_s]R_h}{2}$$

$$E=R_h/2[(H_s+H_a)+H_s-H_a/2+h_s-h_a]$$

(See *symbols, wage formula*)

Key to additional symbols:

h_s=Hours standard for jobs not done in task time

h_a=Hours actual for jobs not done in task time

Note that h_a is greater than h_s

shift. A term applied to a work period where two or more groups of workers are employed at different hours during the operating time of an establishment; e.g., an establishment may operate two shifts of 8 hours each or 16 hours a day. In some industries, the term "trick" or "tour" is used instead of "shift." See also FIXED SHIFT, GRAVEYARD SHIFT, LOBSTER SHIFT, ROTATING SHIFT, SPLIT SHIFT, and SWING SHIFT.

shift differential. Added compensation to workers who are employed on a work schedule other than the regular daytime schedule. Shift differentials may be paid in a number of ways: (1) a fixed amount per hour above the rate paid on the regular day shift; (2) a percentage over earnings at the regular day shift rates; (3) shorter hours and additional monetary compensation above full daily pay.

shop, closed. See CLOSED SHOP.

shop committee. A group of employees elected to consider grievances and other conditions of employment.

shop steward. A union employee in a plant, department or production unit who represents the employees in the respective group in the handling of grievances and determines whether specified work conditions are being maintained. The steward is to the union what the foreman is to the company—the key-man in the whole collective bargaining set-up. Stewards are usually elected by the workers they represent. Describing the steward, a U.S. Department of Labor Bulletin, "Settling Plant Grievances," says: "When collective bargaining is new stewards are often chosen because they have demonstrated outstanding organizing ability during the early stages of the union's growth. The belligerent steward outgrows his defensive attitude (or is replaced by another worker with a more constructive point of view) to the extent that both management and union recognize the importance and responsibility of the position." The shop steward fulfills a function recognized by law. He (or she) is possessed of rights guaranteed by law and by the contractual agreement between his union and the company. Therefore, the steward's function warrants the respectful recognition of foremen.

shop, union. See UNION SHOP.

short hour tours ("T" Tricks). In telephone terminology, tours in Traffic that vary from 6 to 7½ hours, depending upon their ending time, for which 8 hours pay may be received.

"Short-Time Placement." A term used by the United States Employment Service. See PLACEMENT.

short-unit course. A self-contained training program of relatively short duration for the purpose of giving instruction in a single phase of a subject or in the operation of a specific machine.

"Shortage List." A term used by the United States Employment Service. A local office list showing the occupational titles and codes of jobs for which the current demand for applicants cannot be satisfied by selection from the application file.

shut-down. The closing of a plant or other place of business pending settlement of a labor dispute or because of financial difficulties, material shortages, or other reasons.

sick leave. Leave of absence granted with or without pay to ill or injured employees pending recovery. Sometimes certain conditions must be satisfied, either to collect the pay or to keep the job open. These conditions may be a doctor's certificate, or other satisfactory evidence that the employee cannot work; proper notification of the employer that the employee is ill; the cause of illness; and keeping in touch with the employer from time to time as to progress.

sight-conservation. A number of companies have voluntary eye-screening programs to enable employees to check their vision. Other companies support to varying degrees sight conservation measures. "Wise Owl" clubs are active in industry, as well as the National Society for Prevention of Blindness. See "Save Your Sight," published by Public Affairs Committee in cooperation with NSPB, 1790 Broadway, New York 19, N. Y.; publications of Industrial Vision Institute, Purdue University, Lafayette, Indiana. See also INDUSTRIAL VISION RESEARCH.

Simons, Henry C. (1889-1946), professor of economics at the University of Chicago. His writings on trade unionism are mainly confined to a single short article, "Some Reflections on Syndicalism," which appeared in the *Journal of Political Economy*, March 1944. Trade unionism, according to Simons, is monopoly, founded on violence and hence antidemocratic, with the goal of restricting output to raise the price of the commodity it has for sale—labor. The fundamental conflict of interest in society is not between employer and employee but between "every large organized group of laborers and the community as a whole." In contrast, "we generally fail to see . . . the identity of interest between the whole community and enterprisers seeking to keep down costs (i.e., employers). Where enterprise is competitive—and substantial, enduring restraint of competition in product markets is rare— enterprisers represent the community interest effectively."

Simo Chart. (Simultaneous Motion Cycle Chart). A graphical representation of an operation, usually, although not necessarily, made from a motion picture film, in which the basic motions, such as therbligs, used to perform the operation by the right-and-left hand members of the body are separately plotted in columns scaled to time, using standard symbols for the elements.

Simo Chart, Full. An extremely detailed "simo chart," containing columns to represent every body member directly or indirectly entering the operation.

Simo Chart, Simple. A simplified form of "simo chart," usually sufficient for most practical purposes, on which are recorded only the basic motions of the body members immediately or directly engaged in the operations; as the actions of the two hands; or of the hands and

feet; or of the wrists, lower arms, and upper arms.

single firm bargaining. Presumably the commonest form of bargaining in which negotiations are confined to one company. However, unions do not normally permit the conditions in individual firms to fall materially below their competitors, and often negotiations are partly based on industry-wide or area conditions.

single rate. A rate which is the same for all workers on the same job or in the same job classification, and under which the individual worker on a job receives the same rate during the entire time that he is holding the job. The single rate usually is paid to experienced workers in jobs requiring varying degrees of skill. Learners or apprentices may be paid according to rate schedules which start below the single rate and permit the worker to achieve the full job rate over a period of time. In the less skilled jobs, the rates for beginners and experienced workers may be identical because the period of time necessary to become familiar with all the phases of the work is relatively short. Individual workers may occasionally be paid above or below the single rate for special reasons, but such payments are regarded as exceptions to the usual rule. The definition of a "job" or "classification" may be very narrow or very broad, and the single rate may therefore be applicable to as few as one or two workers doing identical jobs, or as many as several thousands performing a number of essentially different jobs which are nevertheless regarded as meriting the same rate of pay.

Single Working Woman Budget. A budget designed to represent a minimum, adequate standard of living for a self-supporting woman without dependents. The generally accepted concept is a woman living alone in a furnished room or boardinghouse with lunches to be eaten at a restaurant, and other meals entirely or alternately at either a boardinghouse or restaurant. Current budget estimates may be obtained from Women's Bureau, U.S. Dept. of Labor.

sit-down. An action whereby employees remain at their work stations but refuse to work. Usually, a sit-down is a strike. Although used in several European countries for sometime previous, it was not until the spread of industrial unionism in the middle 1930's that the sit-down strike became widely known in the United States. The sit-down strike has fallen into disfavor because of adverse public opinion.

"Size-of-Firm Provision." A term used by the United States Employment Service. The provision of a State employment security law which specifies the minimum number of employees and/or the minimum period of employment or minimum pay roll which an employing unit must have before it is liable for contributions.

skill. (1) The ability to use one's knowledge, technical proficiency, developed and/or acquired ability, in devising an efficient method of accomplishing a given objective. (2) Proficiency at following a given method, good or bad, developed as the result of aptitude and practice.

"Skill Level." A term used by the United States Employment Service. An arbitrary range in which are grouped jobs broadly similar to each other according to such factors as knowledge of process, exer-

cise of judgment, manual dexterity, responsibility for product and equipment, length of training period, etc. The most commonly used skill level groupings are: skilled, semi-skilled, and unskilled.

skilled laborer. A craftsman or person engaged in a manual occupation who possesses a thorough and comprehensive knowledge of a process or operation. Skill usually implies a high degree of manual dexterity and the ability to exercise independent judgment. It may include assuming responsibility for a product or equipment.

skilled mechanic. One competent to perform, with a high degree of expertness, the work in one or more specialized divisions of a given trade.

skilled operator. One competent to perform efficiently and expertly one or more kinds of repetitive production or single purpose jobs on machines or other special equipment, demanding manual dexterity.

skill differential. Differences in wage rates paid to workers engaged in occupations requiring varying levels of skill in work performance. May also refer to differentials in rates of workers in the same occupation, higher rates being paid to those who usually perform the more complex tasks. See also PREMIUM RATE.

"Slip Report." A term used by the United States Employment Service. See WAGE REPORT.

slowdown. A less effective form of strike, in which the workers in an organized manner reduce output without actually leaving the plant, in order to force a concession from the employer.

Smith-Connelly War Labor Disputes Act. Federal law of 1943 which provided for government seizures of struck war plants, requiring thirty-day strike notices and strike votes, restricted political contributions by unions, and gave statutory recognition to the National War Labor Board.

Smith-Hughes Act. The basic federal vocational education act, passed in 1917, which established the principles of federal financial aid and cooperation with states in promoting public vocational education of less than college grade in agriculture, trade and industries, and home economics, for persons 14 years of age and over. It includes a permanent appropriation, and is administered by the U.S. Office of Education, Department of Health, Education and Welfare.

snapback method. The procedure of timing, used in making time studies, whereby the stop watch is read and the watch hand returned to zero at the termination of each element or work cycle.

snapback reading. See SNAPBACK METHOD.

social insurance. Public programs under which individuals are compensated, without reference to need, at rates determined by past earnings or service, for part of the wage loss resulting from old age, sickness, disability, unemployment or death. Examples are federal old-age and survivors' insurance and federal-state unemployment insurance.

social legislation. Laws designed to improve and protect the economic and social position of those groups in society which because of age, sex, race, physical or mental defect, or lack of economic power cannot achieve healthful and decent living standards for themselves.

Social Security Account. To operate the Federal Old-Age and Survivors Insurance System, and pay benefits on the basis of the worker's average monthly pay, the Federal Government must have a record of the pay each worker receives in covered employment. The Social Security Administration keeps such a record, taken from the employer's wage reports, which are turned in every 3 months with the social security taxes. The record is kept in the form of a separate social security account for each individual worker, under his name and a number that identifies his account. That number appears with the worker's name on his social security card, which he gets from his local Social Security office. The worker should make sure that every employer for whom he works takes down his social security number exactly as it is printed on the worker's card. The employer must have the number in order to report accurately a worker's wages and social security taxes to the Government. A worker should have only one social security number. If he has more than one number, he should report this fact to his local Social Security office, so that his social security account can be straightened out by bringing all of his recorded wages together under one number. Every worker should take good care of his social security card. For double safety, he should take off the lower half, or stub and put it some place where he can always find it. The number will be good as long as he lives. When he or any of his family files a claim for benefits the number will identify his account. The wages credited to that account will then be used to calculate the benefits that may be due. He can check up on his social security account each year by

(289)

writing to the Social Security Administration and asking for a statement of his
wage credits. Any mistake that might
be found should be reported to the local
office immediately so that a correction
can be made. Mistakes may occur if the
employer has failed to report accurately
and completely the worker's name, his
social security account number, and the
amount of wages paid him. Almost any
mistake can be corrected regardless of
when it is discovered. Some cases, however, cannot be corrected unless the mistake is called to the attention of a Social
Security office within 4 years. A post
card form for convenient use in asking
for a statement of a worker's wage record may be obtained free of charge at
any Social Security Administration field
office. Or write to the Bureau of Old-
Age and Survivors Insurance, Candler
Building, Baltimore 2, Md., giving name,
address, and social security account
number. A statement of the worker's
wage record will be sent in a sealed en-
velope. The receipts furnished by the
employer are another check on the
worker's social security account because
they show wages as well as taxes.

"Social Security Account Number." A
term used by the United States Employment Service. The identification number
assigned to an individual by the Bureau
of Old-Age and Survivors Insurance under the Social Security Act.

Social Security Act. Act of August 14,
1935, and subsequently amended, including 1958 amendments. The Social
Security Act provides for two Nationwide systems of social insurance to protect wage earners and their families
against loss of income due to unemployment, disability, old age, and death: (1)

Old-age and survivors insurance, an all-
Federal system, operated by the United
States Government through the Social
Security Administration and approximately 540 field offices; and (2) Unemployment insurance, a Federal-State plan
under which each State sets up its own
law and State administrative agency,
with the Federal Government paying all
operating costs. Supplementing these,
the Social Security Act provides for public assistance on a Federal-State plan
with monthly cash payments to needy
old people, needy dependent children,
the needy blind, and needy persons who
are permanently and totally disabled.
The act also provides grants to the
States for maternal and child-health
services, services for crippled children,
and child-welfare services, to supplement State and local funds available for
such programs. See also: OLD-AGE AND
SURVIVORS INSURANCE (OASI) under Social Security Act, PUBLIC ASSISTANCE
under Social Security Act, MATERNAL
AND CHILD WELFARE under Social Security Act, RAILROAD RETIREMENT ACT,
BUREAU OF EMPLOYMENT SECURITY, UN-
EMPLOYMENT INSURANCE.

**social security, information about pro-
grams.** Local offices of the appropriate
offices are listed in the telephone book.
The post office will also furnish information. The Federal or State agencies usually have their headquarters in the capital of the State. These agencies usually
have leaflets explaining the program in
more detail. Agencies Administering Sections of the Social Security Act:

Old Age, Disability and Survivors
Insurance
Local and State
Local Social Security Office

Federal

Social Security Administration
U.S. Department of Health, Education, and Welfare
Washington, D. C.

Unemployment Insurance

Local State Employment Office, or
State Employment Security Agency
Bureau of Employment Security
United States Department of Labor
Washington 25, D. C.

Public Assistance

Local Public Welfare Office
or State Public Welfare Agency
Bureau of Public Assistance
Social Security Administration
U.S. Department of Health, Education, and Welfare
Washington, D. C.

Maternal and Child-Health Services

Local Health Department, or
Maternal and Child Health Division
of the State Health Department
Children's Bureau
Social Security Administration
U.S. Department of Health, Education, and Welfare
Washington, D. C.

Services for Crippled Children

Local Health or Welfare Department,
or State Crippled Children's Agency
Children's Bureau

Social Security Administration
U.S. Department of Health, Education, and Welfare
Washington, D. C.

Child-Welfare Services

Local Public Welfare Agency, or
Child Welfare Division of the
Public Welfare Agency
Children's Bureau
U.S. Department of Health, Education, and Welfare
Washington, D. C.

social security number. A series of numbers assigned as a combination to each worker covered by the Social Security plan. The number is the identification of the worker. Against this numerical code all his earnings are reported and credited. It remains through his entire work life as a part of his employment record. After his death, the number serves to identify the benefit payment account of his survivors. In filling out application for a new job, the Social Security number is invariably requested. Some employees have the number engraved on an identification bracelet, or other permanent form.

social security tax, amount of. The following table shows the present rate of the social security tax on the first $4,800 of earnings and the scheduled increases:

Calendar Year	Employer	Employee	Self-Employed
1957-58	2¼%	2¼%	3⅜%
1959	2½%	2½%	3¾%
1960-62	3%	3%	4½%
1963-65	3½%	3½%	5¼%
1965-68	4%	4%	6%
1969 and thereafter	4½%	4½%	6¾%

These taxes are designed to pay the entire cost of old-age, survivors, and disability benefits and the cost of administering the program. The employer must contribute, for each employee, the same amount as deducted from the worker's pay and report wages on a quarterly basis (farmers report the wages of employees annually). The self-employed also report net earnings in connection with their income tax return. Once a year the employer must give the worker a receipt for the tax taken out of his pay. This receipt also shows the amount of wages paid. The employer must also furnish a receipt if and when a worker leaves his job.

social security tax, method of figuring. The chart below shows how the monthly pension varies according to the amount earned by the retiree and at age at which he or she retires:

EXAMPLES OF MONTHLY PAYMENTS BEGINNING AFTER 1958
(For this table all amounts are rounded down to the next lower whole dollar figure)

If average monthly earnings after 1950 are:[1]	$50 or less	$150	$250	[2]$350	[3]$400
For RETIREMENT at 65....⎫ For DISABILITY at 50......⎬	$33	$73	$95	$116	$127
For RETIRED WOMAN WORKER starting at age 62[4]	26	58	76	92	101
For WIDOW, or surviving child, or dependent widower, or parent	33	54	71	87	95
For RETIRED COUPLE, wife starting at age 62[4]	45	100	130	159	174
For RETIRED COUPLE, wife starting at age 65 or WIDOW and 1 child or 2 dependent PARENTS....	49	109	142	174	190
For RETIRED COUPLE, and 1 child or WIDOW and 2 children....	53	120	190	232	254
MAXIMUM FAMILY BENEFIT	53	120	202	254	254
SINGLE lump-sum death payment	$99	$219	$255	$255	$255

[1] In figuring your average, you may omit up to 5 years of lowest earnings, and any period your record was frozen because you were disabled.

[2] Average monthly earnings over $350 will not be possible before the end of 1959.

[3] A $400 monthly average will generally not be possible for any one who has reached the age of 27 before 1959. Payments based on this average cannot be made unless all credits used in figuring the benefit are earned after 1958.

[4] Retirement payments to women are permanently reduced if started before age 65.

The Society for Advancement of Management. The Society was formed in 1936 by the merging of the Taylor Society, organized in 1912 to forward the ideas of Frederick W. Taylor and his associates, who developed the concept of scientific management; and the Society of Industrial Engineers, formed in 1917. A third organization, the Industrial Methods Society, merged with the Society for Advancement of Management in 1946. Located at 74-5th Avenue, New York City. Official publication, "Advanced Management." The purposes of this Society as outlined in the Constitution are, through conferences, seminars, research, publications and other appropriate means (1) To develop efficiency through the study and application of scientific principles and methods of management. (2) To promote and accomplish the various mutual interests of management, investors, labor, government, and the public in improved management. (3) To provide direct means whereby executives, engineers, teachers, public officials and others concerned, are aided in applying scientific methods to management problems, and promoting this common interest. (4) To inspire in manager and employee a constant adherence to the highest ethical conception of individual and collective social responsibility.

sociometry. An approach to the study of sociology. It emphasizes the operational definition of sociological concepts and the description of human relationships and other social phenomena in quantitative or measurative terms. In personnel relations, sociometry enters particularly in connection with personnel testing, where the sociometrist handles the evaluation of scoring.

soldiering. See GOLDBRICKING.

sound and tested going rate. See WAGE RATE BRACKET.

span of control. The number of persons which an executive, officer or supervisor can have reporting directly to himself with efficiency.

"Special Aids for Placing Military Personnel in Civilian Jobs." A term used by the United States Employment Service. Groups of civilian occupations, requiring varying degrees of the same or similar abilities of workers, that are related to an occupation in the army.

"Special Aids for Placing Naval Personnel in Civilian Jobs." A term used by the United States Employment Service. Similar to SPECIAL AIDS FOR PLACING MILITARY PERSONNEL, but prepared for naval personnel.

"Special Job Family." A term used by the United States Employment Service. See JOB FAMILY.

special permit rate. A rate paid to a union worker who comes from another city and is employed under a special permit because of local labor shortages. The rate received is the same as that paid to permanent workers in the area. In the unionized brewery industry, this term refers to the rates paid to special workers who are temporarily employed during the peak summer period. These rates are usually lower than those received by "regular" union workers.

special time allowance. A temporary time value applying to an operation in addition to or in place of a standard allowance in order to compensate for a specified, temporary non-standard production condition.

speed rating. A method of performance rating that compares the speed or tempo with which a worker performs the motions necessary to execute an operation against the observer's concept of standard or normal tempo.

speed-up. A term originated by workers to denote a condition which forces employees to increase production. The term is also used to indicate a situation under which a reduction in rates may cause an increase in output to maintain former earnings.

spendable earnings. In general, the money earnings of workers less various amounts deducted for taxes and other purposes from pay rolls; hence, "spendable earnings" may be identified broadly with "take home" earnings. Term also used in the sense of the earnings available for private spending or saving, but this usage would include certain types of deductions (e.g., union dues) as spendable earnings. "Net spendable average weekly earnings" is a series developed by the Bureau of Labor Statistics in which Federal social security and income taxes are deducted from gross average weekly earnings for workers with specified number of dependents. See also TAKE-HOME PAY.

split shift. The daily working time that is not continuous but split into two or more working periods. "Split shifts" are usually found in industries such as local transportation, which is affected by peaks or rush periods at various times of the day. See also FIXED SHIFT, ROTATING SHIFT, SHIFT, and SWING SHIFT.

"Spot Placement." A term used by the United States Employment Service. See PLACEMENT.

spread (schedule spread). The difference between the top rates of the highest schedule and those of the lowest schedule for any one occupation.

stable workforce. A measure of employment stability defined as that proportion of all workers listed on the annual payroll which was not absent at more than two pay periods. The measure does not distinguish between quits, layoffs, and discharges. It is not widely used currently as a measure of labor stability.

staff organization. A type of organizational set-up in a company where authority flows from the president functionally to the department heads. Each department reports to one staff specialist with regard to personnel, finance, production, or other designated functions. Advantages are that operating or production executives are not required to perform work outside of their specialized fields, and receive expert advice and counsel from staff specialists. Disadvantages are that lines of authority are not sharply defined. See also LINE ORGANIZATION; LINE-AND-STAFF ORGANIZATION.

"Staffing Pattern." A term used by the United States Employment Service. See STAFFING SCHEDULE.

"Staffing Schedule." A term used by the United States Employment Service. An inventory of the jobs in a plant which presents the distribution of jobs as they occur in plant processes and gives a complete record of the manner in which workers are distributed among the jobs.

(294)

staggering shifts. (1) A method of reducing unemployment in a plant by reducing the number of hours of work and establishing two or more shifts in order that there may be work for all. In this system, each worker shares the burden of reduced business or activity of the enterprise through decreased hours and reduced earnings. (2) a method of alleviating the problems of transportation by having the shifts begin and end at 15 minute or half hour intervals. This helps relieve traffic congestion.

standard. (1) Any established or accepted rule, model, or criterion against which comparisons are made. (2) See PERFORMANCE STANDARD, STANDARD TIME, STANDARD HOUR, DIRECT LABOR STANDARD, GUARANTEED TIME STANDARD, and so on.

standard allowance. The established or accepted amount by which the normal time for an operation is increased within an area, plant, or industry to compensate for the usual amount of fatigue and/or personal and/or unavoidable delays.

"Standard Contribution Rate." A term used by the United States Employment Service. See CONTRIBUTION RATES.

standard cost. The normal cost of an operation, process, or product including labor, material, and overhead charges, computed on the basis of past performance costs, estimates, or work measurement.

standard data. See STANDARD TIME DATA.

standard and elemental time. The normal elemental time plus allowances for fatigue and delays.

"Standard Functional Time Distributing Code." A term used by the United States Employment Service. A system in which identifying numbers are assigned to each of the functions in a State employment security agency, so that these identifying numbers, instead of names of functions, can be used by personnel to identify on a record the functions on which they worked for the amount of time shown. See also PERSONNEL FUNCTIONAL TIME DISTRIBUTION SYSTEM.

standard hour. An hour of time during which a specified amount of work of acceptable quality is or can be performed by a qualified workman following the prescribed method, working at normal pace, and experiencing normal fatigue and delays.

standard hour plan. A wage incentive plan having standard times expressed as standard hours. The hourly base wage rate is paid for standard hours earned rather than actual hours worked. Usually the plan provides for a guaranteed minimum wage based on the hours worked if they exceed the standard hours earned.

standard of living. The kind and quantities of goods and services which are considered essential by an individual or group. Technically, standard of living differs from scale or plane of living which is merely the list of things the individual or group consumes at a given time or place. But the term is frequently used in the latter meaning.

standard performance. The performance which must be given by a workman to accomplish his work in the standard time allowed.

standard practice. The established or accepted procedure used within an area, plant, or industry for carrying out a specified task or assignment.

standard rate. A basic rate of pay established for an occupation in a plant, industry, or community through collective bargaining, company regulation, or by law. May also refer to established rates for services rendered in a community in connection with maintenance and repair of automobiles, appliances, buildings, etc.

standard time. (1) The time which is determined to be necessary for a qualified workman, working at a pace which is ordinarily used under capable supervision and experiencing normal fatigue and delays, to do a defined amount of work of specified quality when following the prescribed method. (2) The normal or leveled time plus allowance for fatigue and delays.

standard time data. A compilation of all the elements that are used for performing a given class of work with normal elemental time values for each element. The data are used as a basis for determining time standards on work similar to that from which the data were determined without making actual time studies.

standardizaton. As used in psychological testing, standardization means that a test, through a process of experimentation, has been found to have both validity and reliability.

standardization. A management sponsored program to establish criteria or policies that will promote uniform practices and conditions within the company and permit their control through comparisons. It deals with such areas as work quality and quantity, working conditions, wage rates, and production methods.

start. A THERBLIG (which see) which is defined as: to originate motion or action; often motion from a sudden influence; cause to move or act; to set in motion, as something inanimate; to move from its place; to give a beginning or new direction to; to give a signal for the motion of. The type of the fit between the parts, alignment, weight of the part or tool, friction or mechanical action to be overcome may be the cause of additional time being added to the work cycle.

starting rate. See ENTRANCE RATE.

"State Agency." A term used by the United States Employment Service. The agency of a State government which, under State law, is charged with the responsibility of administering the State employment security program.

State Board of Vocational Education. The agency created by a state having major responsibility for the general supervision of vocational education in the state. It is responsibile for maintaining certain minimum standards in the expenditure of federal funds allotted to the state for vocational education.

State Director of Vocational Education. An administrator designated within the state to be directly responsible to the executive officer of the state board for vocational education for the administration and operation of the total vocational education program in the state.

"State Inventory of Job Openings." A term used by the United States Employment Service. A list of current clearance job openings existing within a State, prepared by the State central office, based on Job Openings for Inventory submitted by its local offices.

state minimum wage laws. State laws in effect in some states provide for the establishment of a floor to wages. After a rate is set for an industry or occupation, no covered employer can pay less. He can, however, pay higher wages. The Fair Labor Standards Act (which see) applies to men and women workers engaged in *interstate commerce,* or in the production of goods for interstate commerce. Employees in local establishments usually must look to their State to set a floor below which wages cannot fall. There are two types of State Minimum Wage laws: One has a "statutory" rate —a rate set by the legislature. The other type fixes no rate in the act but provides for the setting of minimum wages through wage orders. Wage orders generally are issued by the State labor commissioner, based on recommendations of industry or occupation wage boards, composed of representatives of workers, employers, and the public. After holding a public hearing, the commissioner issues the order establishing wages and other standards for the protection of workers in the industry or occupation covered. The procedure for revising wage orders is usually the same as for issuing an original order.

state plan for vocational education. An agreement between a state board for vocational education and the U.S. Office of Education, describing (1) the vocational education program developed by the state to meet its own purposes and conditions and (2) the conditions under which the state will use federal vocational education funds (such conditions must conform to the federal acts and

the official policies of the U.S. Office of Education before programs may be reimbursed from federal funds). The plan is usually revised every five years.

"State Practice." A term used by the United States Employment Service. An established custom or usage accepted or generally applied as an expenditure control in the fiscal administration of the State government.

"Status Determination." A term used by the United States Employment Service. See DETERMINATION.

Status Quo, maintenance of under Railway Labor Act (which see). While conferences over making or revising agreements under the Railway Labor Act are being held and while the National Mediation Board is acting in any dispute, the carrier may not alter rates of pay, rules, or working conditions.

"Status Report." A term used by the United States Employment Service. A report required of all employing units in a State giving the information on which the State employment security agency bases its determination as to whether the employing unit is liable for contributions under the State employment security law. Same as LIABILITY REPORT.

step bonus. A feature of some wage incentive plans whereby a substantial increase is made in incentive payment when the quantity and/or quality of output reaches a specified level. Such increases are ordinarily expressed as percentages of either the base wage rate or the incentive rate.

stenographer. According to the Dictionary of Occupational Titles, (which see) takes dictation in shorthand of correspondence, reports, and other matter and transcribes dictated material, writing it out in long hand or using a typewriter. May be required to be versed in the technical language and terms used in a particular profession. May perform a variety of related clerical duties. May take dictation on a stenotype machine or may transcribe information from a sound producing record.

Stevens Point Plan. A wage incentive system similar to DYER SYSTEM, which see.

steward, union, tips for personal conduct. The following "tips" are taken from "Leadership Training Program for Stewards, Shop Committeemen and Lodge Officers," New York State Council of International Association of Machinists. (1) Don't make threats. If you make threats and they are just a bluff, no one will take you seriously in the future. (2) Take up grievances promptly. Be persistent until the grievance is processed according to procedure. (3) When arguing a case, stick to the issues. Don't fall in love with your own voice. Don't be sarcastic. Argue the merits of the case openly. Don't be led into by-paths. Don't be provoked into losing your temper. (4) Always keep a solid front in the grievance committee. Don't argue with each other in front of the boss. If you should disagree, ask for an intermission. (5) Don't abuse your position. If the contract says you can spend only a certain amount of time on grievances, stick within its provisions. Don't give the boss a chance to charge bad faith.

stoop labor. The hand picking of sugar beets, done to a considerable extent by Mexican nationals.

stop. A THERBLIG (which see) which is defined as: to bring from motion to rest; to prevent egress from or passage through; to give a signal for the discontinuing of a movement or condition.

straight commission. A term generally used to describe a method of payment to salesmen on a percentage basis. This compensates salesmen in proportion to the amount of goods they sell. See also BONUS; COMMISSION EARNINGS; DRAWING ACCOUNT.

straight salary. A term generally used to describe a method of payment to salesmen, assuring a definitely fixed compensation per week, month or other stated period. See also BONUS; COMMISSION EARNINGS; DRAWING ACCOUNT.

straight time rate. See DAY RATE.

straw boss. A colloquial expression for an assistant foreman or other group leader.

stretch out. (1) The act of extending the time taken to do a job by malingering. (2) Term referring to giving a workman additional work to do without a compensating increase in earnings or change in conditions, methods or the like.

strike. An employer-employee relationship in which the employees as a group refuse to work until certain conditions of employment are granted by the employer. The act of going on strike is not synonymous with quitting work, and under present law the employee has numerous guarantees against arbitrary dismissal for engaging in strike or organizing activities.

strikebound. Affected by a strike or operating under striking conditions. As, for example, a strikebound establishment or industry.

strikebreaker. A person usually representing the employer's interests, who attempts to, or who succeeds in breaking a strike.

strikebreaking. The practice of attempting to or of succeeding in terminating or to render a strike ineffective against the will of the majority of striking employees. Strikebreaking may involve the use of violence in breaking through picket lines, in hiring labor spies to break the strike from the inside by creating dissension among the employees, by hiring scab labor, by arousing public and government opinion against the strike.

strike fund. A reserve accumulated by a union for the purpose of providing members with some income in event of a strike as well as to pay in full or in part the expenses connected with the organization and launching of a strike.

strike, industry-wide. A strike of organized employees in an entire industry.

strike notice. A formal advisement by a group of employees to their employer or to an appropriate government agency that as of a certain date strike action will be taken if the grievance is not settled.

strike, jurisdictional. See JURISDICTIONAL STRIKE.

strike, sympathy. A work stoppage called by employees who have no direct grievance against their employer but who are acting in order to bring pressure to bear in favor of other workers involved in a strike on account of some grievance and in order to demonstrate worker solidarity.

strike vote. A poll of workers to determine whether or not they will leave their

operations in order to secure or maintain certain working conditions or demands. It need not be called immediately after the election, but calling of the strike may be left to the discretion of the top union officials or negotiation committee as a final resort to gaining demand.

student learner (student worker). A member of a high school cooperative education program legally employed as a part-time worker and so classified by the Wage and Hour and Public Contracts Divisions of the U. S. Department of Labor for wage and hour regulations purposes.

style development rate. Similar to temporary, experimental, or trial rate. The term is used in the hosiery manufacturing industry and relates to work on new styles for which no piece rates have yet been set. Generally, hourly rates are paid on such work. Usually these hourly rates average close to the workers' previous piece-rate earnings. The style development rates are in effect for a specified time and are then replaced by new piece rates.

subminimum rate. A rate below the minimum established for an occupation, establishment, industry, or area by union agreement, law, or policy. Such rates may be paid to learners and to substandard, superannuated, probationary, or special permit workers.

subsidized time. See MAKE-UP TIME.

subsistence allowance. A payment to a worker for expenses covering meals, lodging, and transportation while in a traveling status for his employer. Such allowances may be based on a fixed amount for meals and lodging plus other expenditures or on the actual expenses incurred for all items. There are also cases where institutional workers (e.g., nurses) receive a subsistence allowance for living outside the institution, since free room and board are incorporated into the wage structure.

"Subject Employer." A term used by the United States Employment Service. An employing unit which is subject to the contribution provisions of a State employment security law.

substandard rate. A rate of pay below the prevailing or standard level for a worker whose efficiency is impaired because of physical or mental handicaps. The term is also used to refer to rates below Federal or State minimum wage levels or below prevailing levels for an occupation in an industry or area. See also HANDICAPPED WORKER RATE.

subtracted time. On a time study conducted using the continuous timing method, the elapsed time obtained for an element of an operation by subtracting from the watch reading recorded at the end of that element during the same cycle.

Suggestion Box. See SUGGESTION, DEFINITION OF.

suggestion boxes. Usually a locked box which is an integral part of a combination unit in a suggestion system that also includes a bulletin board for displaying suggestion poster material and a receptacle holder for suggestion forms. The unit is ordinarily made of wood or a light metal and is comparatively inexpensive. Usually one suggestion box is installed for every twenty-five to fifty employees. Some guides for the proper place to install the suggestion box are: (1) Do not install near entrances or time clocks where traffic is heavy. (2) The location should be well lighted and such that every employee will see it every day. (3) The unit should be in the direct line of vision of passers-by and easily accessible. Dressing rooms, lunchrooms, or smoking rooms where employees congregate and spend some time are very desirable.

suggestion systems, awards for. Suggestion awards are of two general types: (1) merit and recognition awards, and (2) cash or other tangible value items that represent an actual payment for value received. The most common merit awards are suggestion pins, certificates, letters from a high official of the company, etc. Cash or other tangible value awards consist of cash or checks, merchandise awards, or prizes such as all-expense tours or trips. Special dinners at which recognition is expressed are also popular.

suggestion system committee. A committee set up to examine suggestions from employees and to see that the improvements suggested are put into action. Plans of the organization of the committee vary with different companies. The "Suggestion Manual" published by Elliott Service, Mt. Vernon, N. Y. suggests that the committee should include such persons as the following: (1) A representative of top management who is able to place before the committee the company's attitude towards the various ideas submitted. (2) A technically trained person to ascertain the feasibility of the ideas submitted from a technical viewpoint. (3) A cost man to determine the probable savings which might result from an idea, also to determine the cost of installation of equipment or materials necessary for the utilization of the idea. (4) A foreman to represent all men in his group and to pass on the applicability of the idea. (5) A representative of the working force to see that the ideas considered are given fair and just consideration.

suggestion systems, cooperation of supervisors. It is generally accepted that the success of a suggestion system depends to a considerable extent on the cooperation of foremen and supervisors. The Metropolitan Life Insurance Company, in its report, "Suggestion Systems," prepared for its "Policyholders Service Bureau" suggests some supervisory responsibilities in connection with the suggestion plan are: (1) To acquire a thorough knowledge of the system's rules and policies. (2) To investigate promptly all suggestions assigned to them. (3) To exercise judgment and fairness in considering any suggestions referred to them. (4) To encourage employees in their departments to make suggestions, and to instruct them in the kinds of suggestions wanted. (5) To handle with tact any rejections assigned to them by the suggestion committee, and to abstain from criticizing poor ideas. (6) To participate in presenting awards to employees in their departments. (7) To adopt promptly the suggestions accepted by the committee.

suggestion, definition of. There are many good definitions of what constitutes a suggestion. Herman W. Seinwerth, in his *Getting Results from Suggestion Plans,* (McGraw-Hill) gives two representative examples: (1) "A suggestion is any definite proposal intended to be of benefit to the company. The suggestion can be either new and original or involve a new application of an old idea. It may refer to a way to improve the company's policies; its methods of conducting its business or equipment; or any of its activities. Suggestions regarding obvious maintenance repairs, such as carpentry, painting, plumbing, etc. will not be considered unless accompanied by an improved method for doing the work." (2) "A suggestion is a positive constructive idea to improve methods, equipment, and procedures, to make for safer and better working conditions, to reduce the time or cost of an office, factory, or sales operation, or to improve either industrial or public relations." The suggestion must not only call attention to a change but must contain a proposed solution or correction. To put it another way, a suggestion should not merely cite a need for a change but should recommend a way of accomplishing it. Suggestions do not have to be new and original; they may merely involve a new or further application of an old idea. The very basis of a suggestion plan is the feeling of alertness that is generated in all employees to be on the lookout for the correction of mishandling the reinstatement of previously existing practices, the extension of present application of existing practices, etc.

suggestion system, form for. Formal employee suggestion systems usually make use of printed forms to a considerable degree. A classification of these forms according to function might be made as follows: Forms for entering suggestions; Forms for acknowledging suggestions; Forms for recording investigation and appraisal; Forms for notifying suggesters of the disposition of their suggestions;

Certificates of award; Records of suggestion activity; Publicity posters.

suggestion systems, essentials for successful operation. Some generally accepted principles underlying successful operation of suggestion systems include: (1) management must be thoroughly sincere in asking and offering to pay for suggestions; (2) employees must be convinced that the plan's objective is to improve the business; to improve competitive status, etc. so that the success of the business and the job security of employees are further enhanced. The National Industrial Conference Board, in its "Studies in Personnel Policy, No. 43," entitled "Employee Suggestion Systems," summarizes the following rules: (1) Get the wholehearted cooperation of the entire supervisory force. (2) Recognize supervisors' suggestions in some manner. (3) Investigate each suggestion thoroughly. (4) Be sure that decisions of the Suggestion Committee are absolutely impartial. (5) Pay fair awards and err on the side of liberality in case of doubt. (6) Publicize problems on which management is thinking, and ask for ideas on these problems. (7) Insist on fairness and a square deal to every suggester. (8) Eliminate unnecessary delays in answering suggestions and making decisions. (9) Explain to employees how awards are determined. (10) Follow up adopted suggestions to make sure that they are actually put into effect. (11) Conduct a continuous advertising program that keeps the suggestion system constantly before the employees. (12) Select a person of broad experience, recognized ability and fairness to head the suggestion administration. (13) Pattern the suggestion system to the individual organization. (14)

Secure the active interest of the chief executive.

suggestion system, origin of. The National Association of Suggestion Systems, in its book, "Suggestion Systems—A Brief Survey of Modern Theory and Practice," says, "Probably Napoleon's boast that every private in the armies of France carried a Marshall's baton in his knapsack is more than a hint at a systematic attempt to induce thinking and action outside and beyond the natural functions of a private soldier. And the poet's cry that 'Praise from Caesar is praise indeed' has often been construed as a dare to the performance of feats that would prove worthy of that praise. In modern times the Suggestion System, in one form or another, has been known and used for more than half a century. Whether called a Suggestion System, a Bureau of Awards, Bureau of New Ideas, a Committee on Standards, or any of the various other titles under which it has served, the idea has been in more or less constant use among certain organizations over a long period of years. During World War II, a number of joint Labor-Management Committees were set up in response to the request of the chairman of the War Production Board. One function of these committees was to promote suggestions from employees and to further the use of suggestions throughout the war production industry."

suggestion systems, purpose of. The publication, "Maintaining Interest in the Suggestion Plan," (Dartnell Industrial Relations Service) lists the following major purposes: (1) Provide close contact between the employee and his company. Such plans work both ways: They stimulate interest in the company on the part of the employee and they stimulate interest on the part of management in the worker. (2) Provides a creative outlet for the average employee which he may not be able to find in his job. Other benefits to the employee from the installation of the suggestion program include, in some measure, the following: (1) Safety valve—constructive suggestions may take the place of gripes. (2) Self-improvement—the employee is encouraged to develop beyond the requirements of his job. (3) Teamwork—a suggestion to management helps to build esprit de corps. (4) Recognition—the development of pride in accomplishment. (5) Cash award—last, but not least, the award he receives for his suggestion.

suggestion systems, types of. There are two distinct types of suggestion plans—continuous and contest. Under the continuous type of suggestion plan, there is no time limit on the submission of ideas, as it is in the constantly operating. Plans of this nature have the important advantage of always being available to the worker who has a suggestion to make.

suits by and against labor organizations, under Labor Management Act of 1947. Suits for violation of contracts between a labor organization representing employees in an industry affecting interstate commerce are permitted in the Federal district courts. A union in an industry affecting interstate commerce can sue or be sued as an entity. However, if a money judgment is obtained against a union it is enforceable only against union assets—not against assets of individual union members. In addition any person injured in his business or property as a result of certain listed activities of a la-

bor union in an industry affecting interstate commerce, has a right to sue the union and to recover damages. Generally speaking these activities are limited to boycotts, sympathy strikes, and jurisdictional strikes. The same activities are unfair labor practices under section 8 (b) (4) of Title I of the Labor Management Relations Act.

superannuated rate. A rate of pay below the prevailing level for a worker above a certain age. Such rates are frequently allowed in union agreements. At times, the agreement requires the employment of a certain ratio of older workers at superannuated rates. Superannuated workers with long service are sometimes retained in an employed status because of their economic need; also, their services are sometimes sought during periods of labor shortages.

superintendent. See MANAGER, DEPARTMENT.

supervision. (1) Guidance and direction given to one or more individuals performing assigned tasks or operations. (2) The group of individuals within an area, plant, or industry who are responsible for giving guidance and direction to one or more individuals performing assigned tasks.

Supervisors' Policy Manual. A supervisors' policy manual is a series of written policies and practices, organized into manual form for ease and reference. In the looseleaf or "revisable" manual the material is continuously assembled, and a simple code is used to keep all material on the same subject together, regardless of when it is issued or who authorizes it. In the case of a bound manual, information is periodically rounded up for a revision of the booklet. Research Report Number 11, HOW TO PREPARE AND MAINTAIN A SUPERVISORS' MANUAL, issued by the American Management Association, says that the policy manual makes clear to the supervisor: (1) What he may do on his own. (2) What he must clear before taking action. (3) What he may do without prior clearance, but must report for post-audit. (4) The continuity of any activity that originates or winds up in staff departments. Objectives in issuing a manual include: (1) Insure unaltered transmission and daily administration of top management's policies. (2) Provide an authoritative reference guide that stays on the top. (3) Facilitate proper indoctrination of supervisory personnel. (4) Provide follow-through on formal training. (5) Clarify line and staff roles in each activity. (6) Organize communication to avoid friction and misunderstandings. (7) Develop the foreman, management's representative, as the source of information for workers, instead of leaving the role to the shop steward. (8) Reduce or eliminate instances where the company is legally liable for supervisors' discriminatory acts. (9) Strengthen the foreman's identification with top management. (10) Get the personnel job done at the point of employee contact: in the shop.

supervisory attributes. Attributes which are generally conceded to be desirable in supervisors. These include: Good health, education or its equivalent, technical knowledge and experience, ability to direct people.

supervisory control. A specific term used in automation, which designates a control system which furnishes intelligence, usually to a centralized location, to be used by an operator to supervise the control of a process or operation.

supervisory development. See EXECUTIVE DEVELOPMENT.

supervisory job descriptions. Job analysis applied to supervisory jobs. Specifically, such job analysis should result in: (1) improved selection of supervisors; (2) development of supervisory training; (3) more reliable rating of supervisors. Other benefits may also accrue as: (1) Reduction of job content to formal written records; (2) Clarification of responsibility and authority; (3) Improved relations between the supervisor and the supervised; (4) Training in job content for the entire organization; (5) Improved methods of doing the work; (6) Improved system; (7) Proper specialization of jobs; (8) Improved organizational structure; (9) Facilitation of salary administration and job evaluation. The following is a suitable general outline for a supervisory job description: (1) Identification of the Job. (2) Summary of the Function and Purpose of the Job. (3) Classification of Job Duties: (a) Organizing for the job; supervision received; contacts made by supervisor in obtaining materials, equipment, personnel, information; flow of work; methods. (b) Performing the work—description of duties, percentage of time spent on each duty. (c) Following up—resonsibilities, supervision exercised, flow of work. (4) Standards of Quality and Quantity. (5) Working Conditions. "Using Descriptions of Supervisory Jobs," and "Describing the Supervisor's Job," Industrial Relations Section, California Institute of Technology, give complete details on this subject.

supervisory rating. Companies have developed numerous forms for rating supervisors (see "RATING OF SUPERVISORS," Industrial Relations Section, California Institute of Technology). Some general criteria include: *Performance Factors*: Employee Relations; Meeting Quality Standards; Meeting Cost Standards and Budgets; Meeting Schedules; Maintenance; Special Functions, such as working on committees, preparing reports, etc. *Personal Factors*: Leadership; Knowledge; Dependability and Judgment; Initiative and Creativeness; Health; Character Traits; Participation in Community Life. *Capacity and Ambition for Advancement.* Some of the benefits derived from rating supervisors include: Rating aids in determining salaries, promotions, transfers and layoffs; rating improves supervision; rating improves morale; rating checks recruiting, placement, and training.

supervisory selection. The judgment exercised in selecting supervisors is a basic human characteristic which some men have and which others never develop. There are, however, certain procedures and safeguards which can be followed. *Selections of Supervisors,* Industrial Relations Section, California Institute of Technology, suggests that collective judgment of executives is facilitated by using two fact-gathering procedures: (1) Adequate records and centralized information to serve as a factual basis for valid judgment. The records and information

should be of two types: (a) outlining the requirements of the job, and (b) describing the qualifications of the candidates. (2) Demonstration devices to locate the maximum number of supervisory candidates and to test their effectiveness on the job. One company with a thoroughgoing selection program has set up a tentative list of characteristics desired in all supervisors, assigning weights as follows: 25 points for "insight into human nature," defined as "sensitivity to others and understanding of oneself." 25 points for ability in abstract and comprehensive thinking. 20 points for skill in human relations. 15 points for ability to organize and direct. 15 points for emotional control. Other companies and executives have stressed perseverance, the keeping of promises, orderliness, a sense of humor, discretion, fairness, tact, resourcefulness, adaptability.

supervisory training. See FOREMANSHIP TRAINING; "TRAINING WITHIN INDUSTRY." In considering the broad scope of supervisory training the skills of any supervisor can be broken down into groups, for each of which there is appropriate subject matter for training. The bulletin, *Training of Supervisors,* issued by the Industrial Relations Section, California Institute of Technology, has analyzed the areas of training most frequently encountered:

Areas of Training for Supervisors

Following shows the *Skill or Knowledge* with respective *Subject of Training*: *Departmental Operation*: How to perform the jobs to be supervised. Training is usually taken care of through working experience or apprenticeship on the job.
Technical Training: Theory and practice of operation of equipment in department. Usually acquired through education and experience on the job. May require formal technical training.

Company Policies; Organization, Procedures: Duties and responsibilities of a supervisor; Company organization (a) line organization; (b) staff or service groups; Company policies: background and reasons for existence of particular policies.

Production Skills: Methods improvement—Standard procedures, elements of job methods study; Job analysis—Technique of preparing job descriptions and specifications; Production control—Principles of planning and scheduling work, production control procedures; Cost control—Elements of costs, means of control; Quality control—Determining work standards holding output to specifications, preventive quality control.

Industrial Relations Skills: Selection and placement of men—Principles and criteria of selection, use of rating techniques, job specifications, induction procedure; Training and development of men—Teaching methods, creating interest in the work, breaking down the job, presenting jobs in proper sequence for learning; Wage recommendations—Job classification or evaluation, employee rating; Safety and accident prevention—Safety rules and devices, safe work practice, workmen's compensation, conducting a safety program; Employee relations—Elements of human behavior, principles of leadership, grievance procedure, relations with union representatives.

Current Information: A continuous program of acquainting supervisors with changes and improvements in any of the items mentioned above, and the introduction of new developments such as clauses in labor agreements, legislation, new procedures, etc.

supper money. An allowance for meals paid by certain employers to workers who work overtime after termination of the regular working day. It may be paid in addition to the regular overtime rate or it may be the only overtime reward given by the employer. Supper money has been largely supplanted by overtime pay.

"Supplemental Benefit Payment." A term used by the United States Employment Service. A payment issued for the sole purpose of adjusting an underpayment for one or more previous weeks.

supplemental payments. Additional pension usually paid out of current income, given to retired employees.

supplements to wages and salaries. As defined by the U. S. Department of Commerce for national income purposes:

"Supplements to Wages and Salaries is the monetary compensation of employees not commonly regarded as wages and salaries. It consists of employer contributions for social insurance, employer contributions to private pension and welfare funds, compensation for injuries, directors' fees, pay of the military reserve, and a few other minor items of labor income." Term sometimes used more broadly to refer to all supplements to basic wage or salary rates.

survey. A general check or brief investigation of an activity or organization made to evaluate the existing situation and, usually, the opportunities for improvement that are present.

survey, occupational. An investigation and evaluation to gather pertinent information about a single industry or the occupations of an area, to determine prevalent practices, labor supply and turnover, wages, hours worked, or other relevant statistics.

survey, vocational education. A study to obtain necessary information as a basis for the proper development of programs of vocational education. It serves to identify the needs for vocational training, recommend suitable types of classes, assist in the development of new instructional processes and evaluate the results of work already done.

survivor benefits, under Social Security Act. Survivor benefits may be claimed by the widow of an insured wage earner. She is entitled to a benefit equal to three-fourths of her husband's monthly benefit when she reaches 62, if she has not remarried. A younger widow who has children of a fully or currently insured wage earner in her care may receive a similar benefit. In addition, the first child under 18 may receive a benefit equal to three-fourths of the father's monthly benefit amount. Additional children receive one-half. If a fully insured wage earner leaves no widow or children under 18 who could become entitled to benefits, but does leave a father 65 or over who was chiefly dependent on him, then his father may receive an amount equal to three-fourths of his benefit amount. If he leaves a mother, and the insured worker was furnishing at least half of her support, she may become entitled to social security payments at 62. Any person who is entitled to more than one benefit can claim the larger amount. For example, a woman who has a social security account of her own may, of course, qualify for benefits at 62 on her own account. If she is a wife or a widow entitled to benefits on her husband's

account also, she cannot get both, but her benefit is increased to equal the larger amount. See also BENEFITS, SOCIAL SECURITY, TABLE OF.

sweatshop. A factory or shop where labor is employed under unhealthy conditions, for long hours, at excessive high speed and for small wages. Employment of women and children was also characteristic of such establishments. The labor laws protecting workers enacted in the 1930's and since have largely eliminated such abuses.

"sweetheart agreement." An agreement regarding working conditions entered into by a union and an employer. Usually a situation wherein management decides to grant union demands on the condition that the union shall in return assure management of complete cooperation, as in control of costs.

swing shift. An extra or "swing" shift of workers required in establishments where continuous or seven-day operations are scheduled, to provide the other crews with days off. The "swing crew" usually rotates among all of the other shifts. Also refers to the practice of one of three rotating shifts staying on the job through two shift periods, thus "swinging" the shifts into their new assignments. See also FIXED SHIFT, ROTATING SHIFT, SHIFT, and SPLIT SHIFT.

Sylvester Empiric Plan. Similar to EMERSON EFFICIENCY BONUS PLAN, which see.

symbols, wage formula. Accepted symbols used to express the elements for wage terms in algebraic or mathematical formulas include:

H_s; S=The standard or allowed time for completing a particular operation or task.

H_a; T=Actual time worked.

R; R_h; R_p=The rate per hour or per-piece R_p whichever the case may be.

B=Guaranteed rate in per cent of standard or going rate.

N; N_p=The number of pieces which the worker produced.

B_o=Bonus in percent of BH_aR_h, a constant.

Pr; p=Premium percentage.

E=Earnings of the employee in dollars.

W=Wages in percent of standard at task efficiency.

synthesis of elemental times. (1) The act of selecting and combining proper elemental times obtained from time studies or predetermined elemental motion time studies of actual operations in order to obtain the normal or standard time for an operation without making a time study of it. (2) In time formula development, the combining and simplifying of the mathematical or graphical expressions for determining individual elemental times.

synthetic time standard. A time standard developed for an operation by utilizing predetermined elemental time data or standard data rather than by making a time study.

systems engineering. A method of engineering approach which takes into consideration all of the elements in an automatic control system, down to the smallest valve, and the process itself. It is believed to have the most promise as an intelligent approach leading toward fuller industrial automation.

T

Taft-Hartley Act. See LABOR MANAGE-MENT RELATIONS ACT.

take-home pay. Typically, earnings for a pay-roll period, less required deductions, such as withholding taxes, union dues, insurance, etc. See also SPENDABLE EARN-INGS.

Tannenbaum, Frank. (1893–) American author and economist. Tannenbaum was born in Austria, came to the United States in 1905. He took his Ph.D. in 1927. His principal work on labor economics is *The Labor Movement* (1921). The dominant influence in modern society, according to Tannenbaum, is "the machine," which is "the center of gravity in the present-day industrial community." The labor movement is the result, and the machine is the major cause. The main function of the labor movement is to overcome insecurity. To do this, it must control the machine. This need is not entirely economic, he believes. It is also in part psychological.

tardiness. Reporting for work later than the scheduled hour. Just when a worker is considered tardy and when he is considered absent varies with practice. Usually, if he comes in more than half a day or half a shift later, he is considered absent. Methods of reducing tardiness are closely tied in with reducing absenteeism.

tardiness rate. A measure of tardiness commonly represented as the ratio of the average number of tardiness occurrences per day to the average number on the payroll, all figures being on a monthly basis. For purposes of recapitulation and comparison, tardiness rates may be calculated on an annual basis using the same ratios.

target. In piece-rate systems, a rate is set with the objective of making it possible for a worker to earn, on the average, 10, 15, or some other percentage above the base rate. The expected earnings to which the piece rate is geared is referred to as a target.

task. (1) The amount of work established as a standard in any particular instance. (2) A specifically assigned amount of work.

task and bonus plan. Any wage incentive plan that pays a specific percent of the base wage rate in addition to the base wage rate when a specified level of output is maintained or exceeded for a specified period of time.

(309)

Task system. A term used to describe a system of compensation by which a salesman is paid for every call he makes, whether or not he makes a sale. In selling certain articles, the pay may be based on the number of complete demonstrations given by the salesman. The task system is frequently supplemented by a bonus or commission based upon the sales made.

"Tax." A term used by the United States Employment Service. See CONTRIBU-TIONS.

"Tax Credit." A term used by the United States Employment Service. See CREDIT ALLOWANCE.

"Tax Return." A term used by the United States Employment Service. Same as FEDERAL UNEMPLOYMENT TAX RETURN.

"Tax Offset." A term used by the United States Employment Service. Same as CREDIT ALLOWANCE.

"Taxable Wages." A term used by the United States Employment Service. See WAGES.

Taylor Differential Piece-Rate Plan. An incentive wage payment plan whereby one piece rate is established for substandard production, and a higher rate fixed for that production which is above standard; it thus involves use of two rates. The formula suggested for figuring an employee's earnings under the Taylor plan is:

Up to task: $E = N_p \times (R_p)_1$ or $E = RN$
Above task: $E = N_p \times (R_p)_2$ or $E = R'N$
    where N_p = number of pieces
      R or $(R_p)_1$ = low piece-rate
      R^1 or $(R_p)_2$ = high piece-rate

Taylor, Frederick Winslow. (1856-1915) Known as the "Father of Scientific Management." His writings include: *The Adjustment of Wages to Efficiency* (1896), *The Art of Cutting Metals* (1896), *Shop Management* (1911) and *The Principles of Scientific Management* (1911). Taylor came from an old-line and well-to-do family, but when he was prevented from attending college by his poor eyesight, he served his apprenticeship as a patternmaker and machinist. He completed his training in 1878 and went to work for the Midvale Steel Company, in Philadelphia. Since there was no work available as a machinist, he signed on as a laborer to wait his chance at a machinist's job. He earned that chance by serving as an accounts clerk when they needed one. Later, when he asked for the machine job he was put on the lathe. Shortly after that he became the gang boss of the lathe crew. The promotion to gang boss, then foreman, put him on "the other side of the fence." He was now a member of management and since he'd so recently been a worker he knew the practice of "systematic soldiering" was being carried out in the Midvale shop. He set himself to attack the practice and increase the output. "Soldiering" came about through the day-work plan used in those days. Men were hired to work and everybody was paid the same rate, by the day. Naturally, nobody worked faster than the slowest man. There was just no sense in straining when you could get the same pay by taking it easy as the slowest man. "Systematic soldiering," though, resulted from the piecework plan which was supposed to correct the evils of day work. Piecework did provide an incentive, but if the workmen took advantage of it and began to produce more work, they soon found themselves with a rate cut. "Even the most stupid man," Taylor said, "after receiving two or three piecework cuts as a reward for having worked harder, resents this treatment and seeks a remedy for it. Thus begins a war . . . between the workmen and management." A dispute with the workers led him to conduct a series of experiments to determine what constitutes a day's work on any operation. This led to his perfecting those principles of shop management which later became known as scientific management. The latter part of his life was spent practicing the new profession of consulting management engineer in many plants. The scientific management system was not established when Taylor left Midvale, but it was worked out in principle. Taylor's later work keyed in with the work of other pioneers in the field: Carl G. Barth, Dwight V. Merrick, Frank G. Gilbreth, Henry L. Gantt, S. E. Thompson, and many others. Gradually, he developed his ideas of scientific management and, in 1895, he presented a paper entitled "A Piece Work System" before the American Society of Mechanical Engineers. In this paper, for the first time, he published his ideas of management. He said: "The new duties of the managers are grouped under four heads—First: They develop a science for each element of a man's work, which replaces the old rule-of-thumb method. Second: They scientifically select and then train, teach, and develop the workman, whereas in the past he chose his own work and trained himself as best he could. Third: They heartily cooperate with the men so as to insure all of the work being done in accordance with the principles of the

science which has been developed. Fourth: There is an almost equal division of the work and the responsibility between the management and the workmen. The managers take over all work for which they are better fitted than the workmen, while in the past almost all the work and the greater part of the responsibility were thrown upon the men." As for the underlying idea, the first sentence of Chapter 1 of "The Principles of Scientific Management" states it: "The principle object of management should be to secure the maximum prosperity for the employer—coupled with the maximum prosperity for each employee."

technical education. Education to earn a living in an occupation in which success is dependent largely upon technical information and understanding of the laws of science and technology as applied to modern design, production, distribution and service.

technical high school. An educational institution at the secondary level which is vocational in objective, technical in subject matter content, and usually terminal in character.

technical institute. A school at the post-high level, which offers technical education in one or more fields, to prepare people for employment in positions which lie between the skilled trades and professional engineering.

technician. An employee on a level between the skilled tradesman and the professional engineer. His technical knowledge permits him to perform many of the duties formerly assigned to the graduate engineer. Technicians design the mechanism, compute the cost, write the specifications, organize the production, and test the finished product.

technological change. A continuing process induced by such factors as increasing refinement of tools, implements and equipment; more empirical knowledge; new inventions; better techniques and methods, including changes in speed, location of equipment; better utilization of natural environment and materials; greater understanding of the human being, his abilities, skills and motivations. John W. Riegel, in "Management, Labor and Technological Change," (University of Michigan Press) has found at least ten types of technological change taking place in American industry. They include: Equipment designed by specialized machinery manufacturers; new machinery designed by a company; operating old machinery at higher speeds or in new combinations; introduction of new tools and fixtures; new or improved materials; improvement of hand methods; dividing tasks; mechanizing manual work; installing conveyors; relocating processes. The "Council for Technological Advancement," organized by and integrated with Machinery and Allied Products Institute, Chicago, Illinois, continuously conducts research and issues bulletins on trends in technology and employment.

technocracy. A short-lived movement—almost just a fad—originating in 1932 during the depression which stressed the importance of the technician in modern society. A group of "technocrats" was led by Howard Scott, author of the most authoritative book on the subject. Principles underlying technocracy were: (1) under the existing pricing system not a sufficient amount of money is distributed to make it possible to buy the goods pro-duced, and hence our population cannot make full use of technological developments; (2) it is possible to measure social phenomena, and rules of social control may be determined from these measurements; (3) the abundance of money causes a lower bank interest and ultimately banks will charge interest instead of paying it to hold money; (4) politicians have been unsuccessful in managing economic affairs and therefore control of the economy should be vested with engineers and scientists.

technological unemployment. Unemployment resulting from the displacement of men by machinery or by the introduction of more efficient methods of production. Economists generally agree that technological changes cause immediate disturbances in employment. But the long-term effects of such changes appear to be on the positive side. The advent of the automobile age caused unemployment among blacksmiths. But the number of people employed in automobile manufacture today is thousands of times the number of blacksmiths. Dial telephones have been installed all over the United States, yet we have more telephone operators than ever before. Between 1850 and 1953, the population of the United States increased roughly 7 times; in the same period, production increased 25 times, meaning a much higher standard of living for all people with less working hours. This was made possible because work was done with 94 percent mechanization in 1953, contrasted with 6 percent in 1950. Some economists believe that technological developments may, during certain periods, increase total production and productivity per man faster than changes in the economic system can absorb this production, causing depressions and unemployment. Too many other variable factors are involved, however, to make any definitive statements to this effect.

"Telephone Referral." A term used by the United States Employment Service. See REFERRAL.

template (or templet). (1) A gauge or pattern used as a guide to the size and shape of a part to be made. (2) A two-dimensional cutout, representing the area required by a workman; by a machine when operating, or by a bench, desk, or temporary storage bins at the work station and other equipment, used in planning and layout of plant and office facilities.

temporary rate. A rate set tentatively on new work. When new work is started under piece rates in some industries and it is not known whether or not the initial rates can be properly set for the tasks involved, temporary rates are established. These rates are later revised and are made permanent when found to be satisfactory. Sometimes they are called "experimental" or "trial" rates. These are alternate designations in various industries. See also GUARANTEE ON TRIAL RATE and PROTEST PRICE.

temporary standard. A time standard applied to an operation for a limited period pending the development of a more accurate time standard, the development of a new method, or the correction of abnormal conditions affecting the operation.

"Temporary Disability Insurance." A term used by the United States Employment Service. *Temporary Disability Insurance*: A system established by law for the payment of cash benefits to eligible insured workers for unemployment resulting from sickness or accident (generally designed to cover non-occupational disabilities).

"Test Office." A term used by the United States Employment Service. A local office selected by the State agency in which, under special supervisory arrangements, existing methods and administrative techniques for performing local office functions and/or experiments in new methods and techniques are subjected to continuous evaluation.

"Tests." As defined by the United States Employment Service, there are: *Aptitude Test*: A device for measuring the potentiality of an applicant for acquiring vocational proficiency. See also PROFICIENCY TEST below. *Aptitude Test Battery*: A combination of aptitude tests used to measure the potentiality for acquiring one or more occupational skills. See also GENERAL APTITUDE TEST BATTERY below. *General Aptitude Test Battery*: A combination of fifteen aptitude tests measuring ten different aptitudes, used by counselors to determine the applicant's potentiality for acquiring the skills involved in many broad occupational groups. See INDIVIDUAL APTITUDE PROFILE; OCCUPATIONAL APTITUDE PATTERN. *Performance Trade Test*: A proficiency test designed as a replica of the work situation in which the applicant actually demonstrates his skill by doing a work sample. Examples: Typing and dictation tests. *Proficiency Test*: A device to measure the skill or knowledge that a person has acquired in an occupation; for example, sets of oral trade questions, typing and stenographic tests, and

picture trade tests. *Trade Questions*: A
standardized list of questions, the diagnostic value of which is known for a
given occupation, and which are used in
application taking or selection to measure an applicant's knowledge of a given
job.

tests, employment. The use of employment tests is becoming widespread. The
purpose is to discover the extent to
which an applicant possesses the abilities
and qualities which the organization
needs are to impose upon him if he is
placed in a particular work situation.
The introduction of tests has in many
cases been preceded by interpretations
of jobs analyses and of time and motion
studies, conferences with supervisors,
and efforts at converting the results of
observations and comments into probable demands. Employment tests may
be subdivided in many categories. This
publication (Dictionary) uses the following: (which see) INTELLIGENCE TESTS;
TRADE TESTS; PERSONALITY TESTS; VISUAL
SKILL TESTS; MECHANICAL TESTS; INTER-
EST TESTS; CLERICAL TESTS; GENERAL AP-
TITUDE TESTS; EMPLOYMENT APPLICA-
TION FORMS; MISCELLANEOUS TESTS. See
also: *Experience with Employment
Tests*, National Industrial Conference
Board; *Introduction to Occupational
Testing in the Employment Service*, Bu-
reau of Employment Security, U.S. De-
partment of Labor. Books dealing with
personnel testing include: Kaplan, *Ency-
clopedia of Vocational Guidance*, 2
Vols., The Philosophical Library, Inc.;
Buros, O. K., *Mental Measurements
Yearbook*, The Gryphon Press, Highland
Park, N. J.; Ghiselli, E. E., and Brown,
C. W., *Personnel and Industrial Psy-
chology*, McGraw-Hill, New York; Dor-

cus, R. M., and Jones, M. J., *Handbook
of Employee Selection*, McGraw-Hill,
New York; Tiffin, Joseph, *Industrial Psychology*, Prentice-Hall, New York; Stone
and Kendall, *Effective Personnel Selec-
tion Procedures*, Prentice-Hall, New
York; Lawshe, C. H., *Principles of Per-
sonnel Testing*, McGraw-Hill, New York;
Studies in Personnel Policy, No. 32, *Ex-
perience with Employment Tests*, Na-
tional Industrial Conference Board. See
also entries under APTITUDE, APTITUDE
TEST, APTITUDE TEST BATTERY, CRITICAL
SCORE, INDIVIDUAL APTITUDE PROFILE,
NORM, OCCUPATIONAL APTITUDE PAT-
TERN, ORAL TRADE QUESTIONS, PERFORM-
ANCE TRADE TEST, PROFICIENCY, RELI-
ABILITY, VALIDITY, and PUBLISHERS, PER-
SONNEL TESTS.

Therblig. Therblig is the name given to
the minor happenings which occur during a work cycle of an operation. They
are descriptions of body member movements, sense organ use, nerve reactions,
or mind use. The names of the therbligs
are: Search, Find, Select, Acquire, Start,
Stop, Deviate, Transport Loaded, Transport Empty, Grasp, Position, Pre-position, Assemble, Disassemble, Use, Inspect, Hold, Release, Plan, Rest Delay,
Unavoidable Delay, Avoidable Delay,
Nerve Reaction, Mind Decision. The
word therblig is the reversal of the name
of the pioneer in motion study, Frank
B. Gilbreth. The original 17 therbligs
and the therblig Hold have stood the
test of time, and are today the foundation of the teaching and application of
motion study. To these have been added
six more therbligs to define more clearly
the body member movements, sense organs, and mental activities which accom-
pany the body member movements. By
the use of these additional therbligs, Ac-

quire, Start, Stop, Deviate, Nerve Reaction and Mind Decision, the analyst is able to credit the operator with the time value for nerve reaction and mental processes. See entries under each of the above named.

tight rate. See TIGHT STANDARD.

tight standard. (Colloquial). A time standard that provides a qualified workman with insufficient time to do a defined amount of work of specified quality when following the prescribed method, working at normal pace, and experiencing normal fatigue and delays.

time allowance. See ALLOWANCE, SPECIAL TIME ALLOWANCE, and STANDARD TIME.

"Time Factor." A term used by the United States Employment Service. Time spent or determined to be necessary for performance of a unit of work.

"Time Distribution System." A term used by the United States Employment Service. See PERSONNEL FUNCTIONAL TIME DISTRIBUTION SYSTEM.

"Time Distribution Code." A term used by the United States Employment Service. See STANDARD FUNCTIONAL TIME DISTRIBUTION CODE.

time formula. A collection of standard time data arranged in the form of an algebraic expression for determining the standard time for an operation.

time study. The procedure by which the actual elapsed time for performing an operation or subdivisions or elements thereof is determined by the use of a suitable timing device, such as a stopwatch, marstochron, etc., and recorded. The procedure usually but not always includes the adjustment of the actual time as the result of performance rating to derive the time which should be required to perform the task by a workman working at a standard pace and following a standard method under standard conditions. Time study is often accompanied by a searching analysis of the method and equipment used in doing a piece of work and development of the best method of doing it. Phil Carroll, Jr. says ("Timestudy Fundamentals for Foremen," McGraw-Hill): "Timestudy is a major factor in our continuing industrial progress. It is important because it provides the basis for wage incentive. This, in turn, makes a two-way contribution. First, it materially adds to the earning capacity of those working on incentive. Second, it helps to reduce the cost of things we buy. Taken alone, either of these effects is substantial. When both are gained from a single effort, the benefits are multiplied. That is why the two-way effectiveness of timestudy is so generally used by progressive industrial organizations."

time-study comparison sheet. See MASTER TABLE OF DETAIL TIME STUDIES.

time study recap sheet. See MASTER TABLE OF DETAIL TIME STUDIES.

time study summary sheet. See MASTER TABLE OF DETAIL TIME STUDIES.

time taken. See ACTUAL TIME.

time ticket. Any form on which a workman's name and/or identifying number is recorded that serves as the original or source document for information on the operations or types of work he did, when he did them, and the time he used doing them. Other information such as applicable job or order numbers, base wage rates, standard times, and the like is also often recorded.

time used. See ACTUAL TIME.

tip. A gratuity given by a customer or patron in recognition of satisfactory personal service or through custom. Tips are considered as compensation by the Bureau of Internal Revenue, thus constituting taxable income. A substantial proportion of the earnings of some categories of workers in hotels, restaurants, steamships, and barber and beauty shops is realized from tips.

titles, of jobs. A "Dictionary of Occupational Titles," is available through the Department of Labor of the U.S. Government, together with supplements. This gives definitions of thousands of job titles. It is available in libraries.

tool maintenance time. See ALLOWED TIME.

tonnage rate. Pay for a unit of work applicable to incentive workers, and common in such industries as coal mining and basic iron and steel, where output for important categories of workers can be measured on a tonnage basis.

top rate. The maximum amount of basic wages an employee may receive in any week as specified by the contract.

total selected time. The sum of the selected times for the elements of an operation. See SELECTED TIME.

"Total Unemployment." A term used by the United States Employment Service. See WEEK OF UNEMPLOYMENT.

town differential. In telephone or utility terminology, the wage difference between any two towns which have different wage schedules in the contract. This is usually measured by the difference in top pay for the same occupation in the two towns.

town reclassification. Telephone terminology designating the change of an exchange from one wage schedule to another.

trade analysis. A term used in vocational education to describe the procedure of breaking down a trade or occupation to determine the teachable content in terms of operations, tools, processes and technical information to be organized into a course of study and arranged according to a sequence of difficulty.

trade and industrial education. Instruction which is planned for the purpose of developing basic manipulative skills, safety judgment, technical knowledge, and related occupational information for the purpose of fitting young persons for initial employment in industrial occupations and to upgrade or retrain workers employed in industry.

trade extension class. See PART-TIME PROGRAMS, VOCATIONAL.

trade preparatory programs. Education to prepare for entrance into useful employment in industrial occupation and to provide opportunity to continue a general education. It is that type of vocational education given in fulltime day or technical institute classes.

"Trade Questions." A term used by the United States Employment Service. See TESTS.

trade school. A public or private vocational school which trains youth and adults in the skills, technical knowledge, related industrial information, and job judgment necessary for success in one or more skilled trades. These schools provide opportunity also for continuation of general education.

trade test. A measure of the skill or knowledge acquired by an application in an occupation or training course. Trade tests include: Can You Read a Micrometer?—Lawshe—Science Research Associates; Can You Read a Scale?—Science Research Associates; Can You Read a Working Drawing?—Lawshe and Lindahl—Science Research Associates; Purdue Blueprint Reading Test—Owen and Arnold—Science Research Associates; Purdue Test for Electricians—Caldwell et al.—Science Research Associates; Arithmetical Reasoning Test—Cardall—Science Research Associates; Purdue Industrial Mathematics Test— Lawshe and Price—Div. of Applied Psychology, Purdue University; and many others which can be obtained from the publishers, which see.

"Trade Test." A term used by the United States Employment Service. See PROFICIENCY TEST under TESTS.

trade union. A voluntary association of working people organized to maintain or further their rights and interests, with particular respect to wages, hours, and conditions of health, efficiency, security, education, insurance, etc.

Trade Union Advisory Committee on International Affairs. See OFFICE OF INTERNATIONAL LABOR AFFAIRS.

trainee. The term "trainee" applies to workers who receive formal training for occupations requiring a limited degree of skill. The training may include some classroom work. A trainee differs from a learner in that a learner does not receive formal training but learns his job through actual performance, under supervision.

training, supervisory. See SUPERVISORY TRAINING.

"Training Within Industry." An emergency service to the nation's war contractors and essential services offered by the government for five years from 1940 to 1945 during World War II. TWI's programs—Job Instruction, Job Methods, Job Relations and Program Development have permanently become part of American industrial relations as accepted tools of management. These programs are based on the idea of 10 hours of instruction for a group of 10 men, or what has been called the Training Within Industry "package" idea, the contribution of Glenn L. Gardiner, industrialist and author of labor relations and personnel books and publications. See also JOB INSTRUCTION, JOB METHODS, JOB RELATIONS and PROGRAM DEVELOPMENT.

transfer. The shifting of an employee from one department or section of an establishment to another, without any significant change in duties, responsibilities and remuneration. In a *personnel* transfer, the worker is moved to a position more suitable to his capacities. In other words, the transfer is mainly for the worker's own good. In a *production* transfer, the employee is shifted to increase production of the company. In other words, it is the employer who gains most. In a *remedial* transfer, the employee is shifted so that there may be better adjustment between the workers. In other words, where upgrading or promotions might result in conflicts. Transfers may also be *interdepartmental*—from one department or unit to another, or *intradepartmental*—within a department or unit.

"Transfer." A term used by the United States Employment Service. The exchange or reassignment of an employee from one branch, department, shop, or position to another in an employing establishment.

transfer, replacement. The type of transfer which moves a long-service employee to another department, thereby bumping another employee with shorter service. This usually occurs when operations are declining, in order to retain the longer-service employee for as long as possible. It may be formalized in the union agreement.

transients. People who move from one community to another in search of work. They are frequently unskilled, or emotionally unstable, who do not like to remain in the same employment or place of work for a protracted period.

transport empty. A THERBLIG, (which see) which is defined as: the conveying action without carrying anything; the conveying of the transport means from one location to another; the moving of the empty hand in order to obtain a part, object, or tool; the transportation of an intermediate tool or appliance. No load is encountered and no resistance overcome during *transport empty*. *Transport empty* may involve object, parts, or tools held in the hand throughout the work cycle. The operator may retain a pair of tweezers in the hand, as an example. No

useful work is accomplished on the productive part by carrying the tool back to the part to be picked up, moved, or otherwise worked upon, and, as the tool must be returned, this action is considered as *transport empty*. Or, a few parts may be held in the hand and used as their assembly sequence fits into the complete work cycle. Hence there are cases where parts are transported and the action may be truly *transport empty*. It will be noted that *transport empty* is entirely free from interference.

transport loaded. A THERBLIG, (which see) which is defined as: the act of carrying or conveying; the movement of the body in order to carry a load; the act of moving a part or object either through, across, up, down, over, against, or in any direction. *Transport loaded* may be considered the moving of a part, object, or tool from one point to another. The movement may be carry, slide, push, drag, toss, etc. The part, or object, or tool may be transported by means of body members such as the finger, finger and thumb, hand, hands, foot, or knee. The transport action may also be accomplished by the use of an intermediate tool, mechanical device, or container. Such tools as tongs, pliers, tweezers, pushers, probes, stock racks, pans, tote boxes, trays, bins, trucks, etc. may be used to assist in moving a greater quantity of parts at one time. Or they may be used for the purpose of protecting, counting, or sorting the product.

transportation. Moving an object from one place to another, except when such movements are a part of the operation or are caused by the workman at the work station during an operation or an inspection.

travel time. The time spent traveling to and from a designated point and place of work. Such travel includes portal-to-portal in mining, deadheading on railroads, and building tradesmen, mechanics, musicians, etc.

trick. An idiomatic term sometimes used for shift or work period, especially in the railway, telegraph and several other industries.

troubleshooting. A procedure by which work, tests or materials are checked at certain stages of procedure to make certain they are progressing according to schedule. Also known as EXPEDITING, or FOLLOW-UP.

trunk movement. Any motion made by that portion of the human body located above the hips and below the neck, but excepting the arms, hands and fingers.

trustee. A person or committee, or institution (as a bank) in charge of investing money contributed by employer (or employer and employees) for pension benefits. The trustee also manages the fund, makes periodic reports giving details how the money is invested, shows assets, and provides data as to how the fund is being handled. Often the trustee pays the benefits directly to eligible employees.

trust fund. Money irrevocably set aside and built up through investments and interest for the payment of pension benefits. Contributions to the fund by employer (or employer and employees) are invested by the trustee under the terms of the agreement.

trust fund pension plan. Funds, which are actuarially determined, are deposited in an irrevocable trust. The funds are invested in securities, cash, or other property. The fund is administered by a trustee which may be a bank, an individual, or a committee. Pensions are paid out of the fund, or the trustee may purchase an annuity from an insurance company when an employee retires.

"Turnover." For definition used by United States Employment Service, see LABOR TURNOVER.

"Turnover and Absenteeism Records." As used by the United States Employment Service, see PERSONNEL RECORDS.

turnover, causes of. Turnover is caused by external factors, such as difficult transportation, women leaving to get married, men being drafted, etc. over which a company has no control; by internal forces such as discontentment, disaffection, lack of interest, which management seeks to counteract. Say Scott and Clothier in Personnel Management (A. W. Shaw Company) "the very factors, the very causes, the very influences which tend to create those attitudes of mind which lead employees to quit, inevitably react unfavorably upon the mental attitudes of those who remain, undermining interest and morale, destroying efficiency. It is apparent from this that management is interested in labor turnover not so much from the point of view of the cost of replacing the men who leave as it is interested in labor turnover from the point of view of the cost of lessened interest and effectiveness throughout the organization. Any study of the causes of labor turnover, consequently, which leads to constructive action is an attack both upon instability and upon malingering on the part of those who remain."

turnover costs. Expenses resulting from servicing the movement of employees into and out of the organization. Turnover costs are reflected in reduced production volume, increasing operating expenses, administrative costs of hiring and separation of employees. Specifically broken down (Walters, Personnel Relations): (1) Cost of Hiring: Employment office expense; Medical examination cost; Advertising, prorated over number hired. (2) Cost of Training: Training department cost; Foreman's or workman's time with new man. (3) Extra Labor Cost: Day wages in excess of piece rate earnings; High unit cost of production on time basis; Extra men needed to make up for deficiency of new man; Overtime caused by the deficiency of new man. (4) Extra Operating Costs: Additional power due to reduced rate of output; Additional lubrication due to reduced rate of output; Additional heat due to reduced rate of output; Additional service due to reduced rate of output; Greater wear and tear on machinery; Spoiled work beyond normal; Increased accidents due to greater accident frequency during learning period. (5) Extra Investment Costs: Interest, depreciation, insurance, taxes, and repairs on additional plant investment necessary on account of reduced output. (6) Loss of Business: Loss of goodwill and business through products and services by inexperienced employees.

turnover, discount for. Under some types of funding for pension plans, the anticipated cost of the pension plan is reduced by assuming that a certain percentage of employees will leave the organization before retirement for reasons other than death. The rate of withdrawals cannot be determined on the basis of any accurate table, but on experience within the company, or on some other assumption.

turnover, factors in reducing. Job satisfaction has been found to be a key factor in keeping quit rates low. Research by University of Michigan's Institute for Social Research shows that factors in job satisfaction—other than higher pay—include: Recognition—need to feel that one's achievements are made known to others; Achievement—need to feel one has done something worthwhile or important; Autonomy—need to feel one has power over one's actions and has area of prime responsibility; Affiliation—need to be related to people, to have friends and be in communication with others; Evaluation—need to feel that standards for judging one's behavior and performance are reasonable and just.

turnover formula, labor. (According to the Bureau of Labor Statistics) The U.S. Bureau of Labor Statistics computation of turnover based on separation and accession rates is: (1) Compute average number of employees for a month by totaling the number on payroll for the first day, plus the number for last day, and dividing by two; (2) Divide total of separations per month by the total derived in the first step; (3) Multiply by 100; thereby computing the separation rate per 100 employees for a month.

turnover formula, labor (separation basis). The prescribed formula for computation of turnover on separation basis is usually expressed as:

$$T = \frac{\text{total separations x 100}}{\text{average working force}}$$

or:

$$\frac{100\ S}{W}$$

turnover, labor. Mobility of labor, moving in and out of an organization. See other entries under TURNOVER.

turnover, labor, effect on pension costs. According to turnover estimates, certain percentages of employees will not stay in a company until full retirement age and obligation to the company probably will not be as great as if employees stayed to full retirement date. Turnover is also a significant statistic in figuring costs of severance benefits in a pension plan. For actuarial assumptions under a pension plan, turnover rate should be analyzed by age, sex, and length of service.

turnover, statistics regarding. According to the Bureau of Census, about 18% of men and only 11% of women hold more than one job a year. Job mobility is greater among younger workers than those of advanced years.

The Twentieth Century Fund. Located at 330 W. 42nd Street, New York, N. Y. Does research to seek the improvement of economic, industrial, civic and educational conditions. Publishes results of studies in book form; disseminates research findings in popular media, including newspapers, magazines, pamphlets, radio and television programs, motion pictures and filmstrips.

two-handed chart. See RIGHT- AND LEFT-HAND CHART.

typist. According to the Dictionary of Occupational Titles, (which see) typewrites letters, addresses envelopes, copies data from one record to another, fills in report forms, and does miscellaneous typing, all the work being routine or straight copy from rough draft or corrected copy. May make up stencils for use in duplicating machine.

(321)

U

unavoidable delay. A THERBLIG (which see) which is defined as: a temporary stoppage which cannot be avoided; a movement caused by unexpected or unnecessary interference. The *unavoidable* delay or lack of movement results from the operation sequence which causes one body member or sense organ to remain idle as some other body member is working, or an activity caused by a failure or interruption within the work cycle might be considered as *unavoidable delay*.

unavoidable delay allowance. Time included in the production standard to allow for time lost which is essentially outside the workman's control; as, interruption by supervision for instruction, waits for crane, or minor adjustments to machines or tools.

unemployment. A generally accepted definition is the difference between the number of persons in the normal labor force and the number of persons employed.

unemployment compensation. Funds provided to eligible persons temporarily unemployed. Generally refers more specifically to UNEMPLOYMENT COMPENSATION INSURANCE, which see.

unemployment compensation insurance. Protects employees against severe hardships due to unemployment. Unemployment insurance is administered by the respective states. The entire cost is borne by employers who every 3 months send to the State Employment Bureau a check for up to about 4% of their payroll. (The amount varies with the states and with the employer's record of employment. The more layoffs, the higher the employment tax he pays.) The money is accumulated in a trust fund to pay those looking for work. If an employee is laid off, he must notify local State Employment Office of his availability for work. The State Employment Office will help him look for a job. All states require a person to have earned a specified amount of wages, or to have worked a certain period of time, or both, in order to qualify for unemployment insurance. Each state sets its own benefit rates.

"Unemployment Fund." A term used by the United States Employment Service. See FUNDS.

Unemployment Insurance. Act of August 14, 1935, as amended. Under the Social Security Act a nationwide system of insurance has been provided by the States,

(322)

the District of Columbia, Alaska, and Hawaii to protect wage earners and their families against loss of income due to unemployment. The purpose of unemployment insurance is to provide workers with a weekly income to tide them over periods of unemployment between jobs. It does not assure benefits to every unemployed worker but only to those who have been working on a job covered under their State unemployment insurance law for a specified period, who are able and willing to work, and who are unemployed through no fault of their own. The system is not intended to protect persons who are not physically able to work or who do not want to work. In California, New Jersey, New York, and Rhode Island, there is a program for the payment of benefits to workers unable to work because of illness or accident. *Federal-State Program.* Unemployment insurance is a joint Federal-State program operated by the States in partnership with the U. S. Department of Labor. All 48 States, the District of Columbia, Hawaii, and Alaska have enacted unemployment compensation laws, which incorporate certain basic standards set forth in the Social Security Act and the Federal Unemployment Tax Act. *Federal Standards.*—As long as a State law and its operation meet the requiremetns of the Social Security Act and the Federal Unemployment Tax Act, the Federal Government pays the costs of administering the State unemployment insurance law and permits employers in the State to credit the State contribution paid, or from which they are excused under the State experience-rating provisions, against the Federal tax imposed by the Federal Unemployment Tax Act. *State Provisions.*—Each State requires

employers who come under its unemployment insurance law to pay taxes based on their payrolls. With the exception of two States and Alaska, employees make no contribution to State unemployment insurance funds. Benefits are paid out of a fund built up from these taxes. This fund is deposited to the State's account in the United States Treasury. Whatever the State does not draw out remains in the trust fund, where it earns compound interest. The State legislature fixes the rate of tax on employers. States have enacted *experience-rating* provisions, which allow an employer's tax to vary according to the amount of benefits paid to his former workers, or some other method provided in the State law for measuring the risk of unemployment. Each State law specifies the conditions under which workers may receive benefits, the amounts they may receive, and the number of weeks they may draw benefits. *Who receives Unemployment Insurance Coverage?*—In over half the States, only those workers in firms employing 4 or more persons during 20 weeks in the year are covered. In some States, the law covers firms that have only one employee. In general, State unemployment compensation laws cover jobs in factories, shops, mines, mills, stores, offices, restaurants, laundries, banks, American ships, and other places of private industry and commerce. This coverage applies to jobs on ships owned by, or bareboat chartered to, the United States and operated under a general agency agreement. The following are *generally excluded* from State unemployment insurance laws: (a) Railroad workers who are covered by the Federal Railroad Unemployment Insurance Act; (b) Agricultural workers; (c)

Domestic workers; (d) State and municipal workers; (e) Workers in nonprofit educational, religious, or charitable organizations; (f) Casual labor, that is, occasional work not connected with the employer's regular business; and (g) Service by one spouse for the other, by a parent for a child, or by a minor child for a parent. Most States will allow a firm, not covered by the State law, to elect coverage, if the employer is willing to pay the payroll tax. *Eligibility for Benefits.*—In order to be eligible for benefits, every State law requires a worker to have received at least a specified minimum amount of pay or to have worked a minimum number of weeks in a covered employment during a specified period preceding his unemployment. A number of States provide that a worker who has been employed in more than one State, but is not eligible for benefits in any of them, may combine his wage credits if this will enable him to meet the wage and employment requirements under a given State law. As of the end of 1955, more than half the States had subscribed to an extended wage combining plan. Under such a plan a claimant who had been employed in more than one State, and who is eligible for at least minimum benefits under a given State law, may, nevertheless, combine his wage credits from two or more States if this will entitle him to receive higher weekly benefits for a longer period. *Ability To Work.*—In almost all States a worker cannot draw unemployment insurance if he is sick while out of work or if he is unable to work for any other reason. Delaware, Idaho, Maryland, Montana, Nevada, Tennessee, and Vermont pay unemployment benefits to claimants who become unable to work

after they have registered for work and filed a claim for benefits, until they refuse work which would be suitable but for the disability. *Availability for Work.*—The variations in State laws and their interpretation are so great that any generalized statement may be misleading with respect to any given State. The State laws generally require that a worker must be ready and willing to accept suitable work which he does not have good cause for refusing. *Suitable work* generally means work in which a worker is experienced or trained, that is in line with his skill and usual wages, and within reasonable distance of his home. A worker is usually given some time to look for a job in his own field. As the period of unemployment lengthens, the State agency may take the position that less skilled and lower paid work should be considered *suitable*. *Good cause* has been defined as what a reasonable man would do under similar circumstances. Workers may be required to show that they are making active efforts to find suitable work. Some State laws explicitly require evidence of an independent search for work. In other States, such evidence may be required by the local office. In addition to meeting the availability requirements of the law, a worker must register and report regularly at his local employment office. *Disqualifications*: State laws generally contain provisions under which a worker may be disqualified for unemployment insurance benefits if: (a) He quit his job voluntarily—without good cause; (b) He was discharged for misconduct in connection with his work; (c) His unemployment is due to a stoppage of work in his plant which has been caused by a strike or other labor dispute (although unemployed under such conditions, a worker will not be disqualified if he is not participating in the dispute or interested in its outcome and did not belong to the grade or class of workers that were participating in the dispute or were directly interested in its outcome): (d) He refused or failed, without good cause, to apply for or accept an offer of suitable work. Many State laws contain additional disqualifications for quitting because of marriage or other family reasons, or for fraudulent misrepresentation; in many cases, students attending school are disqualified. In all States, disqualification results in at least a postponement of benefits; in some States, it also involves a cancellation of benefit rights or a reduction of benefit rights. In a few States, all benefit rights may be canceled so that a worker cannot draw benefits until he has earned enough wage credits to qualify again. In some other States, a worker is disqualified until he returns to work and earns remuneration for a specified number of weeks. A worker cannot be denied unemployment insurance benefits for refusing to accept new work if the position offered: (a) Is open because of a labor dispute; (b) Provides wages, hours, or other conditions of work substantially less favorable to the worker than those prevailing in the locality for that kind of work; or (c) Is conditioned upon his joining a company union or refraining from joining (or resigning from) a bona fide labor organization. *Amount of Benefits*: The amount of unemployment insurance a worker receives varies according to the State law. The weekly benefit is ordinarily not less than $5 and not more than $30 to $36 without dependents' allowances. The number of weeks of unemployment for which an eligible worker can collect these benefits depends on the State law; in some States duration is uniform; in 37 States, it depends also upon the worker's past employment or earnings. For workers with irregular past employment, it may be as short a period as 6 weeks in some States. The shortest period is that under the Florida act—a little over 4 weeks. The longest period of unemployment for which benefits will be paid ranges from 16 to 30 weeks. The District of Columbia law has included dependents' allowances from the beginning of the program. Michigan, Nevada, and Connecticut added them in 1945, Massachusetts in 1947, and since then Alaska, Illinois, Maryland, North Dakota, Ohio, and Wyoming laws have been amended to include dependents' allowances. Dependents are limited for the most part to minor children but Alaska, the District of Columbia, Illinois, Michigan, and Nevada include, in addition, some dependent spouses, parents, brothers, sisters, and older children. The weekly amounts per dependent vary from $1 to $5 (most often $3), the maximum allowance for dependents from $3 to $25 or, in Massachusetts, to an amount related to past earnings, and the maximum augmented weekly benefit varies from $30 to $70 or, in Massachusetts, to an amount related to past earnings. *Partial Unemployment Benefits.*—All States, except Montana, provide a partial unemployment insurance benefit when a worker's wages and hours have been considerably reduced by slack work. To claim unemployment benefits, a worker must register for work and file a claim for unemployment insurance at the local public

(*continued on p. 330*)

(325)

SIGNIFICANT PROVISIONS OF STATE UNEMPLOYMENT INSURANCE LAWS, OCT. 15, 1956 [1]

Prepared for ready reference and comparative purposes. Because of the impossibility of giving qualifications and alternatives in brief summary form, the State law and State employment security agency should be consulted for authoritative information.

State	Size of firms covered (minimum number employees or size of payroll)	Amount of wages or employment during base period required to qualify for benefits [2]	Maximum weekly benefit amount for total unemployment [3]	Maximum weeks of duration of benefits for total unemployment [4]
Alabama	4 in 20 weeks	35 times wba [2] and $112.01 in 1 quarter.	$25	20
Alaska	1 at any time	1¼ times high-quarter wages but not less than $450.	[3] 45-70	26
Arizona	3 in 20 weeks	30 times wba and wages in 2 quarters.	$30	26
Arkansas	1 in 10 days	30 times wba	26	18
California	1 at any time and over $100 in any quarter.	30 times wba or 1 1/3 times high-quarter wages, if less, but not less than $600 nor more than $750.	33	26
Colorado	4 in 20 weeks	30 times wba	[3] 28-35	[3] 20-26
Connecticut	3 in 13 weeks	$300; and wages in 2 quarters.	[3] 38-52	26
Delaware	1 in 20 weeks	30 times wba	35	26
District of Columbia	1 at any time	1½ times high-quarter wages; $130 and 1 quarter and wages in 2 quarters.	30	26
Florida	4 in 20 weeks or 4 in 8 weeks and payroll in excess of $6,000 in any quarter.	30 times wba (18+, 23+ or 27 if wba is $8, $9 or $10); and wages in 2 quarters.	26	16

See footnotes at end of table.

STATE UNEMPLOYMENT INSURANCE LAWS

State	Size of firms covered (minimum number employees or size of payroll)	Amount of wages or employment during base period required to qualify for benefits [2]	Maximum weekly benefit amount for total unemployment [3]	Maximum weeks of duration of benefits for total unemployment [4]
Georgia	4 in 20 weeks	40-45+ times wba and $150 in 1 quarter.	30	[5] u22
Hawaii	1 at any time	30 times wba	35	u20
Idaho	1 at any time and $150 in any quarter.	25-38+ times wba; $150 in 1 quarter and wages in 2 quarters.	30	26
Illinois	4 in 20 weeks	$550; and $150 in other than high quarter.	[3] 28-40	26
Indiana	4 in 20 weeks	$250; and $150 in last 2 quarters.	30	20
Iowa	4 in 15 weeks	20 times wba	30	24
Kansas	4 in 20 weeks or 25 in one week.	$400, or $200 in 2 quarters.	32	20
Kentucky	4 in 3 quarters of preceding year, with wages of $50 each in each quarter or 4 in 20 weeks.	$450	32	u26
Louisiana	4 in 20 weeks	30 times wba	25	20
Maine	4 in 20 weeks	$300	30	u23
Maryland	1 at any time	30 times wba and $156 in 1 quarter.	[3] 30-38	26
Massachusetts	1 in 13 weeks	$500	35-([3])	26
Michigan	4 in 20 weeks	14 weeks of employment at more than $15	[3] 30-54	26
Minnesota	1 in 20 weeks in cities or 4 in 20 weeks in small towns and places.	$520	33	26

See footnotes at end of table.

STATE UNEMPLOYMENT INSURANCE LAWS

State	Size of firms covered (minimum number employees or size of payroll)	Amount of wages or employment during base period required to qualify for benefits [2]	Maximum weekly benefit amount for total unemployment [3]	Maximum weeks of duration of benefits for total unemployment [4]
Mississippi	4 in 20 weeks	30 times wba	30	u20
Missouri	4 in 20 weeks	Wages in 2 quarters	25	24
Montana	1 in 20 weeks or over $500 in a year	1½ times high-quarter wages and $170 in 1 quarter.	26	u20
Nebraska	4 in 20 weeks	$300 in 2 quarters with at least $100 in each of such quarters.	28	20
Nevada	1 at any time and $225 in any quarter	30 times wba	[3] 30-50	26
New Hampshire	4 in 20 weeks	$400	32	u26
New Jersey	4 in 20 weeks	17 weeks of employment at $15 or more.	35	26
New Mexico	1 at any time and $450 in any quarter or 2 in 13 weeks	30 times wba and $156 in 1 quarter.	30	24
New York	3 at any time	20 weeks of employment at average of $15 or more	36	u26
North Carolina	4 in 20 weeks	$250	30	u26
North Dakota	4 in 20 weeks	36 times wba and wages in 2 quarters.	[3] 26-35	u20
Ohio	3 at any time	20 weeks of employment and $240	[3] 33-39	26
Oklahoma	4 in 20 weeks	20 times wba and wages in 2 quarters.	28	22

See footnotes at end of table.

STATE UNEMPLOYMENT INSURANCE LAWS

State	Size of firms covered (minimum number employees or size of payroll)	Amount of wages or employment during base period required to qualify for benefits [2]	Maximum weekly benefit amount for total unemployment [3]	Maximum weeks of duration of benefits for total unemployment [4]
Oregon	2 in 6 weeks in 1 quarter and $1,800 in a year.	37 times wba or 1½ times high-quarter wages if less, but not less than $700.	35	26
Pennsylvania	1 at any time	32-42 times wba and $120 in 1 quarter	35	u30
Rhode Island	1 at any time	30 times wba	30	26
South Carolina	4 in 20 weeks	1½ times high-quarter wages but not less than $240; and $120 in 1 quarter.	26	22
South Dakota	4 in 20 weeks or $24,000 in a year.	1½ times high-quarter wages and $150 in 1 quarter or wages in 2 quarters if base-period wages are $600 or more.	25	20
Tennessee	4 in 20 weeks	40, 50, and 60 times wba and $75 in 1 quarter.	30	u22
Texas	4 in 20 weeks	$375 with $250 in 1 quarter and $125 in another or $450 with $50 in each of 3 quarters or $1,000 in 1 quarter.	28	24
Utah	1 at any time and $140 in any quarter.	19 weeks of employment and $400.	33	26
Vermont	4 in 20 weeks	30 times wba with 1/3 of wages in last 2 quarters; and $200 in 1 quarter.	28	u26

See footnotes at end of table.

STATE UNEMPLOYMENT INSURANCE LAWS

State	Size of firms covered (minimum number employees or size of payroll)	Amount of wages or employment during base period required to qualify for benefits[2]	Maximum weekly benefit amount for total unemployment[3]	Maximum weeks of duration of benefits for total unemployment[4]
Virginia	4 in 20 weeks	30 times wba ($250 for minimum wba).	28	18
Washington	1 at any time	$800	35	26
West Virginia	4 in 20 weeks	$500	30	u24
Wisconsin	4 in 20 weeks or $10,000 in any quarter or $6,000 in any year.	14 weeks of employment at average of $13 or more.	36	26½
Wyoming	1 at any time and $500 in any year.	26 times wba and $200 in 1 quarter.	[3] 30-36	26

[1] Source: Bureau of Employment Security, U. S. Department of Labor. For more details, see *Comparison of State Unemployment Insurance Laws as of December 1955*, prepared by the Bureau of Employment Security and on sale at the Government Printing Office, Washington 25, D. C., 40¢ a copy.

[2] Weekly benefit amount abbreviated as wba. For example, "30 times wba" means that to qualify for benefits the wages earned during the benefit period must be at least 30 times the amount of the weekly benefit.

[3] When 2 amounts are given, higher includes dependents' allowances except in Colorado where higher amount includes 25 percent additional for certain claimants employed for 5 consecutive years and no benefits received; duration for such claimants is increased to 26 weeks. Although Massachusetts pays dependents' allowances, the maximum augmented benefit is not shown because there is no fixed limit. In Alaska, the maximum for interstate claimants is $25 and no dependents' allowances paid.

[4] Some States afford the same uniform duration to all claimants who are eligible and who remain unemployed. This is indicated by a "u" (uniform) preceding the duration figure. Other States afford benefits for a shorter period for many claimants who lack the base-period wages or employment required to qualify for the maximum duration.

[5] For claimants with 4x high quarter earnings; 20 for others.

employment office serving his community. If the worker cannot locate the office, he can inquire at his local post office, or write to his State employment security agency, usually located in the capital city of the State. A worker's claim generally dates from the time he registers for work and files his claim—not from the date he lost his job or was laid off. *It is important for a worker to register for work and file a claim for unemployment insurance promptly.* An unemployed worker must report to his local employment office regularly as instructed, usually every week, in order to be eligible for continued payments. Also, he must do whatever a man in his situation would reasonably do in order to find work. In almost all States, no benefits are paid for the first week for which claims are filed; only Maryland, Nevada, North Carolina, and Texas have no waiting period. *Interstate Workers.*— A worker may register for work and file a claim for benefits at any local employment office in the country. For example, if he is living in Illinois, but is eligible for unemployment insurance in Arkansas, he can still file a claim in a local Illinois office. This office will forward his claim to Arkansas, which will send directly to the worker any benefits to which he is entitled. *The Right To Appeal*: A worker can appeal any decision made regarding his unemployment insurance claim that he believes is wrong. Usually opportunity for a second administrative appeal before a board of review or commission is also provided. However, there is always a time limit on appeals. In most States a worker must file his appeal within 5 or 7 days after he is notified of the decision on his claim. To file an appeal a worker may write or visit his local employment security office where he filed his claim and give notice that he wishes to appeal. That office will help him fill out any necessary papers and explain to him what he should do next. Generally there is no cost to the worker for administrative appeals, unless he retains counsel. If, after his appeal has been heard, the worker still feels the decision is wrong, he may carry his case to the courts. For further information go to the nearest local public employment office or write to the employment security agency of your State,

in the capital city, or to the Bureau of Employment Security, U.S. Department of Labor, Washington 25, D. C.

"Unemployment Insurance Administration Fund." A term used by the United States Employment Service. See FUNDS.

"Unemployment Trust Fund." A term used by the United States Employment Service. See FUNDS.

"Unemployment Trust Fund Account." A term used by the United States Employment Service. See ACCOUNTS.

"Unencumbered Balance." A term used by the United States Employment Service. The amount of administrative funds previously made available to a State employment security agency against which the State has not actually incurred obligations at the close of a budgetary period.

unfair labor practices of employers, prevention of. Employers are forbidden, under the Labor Management Relations Act (which see) to engage in any of the five unfair labor practices listed below: An employer is defined in the law as including "any person acting as an agent of an employer, directly or indirectly." Employers are forbidden by the law— (1) To interfere with, restrain, or coerce employees in the exercise of rights guaranteed by section 7 (section 8 [a] [1]). Examples of such illegal interference: (a) Threatening employees with loss of jobs or benefits if they should join a union. (b) Threatening to close down the plant if a union should be organized in it. (c) Questioning employees about their union activities or membership in such circumstances as will tend to restrain or coerce the employees. (d) Spying on union gatherings. (e) Granting wage increase deliberately timed to defeat self-organization among employees. (2) To dominate or interfere with the formation or administration of any labor organization or contribute financial or other support to it. Examples of conduct that is illegal under this section: (a) An employer taking an active part in organizing a union to represent employees. (b) An employer bringing pressure upon employees to join a union. (c) An employer playing favorites to one of two or more unions which are competing to represent employees. In remedying such unfair practices, the Board distinguishes between "domination" of a labor organization and conduct which amounts to no more than illegal interference. When a union is found to be dominated by an employer, the Board has announced, it will order the organization completely disestablished as a representative of employees. But, if the organization is found only to have been supported by employer assistance amounting to less than domination, the Board usually orders the employer to stop such support and to withhold recognition from the organization until it has been certified by the Board as a bona fide representative of employees. (3) To discriminate in hiring or tenure of employment or any term or condition of employment to encourage or discourage membership in any labor organization (section 8 [a] [3]). This section, together with section 8 (b) (2), prohibits the "closed shop," in which only persons who already hold membership in a labor organization may be hired. It also prohibits discriminatory hiring hall arrangements by which only persons who have "permits" from a union may be hired. However, a proviso to this section permits an employer and a union to agree to a union shop, in which employees may be required to join the union at the end of 30 days. The type of union-shop agreements that the act permits is discussed under UNION SHOP. Examples of discrimination in employment forbidden by this section: (a) Demoting or discharging an employee because he urged his fellow employees to join or organize a union. (b) Refusing to reinstate an employee (when a job he can qualify for is open) because he took part in a lawful strike. (c) refusing to hire a qualified applicant for a job because he does not belong to a union, or because he belongs to one union rather than to another union. This section does not limit the employer's rights to discharge, transfer, or lay off an employee for genuine economic reasons, or for just cause such as disobedience or bad work. This applies equally to employees who are active union advocates and to those who are not. However, the fact that a lawful reason for the discharge or disciplining of an employee may exist does not entitle an employer to discharge or discipline an employee when the true reason is the employee's union activities or other activities protected by the law. In weighing an employee's charge that he has been discriminated against because of his union activity, the NLRB will want to know: (a) What reason did the company give for taking the action against the employee? (b) Did the company take the same action against other employees for the same reason? (c) Was the employee given any warnings before the company acted? (d) Did the company know that the employee was active in union matters or was a union member? (e) What is the employee's record as to length of employment, efficiency ratings, wage increases, promotions, or words of praise from his supervisor? (f) What was the company's attitude toward unions and particularly the employee's union? (4) To discharge or otherwise discriminate against an employee because he has filed charges or given testimony under the act (section 8 [a] [4]). (5) To refuse to bargain collectively with the representative chosen by a majority of employees in a group that is appropriate for collective bargaining (section 8[a] [5]). Examples of conduct that violates this section: (a) An employer making a wage increase without consulting the representative of employees when they have chosen such a representative. (b) Making a wage increase larger than that offered to the employees' representative. (c) Refusing to put an agreement with the employees' representative into writing. (d) Refusing to deal with the representative of employees because the employees are out on strike.

unfair labor practices of unions, prevention of. See Labor Management Relations Act of 1947. Labor organizations are forbidden to engage in any of 10 unfair labor practices listed in section 8 (b) of the law. This section forbids labor organizations or their agents—(1) To restrain or coerce employees in the exercise of the rights guaranteed by section 7 (section 8 [b] [1] [A]). A proviso in this section states that "this paragraph shall not impair the right of a labor organization to prescribe its own rules with respect to the acquisition or retention of membership." Examples of conduct found to violate this section: (a) Mass picketing in such numbers that nonstriking employees are physically barred from en-

tering the plant. (b) Acts of force or violence on the picket line or in connection with strikes. (c) Threats to do bodily injury to nonstriking employees. (d) Threats by unions or their agents to employees that they will lose their jobs unless they support the union's activities. (2) To restrain or coerce an employer in the selection of his representatives for the purpose of collective bargaining or the adjustment of grievances (section 8 [b] [B]). (3) To cause or attempt to cause an employer to discriminate against an employee to encourage or discourage union membership (section 8 [b] [2]). This section reenforces section 8 [a] [3] in outlawing the "closed shop." It also contains language reenforcing the limits placed on the union shop by section 8 [a] [3]. This language is discussed under "The Union Shop." Examples of conduct violating this section: (a) Causing an employer to discharge an employee because he circulated a petition urging a change in the union's method of selecting shop stewards. (b) Making of a contract that requires an employer to hire only members of the union or persons "satisfactory" to the union. (4) To refuse to bargain collectively with an employer, when the organization is the representative of a majority of employees in a group appropriate for bargaining (section 8 [b] [3]). Examples of conduct violating this section: (a) Insistence upon the inclusion of illegal provisions, such as a closed shop or a discriminatory hiring hall, in a contract. (b) An adamant refusal to make a written contract of reasonable duration. (5) To engage in, or induce or encourage employees to engage in—(a) A strike to force an employer or a self-employed person to join a labor union or an employer organization (section 8 [b] [4] [A]). *(b)* A *secondary* strike or concerted refusal to perform duties in the course of employment to force a neutral employer or person to cease doing business with another employer with whom the union has a dispute (section 8 [b] [4] [A]). Examples of conduct violating this section: Picketing at the separate plant of an employer who continued to deal with a company with which the union has a dispute; a union official calling union members at the place of their employment in a retail market to tell that a wholesaler had been placed on the union's "unfair list." Picketing directed at an entire construction project because one of the subcontractors doing part of the work on the project had nonunion employees. However, the Board and the courts have ruled that this provision does not prohibit picketing of the plant of an employer with whom a union has a direct dispute even though such picketing may encourage employees of other employers, who come to the plant, to refuse to work. An example of conduct of this type which had been held NOT to violate the law: Picketing the plant of an employer with whom it has a direct dispute even though employees of other employers may refuse to cross the picket line. (c) A secondary or "sympathy" strike to force an employer other than their own to recognize or bargain with a labor organization which has not been certified by the Board as the representative of the other employer's employees (section 8 [b] [4] [B]). Example of conduct violating this section: Picketing of a department store by a deliverymen's union in an effort to compel a

separate company which delivered for the store to recognize the union before it had been certified by the Board. (d) A strike to compel an employer to recognize or bargain with one union when another union has been certified by the Board as the representative of the employees (section 8 [b] [4] [C]). (e) A strike to compel an employer to assign particular work to employees in another union, trade, craft, or class (section 8 [b] [4] [D]). This provision outlaws strikes in certain types of "jurisdictional" disputes between unions over what union or craft should be employed to do particular types of work tasks. (6) To require employees under a union-shop agreement to pay, as a condition precedent to becoming a member of the union, "a fee in an amount which the Board finds excessive or discriminatory under all the circumstances" (section 8 [b] [5]). This section further states: *In making such a finding, the Board shall consider, among other relevant factors, the practices and customs of labor organizations in the particular industry, and the wages currently paid to the employees affected.* Example of a fee which the Board found was discriminatory in violation of this section: a) Charging old employees who failed to join the union before the union-shop agreement took effect an initiation fee of $15 while charging employees hired after that date only $5. (7) To cause or attempt to cause an employer to pay or deliver or agree to pay or deliver any money or other thing of value, in the nature of an exaction, for services which are not performed or not to be performed (section 8 [b] [6]). This section prohibits certain practices commonly known as "featherbedding."

"Unfilled Opening." A term used by the United States Employment Service. See OPENING.

unfunded plan. Pensions paid on a "pay-as-you-go" basis from current operating expenses. No provision for setting up a fund for future payments is made.

"Uniform Base Period." A term used by the United States Employment Service. See BASE PERIOD.

"Uniform Benefit Year." A term used by the United States Employment Service. See BENEFIT YEAR.

"Uniform Duration." A term used by the United States Employment Service. See DURATION OF BENEFITS.

"Union Agreement Provisions," Bulletin 686, U. S. Department of Labor, Bureau of Labor Statistics. A handbook which gives sample agreement provisions for labor contracts on such subjects as management prerogatives, shift premiums, overtime, holidays, and scores of others.

union, closed. See CLOSED UNION.

union, craft. See CRAFT UNION.

union, credit. See CREDIT UNION.

union, dual. A union which claims total or partial jurisdiction over employees claimed by another union. See JURISDICTION, UNION.

Union, Federated Labor. A local union directly affiliated with AFL.

union, industrial. See INDUSTRIAL UNION.

Union, international. See INTERNATIONAL UNION.

union label. Printed emblem attached to an article as evidence that it has been produced by union labor under conditions satisfactory to a local or national union; in the printing trades, known as the "bug."

Union, labor. See LABOR UNION.

union, local. See LOCAL INDUSTRIAL UNION.

union, local industrial. See LOCAL INDUSTRIAL UNION.

union rate. An hourly rate, usually a single rate for an occupation or trade, established by agreement reached through collective bargaining. A union rate or scale is usually the minimum rate that may be paid to qualified persons in the job; there are usually no restrictions prohibiting the employer from paying higher rates.

union security. Anything that involves union shop, closed shop, maintenance of membership or payroll deduction of dues.

union shop. A condition of employment whereby employees in the bargaining unit must, as a condition of continued employment, become and remain members in good standing of the union during the life of the collective bargaining contract.

union scale. See UNION RATE.

union shop, as defined under Labor Management Relations Act of 1947. The act permits a union and an employer to make an agreement requiring all employees to join the union in order to retain their jobs, except in States where such agreements are forbidden by State law (section 8 [a] [3] and section 14 [b]). The maximum form of such a union security agreement permitted by the act

(335)

is a requirement that employees in the contract unit acquire membership in the contracting union within a "grace period" of 30 days following (1) their employment, or (2) the effective date of the contract, whichever is later. An agreement which provides a grace period of less than 30 days is invalid, but the Board has held that employees who are already members of the union need not be extended the 30 days' grace. For a union-security agreement to be valid, *all* of the following requirements must be met: (1) The contracting union must be free from employer domination or assistance within the meaning of Section 8 [a] [2]. (2) The agreement must cover employees in an appropriate unit who have legally designated the contracting union as their representative. (3) The contracting union must have complied with the filing and non-Communist affidavit requirements of the act. (4) The union's authority to make the agreement must *not* have been revoked by the employees voting in a union-shop deauthorization poll within the preceding year. (5) The agreement must contain an appropriate 30-day grace period for all employees who are not members of the union when it takes effect. However, under a valid union-security agreement, an employee may be discharged for lack of union membership only when it results in his failure to tender on time "the periodic dues and the initiation fees uniformly required." *Union Shop Deauthorization*: If a majority of employees wish to revoke a union shop, they may do so through a secret-ballot deauthorization referendum conducted by the Board. Section 9 [e] [1] provides for the Board to conduct such a referendum whenever a petition is filed by 30 per-

cent or more of the employees in a bargaining unit covered by a union-shop agreement. For further information write to the Division of Information, National Labor Relations Board, Washington 25, D. C.

union steward. See SHOP STEWARD.

unit appropriate for bargaining, under LABOR MANAGEMENT RELATIONS ACT, THE NATIONAL LABOR RELATIONS BOARD (which see). The Board has the duty under the act to determine what group of employees constitutes a unit appropriate for bargaining with their employer. Such a unit may extend to one or more employers; or it may include one or more plants of the same employer, or it may be a subdivision of a plantwide unit such as a unit of skilled craftsmen, professional employees, plant guards, or clerical employees. In determining whether or not a particular group of employees, constitutes a proper unit for bargaining, the Board considers particularly the following factors: (1) Similarity of skills, wages, hours, and other working conditions among the employees involved; (2) Any history of collective bargaining; (3) Desires of the employees. In addition, the Board may consider the extent to which the employees are organized, but the act forbids the Board from making this a *controlling* factor. Mutuality of interests among the employees is a prime determinant of the appropriate grouping of employees for bargaining. This is evidenced by (1) the similarity of their skills and working conditions, and (2) the unit grouping that the employees and the employer have followed in past bargaining over a substantial period, unless such units were clearly contrary to the act or to Board rules and policies. This latter factor is known as "history of bargaining." The Board's discretion in determining bargaining units is limited by provisions of section 9 (b) that: (1) Professional employees may not be included in a unit of nonprofessional employees, unless a majority of the professional employees vote to be included. [Broadly, the act's definition of a professional employee covers lawyers, doctors, architects, engineers, and others who must have completed "a prolonged course of specialized intellectual instruction and study in an institution of higher learning or a hospital, as distinguished from a general academic education or from an apprenticeship . . ."] (section 2 [12] [a]). (2) No craft unit may be held inappropriate on the ground that a different unit was established by a prior Board decision. (3) Plant guards, who enforce rules for the protection of property or safety on any employer's premises, may not be included with other employees. The act also forbids the Board from certifying a labor organization as the representative of a unit of guards or watchmen if it admits other employees as members, or if it is "affiliated directly or indirectly" with an organization admitting other employees to membership. The Board has held that employees who do guard work only part time may qualify as guards.

unit benefit plan. Plan in which an annuity is purchased from an insurance company for each year of service employee serves with employer. Benefits usually are figured on a fixed percentage of each worker's salary for each year. In some plans of this type, a new annuity is bought each year, depending on the earnings of the employees covered.

United Mine Workers. A labor union distinguished by the personality of its president since 1919, John L. Lewis. Lewis, born in Iowa of Welsh parents, entered the mines at 12, and has been a champion of the miners during a long career. He became head of the United Mine Workers in 1919. In 1935, he took the lead in splitting from the AFL and forming the Committee for Industrial Organization, (later Congress of Industrial Organizations) of which he was president till 1940, when he resigned because of disagreement with President Franklin Delano Roosevelt. He continued, however, as President of the Mine Workers. In 1946, he returned briefly to the AFL, from which he had split some 10 years earlier, but about a year later, the United Mine Workers once more left the fold, and have been independent since. He has done much to advance welfare of pension funds financed wholly or partially by employers.

United States Department of Health, Education and Welfare. See HEALTH, EDUCATION AND WELFARE, U. S. DEPARTMENT OF.

United States Department of Labor. The United States Department of Labor was created by Congress in 1913 to *foster, promote, and develop the welfare of the wage earners of the United States, to improve their working conditions, and to advance their opportunities for profitable employment.* In line with this mandate, one of the primary functions of the Department is to provide informational services to labor and management and to assist them in the improvement of labor standards and working conditions. Those bureaus of the Department, whose activities are mainly of this type, are described below. Other bureaus of the Department are described in connection with the summaries of the laws which they administer. Requests for assistance or publications from any of these bureaus can be made to the U. S. Department of Labor or directly to the appropriate bureau.

United States Employment Service. The United States Employment Service develops policies and maintains methods for the coordination and guidance of a nationwide system of public employment offices operated by State and Territorial agencies affiliated with the United States Employment Service. There are now approximately 1,800 full-time and 2,000 part-time local offices. The United States Employment Service has the responsibility for checking the individual State plans of operation for conformity with Federal laws; promoting uniform methods for operating employment service offices; maintaining a program for referring labor from one area to another; giving technical assistance to the States in legislation and administration; assisting in determining funds necessary for administration of State employment service programs; and maintaining employment service facilities in the District of Columbia. Having operated the widest extremes of labor market conditions, the Employment Service has developed a well-rounded, comprehensive employment service program which evolves around six important functions, namely: (1) *An Effective Placement Service*: An effective placement service and nationwide clearance system makes it possible for workers to obtain information concerning job opportunities in the community and throughout the entire country.

It assists employers in finding workers, and assists workers in finding employment or reemployment in jobs for which they are suited by skills, knowledge, abilities, and interests. This service facilitates the placement of workers in jobs for which their training, experience, and aptitudes fit them. It saves the employer time and effort in recruiting qualified workers, and assists him in preventing unnecessary turnover. In recent years greater attention has been given to the placement problems of the professional workers by encouraging the local offices to stress such placements and by providing specialized convention placement services by the Bureau and cooperating State agencies at conventions of professional groups. The United States Employment Service also participates with the State Employment Security agencies in the operation of a farm placement service. This program provides special services in addition to basic placement facilities available at all local employment offices. These services include the organization and operation of day-haul programs for seasonal agricultural workers, and provide direction for migratory farm workers to a succession of seasonal jobs. The use of Federal, State, and community resources is encouraged to improve the working conditions, housing, health, education, and welfare facilities available to migrant workers and their families. The Employment Service also operates a program which supplements domestic farm labor with foreign workers brought in for temporary jobs when needed. (2) *Employment Counseling and Selective Placement Service.* The technical assistance furnished through the local offices in counseling and testing as well as selective placement services provides the applicant with an opportunity to discover, analyze, and evaluate his potential abilities; to formulate a suitable vocational plan; and to put the plan into effect. Programs for the counseling and placement of special applicant groups, such as youth, older workers, the physically handicapped, and members of minority groups are developed and coordinated by the Employment Service. Major program activities of these special applicant groups will be described later in this section. (3) *Special Services to Veterans.* The public employment service has always had a special obligation to veterans. This originated under the Wagner-Peyser Act of June 6, 1933, which specified that the Bureau was "to maintain a veteran's service to be devoted to securing employment for veterans." The Servicemen's Readjustment Act of 1944, as amended, strengthened the Veterans Employment Service. (4) *Industrial Services.* The failure of workers to retain jobs because of poor selection and assignments caused by inadequate knowledge of job requirements and worker qualifications results in a high turnover and increased unemployment. By assisting employers, labor groups, and organizations in analyzing employment problems involving effective use of skills and abilities of workers, and by aiding them in the application of techniques and materials, the Employment Service can be of service to both the worker and the employer. (5) *Labor Market Information Service.* The Bureau of Employment Security, the State employment security agencies, and the local public employment offices provide information on employment and unemployment trends and labor demand-and-supply relationships with respect to specific areas, industries, and occupations. Local area labor market newsletters are prepared and distributed to employers, unions, and public officers in nearly 600 communities. The majority of these include information on unemployment trends. A monthly summary of trends and developments in new and insured unemployment, together with an analysis of the factors responsible for changes during the month, the amount of benefits paid and the number of beneficiaries, data on claimants exhausting benefit rights, and significant developments on a geographic regional basis, is published each month in the Bureau periodical, "Labor Market and Employment Security." The "Bimonthly Summary of Labor Market Developments in Major Areas," prepared by the Bureau, gives classification of major areas according to adequacy of labor supply. (6) *Community Participation.* The public employment office is an important cog in the economic life of the community. It is actively engaged in analyzing and developing programs and services which may be applied in alleviating problems of extreme unemployment and underemployment, particularly as these problems relate to the Nation's low-income group. Special assistance is provided by the Bureau to areas faced with a chronic labor surplus due to exhaustion of resources, declining industries, technological changes, and rapidly growing populations. The Employment Service, through its operations, is familiar with the problems in the community and can offer important information to the community on local matters affecting employment. In carrying on the foregoing six-point program, the United States Employment Service develops placement and counseling tools including occupational informational materials and tests, and provides services to special applicant groups. *Placement and Counseling Tools.*—The United States Employment Service provides technical tools and information on the content and requirements of jobs. Best known and most widely used is the *Dictionary of Occupational Titles.* Other publications include Job Descriptions, Occupational Guides covering many occupations, and guides for interviewing handicapped applicants. Inquiries concerning these tools and publications should be addressed to the Bureau of Employment Security, U. S. Department of Labor, Washington 25, D.C. The United States Employment Service test development program produces objective tests and related techniques for the measurement of skills, aptitudes, and interests of applicants. *Services to Special Applicant Groups.*—Certain groups such as veterans, the handicapped, older workers, youth, and members of minority groups tend to need special help in locating satisfactory employment. Local employment offices, through the use of specialized techniques and the intensified application of regular services, assist these applicants in resolving their job problems. *Veterans.*—Veterans are given full advantage of all services available through local employment offices and they receive priority in referral to all jobs. Preferential service among veterans is extended to those who are disabled. State and local office Veterans Employment Representative in each State are available to assist veterans in resolving their job problems. Additional special services given veterans include: (1) employment information, registration, and employment counseling services to patients and discharges at Armed

Forces and veterans hospitals, (2) job information and other employment services through Armed Forces separation centers, (3) information and referral service to appropriate agencies through which benefits and services may be obtained, (4) cooperation with employers and government agencies in establishing and maintaining rehabilitation and job training programs for veterans, and (5) job-finding assistance to veterans by maintaining constant contact with employers, veterans organizations, employer organizations, labor organizations, government agencies, civic organizations, and community service groups. *Older Workers.*—Every fourth person in the population and every third person in the labor force in the United States is 45 years of age, or over. This group therefore constitutes about one-third of the applicants for work at the public employment offices. Yet a majority of the job openings listed by employers with the employment service contain age restrictions specifying a preference for younger workers. As a result, the Employment Service must provide intensive counseling and placement services to many older workers to place them in suitable jobs. The Employment Service also draws upon its own resources and those of the entire Department of Labor to develop facts and information concerning the performance and potentialities of older workers in order to educate employers, labor, and the general public, and thereby to promote employment opportunities. Studies are now being conducted of employment patterns, policies, and practices by age, sex, occupation, and industry. Surveys are being made on the productivity, absenteeism, accident, and turnover rates among older workers as compared to younger workers. Provisions in collective bargaining agreements and pension plans that contribute to the hiring and retention of older workers are being analyzed. Demonstration projects are being conducted on counseling and placement methods and costs. By publicizing the results of these studies and extending and improving placement services to older job seekers, the Department of Labor and the Bureau of Employment Security hope to increase job opportunities for older workers and reduce age-restrictive hiring practices. *Youth.*—When a young person first enters the labor market, it is desirable that his aptitudes, interests, and skills all be evaluated; therefore, the local employment offices provide special services to these new entrants to the labor market. These services include, as needed, counseling and testing to determine vocational aptitudes. The Bureau places special emphasis on the program of cooperation between local employment service offices and secondary schools for the employment, counseling, and placement of high school graduates and dropouts. *The Physically Handicapped.*—The Bureau and the State employment services provide all regular services to the physically handicapped, which include placement and counseling and testing, when needed. In addition to this service, the Bureau has developed special guides to be used in interviewing applicants who have pulmonary tuberculosis, heart disease, epilepsy, diabetes, arthritis, nonarticular rheumatism, and orthopedic disorders. The Bureau and State services work with the Veterans Administration, the State rehabilitation agencies, the Bureau of Employee Compensation, and other Federal and State agencies in an effort to expand and improve the services for the handicapped. *Minority Groups.*—The Bureau and State agencies continue to work on the placement problems of job seekers who have difficulty in obtaining employment because of color, religion, or national origin. Every effort is made to improve policies, programs, standards, and methods to insure the equitable employment of workers belonging to the minority groups, based on the principle of worker selection according to skill, experience, ability, and job performance without regard to national origin, race, or religion. The Bureau has entered into plans of cooperation geared to promoting employment opportunities with the Bureau of Indian Affairs, American Friends Service Committee, and National Urban League.

United States Housing Act of 1937; Housing Act of 1949. These laws cover slum clearance, urban renewal, and low-rent public housing. Construction contracts are awarded by local authorities on projects financed with the asistance of loans and grants from the Federal Government. Laborers and mechanics employed in any part of the development of these projects must be paid not less than the wage rates determined by the Secretary of Labor.

United States Office of Education. A division of the federal government, within the Department of Health, Education and Welfare, established by Congress in 1867 for the purpose of advancing the cause of education throughout the nation. The Division of Vocational Education in the Office of Education is responsible for the administration of the vocational education acts, including the allocation of federal funds to the states for vocational education.

(341)

unit annuity. A specified amount of annuity purchased each year for each participant under a group annuity contract. The employee's retirement benefit is the total of these yearly purchases.

unit shop. A school shop designed and equipped to provide training in a single industrial occupation, or a single kind of material or type of work.

"Unit Time." A term used by the United States Employment Service. See TIME FACTOR.

unit trade course. Instruction organized for persons attending full-time school who are preparing for advantageous entrance into a specific trade of industrial pursuit. Courses are based solely on instruction for a particular trade or occupation.

Unlawful Practices in Radio Broadcasting. (Lea Act) passed April 16, 1946. This act prohibits certain types of coercive practices in the radio industry. These practices usually consist of attempts to compel a radio station to employ more persons than are needed or to restrict the use of recorded or other types of programs. The act makes it a criminal offense for any person to use or threaten to use force, violence, intimidation, duress, or other means to compel any radio station to employ or agree to employ more employees than are needed, or to make any extra payment in place of hiring additional employees. It is also made unlawful to use similar pressures to compel a radio station to pay or agree to pay more than once for services performed or to pay for services which are not performed, or to refrain from broadcasting noncompensated, noncommercial, educational and cultural programs or programs of foreign origin. In addition, the act prohibits similar pressure upon any person to exact payment for using recordings, transcriptions, reproductions, or other materials used for broadcasting, to restrict the manufacture and use of recordings and transcriptions, or to exact payment for using transcriptions of programs previously broadcast and paid for. The U. S. Department of Justice is charged with prosecuting violators who are subject to a maximum fine of $1,000 or imprisonment for not more than 1 year, or both.

unrestricted element. An operation element that is completely under the control of the workman.

unrestricted job. A job that is completely under the control of the workman.

unskilled labor. Persons engaged in manual operations, involving the performance of simple duties that may be learned within a short period of time and that require the exercise of little or no independent judgment.

upgrading. An organized procedure of developing and promoting qualified employees designed to secure maximum utilization of each worker's abilities. This usually includes: the selection of likely looking prospects from persons already employed by the company; training designed to furnish such employees with information of a general character, as well as training in the operations involved in the more advanced jobs; effective placement or promotion of these individuals; and continued follow-up for the purposes of continuing and repeating the cycle of selection, training and promotion.

urban wage rate index. Series maintained by the Bureau of Labor Statistics, beginning in 1943, to measure the movement of wage rates in urban areas in manufacturing, major manufacturing industry groups, and selected nonmanufacturing industries.

use. A THERBLIG (which see) which is defined as: to employ for the accomplishment of a purpose; to put into practice; to make use of in the manner for which it is intended; to apply mechanical means which is operated by a force whose time element is not under the control of the operator. *Use* exists in such cases where the tool or machine moves a part, or where the cutting time or mechanical process time is a direct function of the machine or mechanical device and the operator has no control over the speed of its completion. The *use* therblig may be the movement of a positive machine feed or the action of a mechanical, electrical or chemical process, or a mechanical movement of the operator. A hand feed drill press is a good example of this case.

utility management. Personnel techniques and management in utilities present some special problems. First, utilities are generally under government regulation, by such agencies as Public Utility Commissions, Federal Communications Commission, etc. Secondly, utility crews often work away from their base, frequently with little immediate supervision. The problems of utility management have received special attention by Columbia University, which sets up an annual Utility Management Workshop.

V

vacation pay. Payment for a period of time received by workers for vacation purposes. The time period frequently varies with length of service. During busy times or in a tight labor market, workers may be given the option of accepting vacation pay in lieu of time off.

"Valid Claim." A term used by the United States Employment Service. See CLAIM.

validity. A term used in connection with EMPLOYMENT TESTS. A measure of the extent to which a test measures what it is intended to measure; the degree to which test scores are related to occupational success in specified occupations.

"Validity Period." A term used by the United States Employment Service. A specified period of time during which a record is in active status (e.g., an application card or a clearance order).

variable. A factor or condition which can be measured, altered or controlled, i.e. temperature, pressure, flow, liquid level, humidity, weight, chemical composition, color, etc.

variable element. An element for which the leveled or normal time under the same methods and working conditions, will change because of the varying characteristics of the parts being worked upon; as size, weight, shape, density, hardness, viscosity, tolerance requirements, finish, etc.

variable expense. Expenditures that vary in proportion to the volume of production.

variable time element. See VARIABLE ELEMENT.

variance. The difference between any standard or expected value and an actual value. For example, the difference between the established standard cost and the cost actually incurred in performing a job or operation.

"Verification." A term used by the United States Employment Service. The determination from a reliable source, preferably the employer, whether an applicant referred by the local office has been hired by the employer and has entered on the job. In the case of applicants referred to seasonal agricultural openings, verification is considered complete when it is confirmed that a referred worker has been hired, even though confirmation of his entry on the job may be lacking.

vertical union. An organization of laborers which includes all the workers of the various trades and crafts in the same industry; in contrast to a trade union or association of workers who are all in a particular craft. Also known as an *industrial* union. Example, Textile Workers Union of America. Most industrial unions in the U. S. are affiliated with the CIO (now AFL-CIO). This type of union is spoken of as a vertical union since the workers from the lowest to the highest skills are all members. See "Industrial vs. Craft Unionism" by J. E. Johnson, 1937.

vestibule training. A program organized by the employer in his plant for the preliminary training (short, intensive) or "breaking in" of new employees on special machines and operations.

vesting rights. Vesting rights permit the employee covered under a pension plan to receive certain rights to the employer's contributions upon termination of employment. The amount of vesting may depend upon the employee's years of service and/or age. Under the ordinary plan, the employee does not receive the amount due him under the vesting rights in cash, but in an annuity payable upon retirement.

"Veteran." As defined by the United States Employment Service: (1) Served in the active service of the armed forces of the United States during any of the following periods and has been discharged or released under other than dishonorable conditions: Spanish American War—April 21, 1898, to August 12, 1898; Philippine Insurrection—August 13, 1898, to July 4, 1902. (If service was in Moro Province, ending date is July 15 1903.); Boxer Rebellion—June 20, 1900, to May 12, 1901; World War I—April 6, 1917, to November 11, 1918. (If service was in Russia, ending date is April 1, 1920.); World War II—December 7, 1941, to December 31, 1946; Korean Conflict—June 27, 1950 to January 31, 1955. The term "Armed Forces" includes the Air Force, Army, Navy, Naval Reserve (including Fleet Reserve), Marine Corps, Coast Guard, Coast Guard Reserve (exclusive of Coast Guard Reserves, Temporary), WACS (Women's Army Corps only if discharge dated on or after September 30, 1943), Army Nurse Corps, WAVES (Navy), Navy Nurse Corps, Yeoman (F) in the Naval Reserve or Marinette in the Marine Corps Reserve, and SPARS (Coast Guard). (2) Served in the active military or naval service of any Government allied with the United States in World War II and who, at the time of entrance into such active service, was a citizen of the United States, or (3) Served in the U.S. Public Health Service as a commissioned officer and who, during the World War II period of war: (a) was detailed to the Army, Navy, or Coast Guard; or (b) was assigned to duty in the Public Health Service outside the continental limits of the United States, or in Alaska; or (c) was in the U.S. Public Health Service on or after July 29, 1945.

veterans' reemployment rights. Act of June 24, 1948, as amended. The Bureau of Veterans' Reemployment Rights, U.S. Department of Labor, assists former members of the Armed Forces, national guardsmen and reservists who perform training, persons rejected for military service, and others, in the exercise of their statutory reemployment rights in private employment, as provided by

Federal law. The Bureau depends largely on cooperating agencies and on volunteers who serve as reemployment rights advisers, to supply information to ex-servicemen, employers, labor and veterans organizations, and others interested in the reemployment provisions of the various acts. Local offices of the State Employment Services affiliated with the Bureau of Employment Security refer persons desiring specific information or assistance to field offices of the Bureau of Veterans' Reemployment Rights. The Bureau field representative usually assigns a problem involving reemployment rights to a volunteer Reemployment Rights Adviser located in the community where the problem has arisen. Under the supervision of the Bureau's field representative, the Reemployment Rights Adviser assists in resolving controversies with employers over reemployment rights by negotiation and voluntary settlement. These procedures are designed to promote the expeditious settlement of controversies between veterans and employers within the local community. If the controversy is not so resolved, the field representative of the Bureau of Veterans' Reemployment Rights continues negotiations short of legal action, giving all parties the benefit of his knowledge and experience on similar claims, opinions of the Solicitor of Labor, and conclusions reached by the courts. In those cases where a settlement is not reached, ex-servicemen are advised of their right to review by the United States Department of Justice. Upon their written request, the complete file is referred via the Solicitor of Labor and the Department of Justice to the United States Attorney for the district in which the employer has a place of business. The United States Attorney determines if the claim has sufficient merit to justify legal action. *Conditions of Eligibility for Rights With Private Employers*: An ex-serviceman is eligible for statutory reemployment rights: (1) If the position was in the employ of a private employer. (2) If the position was other than a temporary position. (3) If he left the position to enter upon active military or naval service in the land or naval forces of the United States or the Public Health Service. (Any person who enlists, has enlisted or reenlisted subsequent to June 24, 1948, will have reemployment rights if he serves thereafter for not more than 4 years, unless extended by law. Any reservist who, subsequent to June 24, 1948, enters upon active duty, whether or not voluntarily, will have reemployment rights if he serves thereafter for not more than 4 years or is released as soon after the expiration of 4 years as he is able to obtain orders relieving him from active duty.) (4) If he satisfactorily completed his period of training and service or period of active duty and received a certificate to that effect. (5) If he is still qualified to perform the duties of the position. (Under the 1951 amendments to the Universal Military Training and Service Act, the returned serviceman who cannot perform the duties of his former position by reason of disability sustained during service in the Armed Forces is to be restored to such other position, the duties of which he is qualified to perform, as will provide him with a position of like seniority, status and pay, or the nearest approximation thereof consistent with the circumstances of the case.) (6) If he applies for reemployment within 90 days after he is relieved from military training and service or from hospitalization continuing after discharge for a period of not more than 1 year. (7) If the employer's circumstances have not so changed as to make it impossible or unreasonable to reinstate the serviceman to such position or one of like seniority, status and pay. An "active-duty-for-training reservist" under the Reserve Forces Act of 1955 is an enlistee in the Ready Reserve, performing his required initial six (or three) months training duty. He has rights, on meeting the above conditions of eligibility, except that he must apply within 60 days after his release from this active duty for initial training or from hospitalization continuing for not more than 6 months after such release. Other rights are provided for national guardsmen or reservists who perform a tour of training duty but are not "active-duty-for-training reservists" as defined above, and also for persons rejected by the Armed Forces, provided they meet conditions 1 and 2 above and apply within 30 days following the release from training duty or the rejection. *Rights and Benefits Provided.* An ex-serviceman who meets the seven conditions of eligibility: (1) Shall be entitled to reemployment in his former position or one of like seniority, status, and pay without loss of seniority; and (2) Shall be considered as having been on furlough or leave of absence and, upon restoration, shall participate in insurance or other benefits pursuant to established rules and practices dealing with persons on furlough or leave; and (3) Shall not be discharged without cause within 1 year after proper restoration. An "active-duty-for-training reservist" under the Reserve Forces Act of 1955 is entitled to the rights enumerated above except that his protection from

discharge without cause ends 6 months after proper restoration. Any reservist (when not an "active-duty-for-training reservist") or national guardsman who goes on training duty and any rejectee has these rights, i.e., he shall be granted a leave of absence by his employer for the training or for actions related to entering or attempting to enter military service and, on timely application, shall be reinstated in his position without reduction may be made for all employees similarly situated. *For Further Information.* Further information may be obtained from the Bureau of Veterans' Reemployment Rights, U. S. Department of Labor, Washington 25, D. C., field offices of the Bureau, or local employment service offices. Field Letters issued periodically by the Bureau, in cooperation with the Solicitor of Labor, are also available upon request. These contain questions and answers, interpretations, opinions and analyses of court decisions concerning the reemployment rights status.

visual aids. Visual aids most commonly used in employee and supervisory training include: actual objects (a typewriter, a hand tool); models (a miniature loom, templets for a floor layout); demonstrations (switchboard, drill press); blackboards (flannel boards, bulletin boards, charts, graphs, posters, maps); films—slides—photographs. Of course there are many more intricate visual aids as dioramas, installations that flash on colored electric lights, and others described in such books as "Preparation and Use of Visual Aids," by Kenneth B. Haas and Harry Q. Packer. Advantages of visual aids are: (1) they put over a message with the least resistance. (2) the same visual aids can be used over and over again with different groups, with a minimum effort of preparation by the leader. In handling visual aids: (1) try out the visual aids ahead of time: check that they are arranged in proper order; make sure everyone in the group will be able to see them. (2) give points you are making in your own words. Do not read the captions of material on charts verbatim as it is printed. (3) explain the meaning of charts, graphs, etc., even if quite simple: some people in the group may miss the point. (4) use variety in introducing visual aids. It is monotonous to hear a leader repeat ". . . and now we have here." (5) be sure your timing is right; to flip over a chart before explaining detracts attention from what the leader is saying. (6) don't crowd too much information on a poster, slide or picture. (7) don't use pictures or charts that are too complex. (8) don't oversimplify. Some visual material is so childish it insults the intelligence of the group. (9) don't use material—particularly pictures that are out of date. They discredit the entire presentation. (10) don't stand in front of the material being shown. (11) don't assume visual aids will take the place of other training. Generally they only supplement it. (12) Remember that visual aids demand only passive attention. Some people can look at television for hours without being able to tell what they saw.

visual skill, tests of. Among tests used in industry are: Sight Screener—American Optical Company, Southbridge, Mass.; Ortho-Rater—Bausch and Lomb Optical Co., Rochester, N. Y.; Telebinocular—Keystone View Company, Meadville, Pa. See PUBLISHERS, PERSONNEL TESTS.

Vocational Division of the U.S. Office of Education. The Vocational Division of the U.S. Office of Education administers the Smith-Hughes and George-Barden Acts which provide for the promotion of vocational education under a Federal-State-local plan. Under these acts the Vocational Division allots approximately 30 million dollars annually to the States to be used to develop programs of vocational education in trades and industries, distributive occupations, home economics, and agriculture. Funds are distributed to the States on the basis of population, and may be used for salaries of vocational teachers, counselors, teacher trainers, supervisors, and directors; for maintenance of teacher and counselor training for instructional supplies and equipment, and for research in vocational education. Local schools carry out the program under State plans prepared by the State boards for vocational education and approved by the U.S. Office of Education. State plans must stipulate, among other things, that the vocational instruction will be given in schools under public control, will be of less than college grade, and that the purpose will be to fit individuals for useful employment. Principal types of courses made available under these grants are all-day classes which provide preemployment training for young people of high-school age, and part-time and evening classes for apprentices and other workers over 16 years of age. For further information contact your local school, your State Board for Vocational Education, or the Vocational Division of the Office of Education, Department of Health, Education, and Welfare, Washington 25, D. C.

Vocational Education. Education designed to develop skills, abilities, understandings, attitudes, work habits and appreciations, encompassing knowledge and information needed by workers to enter and make progress in employment on a useful and productive basis. It is an integral part of the total education program and contributes toward the development of good citizens by developing their physical, social, civic, cultural and economic competencies.

vocational guidance. See GUIDANCE, VOCATIONAL.

Vocational Rehabilitation for Disabled Korean Veterans. Act of December 28, 1950, as amended. Qualified veterans who have had active service in the U.S. Armed Forces between June 27, 1950 and January 31, 1955, inclusive, may be eligible for training under an extension of the act affording vocational rehabilitation for World War II veterans, if they have been discharged from military or naval service under conditions other than dishonorable; have a disability incurred in, or aggravated by, such service for which compensation is payable under laws administered by the Veterans Administration, or would be but for the receipt of retirement pay; and are found in need of vocational rehabilitation to overcome the handicap of the disability. There is no deadline date for starting training, but there are dates beyond which no training may be given. Most disabled veterans must begin in time to complete their training within 9 years from their separation from Korean conflict period service or by January 31, 1964, whichever is the earlier. These periods may be extended by 4 years in the cases of persons who are unable to pursue vocational rehabilitation training

to completion within the prescribed period because of certain hardship conditions. Monthly subsistence allowance payments are made to veterans during training and they are provided with such tools, equipment, and supplies as are commonly required to be personally owned by other trainees not under Veterans Administration jurisdiction who are pursuing the same training in the particular establishment. For further information contact the nearest regional office of the Veterans Administration.

Vocational Rehabilitation of Disabled World War II Veterans. Act of March 24, 1943, as amended. July 25, 1956, also marked the virtual end of the vocational rehabilitation training program for disabled veterans of World War II. A few disabled World War II veterans who were unable to pursue vocational rehabilitation training to completion before July 25 1956, are permitted to train after that date under certain specific conditions outlined in an amendment to the act. By July 25, 1956, more than 611,000 disabled veterans had entered training under this act. Of this number more than 235,000 had entered on-the-job training programs. On July 31, 1956, only 236 disabled World War II veterans were still pursuing on-the-job training programs under the Vocational Rehabilitation Training Act. For further information, World War II veterans still entitled to benefits under the Servicemen's Readjustment Act or the Vocational Rehabilitation Training Act are advised to contact the nearest regional office of the Veterans Administration.

vocational school. A school which is separately organized under a principal or director, for the purpose of offering training in one or more skilled or semi-skilled trades or occupations. They are designed to meet the needs of secondary school students preparing for employment and to provide up-grading or extension courses for those who are employed.

vocational subject. Any school subject designed to develop specific skills, knowledges, and information which enables the learner to prepare for or to be more efficient in his chosen trade or occupation.

vocational-technical education. Training intended to prepare the student to earn a living in an occupation in which success is largely dependent upon technical information and an understanding of the laws of science and technology as applied to modern design, production, distribution and services.

voluntary checkoff. An agreement between an employee and a company for deducting union dues from the employee's wages.

"Voluntary Election." A term used by the United States Employment Service. See ELECTION, VOLUNTARY.

W

W-4 Form. Employee's Withholding Exemption Certificate. Required in connection with Social Security deductions. See SOCIAL SECURITY.

wage advance plan. Advancing of wages in work-weeks of short duration under plans obligating employers to maintain weekly wages up to a specified minimum level. Wages must be repaid during later weeks in which regular or longer hours are worked. No repayment is required unless the employer provides sufficient work to enable the advance to be repaid. See also ANNUAL WAGE OR EMPLOYMENT GUARANTEE and GUARANTEED WAGE PLAN.

wage and salary structure. The established or existing compensation or ranges of compensation within an area, industry, or plant related to the levels of job values to which they apply. Such compensation or ranges of compensation are usually established in relationship to the predominant wage rates for equal-valued jobs in the surrounding areas, the same industry or profession, or plants with comparable work.

wage and salary survey. The gathering and comparing of base wage or salary rates and/or ranges for comparable jobs within an area, industry, plant or profession.

"Wage and Separation Report." A term used by the United States Employment Service. A report submitted by an employer at the time when a worker is separated from his employment, on which the employer indicates the wages of such worker for a specified period while employed by him and the reasons why the worker was separated.

wage arbitration. The referral of wage disputes between employers and unions to an arbitrator or board of arbitration. The arbitrator's award or decision is customarily binding upon both parties. Arbitration is usually voluntary, both parties having agreed to refer the dispute to a third party for a decision. See also WAGE MEDIATION.

wage assignment. A voluntary transfer by a worker of some of his earned wages or commissions to another party or parties. Such assignments may be used for payment of purchased goods and debts, purchase of saving bonds, and payment of union dues and assessments.

"Wage-Combining Arrangement." A term used by the United States Employment Service. See INTERSTATE ARRANGEMENTS.

(351)

"Wage Credits." A term used by the United States Employment Service. Wages earned in insured work.

wage curve. A plot or graph showing the relationship between jobs, job classes, job evaluation point ratings, or the like and their corresponding wage rates and/or ranges.

wage determination. The process of establishing wage rates and wage structures through collective bargaining, arbitration, individual employer determination, etc. The process may involve comparisons with rates paid by other firms, the use of job evaluation, or other techniques. The term is also applied to findings, orders, or decisions of wage regulatory bodies such as minimum wage boards.

wage differential. Differences in wages among occupations, industries, or areas. Historical wage differentials, to which frequent reference is made, are those which have existed over long periods of time.

wage earner. The time-honored definition of a wage earner has been based upon method of wage payment. Usually, an employee whose income is computed on an hourly or daily basis, a piecework basis, or other comparable basis. Beginning with January 1945, a uniform definition for this general class of workers in manufacturing, cutting across methods of wage payment, has been adopted by all Federal Government agencies and some others in accordance with recommendations from the Division of Statistical Standards of the Bureau of the Budget.

Wage-Hour Law. See FAIR LABOR STANDARDS ACT.

wage incentive. See FINANCIAL INCENTIVE.

wage incentive plan. A method of payment which directly relates earnings to production. A system which enables workmen to increase their earnings by maintaining or exceeding an established standard of performance.

wage increase, across-the-board. A wage increase of a general nature, which simultaneously affects all employees of a company, industry or plant. It may be uniform on the basis of percentage, or in terms of an amount per hour. When an "across-the board" increase is given in an hourly rate in a unionized plant, the salaried workers frequently receive a corresponding percentage increase.

wage inequality. An unjust disparity between rates of workers whose duties and responsibilities are similar or identical. Wage inequalities can be considered either on an intraplant or interplant basis. The elimination of wage inequalities is often accomplished through job review or the adoption of job evaluation plans. During World War II, the concept was a major basis upon which the National War Labor Board was authorized to permit exceptions from the general stabilization of wages. The "wage rate bracket" procedure was an application of the inequality policy. See also WAGE INEQUITY.

wage inequity. An unjust relationship between wage rates of workers or of job classifications. The concept was a major basis upon which the National War Labor Board was authorized to permit exceptions from the general stabilization of wages during World War II. See also WAGE INEQUALITY.

(352)

"Wage-Item, Individual." A term used by the United States Employment Service. A line entry on a list wage report, a single wage slip, or a wage and separation report.

wage leadership. The influence exercised by the wage settlements reached by a large firm or group of firms on other settlements in an industry or labor market. "Follow-the-leader" wage adjustments appear to be particularly significant in some industries. May also relate to a policy adopted by a firm of maintaining a position of wage leadership in an industry or area.

wage level. The level of wages received by workers in an occupation, establishment, industry, or area. Wage levels are generally indicated by average rates.

wage, living. The rate of remuneration for work considered to be sufficient for the necessities of livelihood.

wage mediation. The entrance of a disinterested third party into a wage dispute in an effort to effect a settlement. Unlike arbitration, the mediator merely makes recommendations and assists the disputant parties in reaching a settlement. This is the principal function of the Federal Mediation and Conciliation Service. See also WAGE ARBITRATION.

wage pattern. The wage relationship that exists among the various groups within a specific industry or area.

wage policy. A formalized practice of an establishment or industry relating to elements of wages, such as wage rate scales, shift differentials, overtime provisions, nonproductive bonuses, automatic increments, paid holidays, paid vacations, pensions, and insurance bene-fits. In a broader sense, criteria for wage adjustments are stated in terms of objectives (e.g., stabilization, rising standard of living, etc.) or in terms of prevailing economic conditions.

wage rate. The monetary compensation for a given unit of time or effort by which a worker's pay is calculated. There are several kinds of wage rates, related to the system of wage payment used in an establishment. The principal kinds are hourly rates, daily rates, weekly rates, monthly rates, annual rates and various kinds of incentive rates. See also BASE WAGE RATE.

wage rate bracket. In the administration of wartime wage stabilization policy by the National War Labor Board, the term referred to a range of "sound and tested going rates" for an occupation in a labor market area. The minimum of the range or bracket, the most important point in actual wage administration, was frequently set at the level of the first substantial cluster of rates in a wage distribution. The minimum of the bracket was the point up to which the War Labor Board would permit adjustments in interplant inequity cases.

wage reopening. A provision or clause in a union agreement permitting the question of wages to be reopened for negotiations before the expiration of the agreement.

"Wage Report." A term used by the United States Employment Service. A report by an employer of the wages of individual workers in his employ. *List Report.* A report listing workers and their wages. *Slip Report.* A report consisting of individual slips, one for each worker, showing wage information.

(353)

wage review. A periodic review of the performance of workers to determine or select those who deserve merit increases or advancement to higher paying jobs. See also MERIT INCREASE.

wage scale. A schedule of rates of pay, applicable to an occupation or group of occupations and to a given place of employment or over an entire area of employment.

wage and salary administration. The managing and supervision of the wage structure of an employer. It involves the application of wage and salary adjustments, according to established policies, and the analysis of data such as cost of living, prices, wage and salary surveys, which have a direct bearing on the wage structure and are used in wage negotiations. May also involve the establishment of new rates through job evaluation, job analysis, and time studies.

wage and salary receipts. As defined by the U.S. Department of Commerce for national income purposes: "Wage and Salary Receipts is equal to wages and salaries less employee contributions for social insurance, except that retroactive wages are counted when paid rather than when earned."

"Wage Structure." As defined by the United States Employment Service, the system or pattern of wage rates existing in a given establishment, industry, or occupation, or prevailing in a community.

wage structure. The sum total of the various elements and considerations that characterize a specific rate schedule in an establishment, industry, area, or country as a whole. Typical of such ele-

ments are: (1) relationship between rates of occupations of different skills; (2) relationship between rates of pay for men, women, and workers of different races and color in the same occupations; (3) provisions for extra pay for late shift work, overtime, hazardous, unpleasant, or unhealthful work; (4) interarea and interregional variations in rates of pay; (5) methods of pay; (6) provisions for lunch and rest periods; and (7) supplementary benefits such as vacations, insurance, sick leave, and holiday provisions.

wage survey. A general term used to describe a wage study based on the collection, tabulation, and analysis of original data. Wage surveys are of many types, and the kinds of data collected depend upon the uses to which the surveys are put.

"Wages." Following are the definitions used by the United States Employment Service: *Average Weekly Wages.* (1) For an individual worker, the result obtained by dividing his total wages in a specified period either by the total number of weeks in the period, or by the number of weeks for which wages were payable to him during the period. See also FULL-TIME WEEKLY WAGES below. (2) For a group of workers, the result obtained by dividing the total wages for one or more quarters by the number of weeks in the period, and then dividing by the average monthly employment during the period. *Benefit Wages.* Under a certain type of experience-rating plan, the wages paid by an employer to a benefit recipient, which are used for the purpose of computing the employer's contribution rate. *Full-Time Weekly Wages.* The amount of wages earned by an individual employee throughout a full-time week, or the amount he would have earned had he been employed throughout a full-time week. *Qualifying Wages.* The amount of wages a worker must have earned in insured work within a specified period in order to be an insured worker. See also BENEFIT ELIGIBILITY CONDITIONS. *Taxable Wages.* Wages subject to contribution under a State employment security law, or wages subject to tax under the Federal Unemployment Tax Act.

wages and salaries. As defined by the U.S. Department of Commerce for national income purposes: "Wages and Salaries consist of the monetary remuneration of employees commonly regarded as wages and salaries, inclusive of executives' compensation, commissions, tips, and bonuses, and of payments in kind which represent income to the recipients." More generally, this term refers to remuneration to individuals for productive effort.

Wagner-Peyser Act. Federal act of 1933 which established the United States Employment Service in the Department of Labor for the development of a cooperative nationwide system of state employment services.

waiting list. A list of applications, usually maintained in a file, to provide a source of persons qualified to fill various jobs.

waiting period. Interval between the filing date of a claim for unemployment benefits and the time at which they become payable. Also, the interval between the beginning of time loss due to accident or illness and the date at which workmen's compensation benefits

become payable. See UNEMPLOYMENT INSURANCE; WORKMEN'S COMPENSATION.

"Waiting Period." As defined by the United States Employment Service a period of unemployment during which a claimant may not draw benefits and during which he must meet certain requirements essential to the establishment of his eligibility for benefits during subsequent weeks.

"Waiting Period Claim." A term used by the United States Employment Service. See CLAIM.

"Waiting-Period Credit." A term used by the United States Employment Service. Credit for waiting period or portion of a waiting period.

waiting time. See DEAD TIME.

walkout. The act of work stoppage by a group of workers who have not formally called a strike.

Walsh-Healey Public Contracts Act. Passed June 30, 1936 and subsequently amended. The Public Contracts Act sets basic labor standards for work done on United States Government contracts exceeding $10,000 in value for materials, articles, supplies, equipment or naval vessels. It applies to all employees, except office and custodial, engaged in or connected with the manufacture or furnishing, including the fabrication, assembling, handling, or shipment of materials, supplies, articles, or equipment required under such contracts. The "white collar" exemptions regulations of the Wage-Hour Law apply under the Public Contracts Act too. The Act requires that the contractor be a manufacturer or regular dealer in the articles called for in the contract. While the Act does not generally apply to subcontractors, under special circumstances, as for example, where it is the regular practice in an industry for the prime contractor to manufacture certain items, secondary contractors are covered. Further information may be obtained from the nearest office of the Wage and Hour and Public Contracts Divisions, U.S. Department of Labor, or from the Wage and Hour and Public Contracts Divisions, U.S. Department of Labor, Washington 25, D. C. See also: MINIMUM WAGE RATES, under Walsh-Healey Public Contracts Act; HOURS OF WORK, under Walsh-Healey Public Contracts Act; CHILD LABOR PROVISIONS, under Walsh-Healey Public Contracts Act; CONVICT LABOR PROVISIONS, under Walsh-Healey Public Contracts Act; SAFETY AND HEALTH REQUIREMENTS, under Walsh-Healey Public Contracts Act; HOME WORK DEFINED, under Walsh-Healey Public Contracts Act; LEARNERS, APPRENTICES AND HANDICAPPED WORKERS, EMPLOYMENT OF, under Walsh-Healey Public Contracts Act; EXEMPTIONS, under Walsh-Healey Public Contracts Act; EXCEPTIONS, under Walsh-Healey Public Contracts Act; RECORDS AND POSTING NOTICES, required by Walsh-Healey Public Contracts Act; EMPLOYER LIABILITIES, under Walsh-Healey Public Contracts Act; PENALTIES, under Walsh-Healey Public Contracts Act.

War Manpower Commission. A federal agency, established by Executive Order of the President in April, 1942 for the purpose of directing wartime mobilization and utilization of the nation's manpower; terminated September, 1945. See also "TRAINING WITHIN INDUSTRY."

waste collection. Includes locating, gathering, and transporting surplus materials or scrap, and where practicable, segre-

gating it at the source into types or classes of materials. Although the planning phases of waste collection are management problems, the success of the collection program depends in a large measure on enlisting the cooperation of employees.

waste, of machinery and equipment. Machinery and equipment are wasted through: (1) Improper operation of machines, machine tools and small tools. (2) Rough use or abuse of machinery and tools. (3) Lack of lubrication. (4) Overloading. (5) Wrong speeds. (6) Failure to keep clean. (7) Loss or theft of small tools. (8) Failure to return tools and portable equipment to their proper places. (9) Carelessly using machines or tools for purposes for which they were not designed. (10) Inadequate or makeshift repairs. (11) Using wrong material or supplies. (12) Misuse of equipment such as extension lights, ropes, ladders, trucks, elevators, hose, and especially clothing or protective devices such as safety belts, welders' helmets, goggles. (13) Failing to report promptly all defects or conditions needing correction such as excessive wear of parts, vibration, dust, faulty bearings, minor damage. (14) Neglecting machines which are not in use. (15) Not understanding duties with respect to the care and use of machines and equipment.

waste, of materials and supplies. Materials and supplies are wasted through: (1) Defective workmanship causing breakage or spoilage due to (a) Wrong, inadequate, or defective tools or machines. (b) Employee not physically fit; may have defective vision. (c) Carelessness, indifference, or inattention to work. (d) Failure to understand orders or lack of knowledge of the work. (e) Too much in a hurry to get through. (f) Using sub-standard, defective, or poor quality material not suited to the job. (g) Failure to follow the standard set for the job. (2) Failure of the employee to under-stand the money value of supplies and materials. (3) Carelessness in handling material in process. (4) Improper use of supplies such as light bulbs, paper clips, oil, oilcans, report forms, timecards, sta-tionery, papertowels, nails, screws, (5) Wrong piling or storage. (6) Failure to protect from the weather, heat, mois-ture, acids, dust. (7) Lack of neatness, as storing stationery so it becomes dog-eared. (8) Overloading trucks causing damage to materials transported. (9) Re-quisitioning more material or supplies than needed and failing to return the unused balance. (10) Improper handling of the finished product in storing, crat-ing, unloading, shipping.

waste of space. Space is wasted through: (1) Poor housekeeping. (2) Improper pil-ing of materials and supplies. (3) Col-lecting scrap piles in improper places. (4) Keeping unnecessary materials that should be scrapped. (5) Keeping un-necessary materials and supplies at workplace. (6) Spreading materials and supplies that could be piled. (7) Scatter-ing or placing of tools, materials, sup-plies and portable equipment around work or in aisles or passageways where clear space is needed. (8) Failure to fol-low the established system of routing.

waste of time. Time is wasted: (1) When employees stay home without advance notice. (2) Unnecessary talking and vis-iting. (3) Failure to maintain a steady pace on the job. (4) Failure to ask ques-tions when orders are not clear. (5) Be-ing late for work. (6) Late in starting work. (7) Slowing down towards the end of the shift or the end of the workday in an office. (8) Quitting actual work early and taking unusually long to get ready for leaving in the wash room. (9) Trying to work when not physically fit. (10) Failure to follow instructions. (11) Not keeping tools or office supplies handy. (12) Forgetting where tools were left. (13) Using wrong or defective tools. (14) Doing personal work without per-mission. (15) Not reporting promptly when work is done to ask if other work is to be assigned. (16) Taking more time than needed to fill out reports and rec-ords. (17) Mistakes and inaccuracies necessitating doing work over. (18) Tak-ing time to do a better or finer job than necessary. (19) Not giving all possible cooperation to fellow employees, fore-men, inspectors, the office supervisor, etc. (20) Improper care or operation of machines resulting in lower output, breakdown, or careless looking work. (21) Not reporting promptly when re-pairs are needed. (22) Failure to keep aisles clear. (23) Failure to keep desks, files in order necessitating hunting for papers. (24) Failure to ask for help when needed. (25) Waste motion due to un-systematic personal working habits. (26) Lack of suitable clothing when exposed to heat, cold, weather, causing frequent interruptions for relief. (27) Inappropri-ate dress in the office necessitating "primping." (28) Waiting around, when not necessary, for tools to be repaired, office machines to be fixed, or for work to arrive when other work is available.

waste, of utilities, etc. Electric current, steam, compressed air, water, heat and gas are wasted in the following instances: (1) Failing to shut off when not in use.

(2) Leaving machines running idle. (3) Using more than needed; such as larger portable tools, or larger lights than necessary; too strong gas flame, or improper mixture. (4) Using compressed air for purposes for which it is not intended. (5) Failing to report leaking valves or fittings, arcing switches, escaping gas, and other conditions needing correction, such as faulty bearings, and improper belt tension. (6) Failure to report overheated motors.

waste prevention. Waste prevention measures are designed to reduce, through methods of work, the amount of waste which occurs; the education of employees and the enlistment of employee assistance is essential. Examples of waste prevention include the reduction of breakage and spoilage, correct use of materials and machines, and reduction of the loss of goods in process.

waste reduction. See also WASTE PREVENTION; WASTE COLLECTION; WASTE UTILIZATION; WASTE OF TIME; WASTE OF MATERIALS AND SUPPLIES; WASTE OF MACHINERY AND EQUIPMENT; WASTE OF UTILITIES; WASTE OF SPACE; ACCIDENTS, COST OF. Activities in which companies seek cooperation of employees to reduce waste may be summarized as follows: ("Enlisting Employees in Waste Reduction," Policyholders Service Bureau, Metropolitan Life Insurance Company). *Waste of Labor*: This includes the reduction of absence and tardiness, the elimination of slowdowns, improvement of health, accident prevention, correct use of tools, conformance with the most efficient work methods, and increased employee cooperation with other employees and management. *Waste of Materials*: Reduction in the waste of materials involves more careful workmanship, reduced spoilage, conservation of material being processed, care in the collection and segregation of scrap, the return of unused materials to stock and systematic storage and handling. Employee cooperation is sought both in improving work methods leading to these ends, and in adhering to those already prescribed. *Waste of Facilities*: Plant facilities include machinery, tools, building and building equipment. Employee cooperation is sought in prompt and effective handling of maintenance, proper lubrication, correct use of machinery and equipment, minimizing breakage, eliminating the loss of tools, methodical arrangement of hand tools and portable equipment, the prompt return of tools to cribs, and efficient utilization of aisles and other floor space. *Waste of Services*: Employees are frequently enlisted in efforts to conserve water, electricity, gas, steam, and compressed air. If two or more services are available for the same purpose, the most economical one is selected. Efforts are made to have petcocks, faucets, switches, etc. turned off when services are not being used. Defective fixtures and equipment are either fixed or reported promptly, and maintenance men are urged to make repairs without unnecessary delay.

waste utilization. Includes the dismantling and sorting of the materials collected, the selection of usable items for further use, the conversion of usable items to a form convenient for scrap; and the disposition of items not required by the plant. These activities are commonly conducted by a salvage department, and the purchasing department is usually responsible for sales to outside concerns.

Webb, Sidney James (the first Baron Passfield) and **Beatrice Potter Webb.** James S. Webb lived from 1859 to 1947. He was a British labor leader and intellectual leader of the Fabian Socialists. See FABIANISM. The essence of the Webbs' position is that trade unionism is the extension of democracy from the political sphere to that of industry and the overcoming of managerial dictatorship. Unionism thus serves to strengthen the liberties of the individual worker by giving him representation in a bargaining situation, the outcome of which will determine his standard of living and his working environment. In the absence of such representation, all the dimensions of the employer-employee relationship are imposed upon the workingman from above, and he is forced to accept because he has no "reservation price" below which he may sell his services. He *must* work, and his bargaining power is nonexistent. The result is a servile condition incompatible with the precepts of a free society.

"Week." A term used by the United States Employment Service. *Calendar Week*: A period of 7 consecutive days usually ending at Saturday midnight, used by some State employment security agencies as a unit in the measurement of employment or unemployment. *Compensable Week*: A week for which benefits have been claimed. *Flexible Week*: A period of 7 consecutive days used by most State employment security agencies as a unit in the measurement of employment or unemployment, the beginning date of which varies with respect to individual claimants. *Full-time Week*: The number of hours or days per week currently established by schedule, custom, or otherwise, as constituting a week of full-time work for the kind of service an individual performs for an employing unit.

"Week of Unemployment." A term used by the United States Employment Service. A week in which an individual performs less than full-time work for any employing unit if the wages payable to him with respect to such week are less than a specified amount (usually the weekly benefit amount). *Week of Partial Unemployment*: A week in which an individual worked less than his regular full-time hours for his regular employer, because of lack of work, and earned less than his weekly benefit amount (plus the partial earnings allowance, if any, in the State's definition of unemployment) but more than the partial earnings allowance, so that if eligible for benefits he receives less than his full weekly benefit amount. *Week of Part-Total Unemployment*: A week of otherwise total unemployment during which an individual has odd jobs and/or subsidiary work with earnings in excess of the amount specified in the State law as allowable without resulting in a reduction in the individual's benefit payment. *Week of Total Unemployment*: A week in which an individual performs no work and earns no wages or has less than full-time work and earns not more than the partial earnings allowance, so that if eligible for benefits he receives his full weekly benefit amount.

"Weekly Benefit Amount." A term used by the United States Employment Service. See BENEFIT AMOUNT.

Wennerlund Plan. A wage incentive plan like that of the Emerson Graduated Bonus Plan in that its bonus begins well below standard output (at 76% of the latter), and also in that this bonus increases, with each one percent gain in efficiency, according to Wennerlund's empirical table, until at the point of attainment of task the bonus is 20% of the worker's base rate. Beyond this point Wennerlund's plan is a 100% bonus scheme, paying in direct proportion to output, i.e. paying for all the time the workman saves at the same hourly rate as it pays him when the times he takes is just equal to the time allowed. As Wennerlund's formula put it, for each added one percent of efficiency beyond 100, the workman gets an additional 1.2% of his hourly base rate for the time he actually works.

wetbacks. Workers from Mexico who gain illegal entrance into the United States by swimming the Rio Grande and hence have "wet backs" upon arrival. See MEXICAN FARM LABOR. A study of conditions of Mexican workers is called "Strangers in Our Fields," published by the U.S. Section of the Joint United States-Mexico Trade Union Committee, Room 504, 815 Sixteenth Street, N.W., Washington 6, D. C.

white collar unionization. Much work on this point has been done at the Industrial Relations Center of the University of Chicago. In general, reasons for unionization include: (1) Fear on the part of employees that they will lose their jobs, particularly in view of the increasing trend to mechanization. (2) Neglecting the importance of women because of the feeling that they won't be long with the company anyway. (3) Withholding information—white collar people want to be "in the know." (4) Too close supervision. (5)Job inequities. (6) Extensive job dis-

locations, particularly when mechanization occurs. Reasons for resistance to unionism include: (1) Turnover among women, which is high. Women prefer saving money to paying union dues. (2) Office people are usually close to the boss. (3) Office people don't want to be dealt with in a group, through a spokesman. (4) Office people are realistic. They may not like paying dues for something in which they do not immediately participate. (5) Office people do not like the idea of using force or intimidation. See: *Satisfying the Salaried Employee*, Industrial Relations Division, National Association of Manufacturers; *White Collar Report*, published by Bureau of National Affairs, Inc., Washington, D. C.

wink. A unit of time equal to 1/2000 minute which the Gilbreths developed and used in motion and time study.

wildcat strike. A popular term to designate a strike unauthorized by union officials or one initiated by a minority number of workers in an organization.

wink counter. An electrically or mechanically driven timing device indicating time in winks.

withholding tax. A tax collected at the source of the income through deductions from wages and salaries. Under the present federal income tax, the employer, in most cases, acts as collecting agent for the government by deducting the employee's income tax from each pay check. This also applies to the taxes withheld under the Social Security program, which are collected by the employer.

wives, as factors in husband's job. The relationship of the wife to her husband's job, has two facets gaining more attention. (1) The type of wife considered important if a man is to achieve managerial success. Companies frequently insist on interviewing the wife before hiring an executive for a higher position, or for service in other countries. Corporation officials sketch the ideal wife as a woman who is (1) highly adaptable, (2) highly gregarious, (3) realizes her husband belongs to the corporation. "The Wives of Management" by William H. Whyte, Jr., *Fortune Magazine*, October-November 1951 initiated much subsequent literature on the subject. (2) The need to keep the wife's morale high and to acquaint her with her husband's company. All types of letters, activities, open house get-togethers, are used by companies to keep wives in contact with their husband's jobs. This is particularly true in lower-ranked positions. Some of these activities, and other details, are outlined in "Communicating With Employees' Wives," July 1956, confidential bulletin of Opinion Research Corporation.

"Wobblies." See INDUSTRIAL WORKERS OF THE WORLD.

women, in industry. Through half a century, the women's share of the U. S. labor force has grown mightily to reach a 33% level in the 1950's. Meanwhile, the women's battle for equality in industry has never stopped. One of the biggest forces behind that battle has been the Women's Bureau of the Department of Labor, Washington 4, D.C. which issues numerous bulletins and statistics. An exhaustive study made by the National Manpower Council called "Womanpower" was published by the Columbia University Press in 1957.

Women's Bureau. An agency of the U. S. Department of Labor which studies and reports on all problems affecting women workers. It promotes standards and policies to improve their working conditions for profitable employment. It supports enactment and better administration of labor laws and other legislation for women. Its research reports deal with employment, hours, wages, wage levels, and working conditions of women; problems of hiring, advancement and lay-off; employment and training opportunities; social problems related to women's employment, such as responsibility for dependents, and nature of their attachment to the labor force; labor legislation for women; legislation relation to women's civil and political status. An equally important Bureau function is its technical and advisory services to State labor departments, civic organizations, unions and Federal authorities on labor legislation for women, including the preparation of draft legislation and on the administration and enforcement of laws on minimum wages, equal pay, maximum hours, maternity legislation, other working conditions standards, legislation relating to civil and political status, including jury service, guardianship, control of earnings, and related subjects.

women, working. The trend of women in the labor force is growing rapidly. Statistics change from year to year, but generally, the rule of "one-third" applies. About one-third of all women in the U. S. over 14 years of age are in the labor force. About one-third of all married women are working; two-thirds of all working women are married—one-third only are single. Also, one-third of all working women are over forty-five years of age. Most of the single women are in clerical or professional occupations; there is a higher percentage of married women who are operatives. An annual "Handbook on Women Workers," is published by the U. S. Dept. of Labor.

work cycle. (1) A pattern of motions and/or processes that is repeated with negligible variation each time an operation is performed. (2) A succession of operations and/or processes that is repeated with negligible variation each time a unit of production is completed.

worker analysis. Determination of skills, aptitudes, interests, and other characteristics of successful workers in an occupation, and determination of suitability of applicants for employment in specific occupations.

workers, covered, under Fair Labor Standards Act. Workers considered "engaged in (interstate) commerce" include those in telephone, radio, television, and railroad jobs; in the purchasing or ordering of goods from other States; in unloading, unpacking, checking, or otherwise, handling goods on receipt directly from outside the State; in maintaining records of such interstate activities; and workers who regularly travel across State lines in the performance of their duties, or who regularly make use of instrumentalities of commerce such as the telephone, telegraph, and the mails for interstate communication. Workers considered "engaged in the production of goods for (interstate) commerce" are those who manufacture, mine, handle, transport, or in any other manner work on such goods, *OR* are employed "in any closely related process or occupation directly essential to the production."

workers, exempt, under Fair Labor Standards Act. The act specifies a number of exemptions from its minimum-wage and overtime requirements. Some of these exemptions apply to both minimum-wage and overtime-pay provisions, and some apply to overtime provisions only. (See below for different, limited exemptions which apply to the child-labor provisions.) Workers in agriculture as defined in sec. 3 (f) of the act are exempt from the minimum-wage and overtime provisions of the act. Under the retail or service establishment exemption, all workers employed by such an establishment—including those who individually may be engaged in interstate commerce activities—are exempt from the act's minimum-wage and overtime provisions. This exemption applies to workers employed in local establishments such as grocery stores, variety stores, department stores, drug stores, restaurants, barber shops, beauty parlors, hotels, motion picture theaters, hospitals, nursing homes, and filling stations. The so-called "white-collar" exemptions provide for minimum-wage and overtime exemptions for employees engaged in bona fide "executive," "administrative," "professional," "local retailing," and "outside salesman" capacities, as defined in regulations issued by the Department of Labor. Among others, supervisors may be found exempt as "executive employees" under these regulations. There are also both minimum-wage and overtime exemptions for seamen; for employees of taxicabs and of local street and bus carriers; for workers employed in the publication of small newspapers and in newspaper deliveries to the consumer; and for employees of small lumbering establishments, small telephone exchanges and small telegraph agencies located in retail establishments. Workers engaged in fishing and fish processing (other than canning) and workers engaged in specified handling and processing of agricultural commodities within "the area of production" are similarly exempt. The act also exempts from the overtime provisions only, employees of air carriers and railroads, and certain employees of motor carriers whose hours of work are subject to regulation by the Interstate Commerce Commission. The overtime exemption also applies to workers engaged in canning fish, to outside buyers of some farm commodities and to employees employed at a place where the employer is engaged in the first processing of certain farm commodities. In addition to these exemptions, the act has provision for limited seasonal exemptions from the overtime provision. A 14-week exemption is permitted employees of employers engaged in the first processing within the area of production of agricultural products during seasonal operations and to employees of a first processor or canner of perishable or seasonal fresh fruits and vegetables. The administrator may also grant a 14-week exemption for employees in any seasonal industry. Under the American Samoan Amendments of August 1956, covered employees in American Samoa are exempt from the minimum wage rate. With respect to such employees, the Secretary of Labor, after a public hearing, may modify the overtime provision, if he finds "economic conditions warrant such action."

worker, migratory. A worker who finds casual employment in different places at various times of the year, so that he must travel from one job to another. The concept includes both essential farm workers and industrial workers such as those employed in the oil and construction industries, whose employment entails frequently migration from one place to another. Major paths of migration are: (1) The Atlantic Coast movement. Negro families are transported by truck from Florida north. Major work areas in North Carolina, Virginia, Maryland, New Jersey and New York. Major crops, potatoes, snap beans, fruit. (2) The Eastern fruit migration. Anglo-Saxon families from Kentucky, Arkansas, Oklahoma and other southern States move north to pick cherries, peaches, tomatoes, and apples in Michigan, Wisconsin, Indiana, and New York. (3) The sugar beet migration. Latin-American families are recruited in Texas to thin and harvest sugar beets. Major work areas are in Michigan, Nebraska, Colorado, Idaho and Montana. Workers also harvest pickles, tomatoes, peas and fruit. (4) The wheat migration. Combine operators move northward with the wheat harvest. Operations start in Texas and move northward through Oklahoma, Kansas, Nebraska and South and North Dakota. (5) The cotton migration. Latin-American workers move with the cotton harvest from south Texas to the northern parts of the State. Some then go eastward to the Mississippi Delta, others westward to New Mexico, Arizona and California. (6) The Pacific Coast movements. Most of the movement is by Anglo-Saxon and Latin-American families from one crop to another in California or in the northwest. Some workers move annually from Oklahoma, Texas, or Arkansas, others from Arizona. Major crops are cotton, tomatoes, grapes, peaches, and pears. See OKIES, STOOP LABOR, WETBACKS.

(363)

work experience. Employment undertaken by a student while attending school. The job may be of the type that provides practical experience in the work-a-day world as part of the requirements of a school course, or it may be a job without any correlation to the school program.

work-factor. A system of predetermined motion time standards employing the Work-Factor as an index of motion difficulty (that is, demonstrating that time is proportional to specific factors in work, such as body member, distance, direction, weight, control and the like, and the relationship is consistent and interchangeable). The system is used for determining efficient methods and setting performance time standards.

working area. See MAXIMUM WORKING AREA, NORMAL WORKING AREA, and PRODUCTION CENTER.

working class. The manual labor group in modern industrial society, occupying the lower ranks among the classes in point of income, status and surrounding conditions, and by reason of the common concerns and problems arising out of its position, tending to form a more or less cohesive secondary group.

working conditions. Factors such as light, temperature, smoke, safety, hazards, noise, dust and the like that affect the performance of a job or the general well-being of the employee.

working force. Same as AVERAGE WORKING FORCE.

working papers. See EMPLOYMENT CERTIFICATES.

"Work Load." A term used by the United States Employment Service. The measure of the volume of work for each functional area of operation in the State agency, e.g. the number of contribution (payroll) reports processed, the number of claims taken, the number of applications for employment, etc.

work measurement. A more comprehensive term to designate "time study." The term was popularized by Dr. Adam Abruzzi, who says: . . . "The procedures of work measurement should be based on the rules of the scientific method, not on the bargaining process. It seems to me that we can no longer tolerate taking empirical action about productivity problems on the basis of the subjective judgments of the individuals acting as advocates of vested viewpoints. Instead, we need objective principles and procedures so that the estimates we make and the action we take will be sound in a scientific sense." See Abruzzi, Adam, *Work Measurement*. New York: Columbia University Press, 1952.

workmen's compensation. State regulated insurance systems providing payments to workers or their relatives for occupational injuries or fatalities. The first Workmen's Compensation Law passed in Maryland in 1902 was declared unconstitutional and the first successful law was passed in Washington in 1911. Most of the industrial states have had this type of legislation for some time. Not until 1948, however, when Mississippi passed such a law, were all 48 states covered and ready to provide for workmen's compensation covering hazards incident to on-the-job accidents and occupational diseases. Three types of insurance plans are in effect: private insurance, self insurance and public insurance systems. Coverage and benefits vary from state to state. A general description of Workmen's Compensation can be found in *Personnel Handbook* (Ronald Press); specific information should be obtained from the *Workmen's Compensation Board*, with offices in State capitals, and in many larger cities.

workplace. See WORK STATION.

work sampling study. A statistical sampling technique employed to determine the proportion of delays or other classifications of activity present in the total work cycle.

work simplification. Reorganization of work methods, materials, tools, equipment and working conditions in order to reduce fatigue and increase output.

work station. That section of a production center where the workman performs his assigned tasks including the space required for his auxiliary equipment as: tools; a workbench; a machine with any stands, containers, conveyors, etc., for the material being worked on.

work station layout. The arrangement of the tools, fixtures, bins, chutes, and other equipment at a specific work station.

work stoppage. The cessation of work initiated by an organized group of employees in order to coerce an employer or to force a concession.

work task. See TASK.

work week. Unless otherwise specified, generally it is assumed that this consists of any eight-hour days in a calendar week.

World Federation of Trade Unions (WFTU). International organization of labor unions (including the CIO) formed in 1945 to represent labor in the negotiation of peace treaties and formation of the United Nations.

written standard practice. A standard practice that has been recorded and approved by the proper authority or authorities. See STANDARD PRACTICE.

Y

yellow-dog contract. An agreement which an employer requires an applicant for employment to sign as a condition of employment, binding the employee not to join a union.

Young Presidents' Organization. This organization has its headquarters at 58th St. and 5th Avenue, New York. It is a group of men and women who became presidents of their companies before they were forty years old. To be eligible for membership, an applicant must be president of a corporation with a gross annual revenue of at least $1,000,000 and a minimum of 50 employees, or if president of a non-industrial corporation, an applicant may be eligible if he has 25 employees and gross annual revenue of at least $2,000,000. Provisions are made in the By-Laws for applicants who are president of two or more corporations, no one of which alone would meet the above requirements. Presidents of banking corporations with average deposits of $15,000,000 or more and a minimum of 25 employees are also eligible. An applicant must have been elected president of his corporation while not more than 39 years of age; and he must not be more than 43 years of age at the time he applies for membership. Founded in 1950, YPO now has attracted more than 1100 members from 43 states, the District of Columbia, Alaska, Territory of Hawaii, Virgin Islands, and two provinces of Canada. A number became presidents of their firms in their 20's and the average age of all members is 38. Many president-members of YPO founded their own companies using their own savings or borrowed money to do it. Others came up through the ranks of established firms. Still others were elected presidents of firms founded by their fathers, grandfathers and other family members. Nearly every form of business activity is represented in YPO with slightly more than half of the members engaged in some form of manufacturing. The typical company has approximately $3.5 million in gross revenue and employs 250 people. Altogether YPO companies employ over 400,000 people and have gross income totaling about $6.5 billion. Throughout the U. S. and Canada YPO members are organized into 27 chapters, most of which hold monthly meetings to discuss management topics of common interest.